THE PHANTOM PIPER

COLLECTED COMIC STRIPS
from the pages of

BBC

—ĐOCTOR WHO—
MAGAZINE™

panini COMICS

Contents

5

41

89

Editor/Designer **SCOTT GRAY**
Cover pencils and inks **DAVID A ROACH**   Cover colours **JAMES OFFREDI**

Head of Production **MARK IRVINE**   Managing Editor **ALAN O'KEEFE**   Managing Director **MIKE RIDDELL**

Special thanks to **PETER CAPALDI, PEARL MACKIE, STEVEN MOFFAT, BRIAN MINCHIN, EDWARD RUSSELL, RICHARD ATKINSON, PERI GODBOLD, PETER WARE, EMILY COOK, ROSANNA STEWART, ANGELA HART, TOM SPILSBURY, MARCUS HEARN** and all the writers and artists whose work is presented herein.

Doctor Who Graphic Novel #27: *The Phantom Piper*. Published by Panini UK. Office of publication: Brockbourne House, 77 Mount Ephraim, Tunbridge Wells, Kent TN4 8BS. All *Doctor Who* material is © BBCtv. *Doctor Who* logo © BBC 2018. Tardis image © BBC 1963. DOCTOR WHO and TARDIS and the DOCTOR WHO and TARDIS logos are trademarks of the British Broadcasting Corporation and are used under licence. Licensed by BBC Studios Limited. All commentaries are © 2018 their respective authors. All rights reserved. All other material is © Panini UK unless otherwise indicated. No similarity between any of the fictional names, characters persons and/or institutions herein with those of any living or dead persons or institutions is intended and any such similarity is purely coincidental. Nothing may be reproduced by any means in whole or part without the written permission of the publishers. This book may not be sold, except by authorised dealers, and is sold subject to the condition that it shall not be sold or distributed with any part of its cover or markings removed, nor in a mutilated condition. Printed in the UK. ISBN: 978-1-84653-926-8

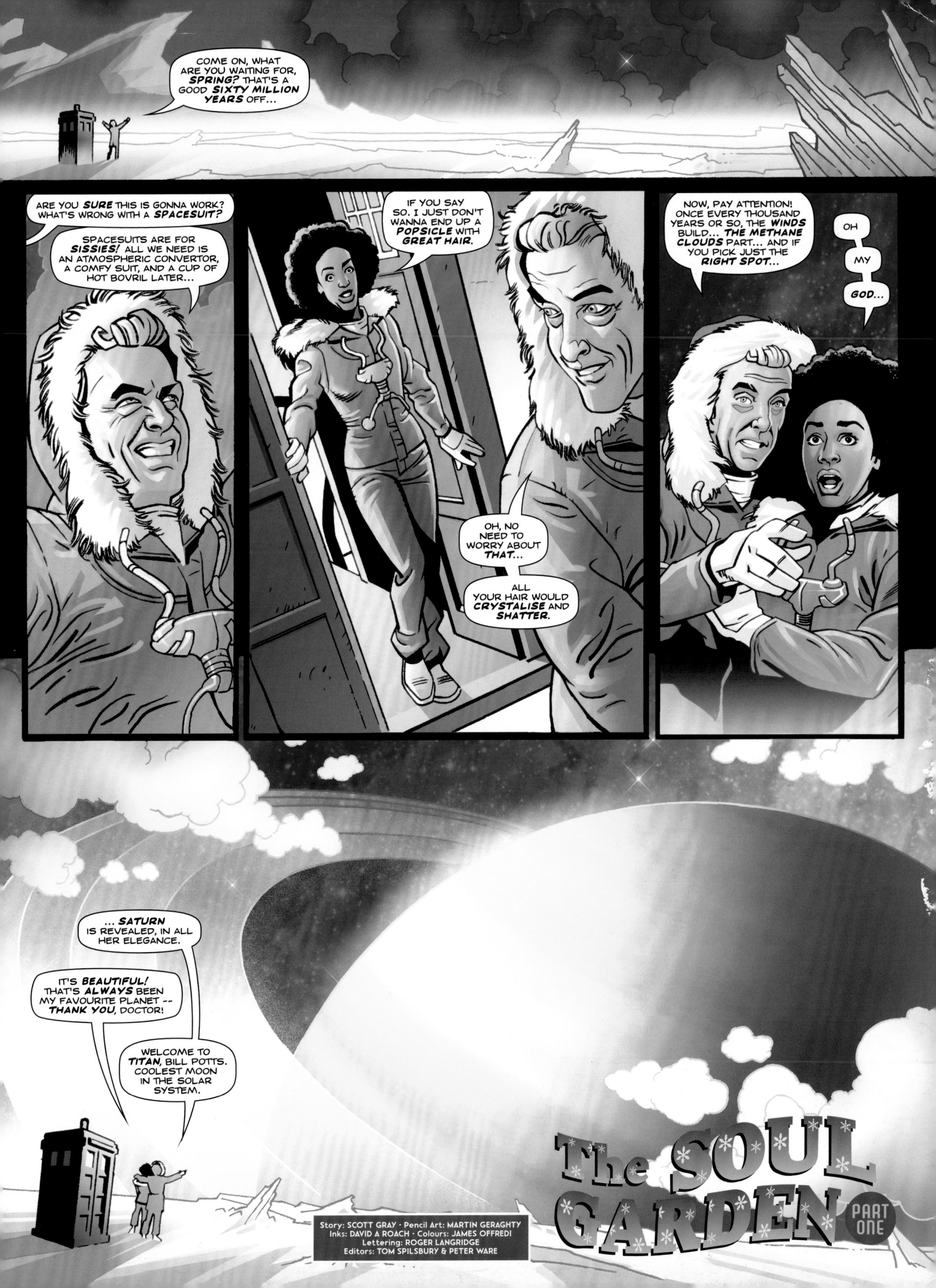
COME ON, WHAT ARE YOU WAITING FOR, SPRING? THAT'S A GOOD SIXTY MILLION YEARS OFF...
ARE YOU SURE THIS IS GONNA WORK? WHAT'S WRONG WITH A SPACESUIT?
SPACESUITS ARE FOR SISSIES! ALL WE NEED IS AN ATMOSPHERIC CONVERTOR, A COMFY SUIT, AND A CUP OF HOT BOVRIL LATER...
IF YOU SAY SO. I JUST DON'T WANNA END UP A POPSICLE WITH GREAT HAIR.
OH, NO NEED TO WORRY ABOUT THAT...
ALL YOUR HAIR WOULD CRYSTALISE AND SHATTER.
NOW, PAY ATTENTION! ONCE EVERY THOUSAND YEARS OR SO, THE WINDS BUILD... THE METHANE CLOUDS PART... AND IF YOU PICK JUST THE RIGHT SPOT...
OH
MY
GOD...
... SATURN IS REVEALED, IN ALL HER ELEGANCE.
IT'S BEAUTIFUL! THAT'S ALWAYS BEEN MY FAVOURITE PLANET -- THANK YOU, DOCTOR!
WELCOME TO TITAN, BILL POTTS. COOLEST MOON IN THE SOLAR SYSTEM.
The SOUL GARDEN PART ONE
Story: SCOTT GRAY • Pencil Art: MARTIN GERAGHTY
Inks: DAVID A ROACH • Colours: JAMES OFFREDI
Lettering: ROGER LANGRIDGE
Editors: TOM SPILSBURY & PETER WARE

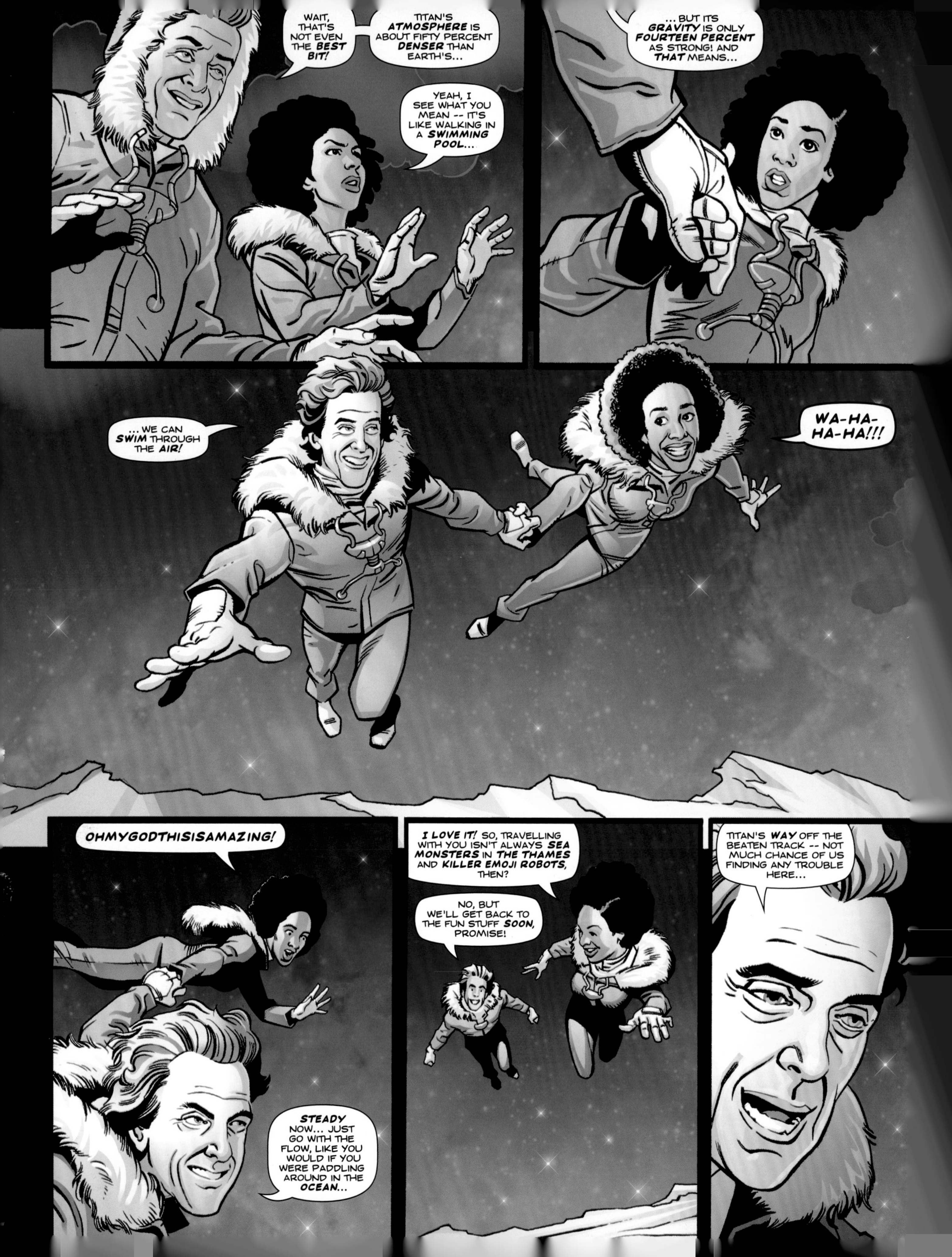
WAIT, THAT'S NOT EVEN THE BEST BIT!
TITAN'S ATMOSPHERE IS ABOUT FIFTY PERCENT DENSER THAN EARTH'S...
YEAH, I SEE WHAT YOU MEAN -- IT'S LIKE WALKING IN A SWIMMING POOL...
... BUT ITS GRAVITY IS ONLY FOURTEEN PERCENT AS STRONG! AND THAT MEANS...
... WE CAN SWIM THROUGH THE AIR!
WA-HA-HA-HA!!!
OHMYGODTHISISAMAZING!
STEADY NOW... JUST GO WITH THE FLOW, LIKE YOU WOULD IF YOU WERE PADDLING AROUND IN THE OCEAN...
I LOVE IT! SO, TRAVELLING WITH YOU ISN'T ALWAYS SEA MONSTERS IN THE THAMES AND KILLER EMOJI ROBOTS, THEN?
NO, BUT WE'LL GET BACK TO THE FUN STUFF SOON, PROMISE!
TITAN'S WAY OFF THE BEATEN TRACK -- NOT MUCH CHANCE OF US FINDING ANY TROUBLE HERE...

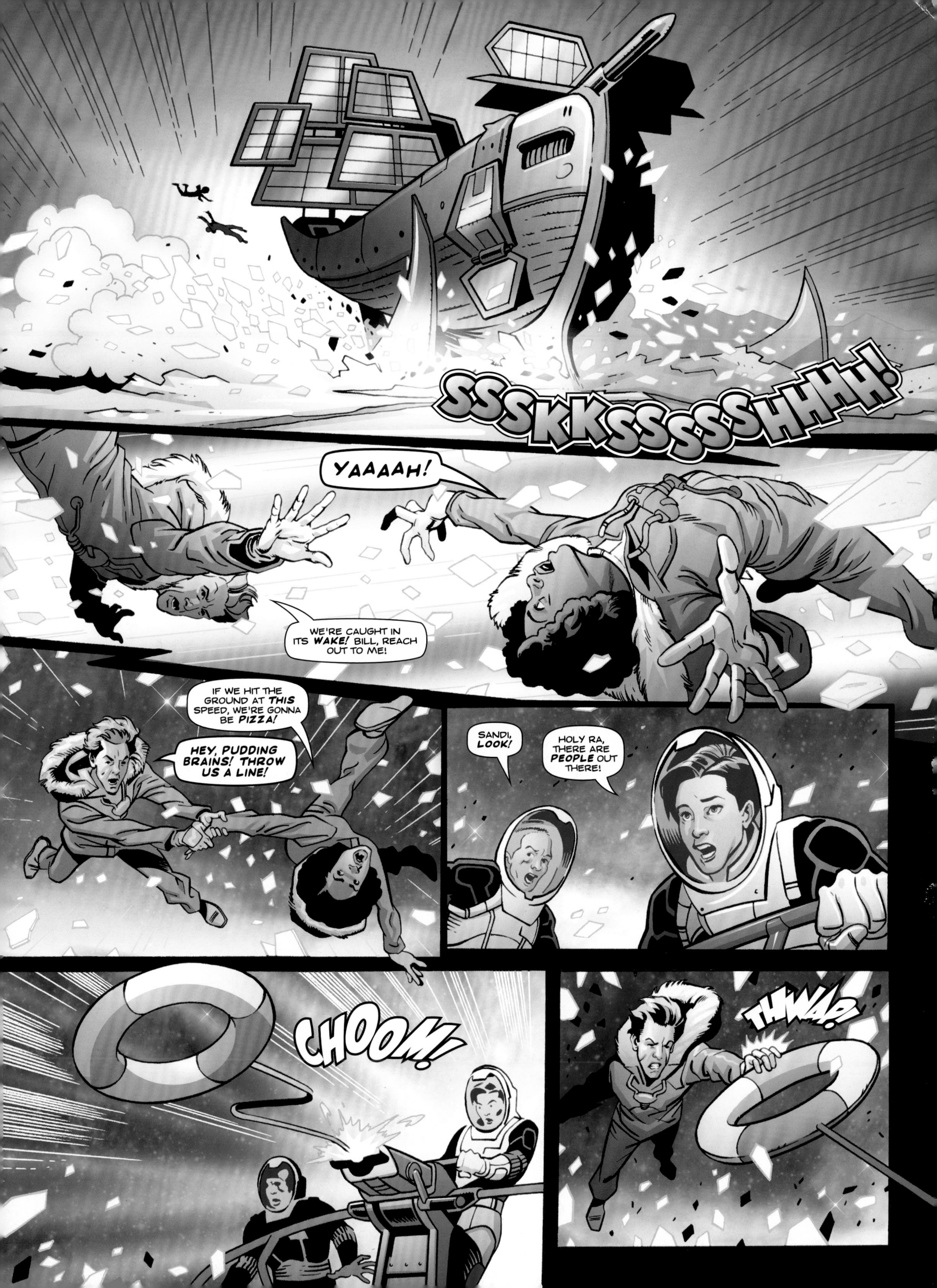
SSSKKSSSSSHHHH!
YAAAAH!
WE'RE CAUGHT IN ITS WAKE! BILL, REACH OUT TO ME!
IF WE HIT THE GROUND AT THIS SPEED, WE'RE GONNA BE PIZZA!
HEY, PUDDING BRAINS! THROW US A LINE!
SANDI, LOOK!
HOLY RA, THERE ARE PEOPLE OUT THERE!
CHOOM!
THWAP!

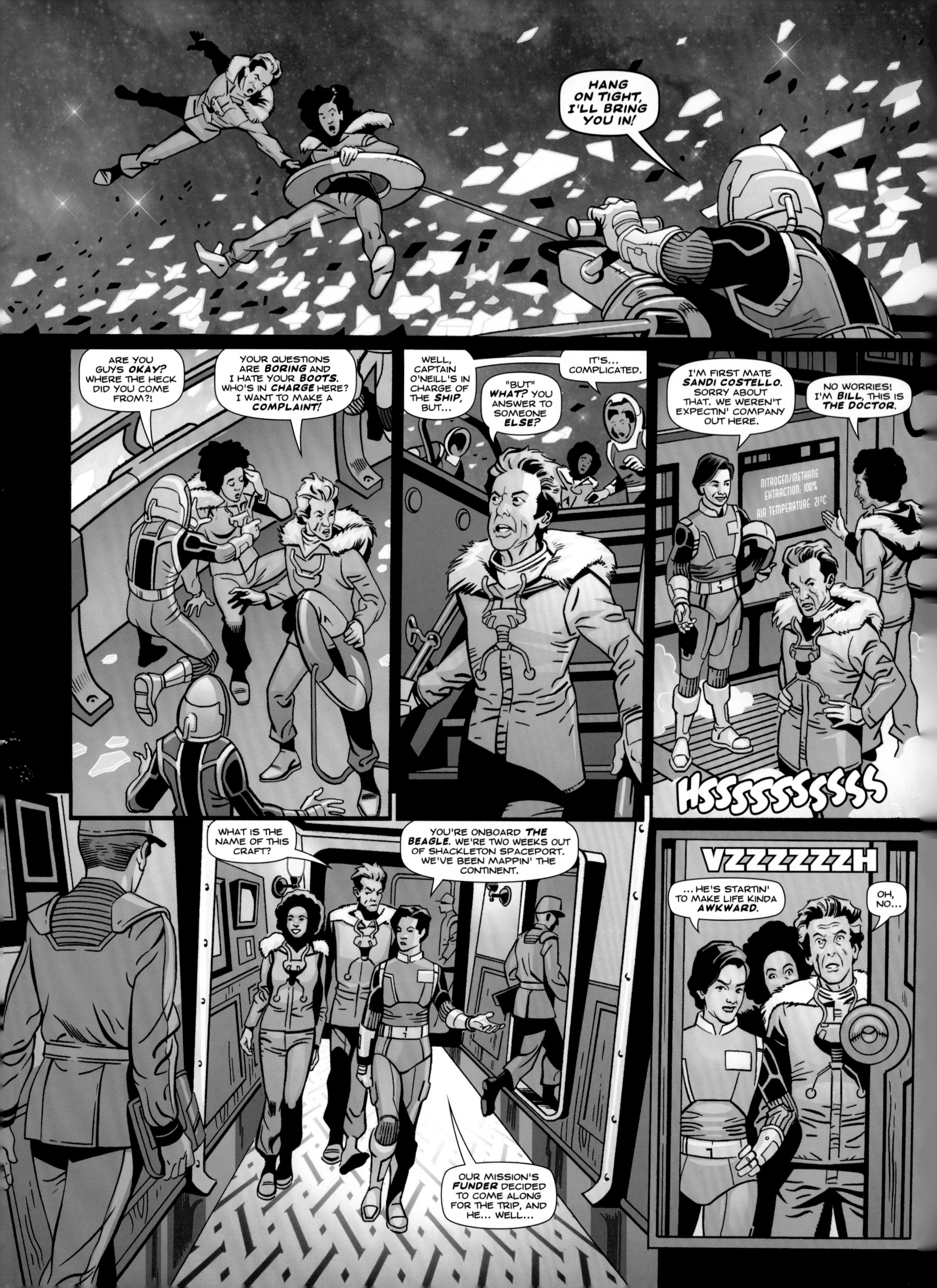
HANG ON TIGHT, I'LL BRING YOU IN!
ARE YOU GUYS OKAY? WHERE THE HECK DID YOU COME FROM?!
YOUR QUESTIONS ARE BORING AND I HATE YOUR BOOTS. WHO'S IN CHARGE HERE? I WANT TO MAKE A COMPLAINT!
WELL, CAPTAIN O'NEILL'S IN CHARGE OF THE SHIP, BUT...
"BUT" WHAT? YOU ANSWER TO SOMEONE ELSE?
IT'S... COMPLICATED.
I'M FIRST MATE SANDI COSTELLO. SORRY ABOUT THAT. WE WEREN'T EXPECTIN' COMPANY OUT HERE.
NO WORRIES! I'M BILL, THIS IS THE DOCTOR.
NITROGEN/METHANE EXTRACTION: 100%
AIR TEMPERATURE: 21°C
HSSSSSSSSSS
WHAT IS THE NAME OF THIS CRAFT?
YOU'RE ONBOARD THE BEAGLE. WE'RE TWO WEEKS OUT OF SHACKLETON SPACEPORT. WE'VE BEEN MAPPIN' THE CONTINENT.
OUR MISSION'S FUNDER DECIDED TO COME ALONG FOR THE TRIP, AND HE... WELL...
VZZZZZZZH
... HE'S STARTIN' TO MAKE LIFE KINDA AWKWARD.
OH, NO...

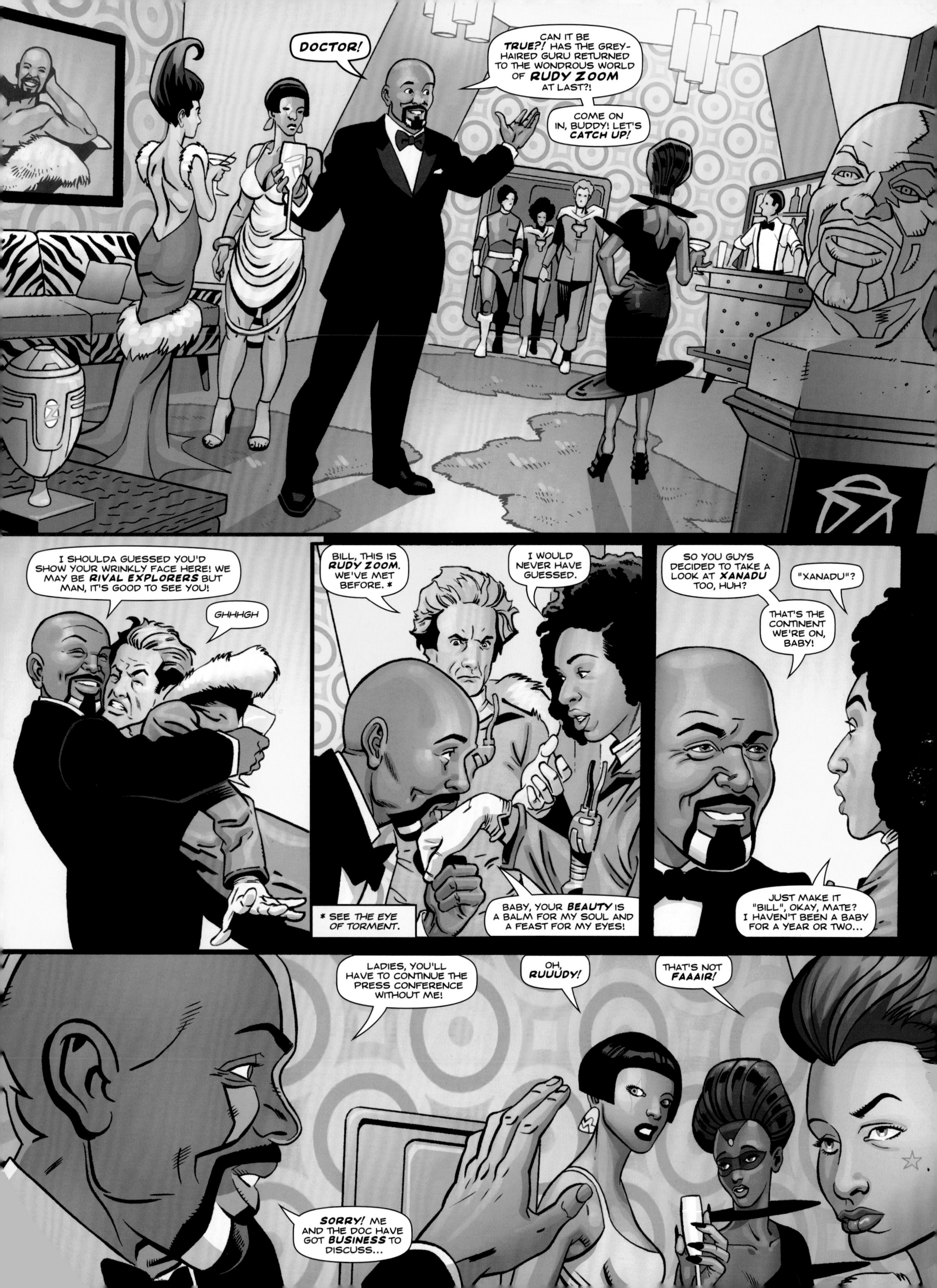
DOCTOR!
CAN IT BE TRUE?! HAS THE GREY-HAIRED GURU RETURNED TO THE WONDROUS WORLD OF RUDY ZOOM AT LAST?!
COME ON IN, BUDDY! LET'S CATCH UP!
I SHOULDA GUESSED YOU'D SHOW YOUR WRINKLY FACE HERE! WE MAY BE RIVAL EXPLORERS BUT MAN, IT'S GOOD TO SEE YOU!
GHHHGH
BILL, THIS IS RUDY ZOOM. WE'VE MET BEFORE. *
I WOULD NEVER HAVE GUESSED.
BABY, YOUR BEAUTY IS A BALM FOR MY SOUL AND A FEAST FOR MY EYES!
* SEE THE EYE OF TORMENT.
SO YOU GUYS DECIDED TO TAKE A LOOK AT XANADU TOO, HUH?
"XANADU"?
THAT'S THE CONTINENT WE'RE ON, BABY!
JUST MAKE IT "BILL", OKAY, MATE? I HAVEN'T BEEN A BABY FOR A YEAR OR TWO...
LADIES, YOU'LL HAVE TO CONTINUE THE PRESS CONFERENCE WITHOUT ME!
OH, RUUUDY!
THAT'S NOT FAAAIR!
SORRY! ME AND THE DOC HAVE GOT BUSINESS TO DISCUSS...

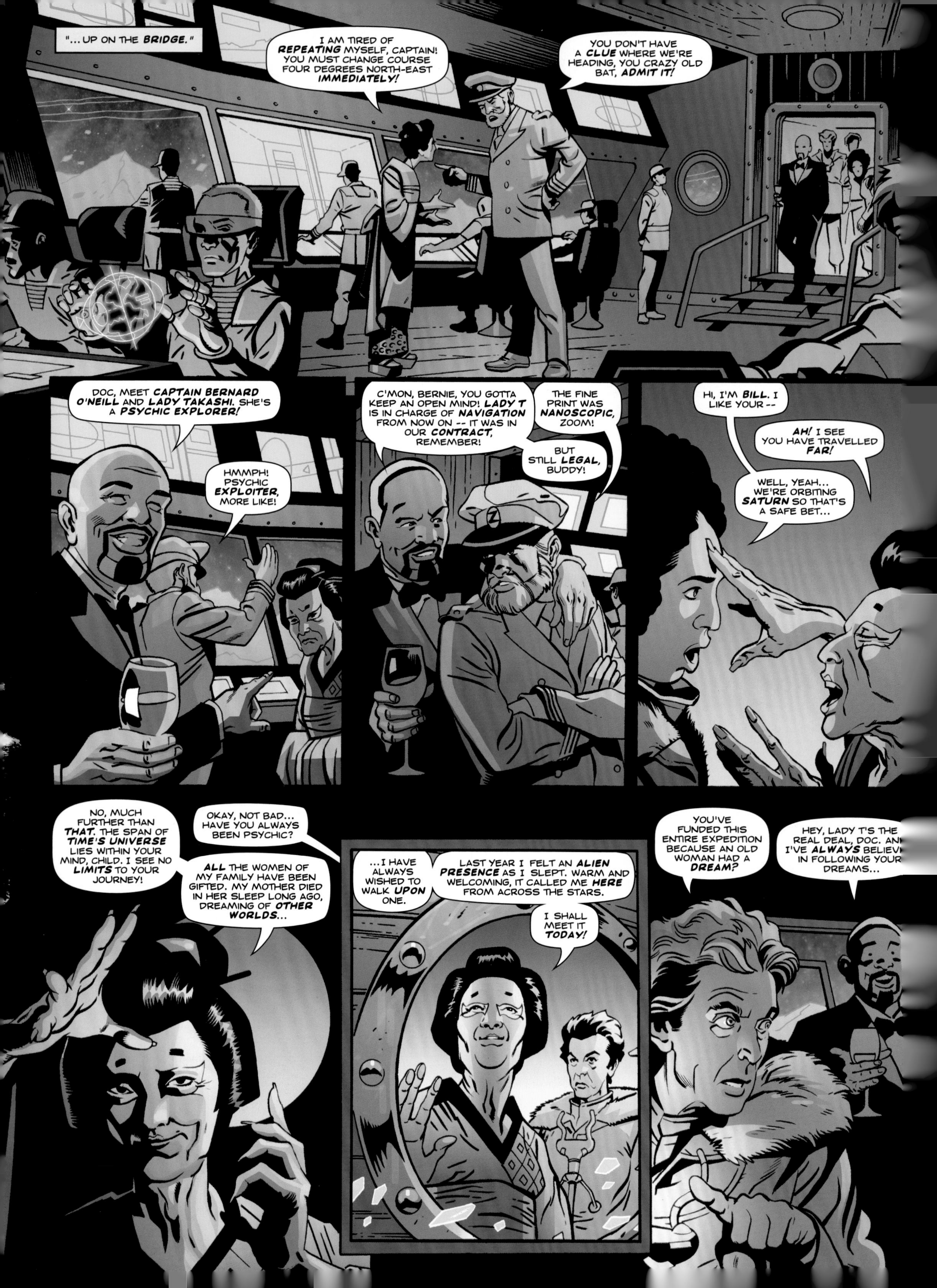
"...UP ON THE BRIDGE."
I AM TIRED OF REPEATING MYSELF, CAPTAIN! YOU MUST CHANGE COURSE FOUR DEGREES NORTH-EAST IMMEDIATELY!
YOU DON'T HAVE A CLUE WHERE WE'RE HEADING, YOU CRAZY OLD BAT, ADMIT IT!
DOC, MEET CAPTAIN BERNARD O'NEILL AND LADY TAKASHI. SHE'S A PSYCHIC EXPLORER!
HMMPH! PSYCHIC EXPLOITER, MORE LIKE!
C'MON, BERNIE, YOU GOTTA KEEP AN OPEN MIND! LADY T IS IN CHARGE OF NAVIGATION FROM NOW ON -- IT WAS IN OUR CONTRACT, REMEMBER!
THE FINE PRINT WAS NANOSCOPIC, ZOOM!
BUT STILL LEGAL, BUDDY!
HI, I'M BILL. I LIKE YOUR --
AH! I SEE YOU HAVE TRAVELLED FAR!
WELL, YEAH... WE'RE ORBITING SATURN SO THAT'S A SAFE BET...
NO, MUCH FURTHER THAN THAT. THE SPAN OF TIME'S UNIVERSE LIES WITHIN YOUR MIND, CHILD. I SEE NO LIMITS TO YOUR JOURNEY!
OKAY, NOT BAD... HAVE YOU ALWAYS BEEN PSYCHIC?
ALL THE WOMEN OF MY FAMILY HAVE BEEN GIFTED. MY MOTHER DIED IN HER SLEEP LONG AGO, DREAMING OF OTHER WORLDS...
...I HAVE ALWAYS WISHED TO WALK UPON ONE.
LAST YEAR I FELT AN ALIEN PRESENCE AS I SLEPT. WARM AND WELCOMING, IT CALLED ME HERE FROM ACROSS THE STARS.
I SHALL MEET IT TODAY!
YOU'VE FUNDED THIS ENTIRE EXPEDITION BECAUSE AN OLD WOMAN HAD A DREAM?
HEY, LADY T'S THE REAL DEAL, DOC. AN I'VE ALWAYS BELIEV IN FOLLOWING YOUR DREAMS...

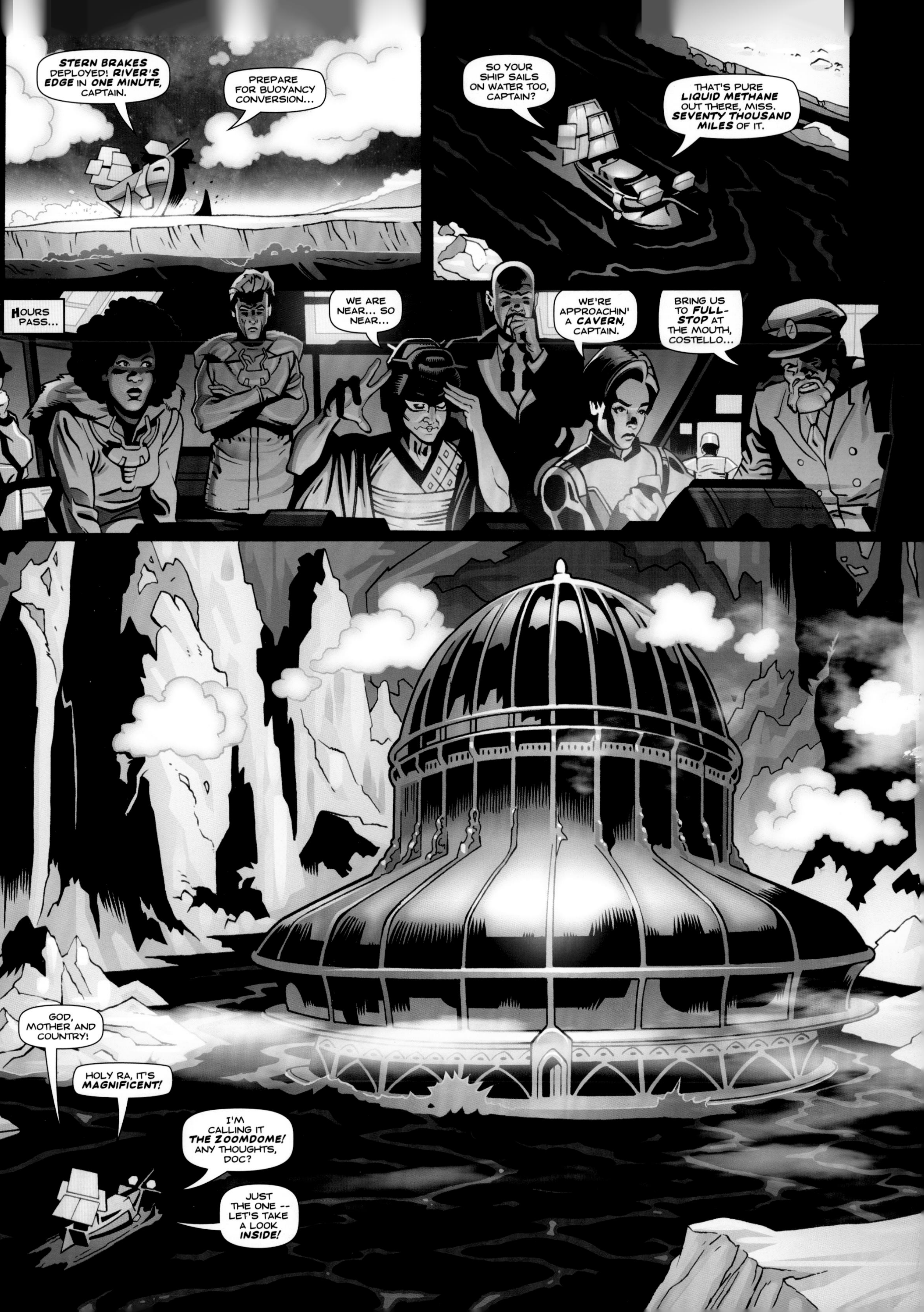
STERN BRAKES DEPLOYED! RIVER'S EDGE IN ONE MINUTE, CAPTAIN.
PREPARE FOR BUOYANCY CONVERSION...
SO YOUR SHIP SAILS ON WATER TOO, CAPTAIN?
THAT'S PURE LIQUID METHANE OUT THERE, MISS. SEVENTY THOUSAND MILES OF IT.
HOURS PASS...
WE ARE NEAR... SO NEAR...
WE'RE APPROACHIN' A CAVERN, CAPTAIN.
BRING US TO FULL-STOP AT THE MOUTH, COSTELLO...
GOD, MOTHER AND COUNTRY!
HOLY RA, IT'S MAGNIFICENT!
I'M CALLING IT THE ZOOMDOME! ANY THOUGHTS, DOC?
JUST THE ONE -- LET'S TAKE A LOOK INSIDE!

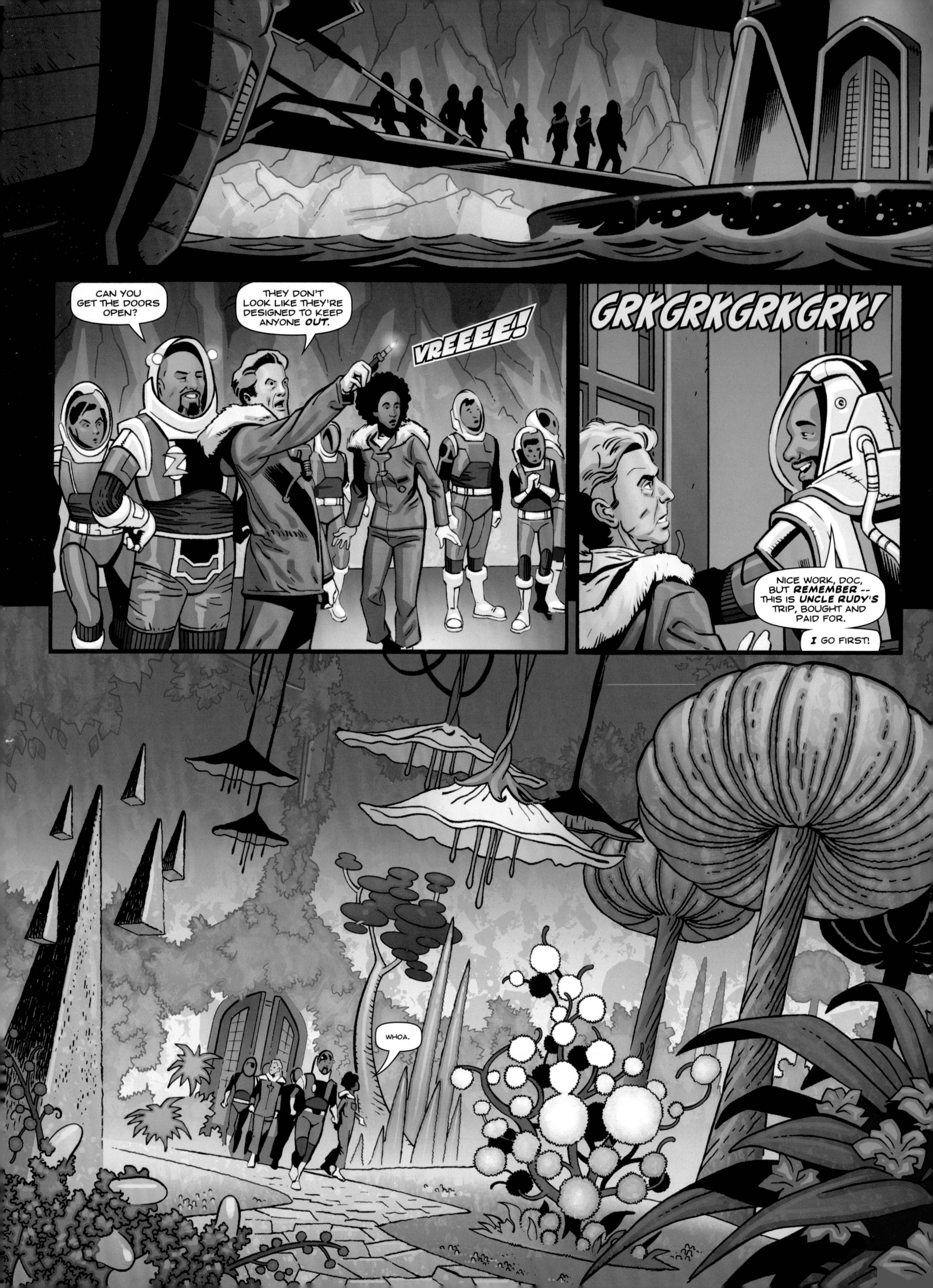
CAN YOU GET THE DOORS OPEN?
THEY DON'T LOOK LIKE THEY'RE DESIGNED TO KEEP ANYONE OUT.
VREEEEE!
GRKGRKGRKGRK!
NICE WORK, DOC, BUT REMEMBER -- THIS IS UNCLE RUDY'S TRIP, BOUGHT AND PAID FOR.
I GO FIRST!
WHOA.

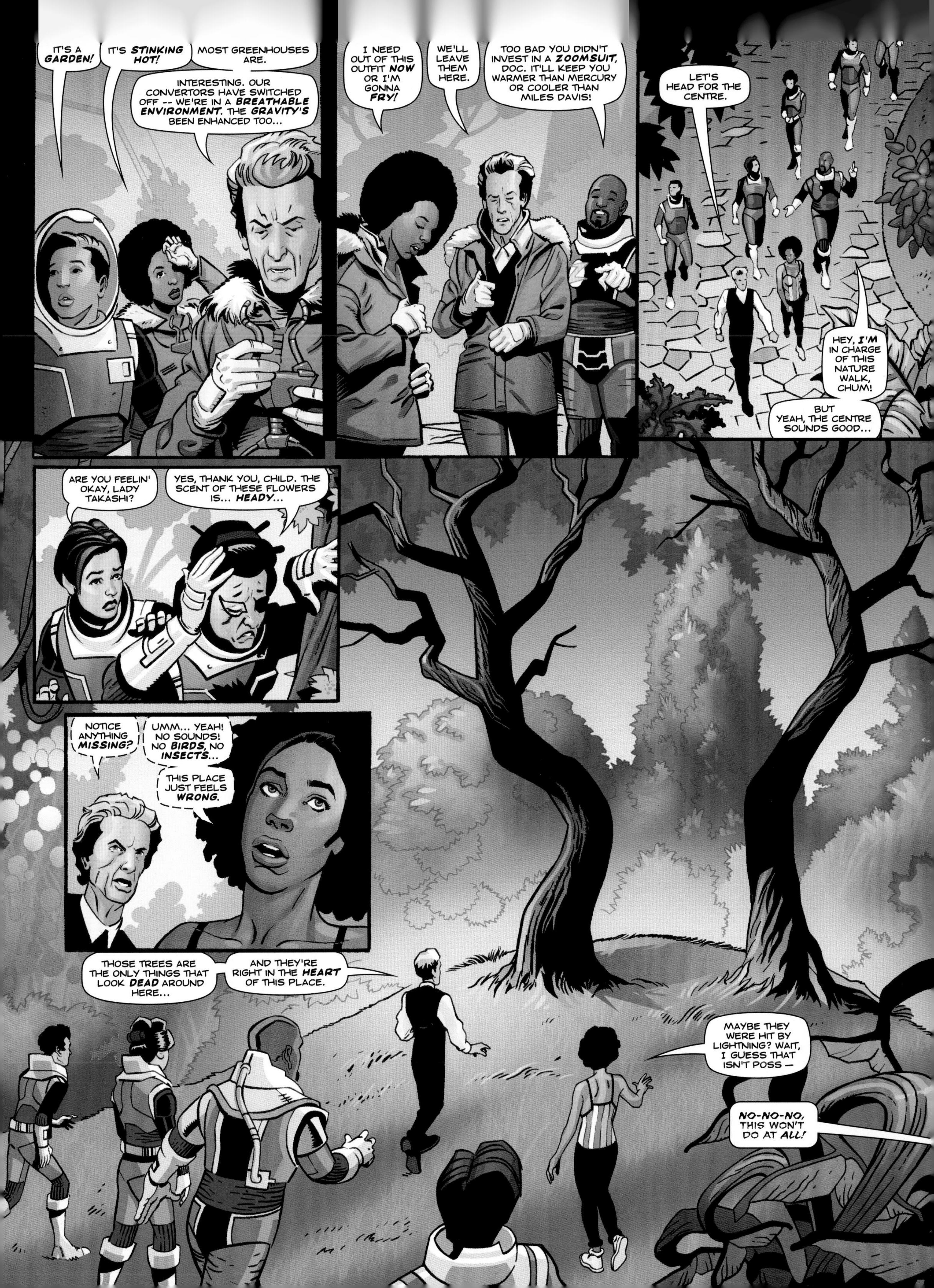
IT'S A GARDEN!
IT'S STINKING HOT!
MOST GREENHOUSES ARE.
INTERESTING. OUR CONVERTORS HAVE SWITCHED OFF -- WE'RE IN A BREATHABLE ENVIRONMENT. THE GRAVITY'S BEEN ENHANCED TOO...
I NEED OUT OF THIS OUTFIT NOW OR I'M GONNA FRY!
WE'LL LEAVE THEM HERE.
TOO BAD YOU DIDN'T INVEST IN A ZOOMSUIT, DOC. IT'LL KEEP YOU WARMER THAN MERCURY OR COOLER THAN MILES DAVIS!
LET'S HEAD FOR THE CENTRE.
HEY, I'M IN CHARGE OF THIS NATURE WALK, CHUM!
BUT YEAH, THE CENTRE SOUNDS GOOD...
ARE YOU FEELIN' OKAY, LADY TAKASHI?
YES, THANK YOU, CHILD. THE SCENT OF THESE FLOWERS IS... HEADY...
NOTICE ANYTHING MISSING?
UMM... YEAH! NO SOUNDS! NO BIRDS, NO INSECTS...
THIS PLACE JUST FEELS WRONG.
THOSE TREES ARE THE ONLY THINGS THAT LOOK DEAD AROUND HERE...
AND THEY'RE RIGHT IN THE HEART OF THIS PLACE.
MAYBE THEY WERE HIT BY LIGHTNING? WAIT, I GUESS THAT ISN'T POSS —
NO-NO-NO, THIS WON'T DO AT ALL!

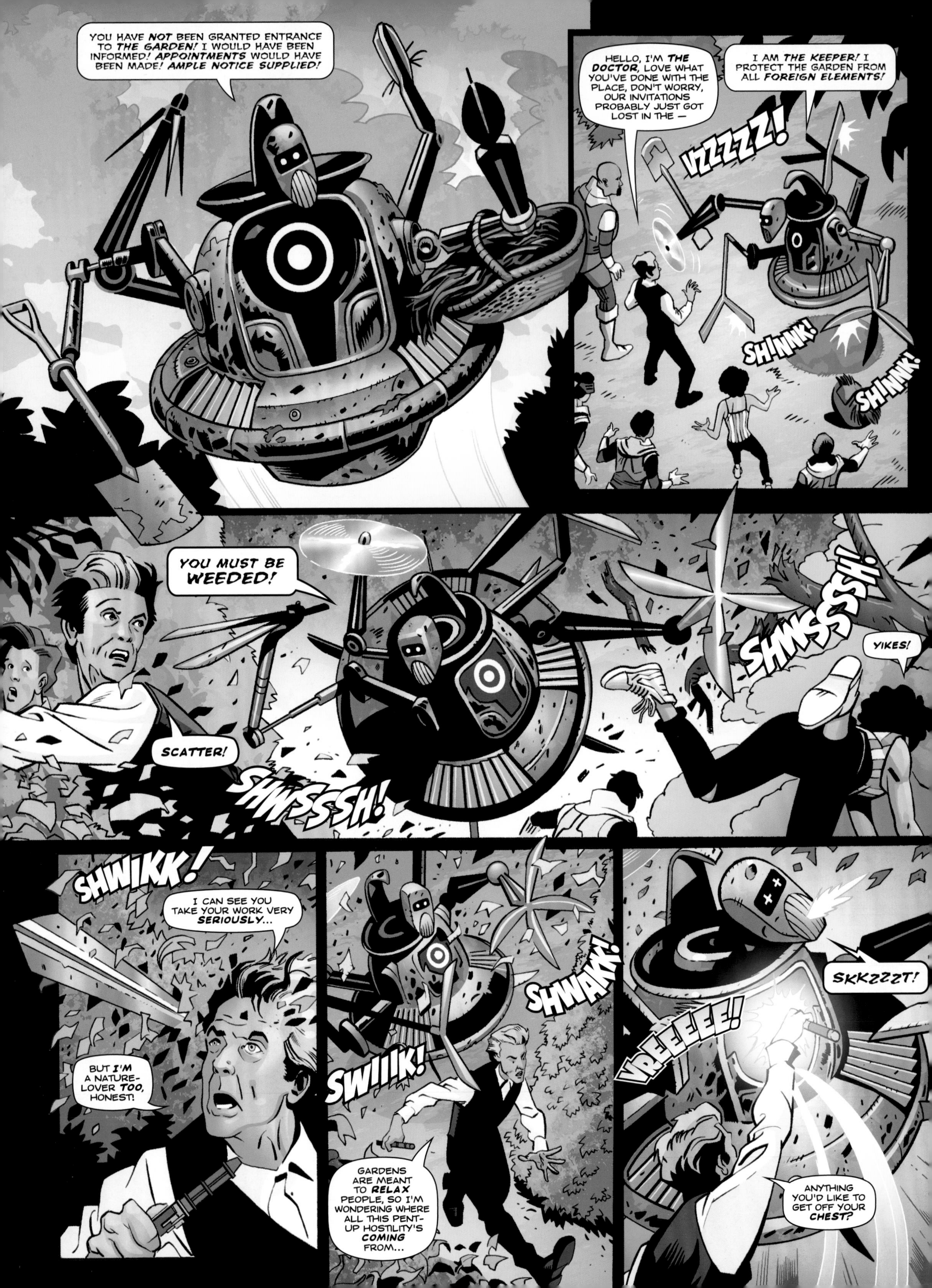
YOU HAVE NOT BEEN GRANTED ENTRANCE TO THE GARDEN! I WOULD HAVE BEEN INFORMED! APPOINTMENTS WOULD HAVE BEEN MADE! AMPLE NOTICE SUPPLIED!
HELLO, I'M THE DOCTOR, LOVE WHAT YOU'VE DONE WITH THE PLACE, DON'T WORRY, OUR INVITATIONS PROBABLY JUST GOT LOST IN THE —
I AM THE KEEPER! I PROTECT THE GARDEN FROM ALL FOREIGN ELEMENTS!
VZZZZZ!
SHINNK!
SHINNK!
YOU MUST BE WEEDED!
SHWSSSH!
YIKES!
SCATTER!
SHWSSSH!
SHWIKK!
I CAN SEE YOU TAKE YOUR WORK VERY SERIOUSLY...
BUT I'M A NATURE-LOVER TOO, HONEST!
SHWAKK!
SWIIIK!
GARDENS ARE MEANT TO RELAX PEOPLE, SO I'M WONDERING WHERE ALL THIS PENT-UP HOSTILITY'S COMING FROM...
SKKZZZT!
VREEEEE!
ANYTHING YOU'D LIKE TO GET OFF YOUR CHEST?

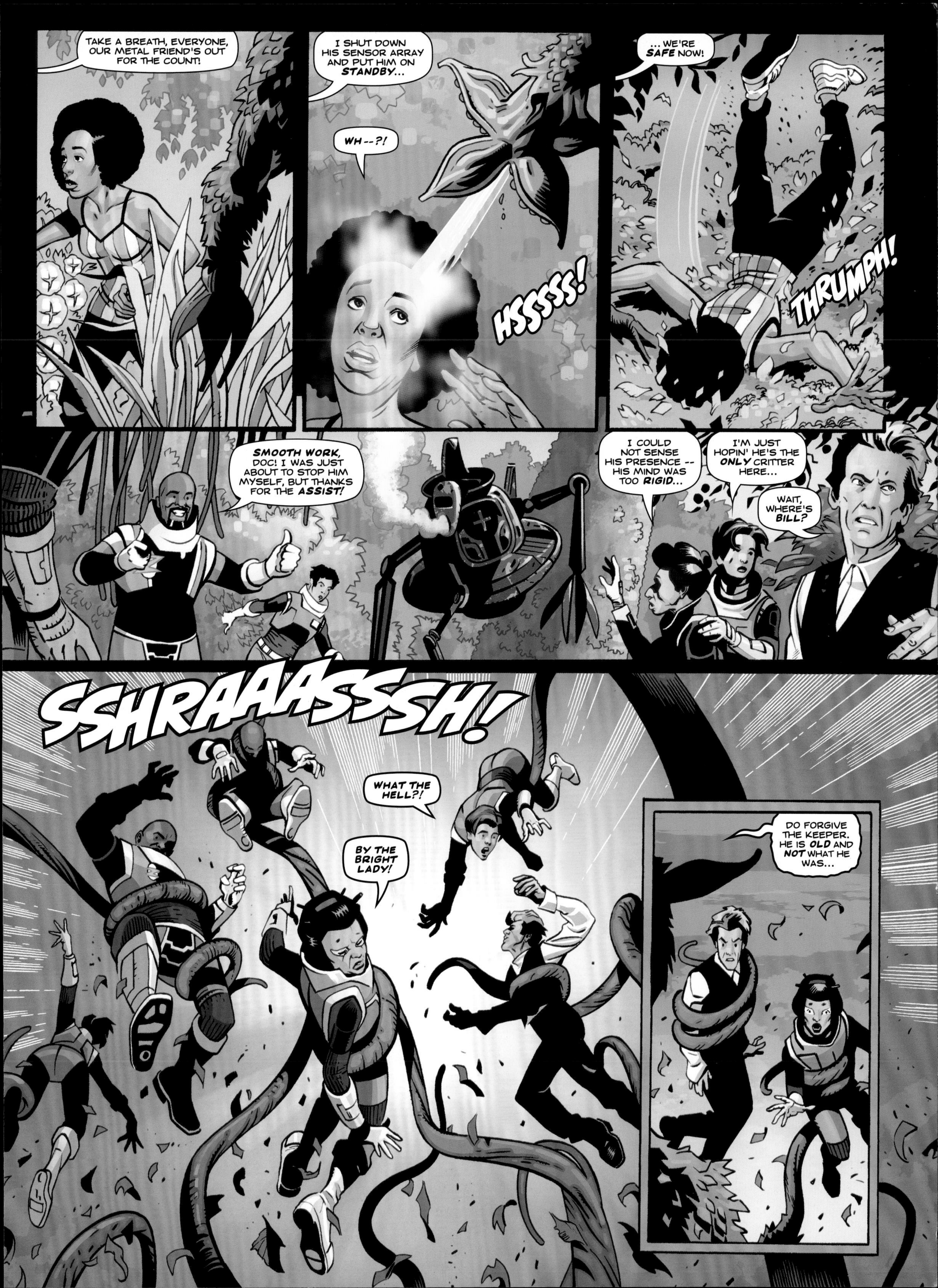

TAKE A BREATH, EVERYONE, OUR METAL FRIEND'S OUT FOR THE COUNT!
I SHUT DOWN HIS SENSOR ARRAY AND PUT HIM ON STANDBY...
WH--?!
HSSSSS!
...WE'RE SAFE NOW!
THRUMPH!
SMOOTH WORK, DOC! I WAS JUST ABOUT TO STOP HIM MYSELF, BUT THANKS FOR THE ASSIST!
I COULD NOT SENSE HIS PRESENCE -- HIS MIND WAS TOO RIGID...
I'M JUST HOPIN' HE'S THE ONLY CRITTER HERE...
WAIT, WHERE'S BILL?
SSHRAAASSSH!
WHAT THE HELL?!
BY THE BRIGHT LADY!
DO FORGIVE THE KEEPER. HE IS OLD AND NOT WHAT HE WAS...

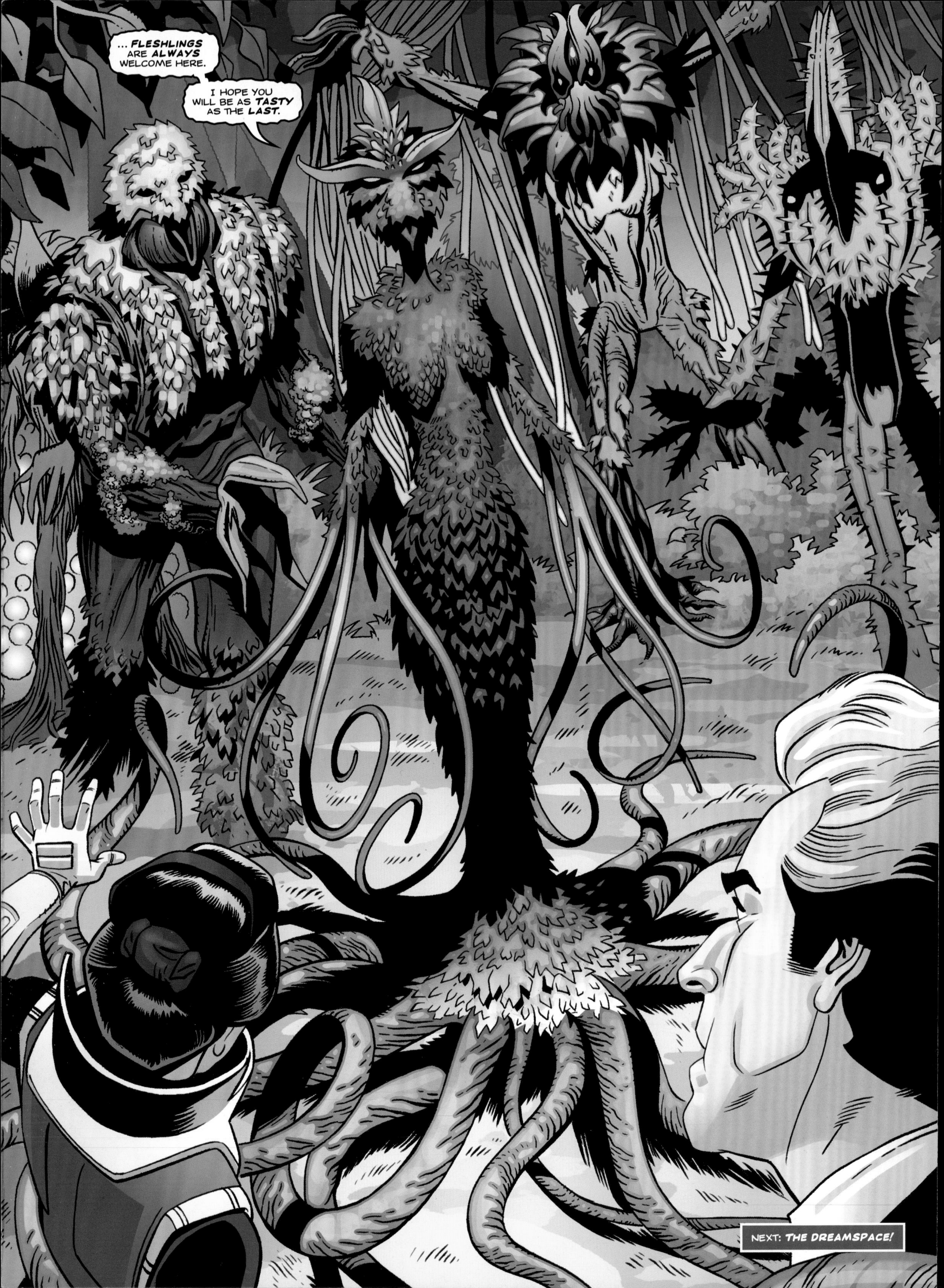
... FLESHLINGS ARE ALWAYS WELCOME HERE.
I HOPE YOU WILL BE AS TASTY AS THE LAST.
NEXT: THE DREAMSPACE!

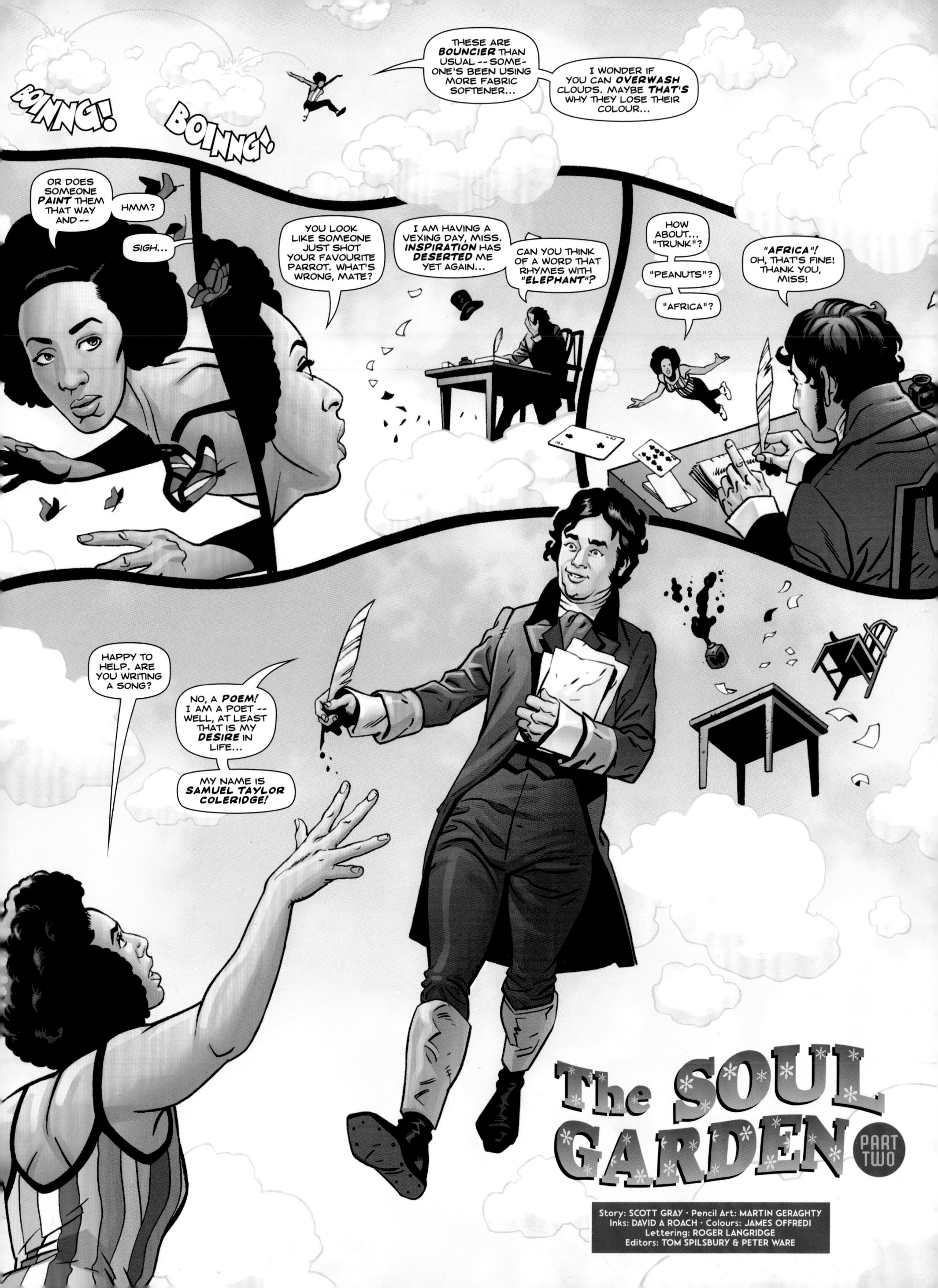
BOINNG!
BOINNG!
THESE ARE BOUNCIER THAN USUAL -- SOME-ONE'S BEEN USING MORE FABRIC SOFTENER...
I WONDER IF YOU CAN OVERWASH CLOUDS. MAYBE THAT'S WHY THEY LOSE THEIR COLOUR...
OR DOES SOMEONE PAINT THEM THAT WAY AND --
HMM?
SIGH...
YOU LOOK LIKE SOMEONE JUST SHOT YOUR FAVOURITE PARROT. WHAT'S WRONG, MATE?
I AM HAVING A VEXING DAY, MISS. INSPIRATION HAS DESERTED ME YET AGAIN...
CAN YOU THINK OF A WORD THAT RHYMES WITH "ELEPHANT"?
HOW ABOUT... "TRUNK"?
"PEANUTS"?
"AFRICA"?
"AFRICA"! OH, THAT'S FINE! THANK YOU, MISS!
HAPPY TO HELP. ARE YOU WRITING A SONG?
NO, A POEM! I AM A POET -- WELL, AT LEAST THAT IS MY DESIRE IN LIFE...
MY NAME IS SAMUEL TAYLOR COLERIDGE!
The SOUL GARDEN PART TWO
Story: SCOTT GRAY · Pencil Art: MARTIN GERAGHTY
Inks: DAVID A ROACH · Colours: JAMES OFFREDI
Lettering: ROGER LANGRIDGE
Editors: TOM SPILSBURY & PETER WARE

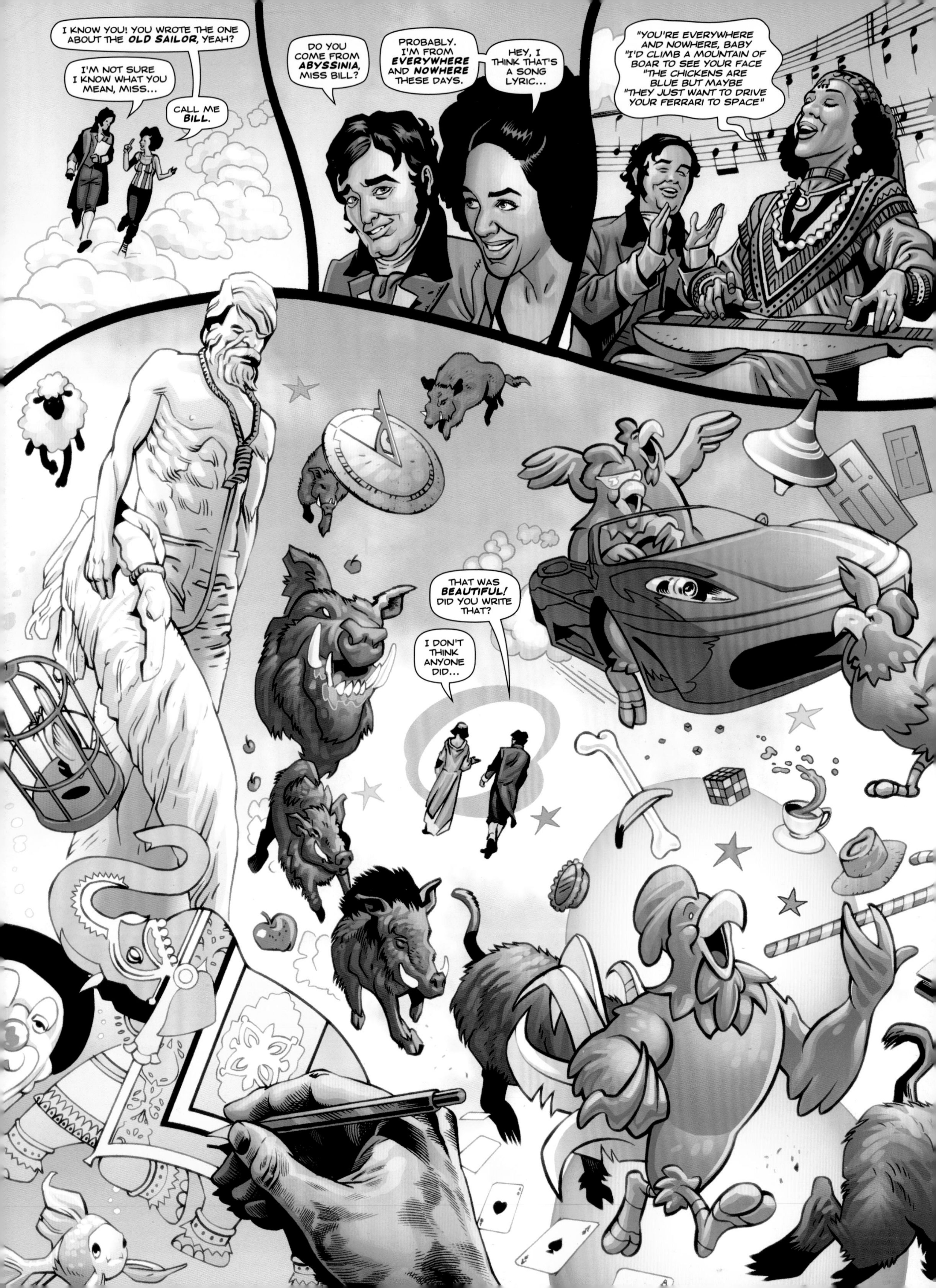
I KNOW YOU! YOU WROTE THE ONE ABOUT THE OLD SAILOR, YEAH?
I'M NOT SURE I KNOW WHAT YOU MEAN, MISS...
CALL ME BILL.
DO YOU COME FROM ABYSSINIA, MISS BILL?
PROBABLY. I'M FROM EVERYWHERE AND NOWHERE THESE DAYS.
HEY, I THINK THAT'S A SONG LYRIC...
"YOU'RE EVERYWHERE AND NOWHERE, BABY "I'D CLIMB A MOUNTAIN OF BOAR TO SEE YOUR FACE "THE CHICKENS ARE BLUE BUT MAYBE "THEY JUST WANT TO DRIVE YOUR FERRARI TO SPACE"
THAT WAS BEAUTIFUL! DID YOU WRITE THAT?
I DON'T THINK ANYONE DID...

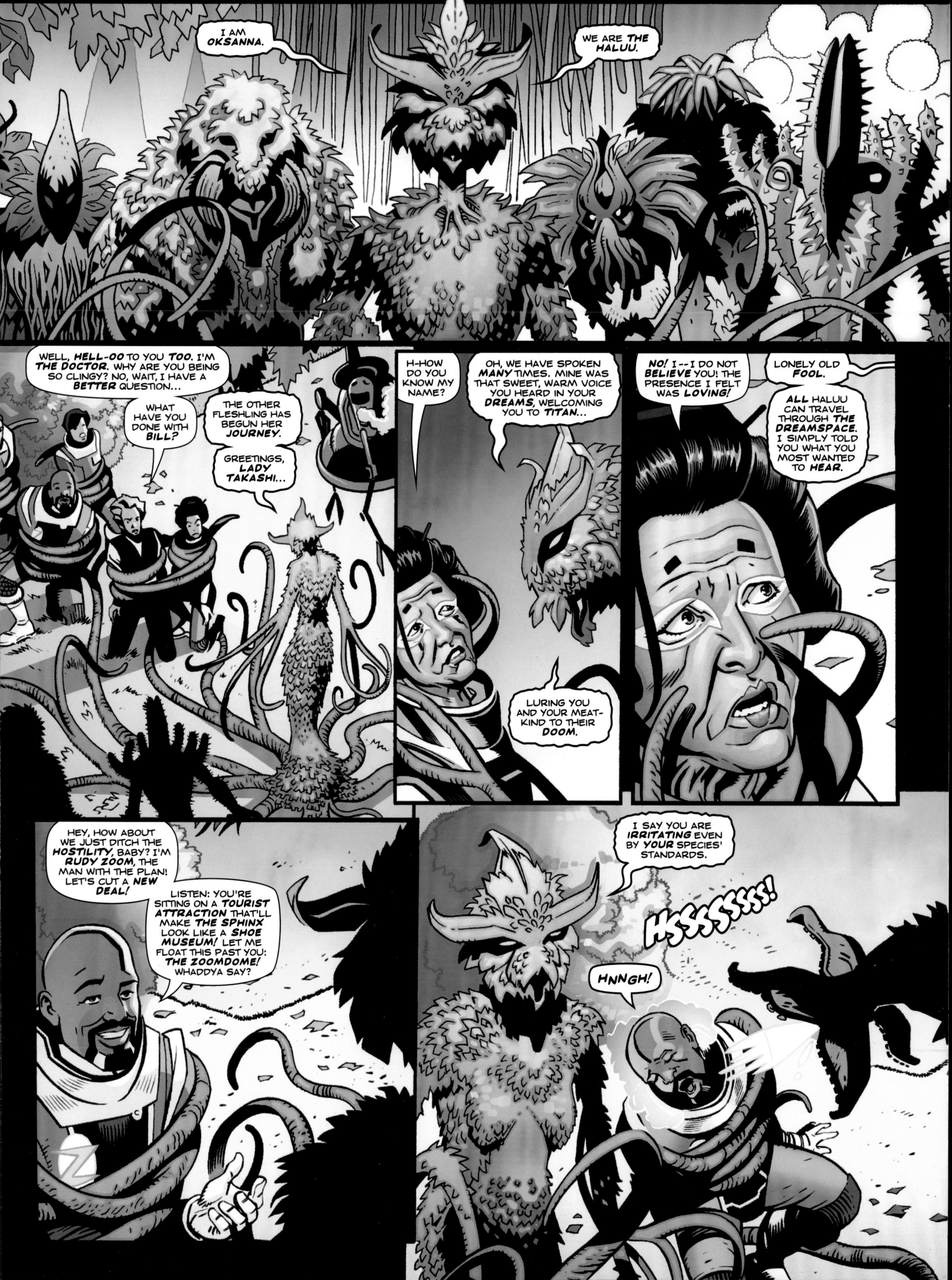
I AM OKSANNA.
WE ARE THE HALUU.
WELL, HELL-OO TO YOU TOO. I'M THE DOCTOR. WHY ARE YOU BEING SO CLINGY? NO, WAIT, I HAVE A BETTER QUESTION...
WHAT HAVE YOU DONE WITH BILL?
THE OTHER FLESHLING HAS BEGUN HER JOURNEY.
GREETINGS, LADY TAKASHI...
H-HOW DO YOU KNOW MY NAME?
OH, WE HAVE SPOKEN MANY TIMES. MINE WAS THAT SWEET, WARM VOICE YOU HEARD IN YOUR DREAMS, WELCOMING YOU TO TITAN...
LURING YOU AND YOUR MEAT-KIND TO THEIR DOOM.
NO! I -- I DO NOT BELIEVE YOU! THE PRESENCE I FELT WAS LOVING!
LONELY OLD FOOL.
ALL HALUU CAN TRAVEL THROUGH THE DREAMSPACE. I SIMPLY TOLD YOU WHAT YOU MOST WANTED TO HEAR.
HEY, HOW ABOUT WE JUST DITCH THE HOSTILITY, BABY? I'M RUDY ZOOM, THE MAN WITH THE PLAN! LET'S CUT A NEW DEAL!
LISTEN: YOU'RE SITTING ON A TOURIST ATTRACTION THAT'LL MAKE THE SPHINX LOOK LIKE A SHOE MUSEUM! LET ME FLOAT THIS PAST YOU: THE ZOOMDOME! WHADDYA SAY?
I SAY YOU ARE IRRITATING EVEN BY YOUR SPECIES' STANDARDS.
HSSSSSSSS!
HNNGH!

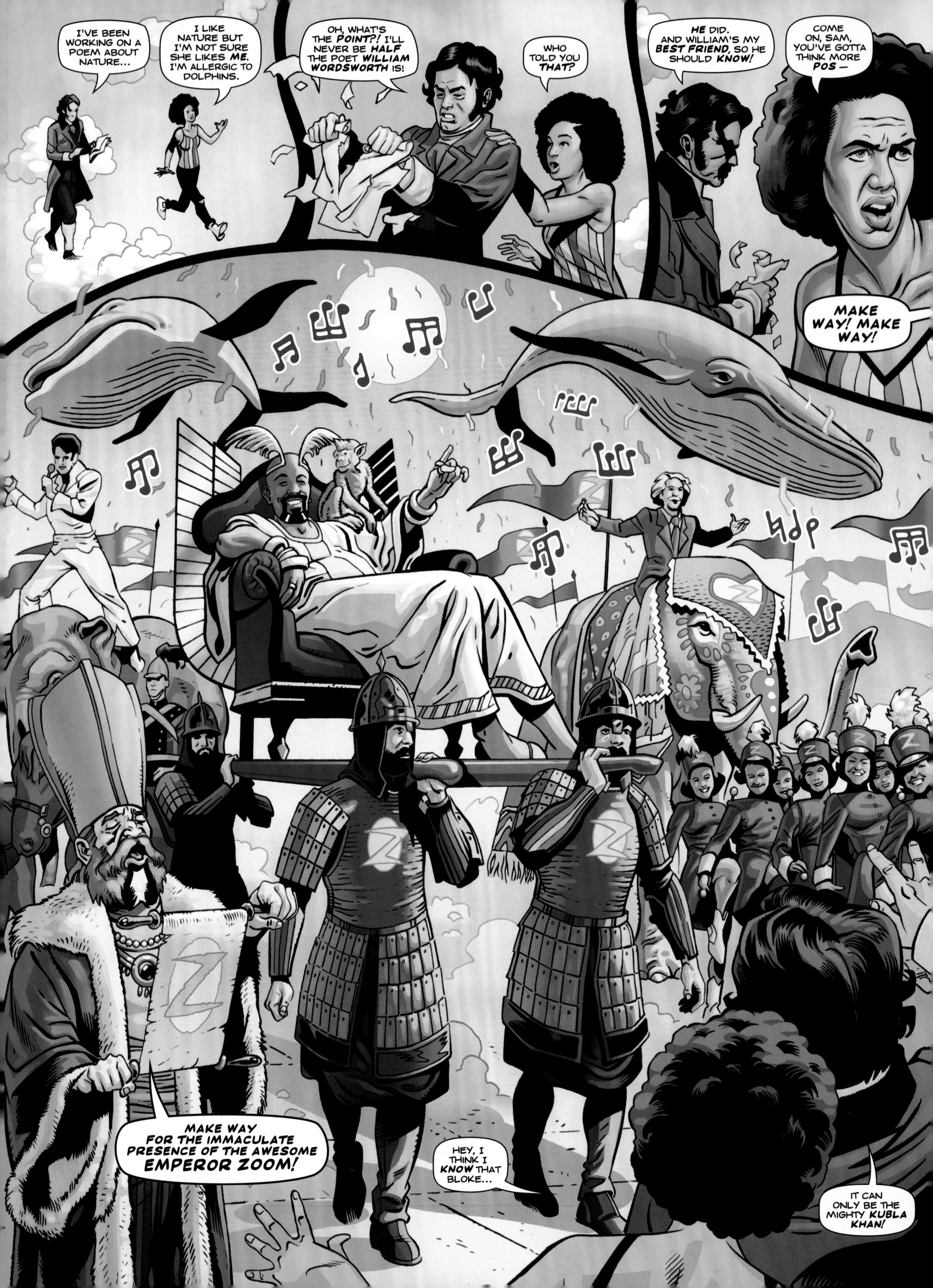

I'VE BEEN WORKING ON A POEM ABOUT NATURE...
I LIKE NATURE BUT I'M NOT SURE SHE LIKES ME. I'M ALLERGIC TO DOLPHINS.
OH, WHAT'S THE POINT?! I'LL NEVER BE HALF THE POET WILLIAM WORDSWORTH IS!
WHO TOLD YOU THAT?
HE DID. AND WILLIAM'S MY BEST FRIEND, SO HE SHOULD KNOW!
COME ON, SAM, YOU'VE GOTTA THINK MORE POS —
MAKE WAY! MAKE WAY!
MAKE WAY FOR THE IMMACULATE PRESENCE OF THE AWESOME EMPEROR ZOOM!
HEY, I THINK I KNOW THAT BLOKE...
IT CAN ONLY BE THE MIGHTY KUBLA KHAN!

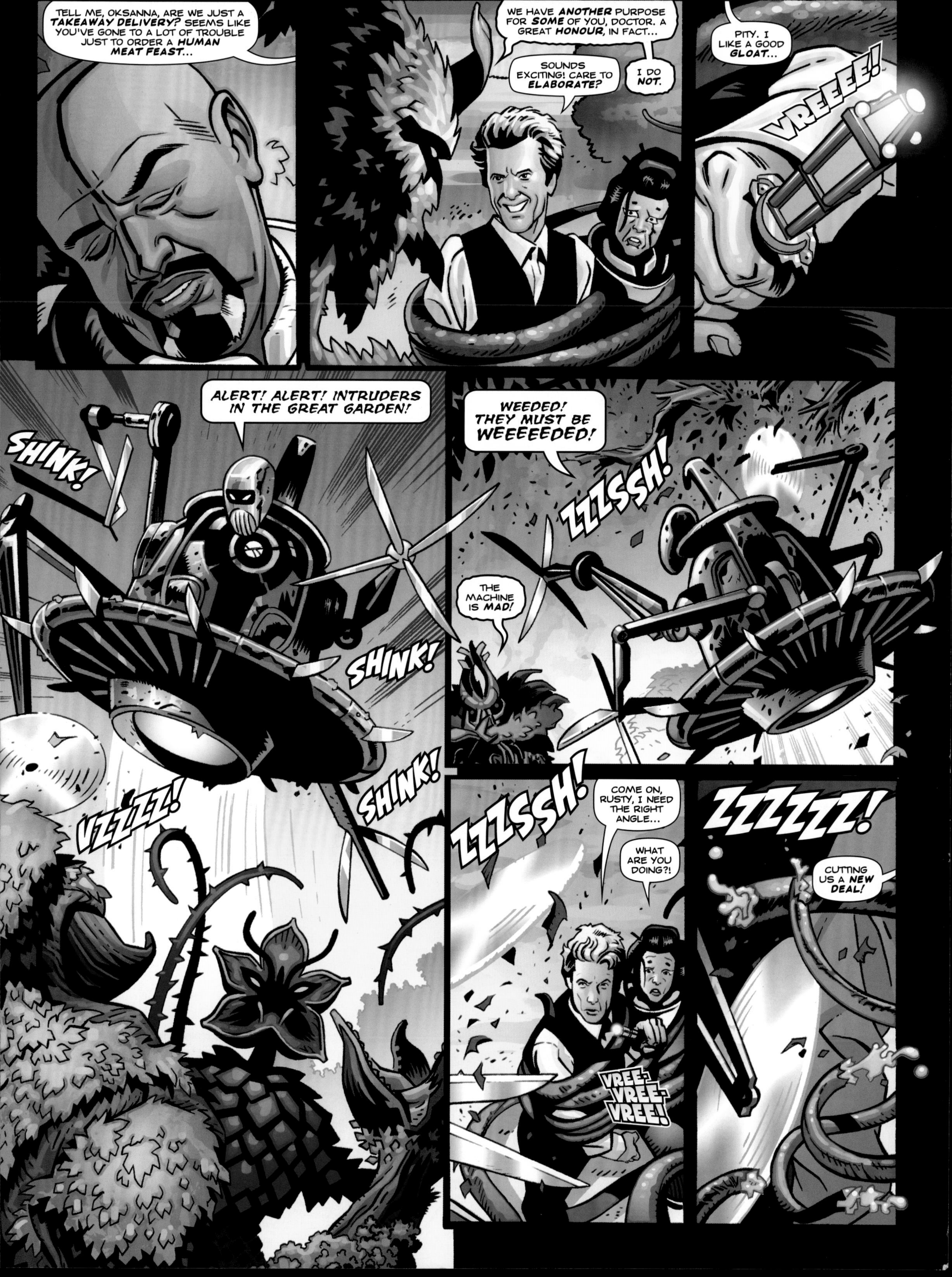

TELL ME, OKSANNA, ARE WE JUST A TAKEAWAY DELIVERY? SEEMS LIKE YOU'VE GONE TO A LOT OF TROUBLE JUST TO ORDER A HUMAN MEAT FEAST...
WE HAVE ANOTHER PURPOSE FOR SOME OF YOU, DOCTOR. A GREAT HONOUR, IN FACT...
SOUNDS EXCITING! CARE TO ELABORATE?
I DO NOT.
PITY. I LIKE A GOOD GLOAT...
VREEEE!
ALERT! ALERT! INTRUDERS IN THE GREAT GARDEN!
SHINK!
SHINK!
SHINK!
VZZZZ!
WEEDED! THEY MUST BE WEEEEEDED!
ZZZSSH!
THE MACHINE IS MAD!
ZZZSSH!
COME ON, RUSTY, I NEED THE RIGHT ANGLE...
WHAT ARE YOU DOING?!
VREE-VREE-VREE!
ZZZZZZ!
CUTTING US A NEW DEAL!

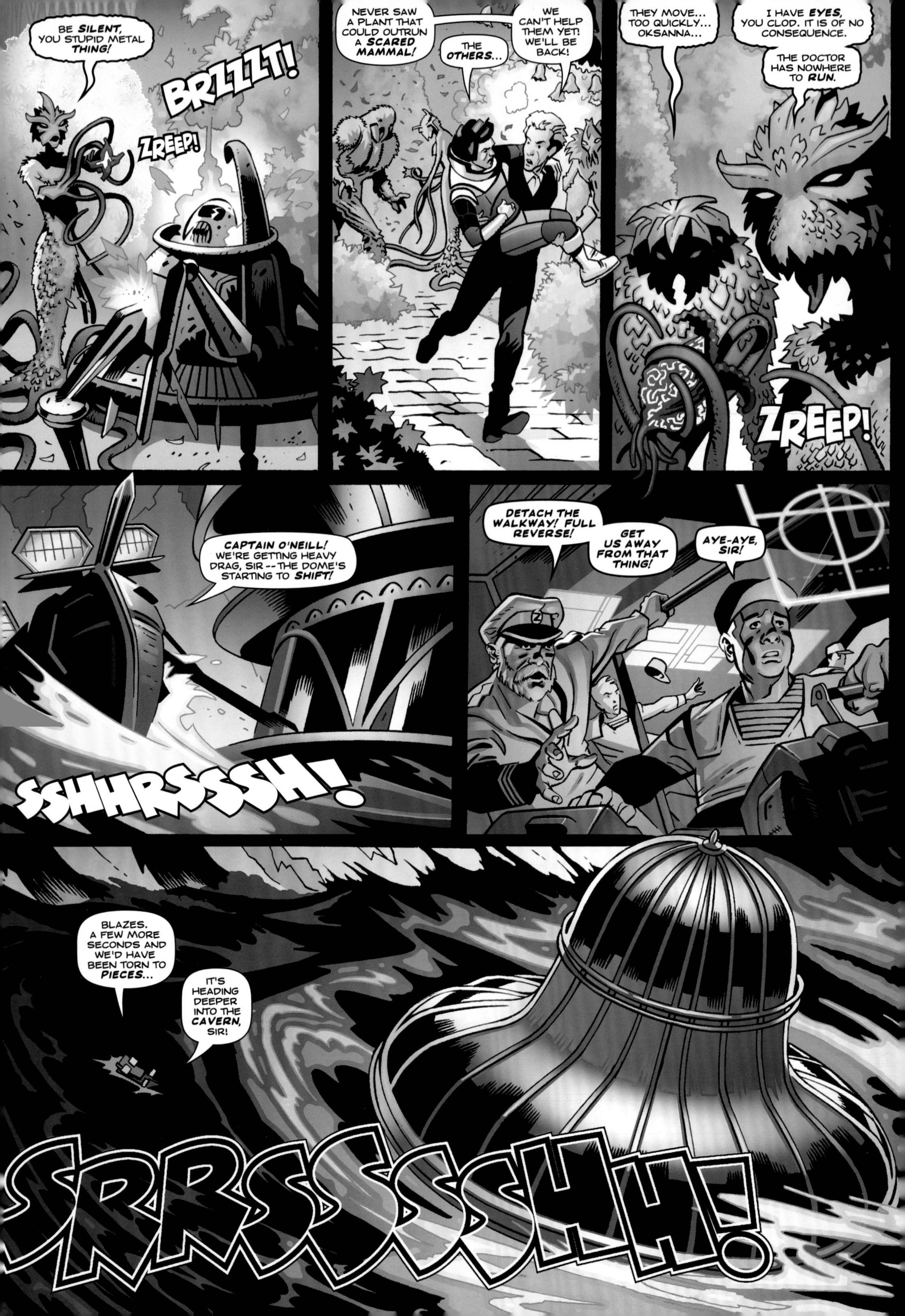
BE SILENT, YOU STUPID METAL THING!
BRZZZT!
ZREEP!
NEVER SAW A PLANT THAT COULD OUTRUN A SCARED MAMMAL!
THE OTHERS...
WE CAN'T HELP THEM YET! WE'LL BE BACK!
THEY MOVE... TOO QUICKLY... OKSANNA...
I HAVE EYES, YOU CLOD. IT IS OF NO CONSEQUENCE.
THE DOCTOR HAS NOWHERE TO RUN.
ZREEP!
CAPTAIN O'NEILL! WE'RE GETTING HEAVY DRAG, SIR -- THE DOME'S STARTING TO SHIFT!
SSHRSSSH!
DETACH THE WALKWAY! FULL REVERSE!
GET US AWAY FROM THAT THING!
AYE-AYE, SIR!
BLAZES. A FEW MORE SECONDS AND WE'D HAVE BEEN TORN TO PIECES...
IT'S HEADING DEEPER INTO THE CAVERN, SIR!
SRRSSSSHH!

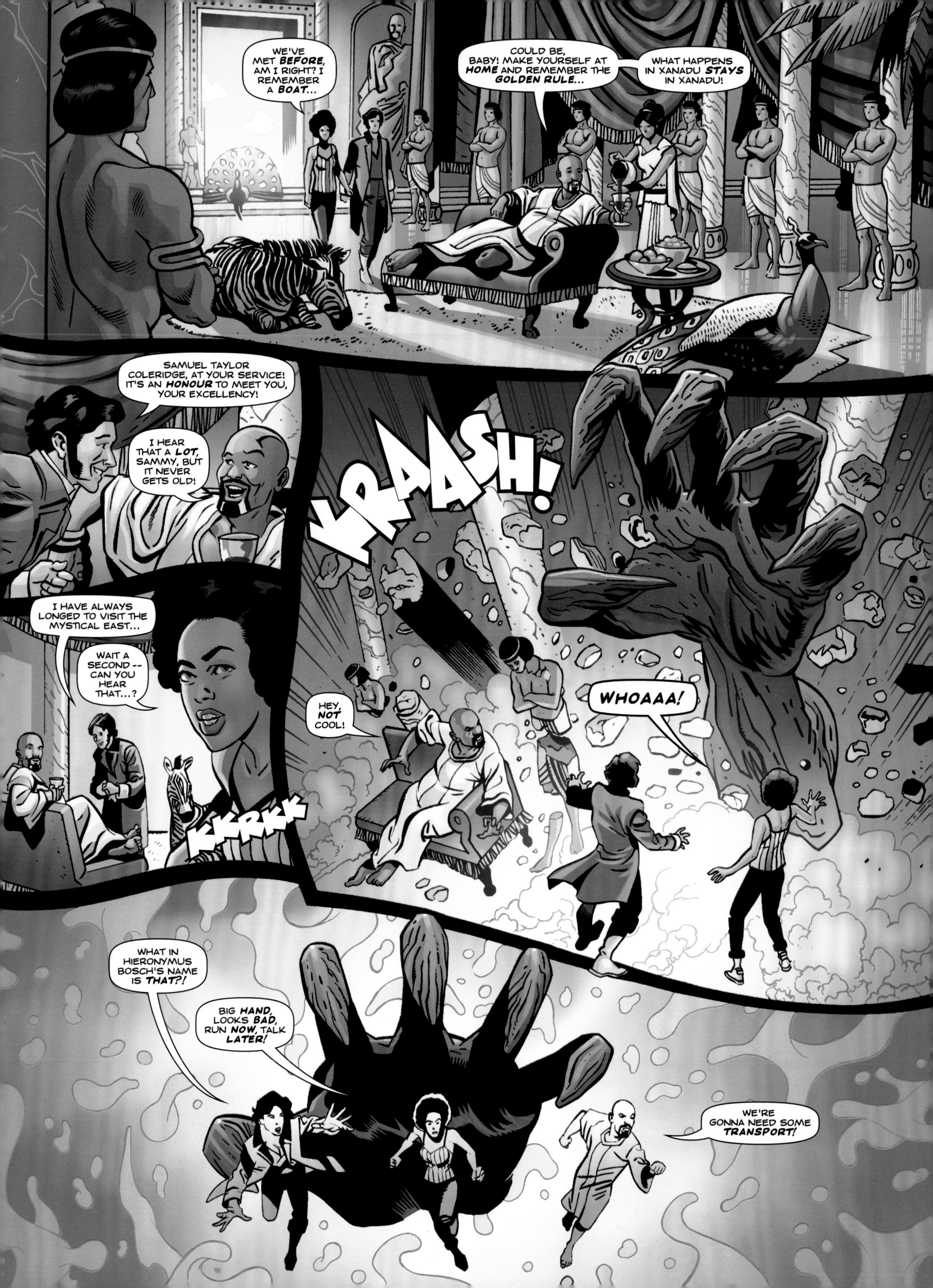

WE'VE MET BEFORE, AM I RIGHT? I REMEMBER A BOAT...
COULD BE, BABY! MAKE YOURSELF AT HOME AND REMEMBER THE GOLDEN RULE...
WHAT HAPPENS IN XANADU STAYS IN XANADU!
SAMUEL TAYLOR COLERIDGE, AT YOUR SERVICE! IT'S AN HONOUR TO MEET YOU, YOUR EXCELLENCY!
I HEAR THAT A LOT, SAMMY, BUT IT NEVER GETS OLD!
I HAVE ALWAYS LONGED TO VISIT THE MYSTICAL EAST...
WAIT A SECOND -- CAN YOU HEAR THAT...?
KKRKK
KRAASH!
HEY, NOT COOL!
WHOAAA!
WHAT IN HIERONYMUS BOSCH'S NAME IS THAT?!
BIG HAND, LOOKS BAD, RUN NOW, TALK LATER!
WE'RE GONNA NEED SOME TRANSPORT!

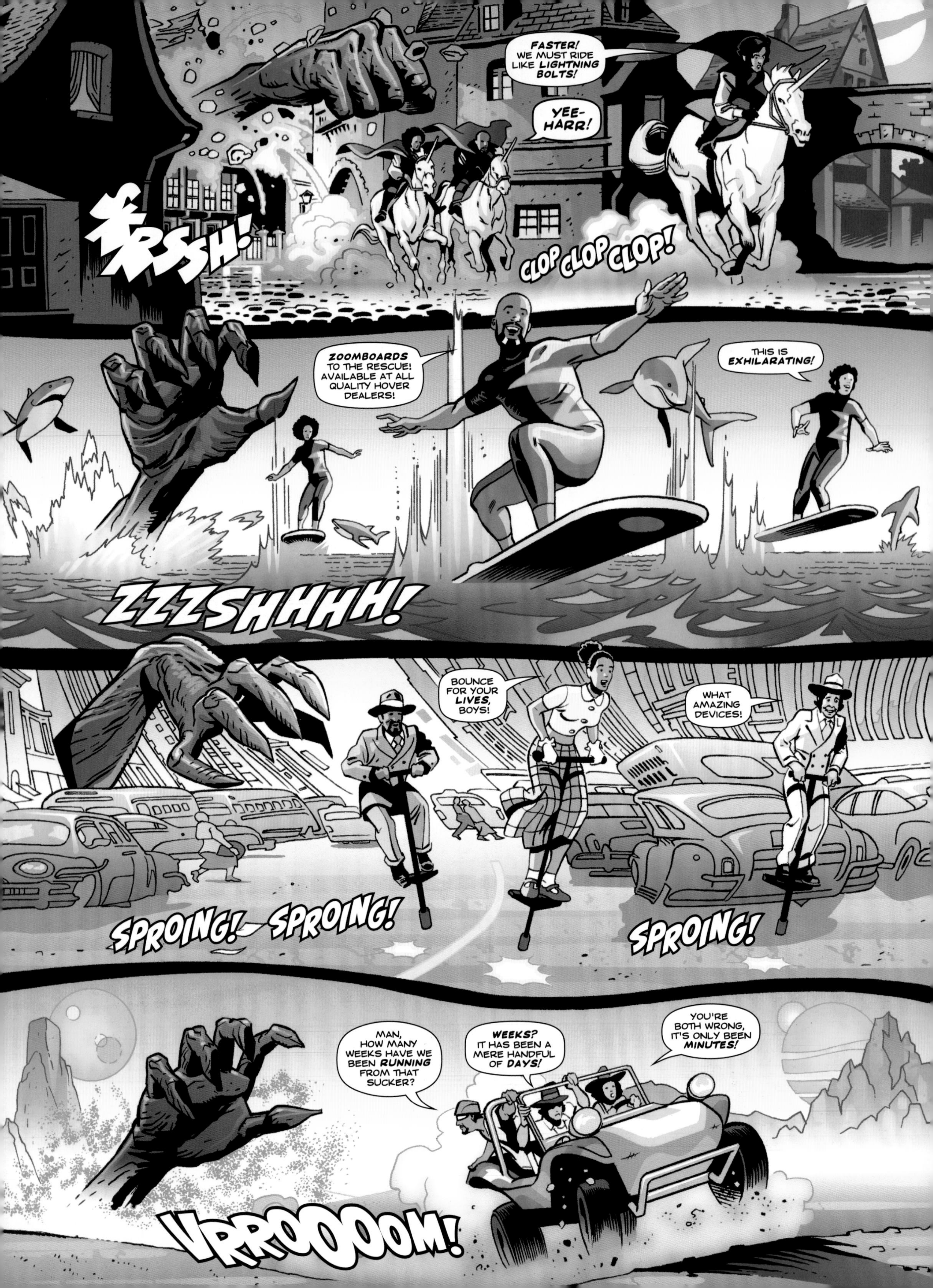
FASTER! WE MUST RIDE LIKE LIGHTNING BOLTS!
YEE-HARR!
FRSSH!
CLOP CLOP CLOP!
ZOOMBOARDS TO THE RESCUE! AVAILABLE AT ALL QUALITY HOVER DEALERS!
THIS IS EXHILARATING!
ZZZSHHHH!
BOUNCE FOR YOUR LIVES, BOYS!
WHAT AMAZING DEVICES!
SPROING! SPROING!
SPROING!
MAN, HOW MANY WEEKS HAVE WE BEEN RUNNING FROM THAT SUCKER?
WEEKS? IT HAS BEEN A MERE HANDFUL OF DAYS!
YOU'RE BOTH WRONG, IT'S ONLY BEEN MINUTES!
VRROOOOM!

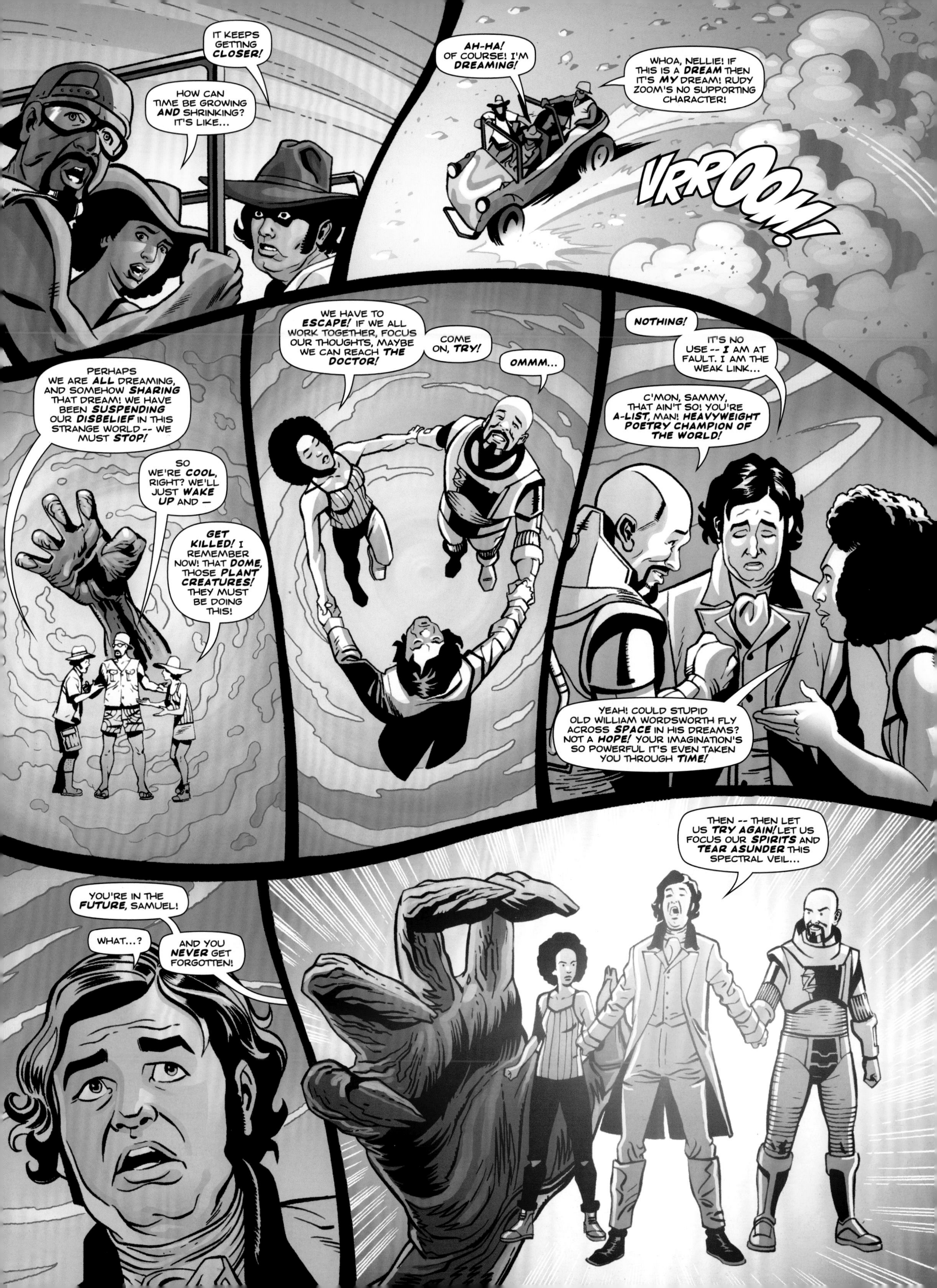
IT KEEPS GETTING CLOSER!
HOW CAN TIME BE GROWING AND SHRINKING? IT'S LIKE...
AH-HA! OF COURSE! I'M DREAMING!
WHOA, NELLIE! IF THIS IS A DREAM THEN IT'S MY DREAM! RUDY ZOOM'S NO SUPPORTING CHARACTER!
VRROOM!
PERHAPS WE ARE ALL DREAMING, AND SOMEHOW SHARING THAT DREAM! WE HAVE BEEN SUSPENDING OUR DISBELIEF IN THIS STRANGE WORLD -- WE MUST STOP!
SO WE'RE COOL, RIGHT? WE'LL JUST WAKE UP AND —
GET KILLED! I REMEMBER NOW! THAT DOME, THOSE PLANT CREATURES! THEY MUST BE DOING THIS!
WE HAVE TO ESCAPE! IF WE ALL WORK TOGETHER, FOCUS OUR THOUGHTS, MAYBE WE CAN REACH THE DOCTOR!
COME ON, TRY!
OMMM...
NOTHING!
IT'S NO USE -- I AM AT FAULT. I AM THE WEAK LINK...
C'MON, SAMMY, THAT AIN'T SO! YOU'RE A-LIST, MAN! HEAVYWEIGHT POETRY CHAMPION OF THE WORLD!
YEAH! COULD STUPID OLD WILLIAM WORDSWORTH FLY ACROSS SPACE IN HIS DREAMS? NOT A HOPE! YOUR IMAGINATION'S SO POWERFUL IT'S EVEN TAKEN YOU THROUGH TIME!
YOU'RE IN THE FUTURE, SAMUEL!
WHAT...?
AND YOU NEVER GET FORGOTTEN!
THEN -- THEN LET US TRY AGAIN! LET US FOCUS OUR SPIRITS AND TEAR ASUNDER THIS SPECTRAL VEIL...

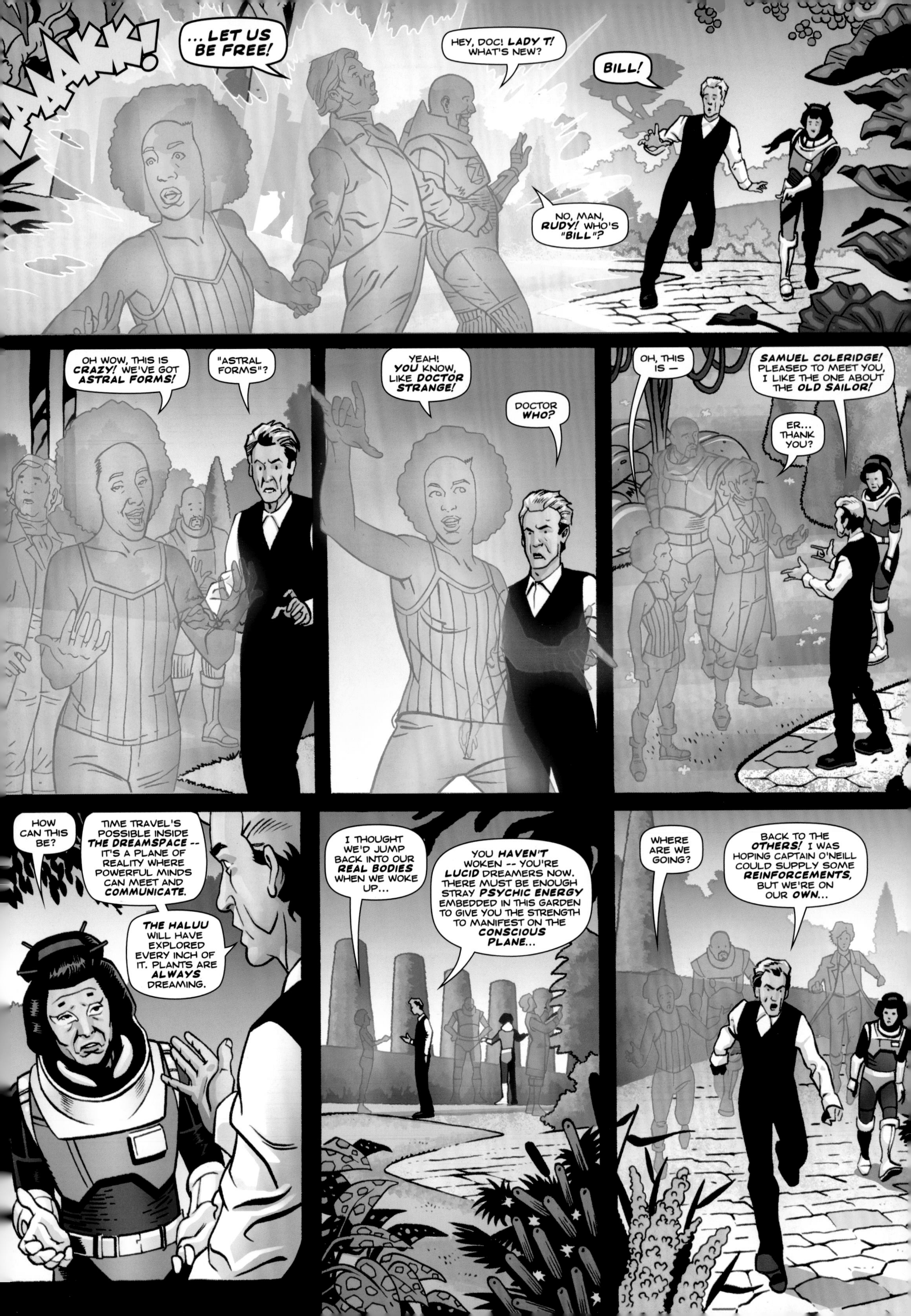
AAAKK!
...LET US BE FREE!
HEY, DOC! LADY T! WHAT'S NEW?
BILL!
NO, MAN, RUDY! WHO'S "BILL"?
OH WOW, THIS IS CRAZY! WE'VE GOT ASTRAL FORMS!
"ASTRAL FORMS"?
YEAH! YOU KNOW, LIKE DOCTOR STRANGE!
DOCTOR WHO?
OH, THIS IS —
SAMUEL COLERIDGE! PLEASED TO MEET YOU, I LIKE THE ONE ABOUT THE OLD SAILOR!
ER... THANK YOU?
HOW CAN THIS BE?
TIME TRAVEL'S POSSIBLE INSIDE THE DREAMSPACE -- IT'S A PLANE OF REALITY WHERE POWERFUL MINDS CAN MEET AND COMMUNICATE.
THE HALUU WILL HAVE EXPLORED EVERY INCH OF IT. PLANTS ARE ALWAYS DREAMING.
I THOUGHT WE'D JUMP BACK INTO OUR REAL BODIES WHEN WE WOKE UP...
YOU HAVEN'T WOKEN -- YOU'RE LUCID DREAMERS NOW. THERE MUST BE ENOUGH STRAY PSYCHIC ENERGY EMBEDDED IN THIS GARDEN TO GIVE YOU THE STRENGTH TO MANIFEST ON THE CONSCIOUS PLANE...
WHERE ARE WE GOING?
BACK TO THE OTHERS! I WAS HOPING CAPTAIN O'NEILL COULD SUPPLY SOME REINFORCEMENTS, BUT WE'RE ON OUR OWN...

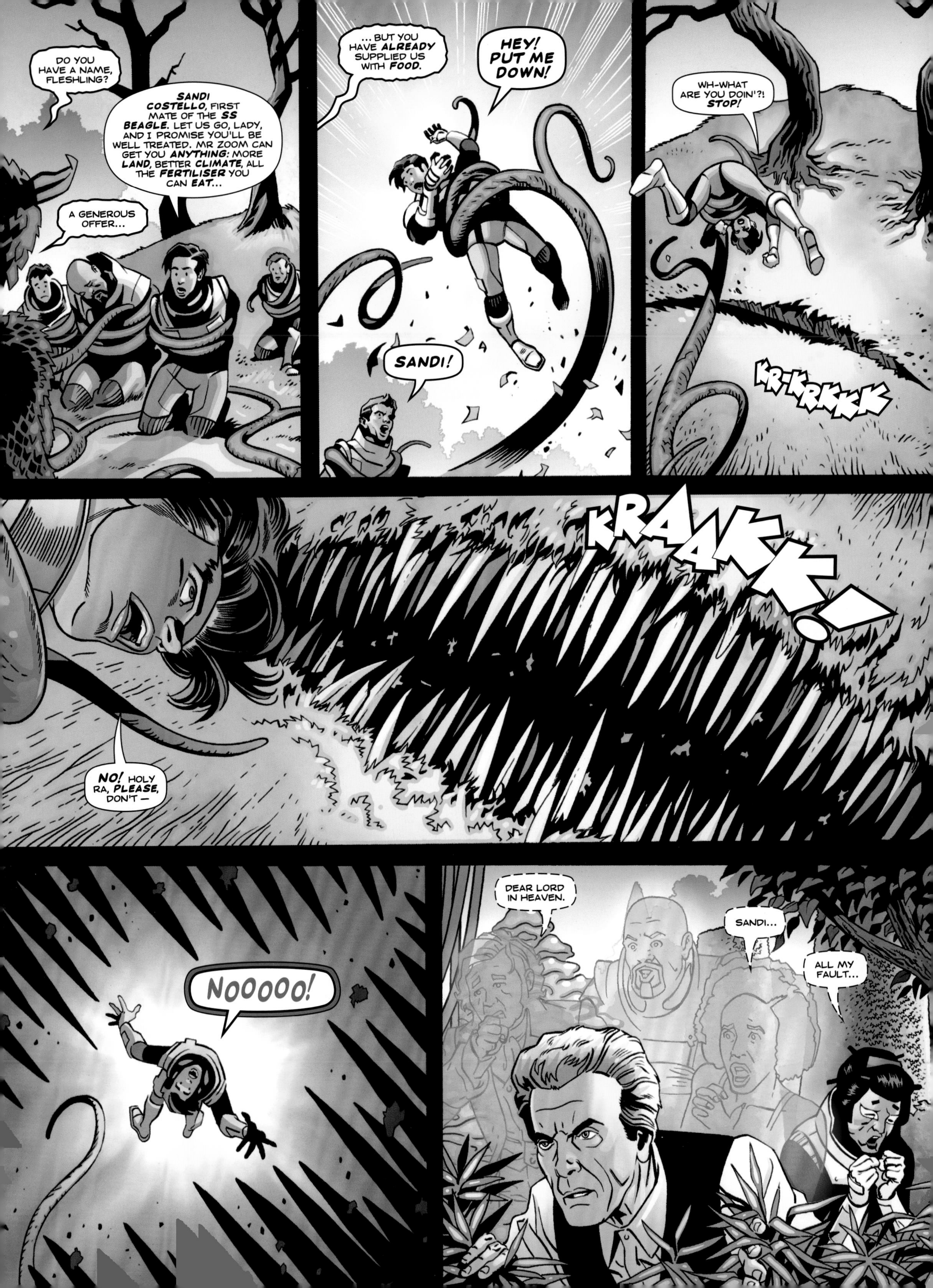
DO YOU HAVE A NAME, FLESHLING?
SANDI COSTELLO, FIRST MATE OF THE SS BEAGLE. LET US GO, LADY, AND I PROMISE YOU'LL BE WELL TREATED. MR ZOOM CAN GET YOU ANYTHING: MORE LAND, BETTER CLIMATE, ALL THE FERTILISER YOU CAN EAT...
A GENEROUS OFFER...
...BUT YOU HAVE ALREADY SUPPLIED US WITH FOOD.
HEY! PUT ME DOWN!
SANDI!
WH-WHAT ARE YOU DOIN'?! STOP!
KR-KRKKK
KRAAKK!
NO! HOLY RA, PLEASE, DON'T —
NOOOOO!
DEAR LORD IN HEAVEN.
SANDI...
ALL MY FAULT...

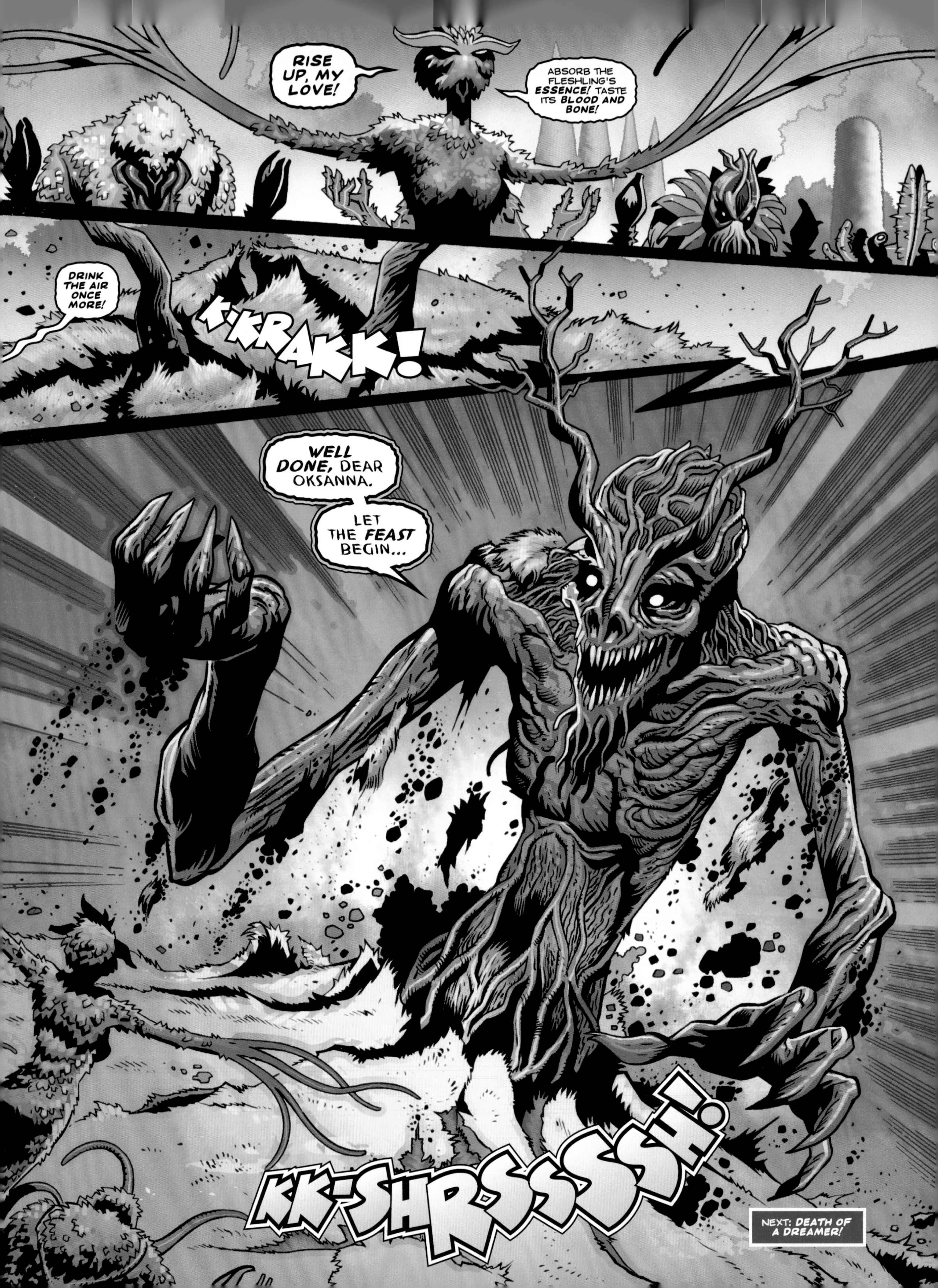
RISE UP, MY LOVE!
ABSORB THE FLESHLING'S ESSENCE! TASTE ITS BLOOD AND BONE!
DRINK THE AIR ONCE MORE!
K-KRAKK!
WELL DONE, DEAR OKSANNA.
LET THE FEAST BEGIN...
KK-SHRSSSSH!
NEXT: DEATH OF A DREAMER!

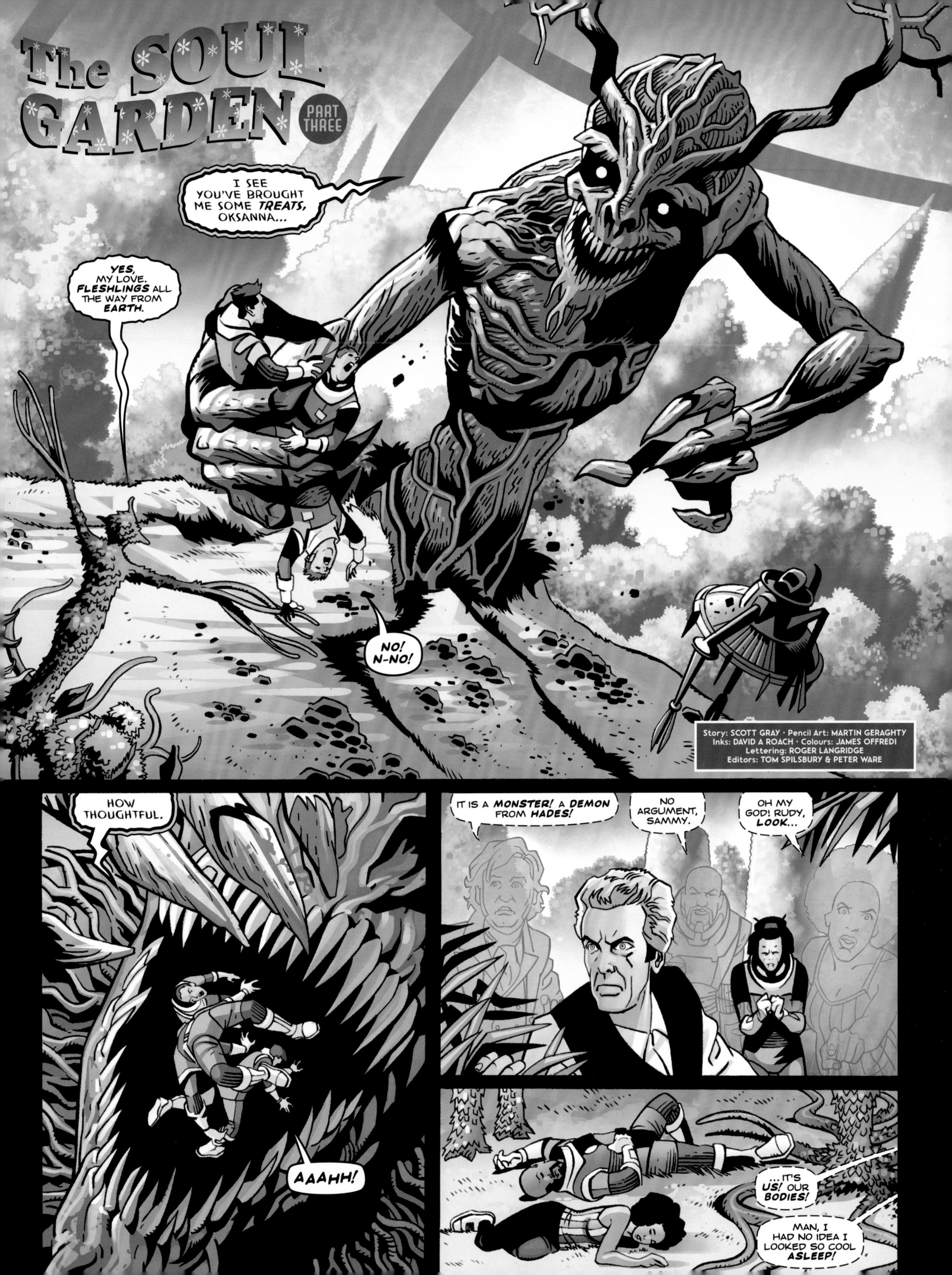
The SOUL GARDEN
PART THREE
I SEE YOU'VE BROUGHT ME SOME TREATS, OKSANNA...
YES, MY LOVE. FLESHLINGS ALL THE WAY FROM EARTH.
NO! N-NO!
Story: SCOTT GRAY · Pencil Art: MARTIN GERAGHTY
Inks: DAVID A ROACH · Colours: JAMES OFFREDI
Lettering: ROGER LANGRIDGE
Editors: TOM SPILSBURY & PETER WARE
HOW THOUGHTFUL.
AAAHH!
IT IS A MONSTER! A DEMON FROM HADES!
NO ARGUMENT, SAMMY.
OH MY GOD! RUDY, LOOK...
... IT'S US! OUR BODIES!
MAN, I HAD NO IDEA I LOOKED SO COOL ASLEEP!

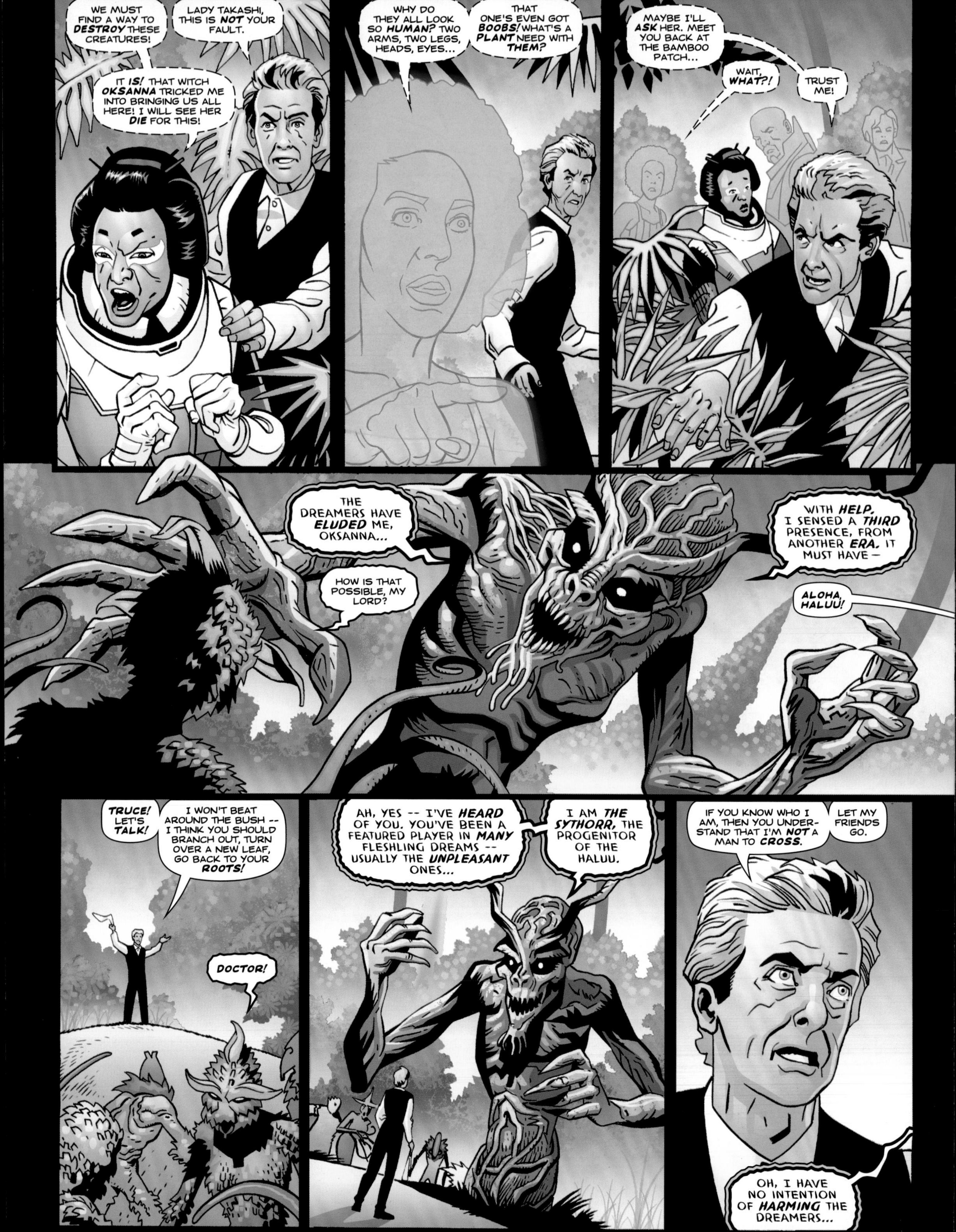

WE MUST FIND A WAY TO DESTROY THESE CREATURES!
LADY TAKASHI, THIS IS NOT YOUR FAULT.
IT IS! THAT WITCH OKSANNA TRICKED ME INTO BRINGING US ALL HERE! I WILL SEE HER DIE FOR THIS!
WHY DO THEY ALL LOOK SO HUMAN? TWO ARMS, TWO LEGS, HEADS, EYES...
THAT ONE'S EVEN GOT BOOBS! WHAT'S A PLANT NEED WITH THEM?
MAYBE I'LL ASK HER. MEET YOU BACK AT THE BAMBOO PATCH...
WAIT, WHAT?!
TRUST ME!
THE DREAMERS HAVE ELUDED ME, OKSANNA...
HOW IS THAT POSSIBLE, MY LORD?
WITH HELP. I SENSED A THIRD PRESENCE, FROM ANOTHER ERA. IT MUST HAVE—
ALOHA, HALUU!
TRUCE! LET'S TALK!
I WON'T BEAT AROUND THE BUSH -- I THINK YOU SHOULD BRANCH OUT, TURN OVER A NEW LEAF, GO BACK TO YOUR ROOTS!
DOCTOR!
AH, YES -- I'VE HEARD OF YOU. YOU'VE BEEN A FEATURED PLAYER IN MANY FLESHLING DREAMS -- USUALLY THE UNPLEASANT ONES...
I AM THE SYTHORR, THE PROGENITOR OF THE HALUU.
IF YOU KNOW WHO I AM, THEN YOU UNDERSTAND THAT I'M NOT A MAN TO CROSS.
LET MY FRIENDS GO.
OH, I HAVE NO INTENTION OF HARMING THE DREAMERS...

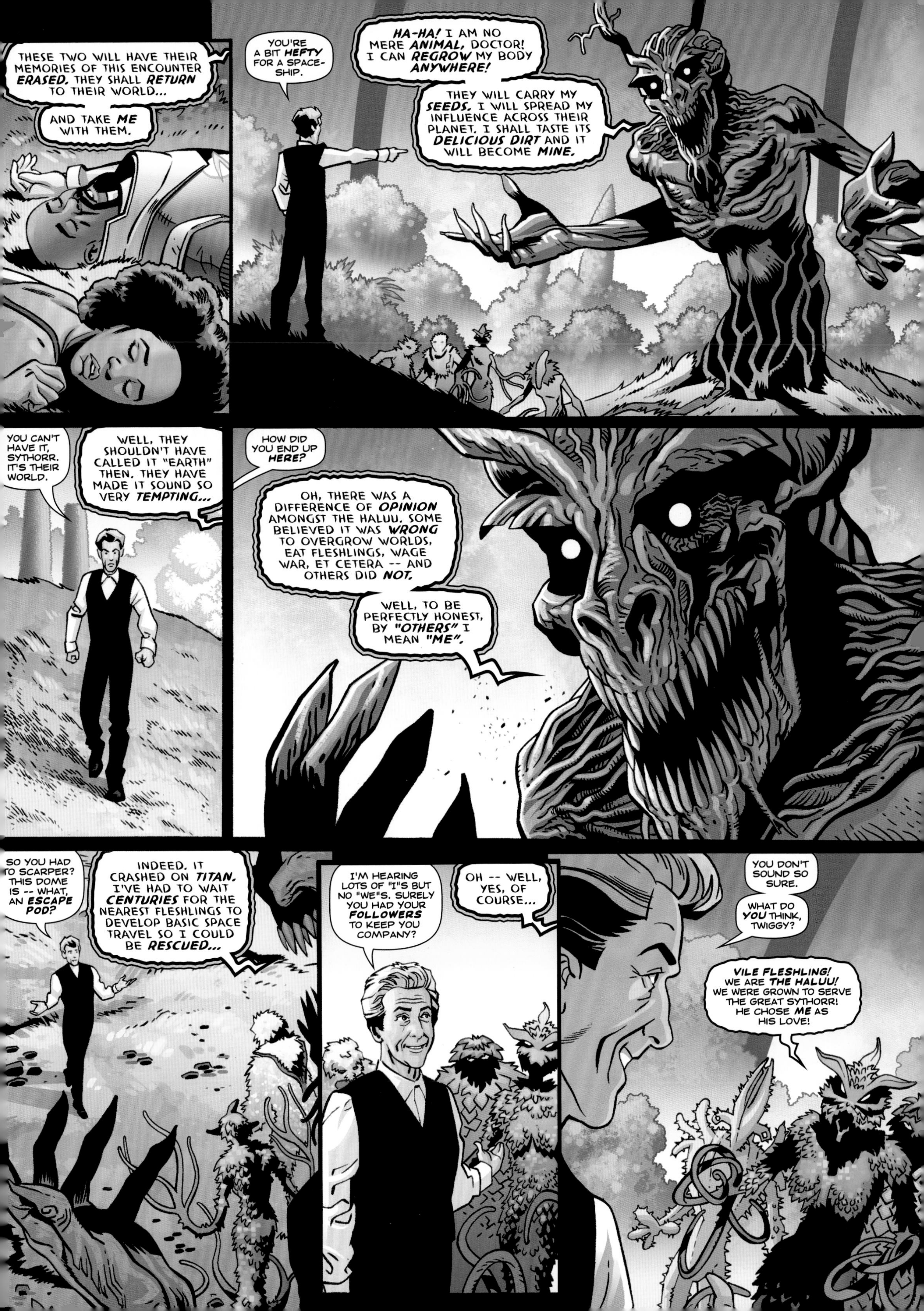
THESE TWO WILL HAVE THEIR MEMORIES OF THIS ENCOUNTER ERASED. THEY SHALL RETURN TO THEIR WORLD...
AND TAKE ME WITH THEM.
YOU'RE A BIT HEFTY FOR A SPACE-SHIP.
HA-HA! I AM NO MERE ANIMAL, DOCTOR! I CAN REGROW MY BODY ANYWHERE!
THEY WILL CARRY MY SEEDS. I WILL SPREAD MY INFLUENCE ACROSS THEIR PLANET. I SHALL TASTE ITS DELICIOUS DIRT AND IT WILL BECOME MINE.
YOU CAN'T HAVE IT, SYTHORR. IT'S THEIR WORLD.
WELL, THEY SHOULDN'T HAVE CALLED IT "EARTH" THEN. THEY HAVE MADE IT SOUND SO VERY TEMPTING...
HOW DID YOU END UP HERE?
OH, THERE WAS A DIFFERENCE OF OPINION AMONGST THE HALUU. SOME BELIEVED IT WAS WRONG TO OVERGROW WORLDS, EAT FLESHLINGS, WAGE WAR, ET CETERA -- AND OTHERS DID NOT.
WELL, TO BE PERFECTLY HONEST, BY "OTHERS" I MEAN "ME".
SO YOU HAD TO SCARPER? THIS DOME IS -- WHAT, AN ESCAPE POD?
INDEED. IT CRASHED ON TITAN. I'VE HAD TO WAIT CENTURIES FOR THE NEAREST FLESHLINGS TO DEVELOP BASIC SPACE TRAVEL SO I COULD BE RESCUED...
I'M HEARING LOTS OF "I"S BUT NO "WE"S. SURELY YOU HAD YOUR FOLLOWERS TO KEEP YOU COMPANY?
OH -- WELL, YES, OF COURSE...
YOU DON'T SOUND SO SURE.
WHAT DO YOU THINK, TWIGGY?
VILE FLESHLING! WE ARE THE HALUU! WE WERE GROWN TO SERVE THE GREAT SYTHORR! HE CHOSE ME AS HIS LOVE!

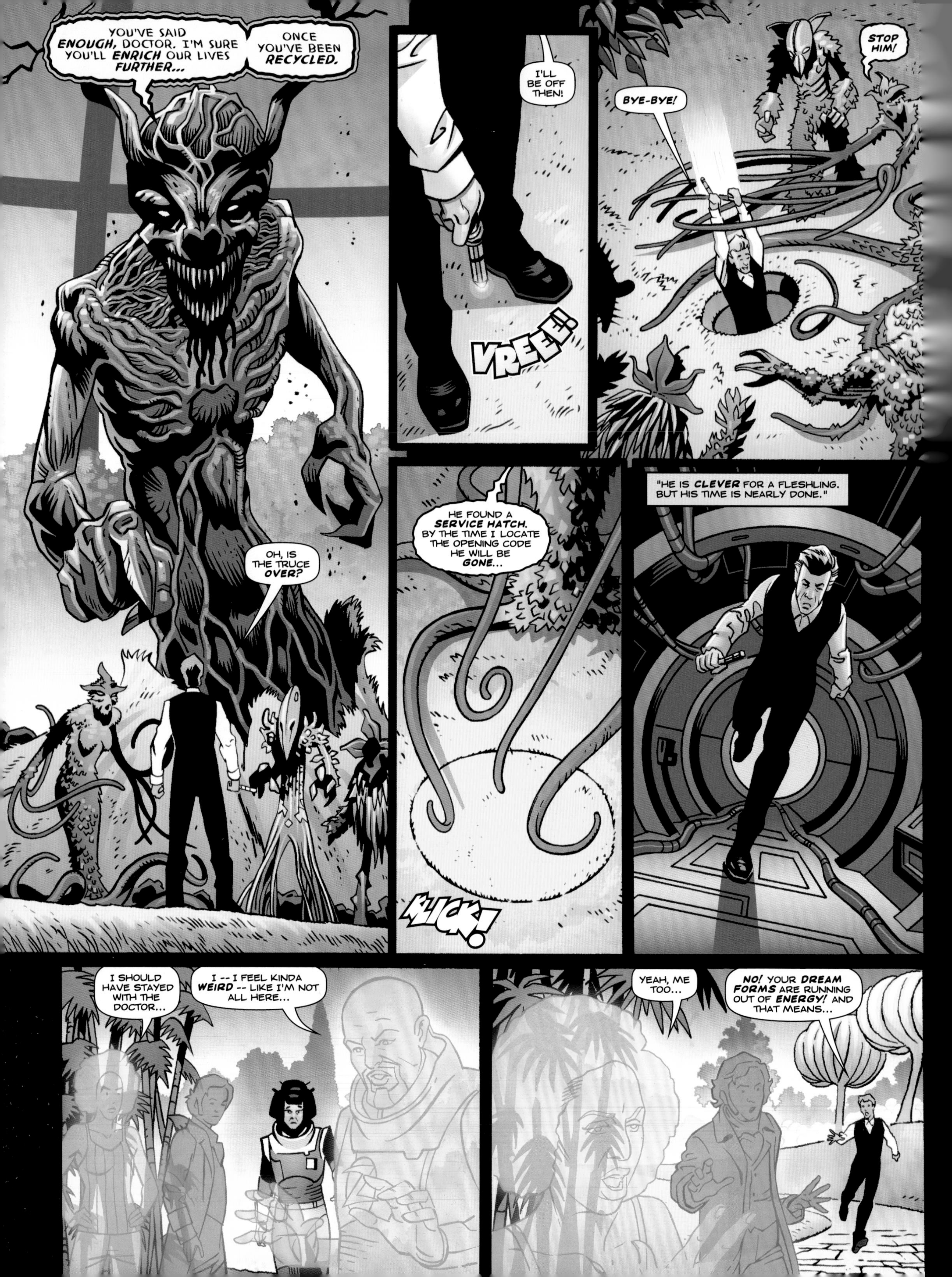

YOU'VE SAID ENOUGH, DOCTOR. I'M SURE YOU'LL ENRICH OUR LIVES FURTHER...
ONCE YOU'VE BEEN RECYCLED.
OH, IS THE TRUCE OVER?
I'LL BE OFF THEN!
VREEE!
BYE-BYE!
STOP HIM!
HE FOUND A SERVICE HATCH. BY THE TIME I LOCATE THE OPENING CODE HE WILL BE GONE...
KLICK!
"HE IS CLEVER FOR A FLESHLING. BUT HIS TIME IS NEARLY DONE."
I SHOULD HAVE STAYED WITH THE DOCTOR...
I -- I FEEL KINDA WEIRD -- LIKE I'M NOT ALL HERE...
YEAH, ME TOO...
NO! YOUR DREAM FORMS ARE RUNNING OUT OF ENERGY! AND THAT MEANS...

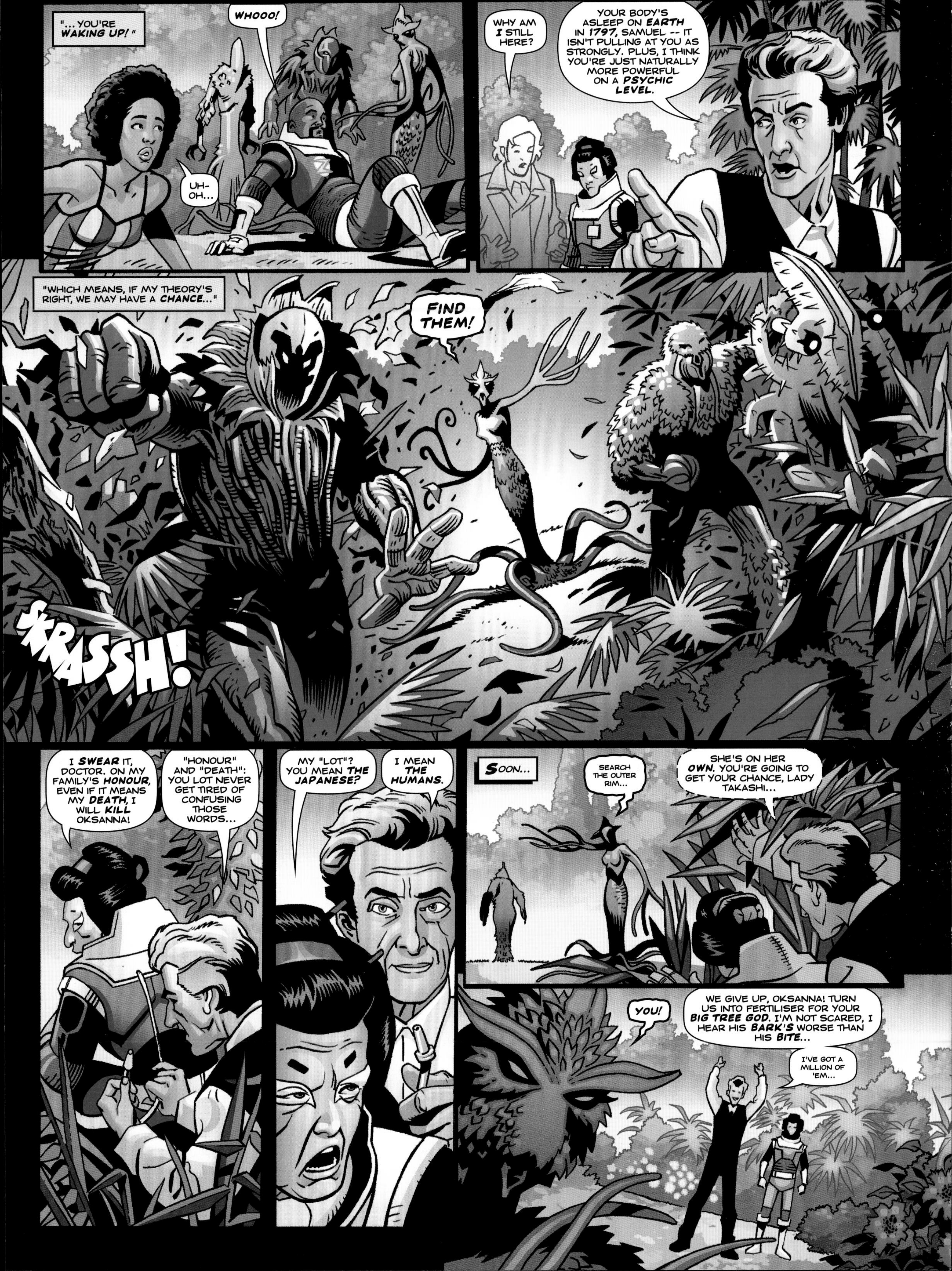
"...YOU'RE WAKING UP!"
WHOOO!
UH-OH...
WHY AM I STILL HERE?
YOUR BODY'S ASLEEP ON EARTH IN 1797, SAMUEL -- IT ISN'T PULLING AT YOU AS STRONGLY. PLUS, I THINK YOU'RE JUST NATURALLY MORE POWERFUL ON A PSYCHIC LEVEL.
"WHICH MEANS, IF MY THEORY'S RIGHT, WE MAY HAVE A CHANCE..."
FIND THEM!
SKRASSH!
I SWEAR IT, DOCTOR. ON MY FAMILY'S HONOUR, EVEN IF IT MEANS MY DEATH, I WILL KILL OKSANNA!
"HONOUR" AND "DEATH": YOU LOT NEVER GET TIRED OF CONFUSING THOSE WORDS...
MY "LOT"? YOU MEAN THE JAPANESE?
I MEAN THE HUMANS.
SOON...
SEARCH THE OUTER RIM...
SHE'S ON HER OWN. YOU'RE GOING TO GET YOUR CHANCE, LADY TAKASHI...
YOU!
WE GIVE UP, OKSANNA! TURN US INTO FERTILISER FOR YOUR BIG TREE GOD. I'M NOT SCARED, I HEAR HIS BARK'S WORSE THAN HIS BITE...
I'VE GOT A MILLION OF 'EM...

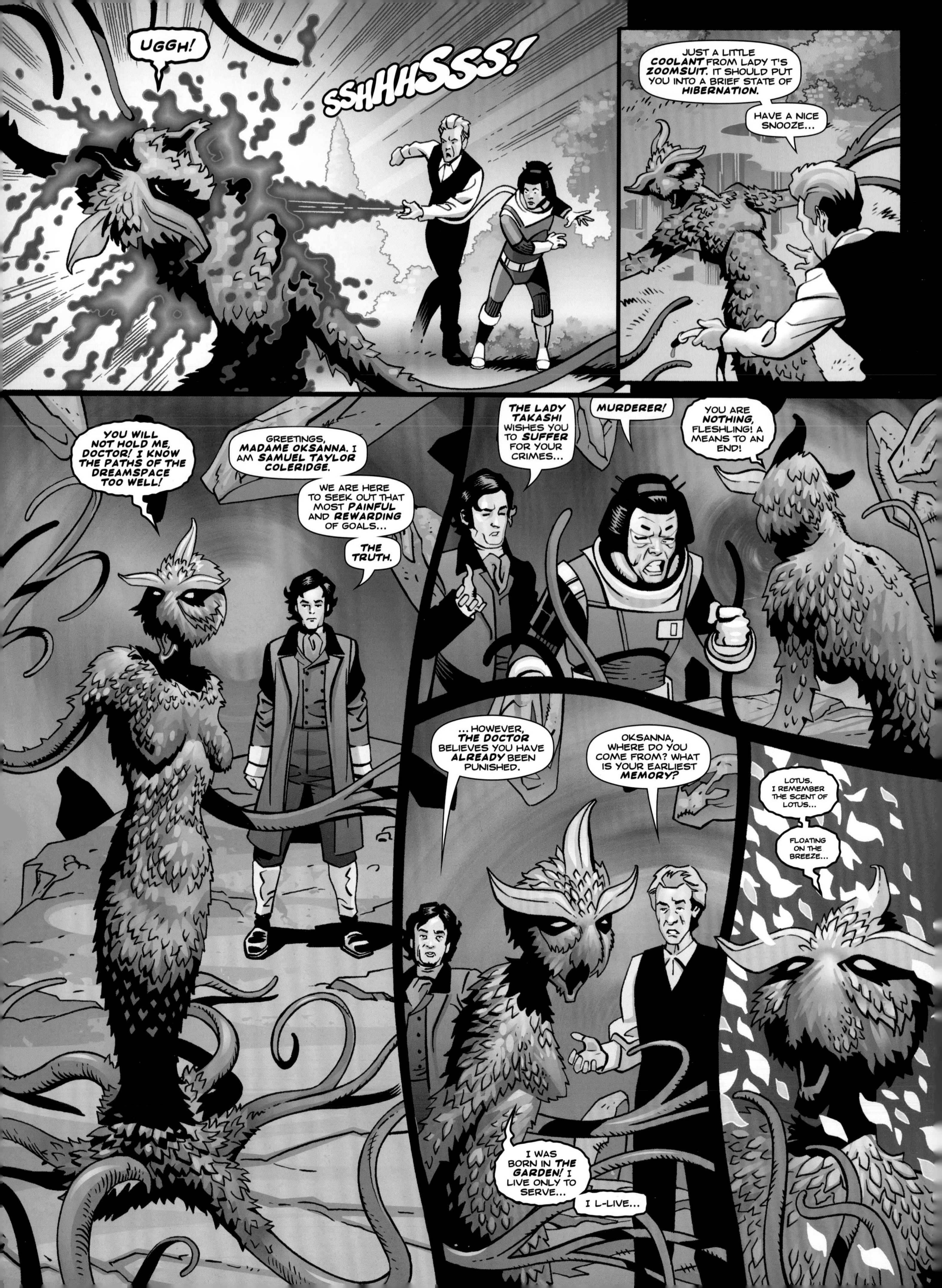
UGGH!
SSHHHSSS!
JUST A LITTLE COOLANT FROM LADY T'S ZOOMSUIT. IT SHOULD PUT YOU INTO A BRIEF STATE OF HIBERNATION.
HAVE A NICE SNOOZE...
YOU WILL NOT HOLD ME, DOCTOR! I KNOW THE PATHS OF THE DREAMSPACE TOO WELL!
GREETINGS, MADAME OKSANNA. I AM SAMUEL TAYLOR COLERIDGE.
WE ARE HERE TO SEEK OUT THAT MOST PAINFUL AND REWARDING OF GOALS...
THE TRUTH.
THE LADY TAKASHI WISHES YOU TO SUFFER FOR YOUR CRIMES...
MURDERER!
YOU ARE NOTHING, FLESHLING! A MEANS TO AN END!
... HOWEVER, THE DOCTOR BELIEVES YOU HAVE ALREADY BEEN PUNISHED.
OKSANNA, WHERE DO YOU COME FROM? WHAT IS YOUR EARLIEST MEMORY?
I WAS BORN IN THE GARDEN! I LIVE ONLY TO SERVE...
I L-LIVE...
LOTUS. I REMEMBER THE SCENT OF LOTUS...
FLOATING ON THE BREEZE...

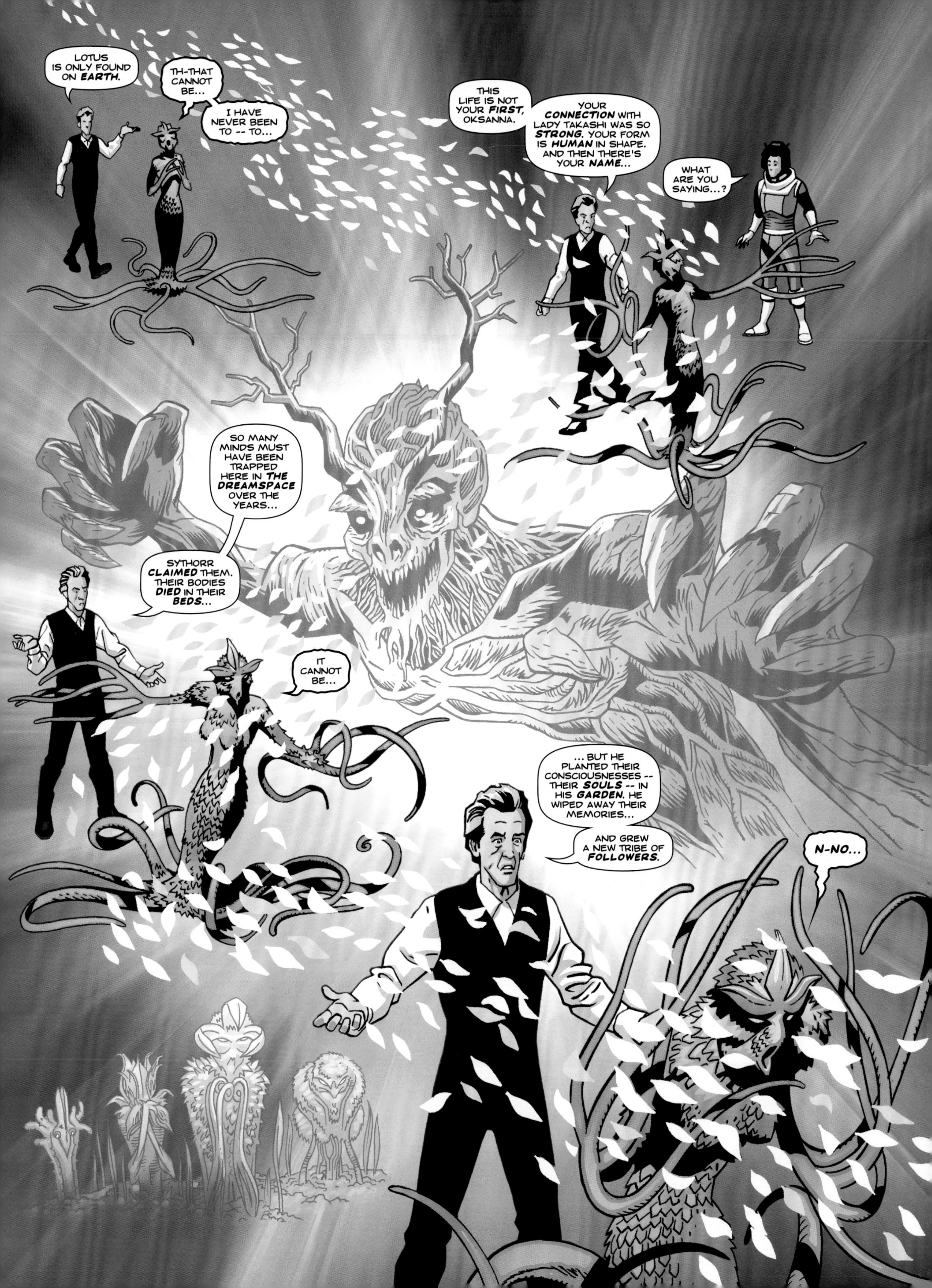

LOTUS IS ONLY FOUND ON EARTH.
TH-THAT CANNOT BE...
I HAVE NEVER BEEN TO -- TO...
THIS LIFE IS NOT YOUR FIRST, OKSANNA.
YOUR CONNECTION WITH LADY TAKASHI WAS SO STRONG. YOUR FORM IS HUMAN IN SHAPE. AND THEN THERE'S YOUR NAME...
WHAT ARE YOU SAYING...?
SO MANY MINDS MUST HAVE BEEN TRAPPED HERE IN THE DREAMSPACE OVER THE YEARS...
SYTHORR CLAIMED THEM. THEIR BODIES DIED IN THEIR BEDS...
IT CANNOT BE...
... BUT HE PLANTED THEIR CONSCIOUSNESSES -- THEIR SOULS -- IN HIS GARDEN. HE WIPED AWAY THEIR MEMORIES...
AND GREW A NEW TRIBE OF FOLLOWERS.
N-NO...

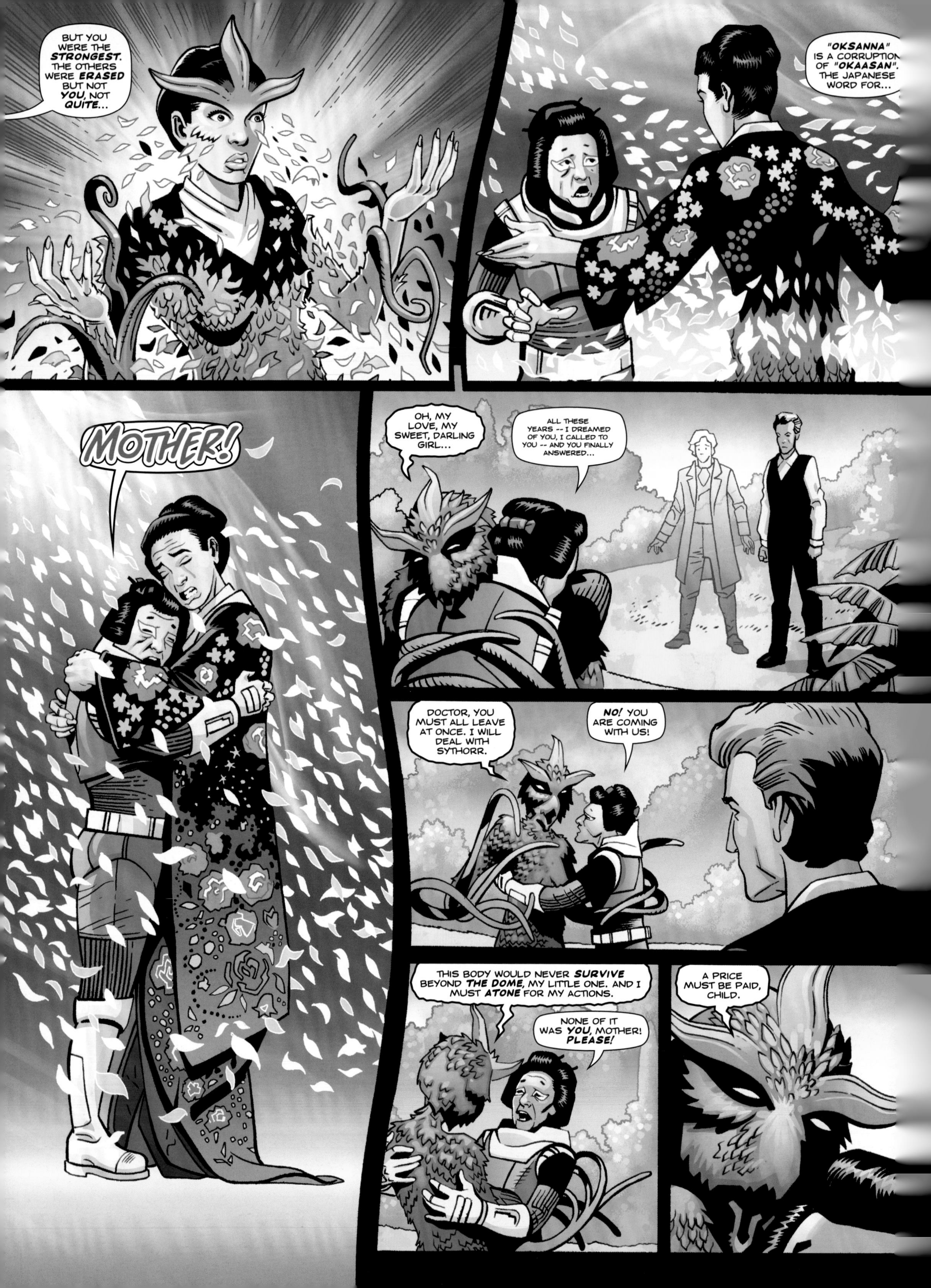
BUT YOU WERE THE STRONGEST. THE OTHERS WERE ERASED BUT NOT YOU, NOT QUITE...
"OKSANNA" IS A CORRUPTION OF "OKAASAN". THE JAPANESE WORD FOR...
MOTHER!
OH, MY LOVE, MY SWEET, DARLING GIRL...
ALL THESE YEARS -- I DREAMED OF YOU, I CALLED TO YOU -- AND YOU FINALLY ANSWERED...
DOCTOR, YOU MUST ALL LEAVE AT ONCE. I WILL DEAL WITH SYTHORR.
NO! YOU ARE COMING WITH US!
THIS BODY WOULD NEVER SURVIVE BEYOND THE DOME, MY LITTLE ONE. AND I MUST ATONE FOR MY ACTIONS.
NONE OF IT WAS YOU, MOTHER! PLEASE!
A PRICE MUST BE PAID, CHILD.

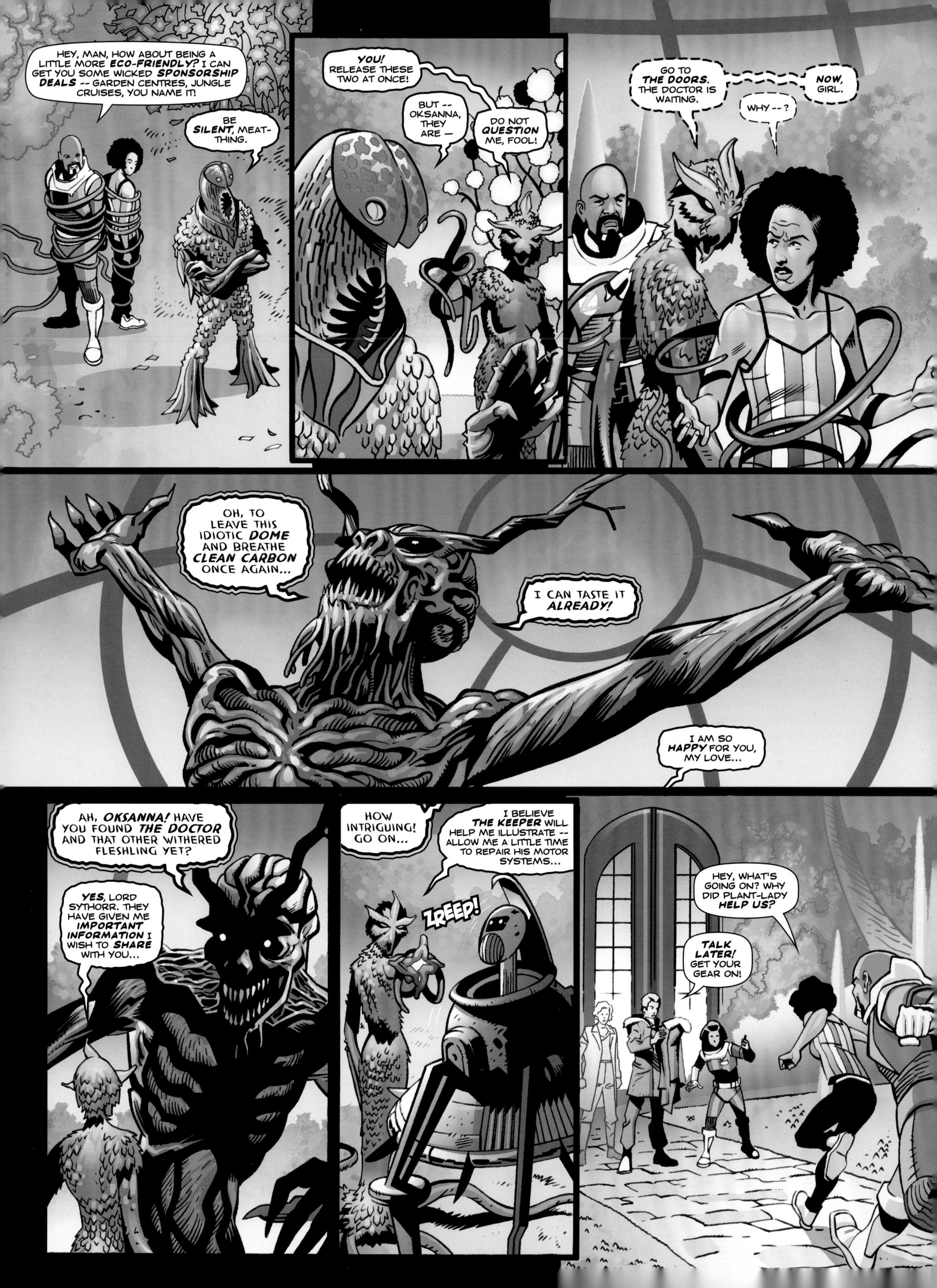
HEY, MAN, HOW ABOUT BEING A LITTLE MORE ECO-FRIENDLY? I CAN GET YOU SOME WICKED SPONSORSHIP DEALS -- GARDEN CENTRES, JUNGLE CRUISES, YOU NAME IT!
BE SILENT, MEAT-THING.
YOU! RELEASE THESE TWO AT ONCE!
BUT -- OKSANNA, THEY ARE —
DO NOT QUESTION ME, FOOL!
GO TO THE DOORS. THE DOCTOR IS WAITING.
NOW, GIRL.
WHY -- ?
OH, TO LEAVE THIS IDIOTIC DOME AND BREATHE CLEAN CARBON ONCE AGAIN...
I CAN TASTE IT ALREADY!
I AM SO HAPPY FOR YOU, MY LOVE...
AH, OKSANNA! HAVE YOU FOUND THE DOCTOR AND THAT OTHER WITHERED FLESHLING YET?
YES, LORD SYTHORR. THEY HAVE GIVEN ME IMPORTANT INFORMATION I WISH TO SHARE WITH YOU...
HOW INTRIGUING! GO ON...
I BELIEVE THE KEEPER WILL HELP ME ILLUSTRATE -- ALLOW ME A LITTLE TIME TO REPAIR HIS MOTOR SYSTEMS...
ZREEP!
HEY, WHAT'S GOING ON? WHY DID PLANT-LADY HELP US?
TALK LATER! GET YOUR GEAR ON!

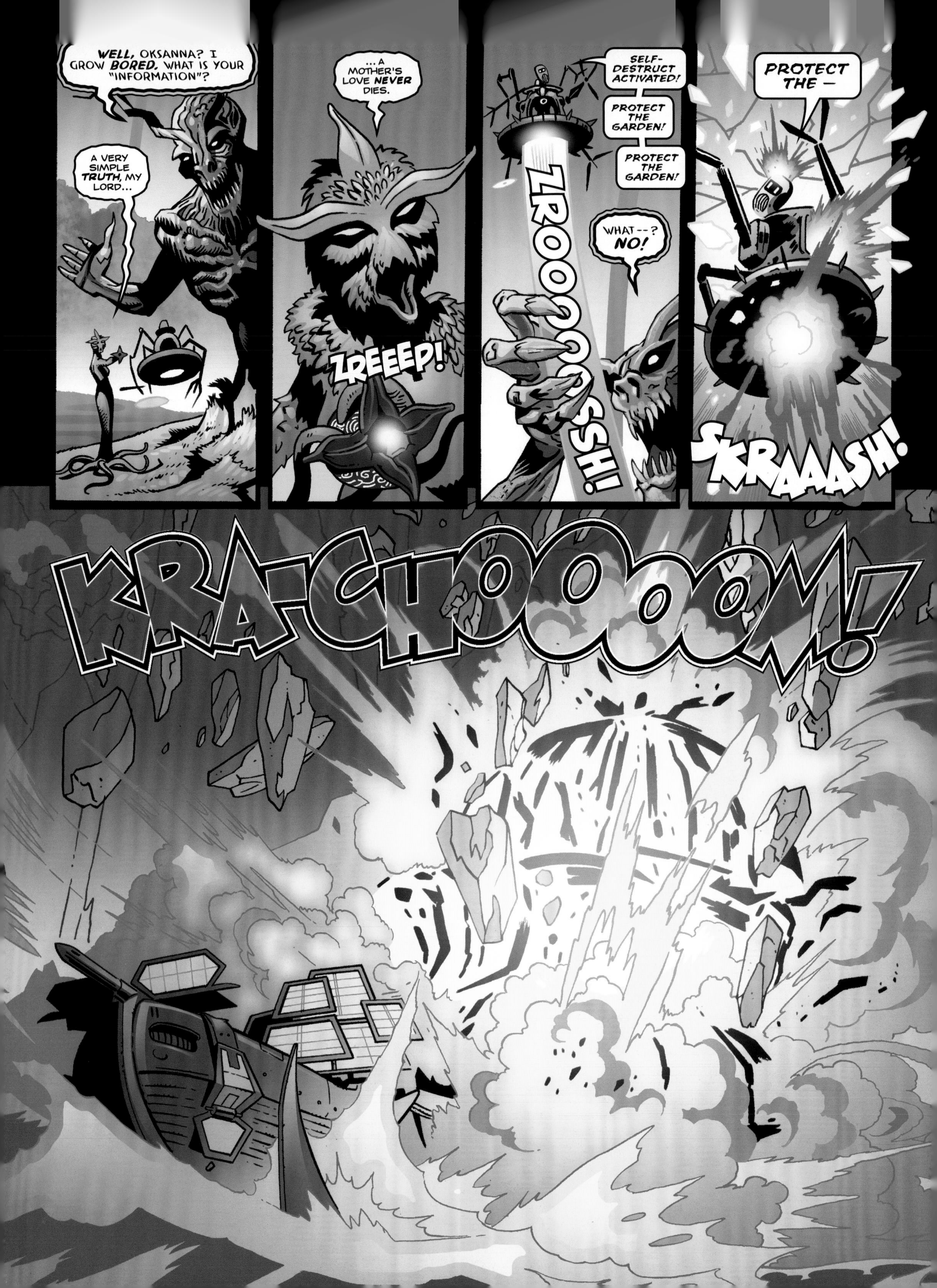
WELL, OKSANNA? I GROW BORED. WHAT IS YOUR "INFORMATION"?
A VERY SIMPLE TRUTH, MY LORD...
... A MOTHER'S LOVE NEVER DIES.
ZREEEP!
SELF-DESTRUCT ACTIVATED!
PROTECT THE GARDEN!
PROTECT THE GARDEN!
WHAT--? NO!
ZLROOOOOOSSH!
PROTECT THE —
SKRAAAASH!
KRA-CHOOOOOM!

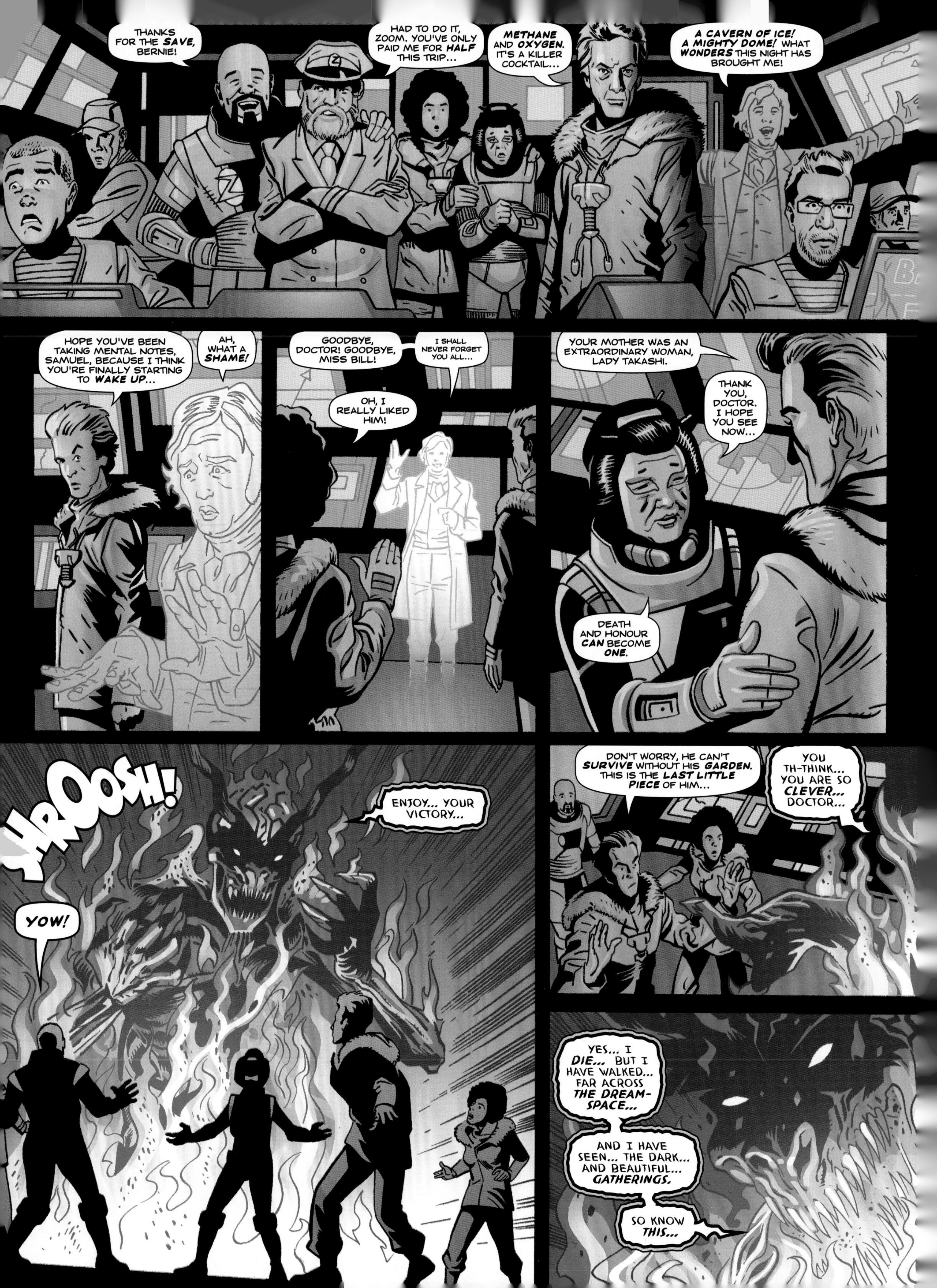
THANKS FOR THE SAVE, BERNIE!
HAD TO DO IT, ZOOM. YOU'VE ONLY PAID ME FOR HALF THIS TRIP...
METHANE AND OXYGEN. IT'S A KILLER COCKTAIL...
A CAVERN OF ICE! A MIGHTY DOME! WHAT WONDERS THIS NIGHT HAS BROUGHT ME!
HOPE YOU'VE BEEN TAKING MENTAL NOTES, SAMUEL, BECAUSE I THINK YOU'RE FINALLY STARTING TO WAKE UP...
AH, WHAT A SHAME!
GOODBYE, DOCTOR! GOODBYE, MISS BILL!
I SHALL NEVER FORGET YOU ALL...
OH, I REALLY LIKED HIM!
YOUR MOTHER WAS AN EXTRAORDINARY WOMAN, LADY TAKASHI.
THANK YOU, DOCTOR. I HOPE YOU SEE NOW...
DEATH AND HONOUR CAN BECOME ONE.
SHROOSH!
ENJOY... YOUR VICTORY...
YOW!
DON'T WORRY, HE CAN'T SURVIVE WITHOUT HIS GARDEN. THIS IS THE LAST LITTLE PIECE OF HIM...
YOU TH-THINK... YOU ARE SO CLEVER... DOCTOR...
YES... I DIE... BUT I HAVE WALKED... FAR ACROSS THE DREAM-SPACE...
AND I HAVE SEEN... THE DARK... AND BEAUTIFUL... GATHERINGS.
SO KNOW THIS...

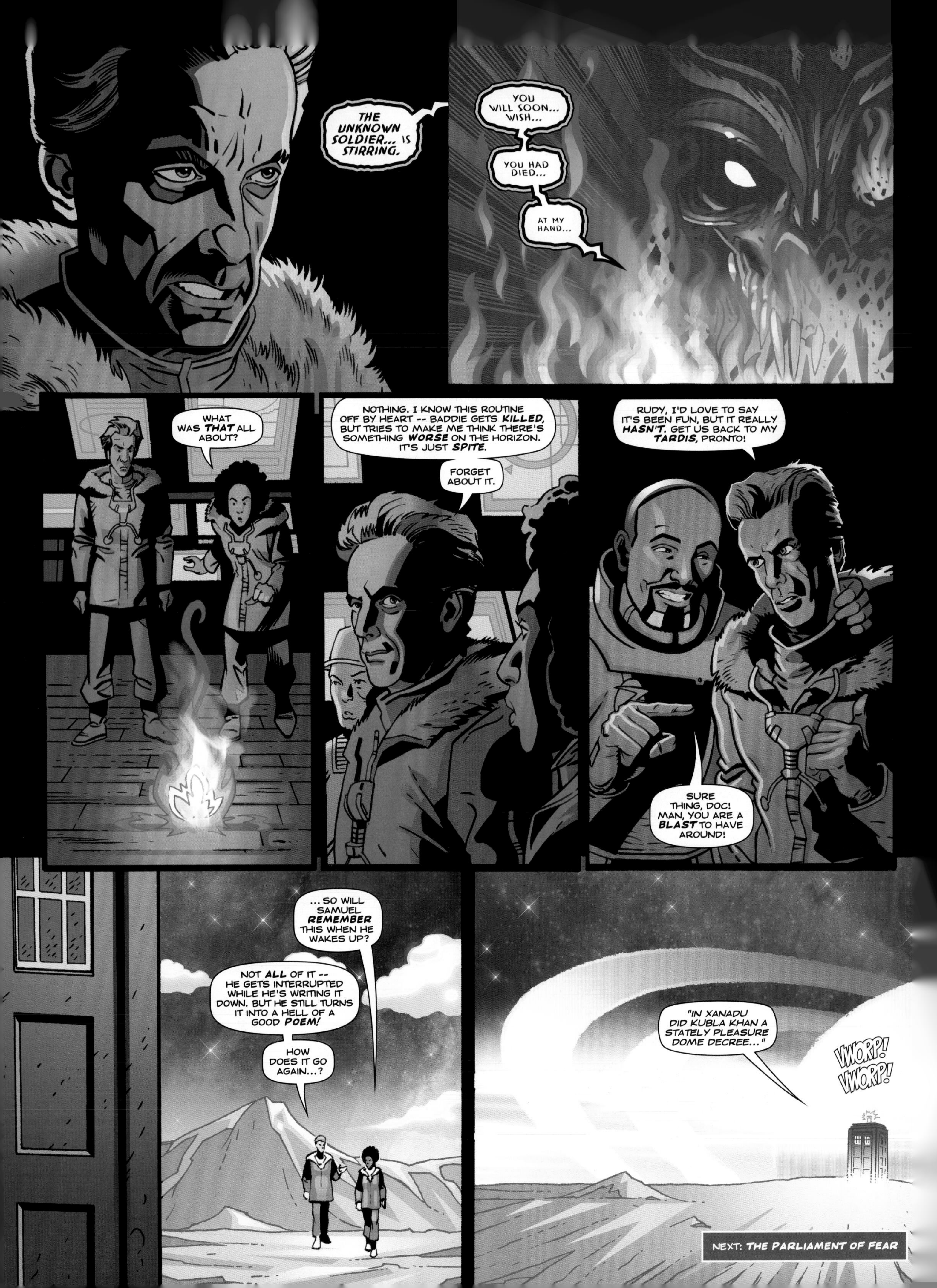

THE UNKNOWN SOLDIER... IS STIRRING.
YOU WILL SOON... WISH...
YOU HAD DIED...
AT MY HAND...
WHAT WAS THAT ALL ABOUT?
NOTHING. I KNOW THIS ROUTINE OFF BY HEART -- BADDIE GETS KILLED, BUT TRIES TO MAKE ME THINK THERE'S SOMETHING WORSE ON THE HORIZON. IT'S JUST SPITE.
FORGET ABOUT IT.
RUDY, I'D LOVE TO SAY IT'S BEEN FUN, BUT IT REALLY HASN'T. GET US BACK TO MY TARDIS, PRONTO!
SURE THING, DOC! MAN, YOU ARE A BLAST TO HAVE AROUND!
...SO WILL SAMUEL REMEMBER THIS WHEN HE WAKES UP?
NOT ALL OF IT -- HE GETS INTERRUPTED WHILE HE'S WRITING IT DOWN. BUT HE STILL TURNS IT INTO A HELL OF A GOOD POEM!
HOW DOES IT GO AGAIN...?
"IN XANADU DID KUBLA KHAN A STATELY PLEASURE DOME DECREE..."
VWORP! VWORP!
NEXT: THE PARLIAMENT OF FEAR

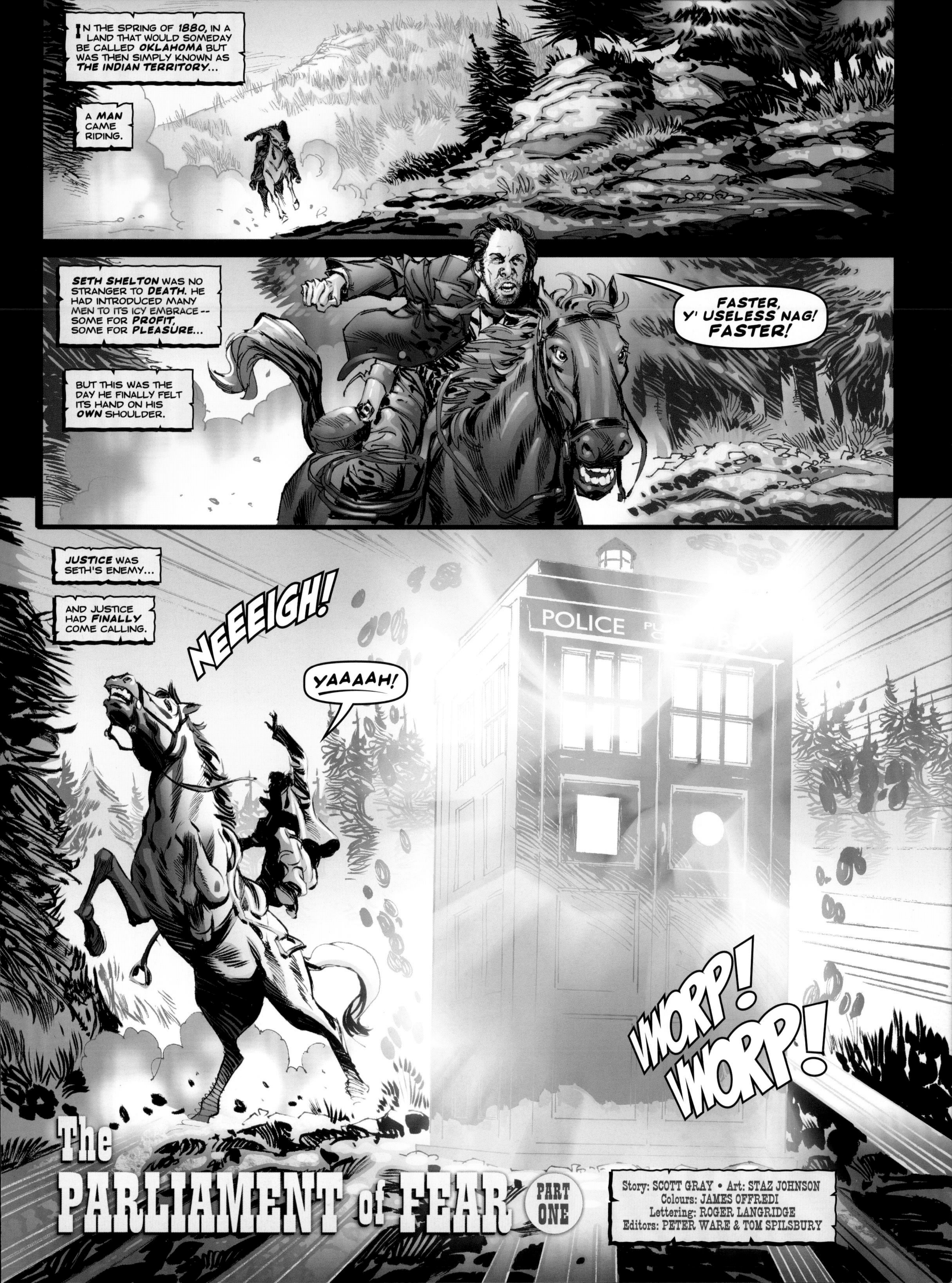
IN THE SPRING OF 1880, IN A LAND THAT WOULD SOMEDAY BE CALLED OKLAHOMA BUT WAS THEN SIMPLY KNOWN AS THE INDIAN TERRITORY...
A MAN CAME RIDING.
SETH SHELTON WAS NO STRANGER TO DEATH. HE HAD INTRODUCED MANY MEN TO ITS ICY EMBRACE -- SOME FOR PROFIT, SOME FOR PLEASURE...
BUT THIS WAS THE DAY HE FINALLY FELT ITS HAND ON HIS OWN SHOULDER.
FASTER, Y' USELESS NAG! FASTER!
JUSTICE WAS SETH'S ENEMY...
AND JUSTICE HAD FINALLY COME CALLING.
NEEEIGH!
YAAAAH!
POLICE
VWORP! VWORP!
The PARLIAMENT of FEAR
PART ONE
Story: SCOTT GRAY • Art: STAZ JOHNSON
Colours: JAMES OFFREDI
Lettering: ROGER LANGRIDGE
Editors: PETER WARE & TOM SPILSBURY

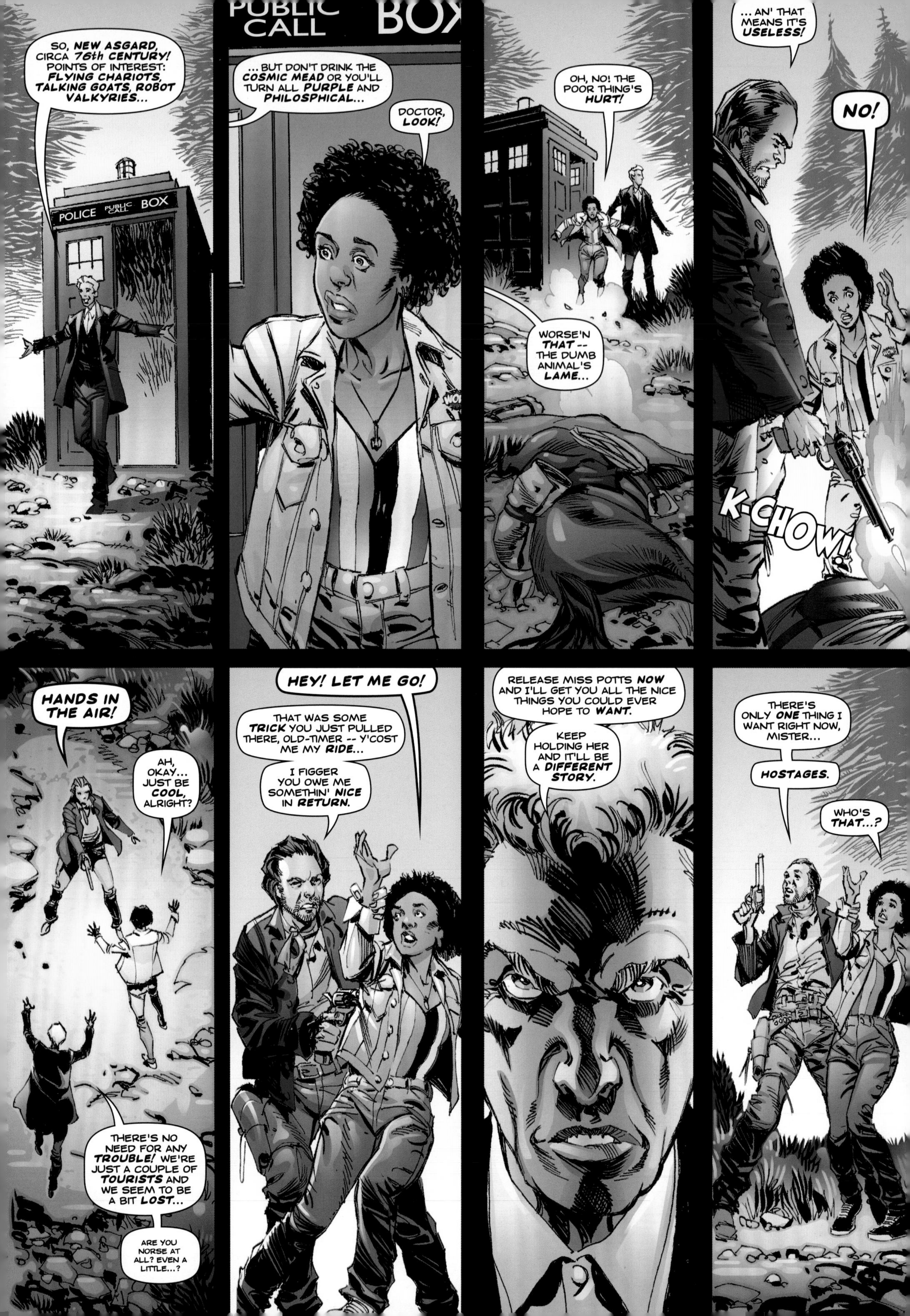
SO, NEW ASGARD, CIRCA 76th CENTURY! POINTS OF INTEREST: FLYING CHARIOTS, TALKING GOATS, ROBOT VALKYRIES...
POLICE PUBLIC CALL BOX
PUBLIC CALL BOX
... BUT DON'T DRINK THE COSMIC MEAD OR YOU'LL TURN ALL PURPLE AND PHILOSPHICAL...
DOCTOR, LOOK!
OH, NO! THE POOR THING'S HURT!
WORSE'N THAT -- THE DUMB ANIMAL'S LAME...
... AN' THAT MEANS IT'S USELESS!
NO!
K-CHOW!
HANDS IN THE AIR!
AH, OKAY... JUST BE COOL, ALRIGHT?
THERE'S NO NEED FOR ANY TROUBLE! WE'RE JUST A COUPLE OF TOURISTS AND WE SEEM TO BE A BIT LOST...
ARE YOU NORSE AT ALL? EVEN A LITTLE...?
HEY! LET ME GO!
THAT WAS SOME TRICK YOU JUST PULLED THERE, OLD-TIMER -- Y'COST ME MY RIDE...
I FIGGER YOU OWE ME SOMETHIN' NICE IN RETURN.
RELEASE MISS POTTS NOW AND I'LL GET YOU ALL THE NICE THINGS YOU COULD EVER HOPE TO WANT.
KEEP HOLDING HER AND IT'LL BE A DIFFERENT STORY.
THERE'S ONLY ONE THING I WANT RIGHT NOW, MISTER...
HOSTAGES.
WHO'S THAT...?

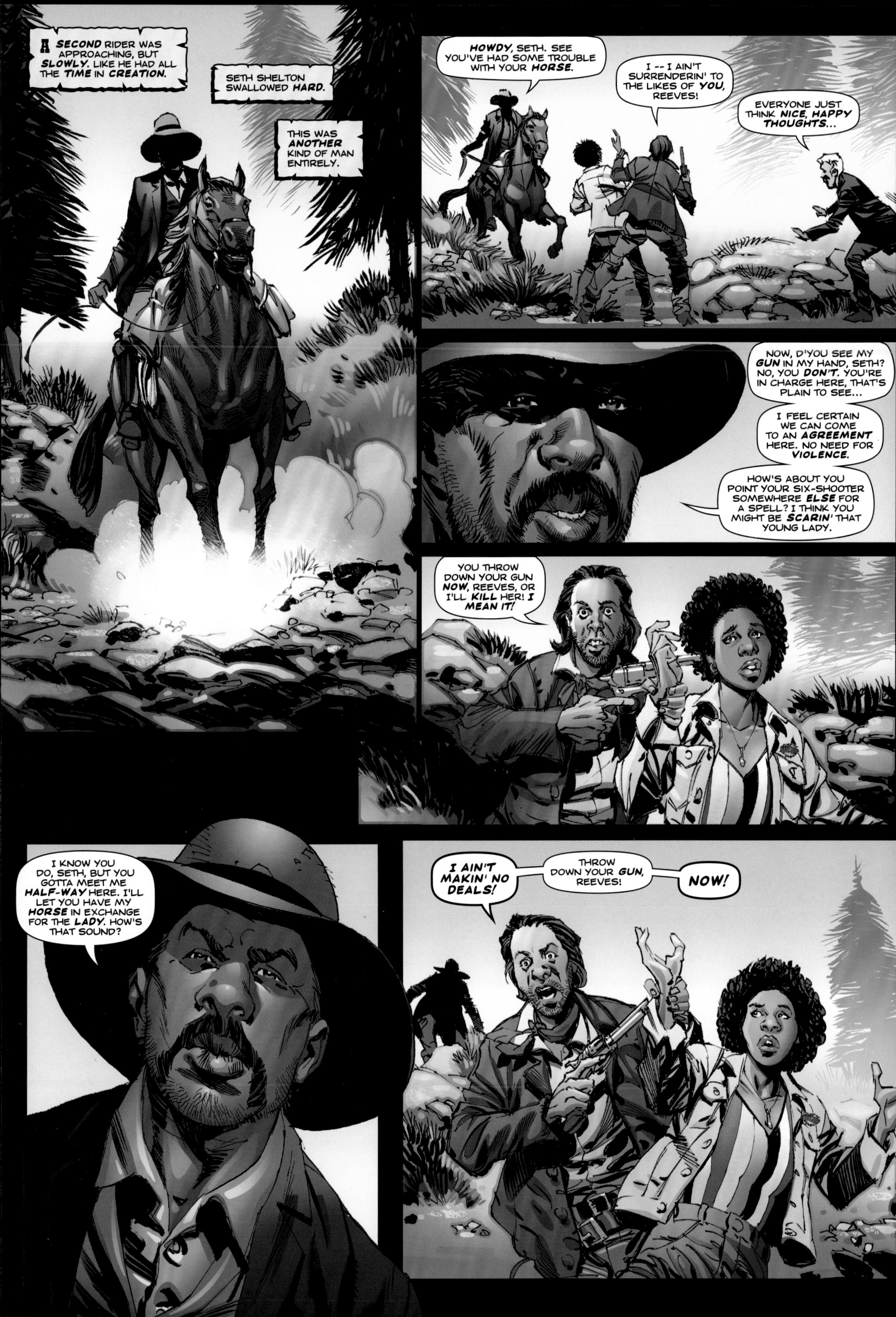
A SECOND RIDER WAS APPROACHING, BUT SLOWLY. LIKE HE HAD ALL THE TIME IN CREATION.
SETH SHELTON SWALLOWED HARD.
THIS WAS ANOTHER KIND OF MAN ENTIRELY.
HOWDY, SETH. SEE YOU'VE HAD SOME TROUBLE WITH YOUR HORSE.
I -- I AIN'T SURRENDERIN' TO THE LIKES OF YOU, REEVES!
EVERYONE JUST THINK NICE, HAPPY THOUGHTS...
NOW, D'YOU SEE MY GUN IN MY HAND, SETH? NO, YOU DON'T. YOU'RE IN CHARGE HERE, THAT'S PLAIN TO SEE...
I FEEL CERTAIN WE CAN COME TO AN AGREEMENT HERE. NO NEED FOR VIOLENCE.
HOW'S ABOUT YOU POINT YOUR SIX-SHOOTER SOMEWHERE ELSE FOR A SPELL? I THINK YOU MIGHT BE SCARIN' THAT YOUNG LADY.
YOU THROW DOWN YOUR GUN NOW, REEVES, OR I'LL KILL HER! I MEAN IT!
I KNOW YOU DO, SETH, BUT YOU GOTTA MEET ME HALF-WAY HERE. I'LL LET YOU HAVE MY HORSE IN EXCHANGE FOR THE LADY. HOW'S THAT SOUND?
I AIN'T MAKIN' NO DEALS!
THROW DOWN YOUR GUN, REEVES!
NOW!

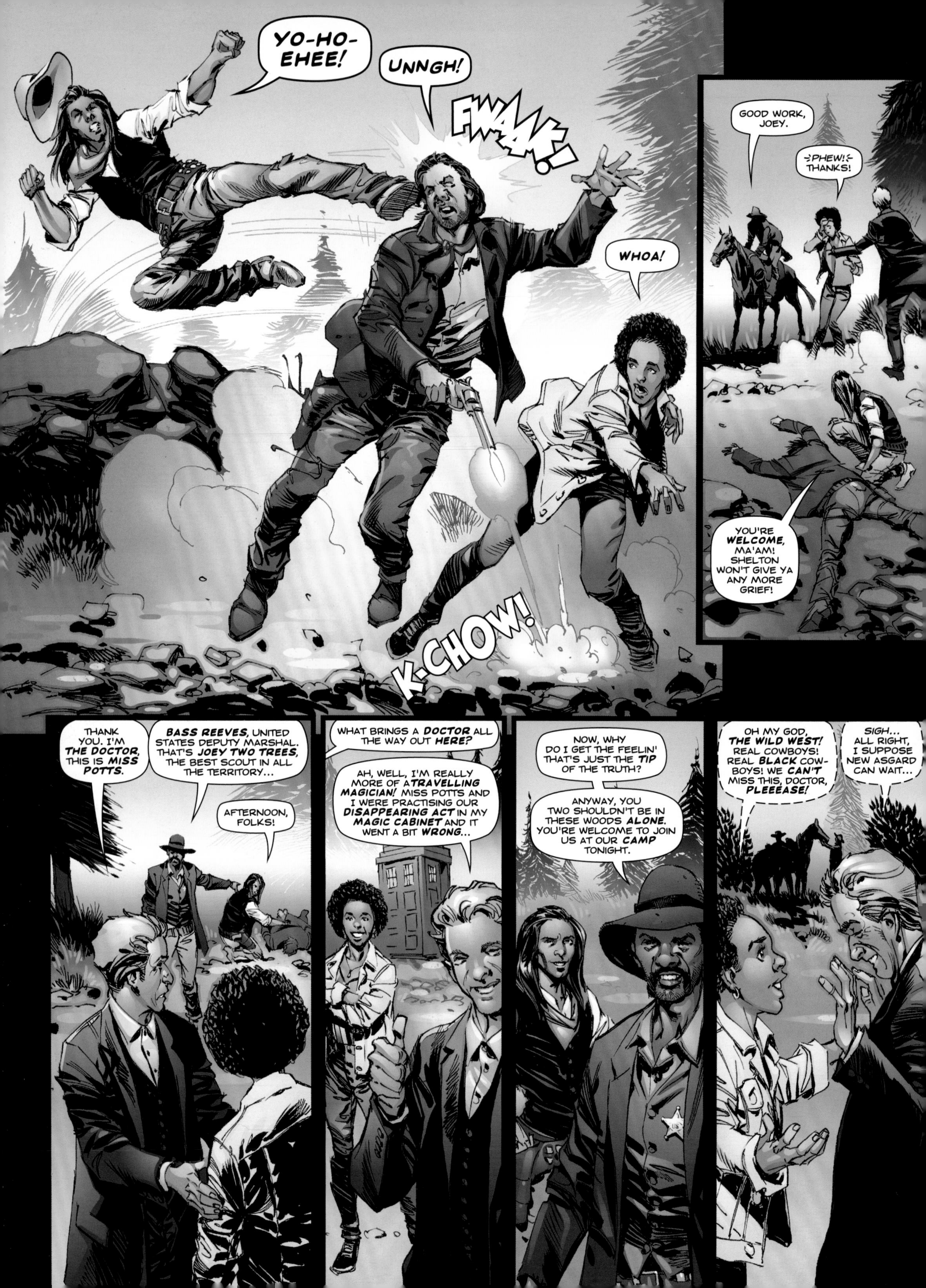
YO-HO-EHEE!
UNNGH!
FWAAK!
WHOA!
K-CHOW!
GOOD WORK, JOEY.
PHEW! THANKS!
YOU'RE WELCOME, MA'AM! SHELTON WON'T GIVE YA ANY MORE GRIEF!
THANK YOU. I'M THE DOCTOR, THIS IS MISS POTTS.
BASS REEVES, UNITED STATES DEPUTY MARSHAL. THAT'S JOEY TWO TREES, THE BEST SCOUT IN ALL THE TERRITORY...
AFTERNOON, FOLKS!
WHAT BRINGS A DOCTOR ALL THE WAY OUT HERE?
AH, WELL, I'M REALLY MORE OF A TRAVELLING MAGICIAN! MISS POTTS AND I WERE PRACTISING OUR DISAPPEARING ACT IN MY MAGIC CABINET AND IT WENT A BIT WRONG...
NOW, WHY DO I GET THE FEELIN' THAT'S JUST THE TIP OF THE TRUTH?
ANYWAY, YOU TWO SHOULDN'T BE IN THESE WOODS ALONE. YOU'RE WELCOME TO JOIN US AT OUR CAMP TONIGHT.
OH MY GOD, THE WILD WEST! REAL COWBOYS! REAL BLACK COWBOYS! WE CAN'T MISS THIS, DOCTOR, PLEEEASE!
SIGH... ALL RIGHT, I SUPPOSE NEW ASGARD CAN WAIT...

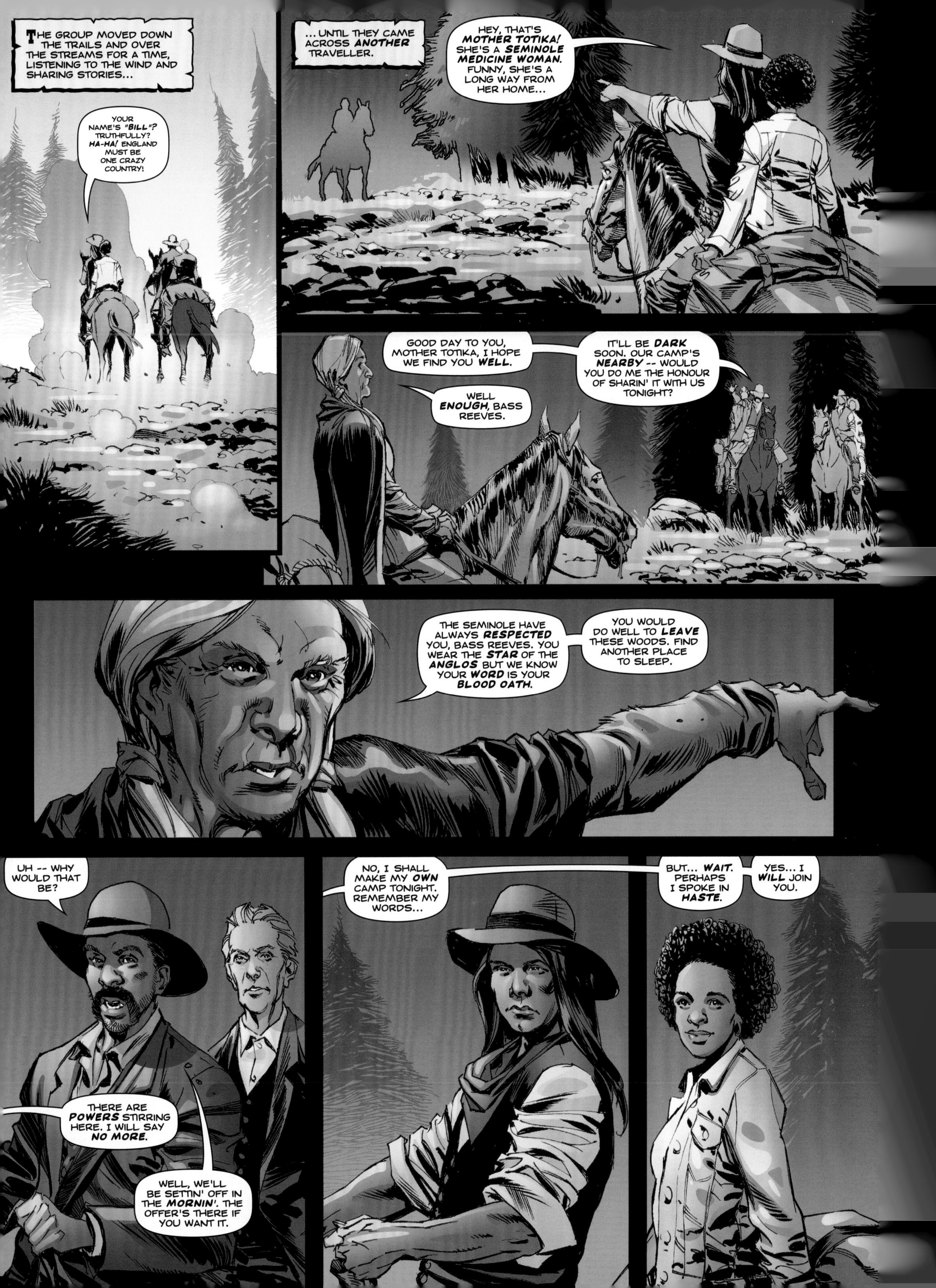
THE GROUP MOVED DOWN THE TRAILS AND OVER THE STREAMS FOR A TIME, LISTENING TO THE WIND AND SHARING STORIES...
YOUR NAME'S "BILL"? TRUTHFULLY? HA-HA! ENGLAND MUST BE ONE CRAZY COUNTRY!
...UNTIL THEY CAME ACROSS ANOTHER TRAVELLER.
HEY, THAT'S MOTHER TOTIKA! SHE'S A SEMINOLE MEDICINE WOMAN. FUNNY, SHE'S A LONG WAY FROM HER HOME...
GOOD DAY TO YOU, MOTHER TOTIKA, I HOPE WE FIND YOU WELL.
WELL ENOUGH, BASS REEVES.
IT'LL BE DARK SOON. OUR CAMP'S NEARBY -- WOULD YOU DO ME THE HONOUR OF SHARIN' IT WITH US TONIGHT?
THE SEMINOLE HAVE ALWAYS RESPECTED YOU, BASS REEVES. YOU WEAR THE STAR OF THE ANGLOS BUT WE KNOW YOUR WORD IS YOUR BLOOD OATH.
YOU WOULD DO WELL TO LEAVE THESE WOODS. FIND ANOTHER PLACE TO SLEEP.
UH -- WHY WOULD THAT BE?
THERE ARE POWERS STIRRING HERE. I WILL SAY NO MORE.
WELL, WE'LL BE SETTIN' OFF IN THE MORNIN'. THE OFFER'S THERE IF YOU WANT IT.
NO, I SHALL MAKE MY OWN CAMP TONIGHT. REMEMBER MY WORDS...
BUT... WAIT. PERHAPS I SPOKE IN HASTE.
YES... I WILL JOIN YOU.

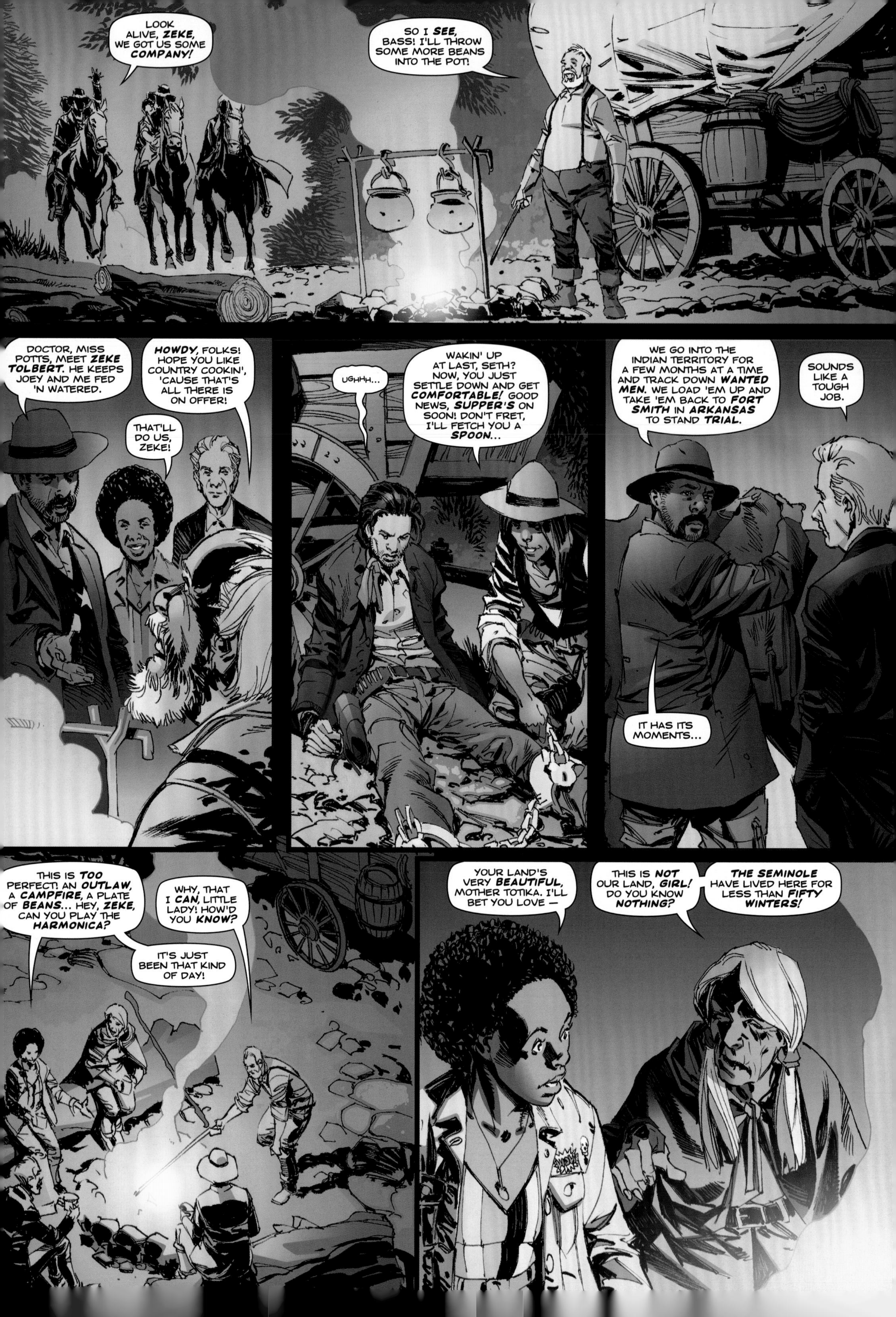
LOOK ALIVE, ZEKE, WE GOT US SOME COMPANY!
SO I SEE, BASS! I'LL THROW SOME MORE BEANS INTO THE POT!
DOCTOR, MISS POTTS, MEET ZEKE TOLBERT. HE KEEPS JOEY AND ME FED 'N WATERED.
HOWDY, FOLKS! HOPE YOU LIKE COUNTRY COOKIN', 'CAUSE THAT'S ALL THERE IS ON OFFER!
THAT'LL DO US, ZEKE!
UGHHH...
WAKIN' UP AT LAST, SETH? NOW, YOU JUST SETTLE DOWN AND GET COMFORTABLE! GOOD NEWS, SUPPER'S ON SOON! DON'T FRET, I'LL FETCH YOU A SPOON...
WE GO INTO THE INDIAN TERRITORY FOR A FEW MONTHS AT A TIME AND TRACK DOWN WANTED MEN. WE LOAD 'EM UP AND TAKE 'EM BACK TO FORT SMITH IN ARKANSAS TO STAND TRIAL.
SOUNDS LIKE A TOUGH JOB.
IT HAS ITS MOMENTS...
THIS IS TOO PERFECT! AN OUTLAW, A CAMPFIRE, A PLATE OF BEANS... HEY, ZEKE, CAN YOU PLAY THE HARMONICA?
WHY, THAT I CAN, LITTLE LADY! HOW'D YOU KNOW?
IT'S JUST BEEN THAT KIND OF DAY!
YOUR LAND'S VERY BEAUTIFUL, MOTHER TOTIKA. I'LL BET YOU LOVE —
THIS IS NOT OUR LAND, GIRL! DO YOU KNOW NOTHING?
THE SEMINOLE HAVE LIVED HERE FOR LESS THAN FIFTY WINTERS!

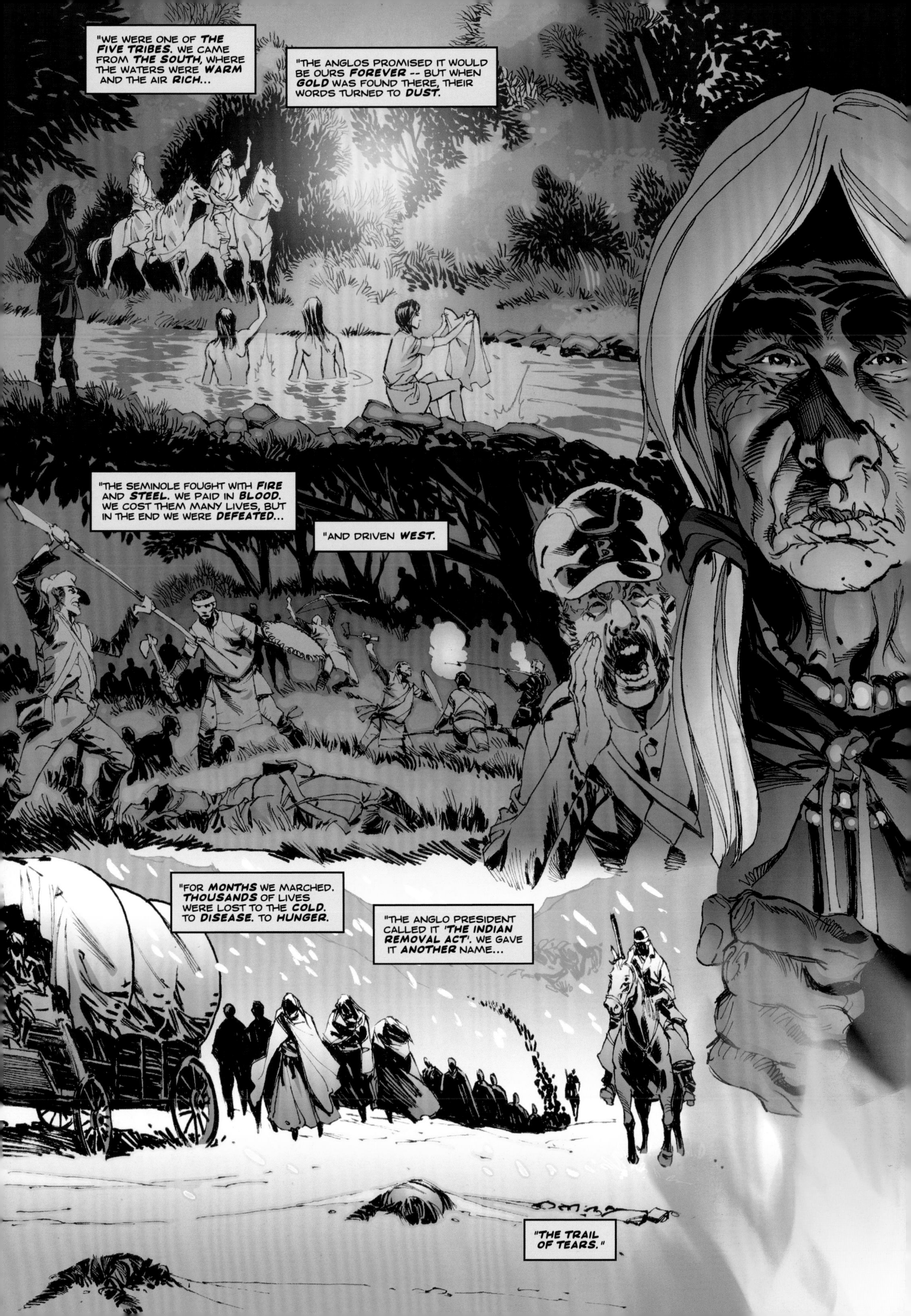
"WE WERE ONE OF THE FIVE TRIBES. WE CAME FROM THE SOUTH, WHERE THE WATERS WERE WARM AND THE AIR RICH...
"THE ANGLOS PROMISED IT WOULD BE OURS FOREVER -- BUT WHEN GOLD WAS FOUND THERE, THEIR WORDS TURNED TO DUST.
"THE SEMINOLE FOUGHT WITH FIRE AND STEEL. WE PAID IN BLOOD. WE COST THEM MANY LIVES, BUT IN THE END WE WERE DEFEATED...
"AND DRIVEN WEST.
"FOR MONTHS WE MARCHED. THOUSANDS OF LIVES WERE LOST TO THE COLD. TO DISEASE. TO HUNGER.
"THE ANGLO PRESIDENT CALLED IT 'THE INDIAN REMOVAL ACT'. WE GAVE IT ANOTHER NAME...
"THE TRAIL OF TEARS."

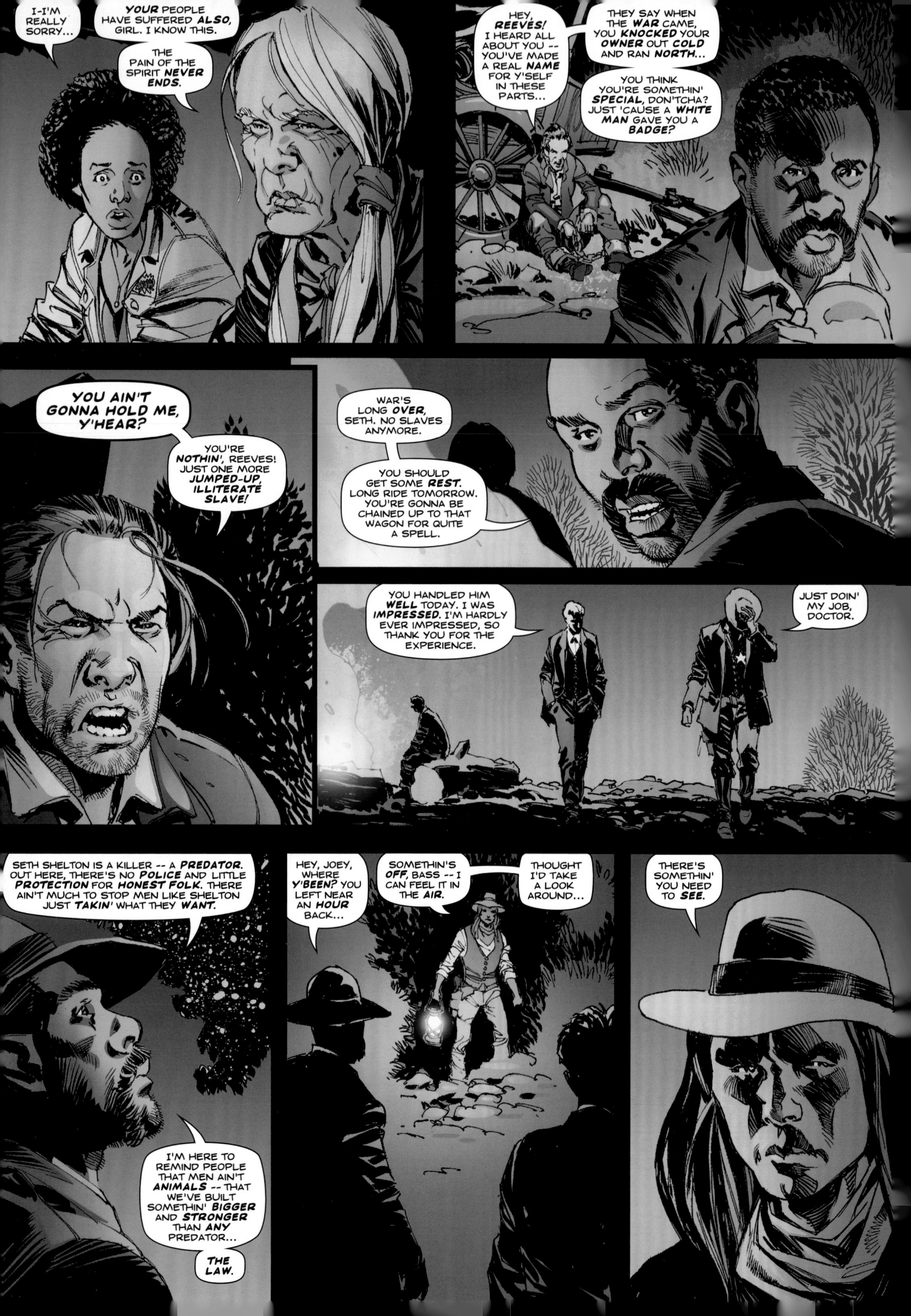

I-I'M REALLY SORRY...
YOUR PEOPLE HAVE SUFFERED ALSO, GIRL. I KNOW THIS.
THE PAIN OF THE SPIRIT NEVER ENDS.
HEY, REEVES! I HEARD ALL ABOUT YOU -- YOU'VE MADE A REAL NAME FOR Y'SELF IN THESE PARTS...
THEY SAY WHEN THE WAR CAME, YOU KNOCKED YOUR OWNER OUT COLD AND RAN NORTH...
YOU THINK YOU'RE SOMETHIN' SPECIAL, DON'TCHA? JUST 'CAUSE A WHITE MAN GAVE YOU A BADGE?
YOU AIN'T GONNA HOLD ME, Y'HEAR?
YOU'RE NOTHIN', REEVES! JUST ONE MORE JUMPED-UP, ILLITERATE SLAVE!
WAR'S LONG OVER, SETH. NO SLAVES ANYMORE.
YOU SHOULD GET SOME REST. LONG RIDE TOMORROW. YOU'RE GONNA BE CHAINED UP TO THAT WAGON FOR QUITE A SPELL.
YOU HANDLED HIM WELL TODAY. I WAS IMPRESSED. I'M HARDLY EVER IMPRESSED, SO THANK YOU FOR THE EXPERIENCE.
JUST DOIN' MY JOB, DOCTOR.
SETH SHELTON IS A KILLER -- A PREDATOR. OUT HERE, THERE'S NO POLICE AND LITTLE PROTECTION FOR HONEST FOLK. THERE AIN'T MUCH TO STOP MEN LIKE SHELTON JUST TAKIN' WHAT THEY WANT.
I'M HERE TO REMIND PEOPLE THAT MEN AIN'T ANIMALS -- THAT WE'VE BUILT SOMETHIN' BIGGER AND STRONGER THAN ANY PREDATOR...
THE LAW.
HEY, JOEY, WHERE Y'BEEN? YOU LEFT NEAR AN HOUR BACK...
SOMETHIN'S OFF, BASS -- I CAN FEEL IT IN THE AIR.
THOUGHT I'D TAKE A LOOK AROUND...
THERE'S SOMETHIN' YOU NEED TO SEE.

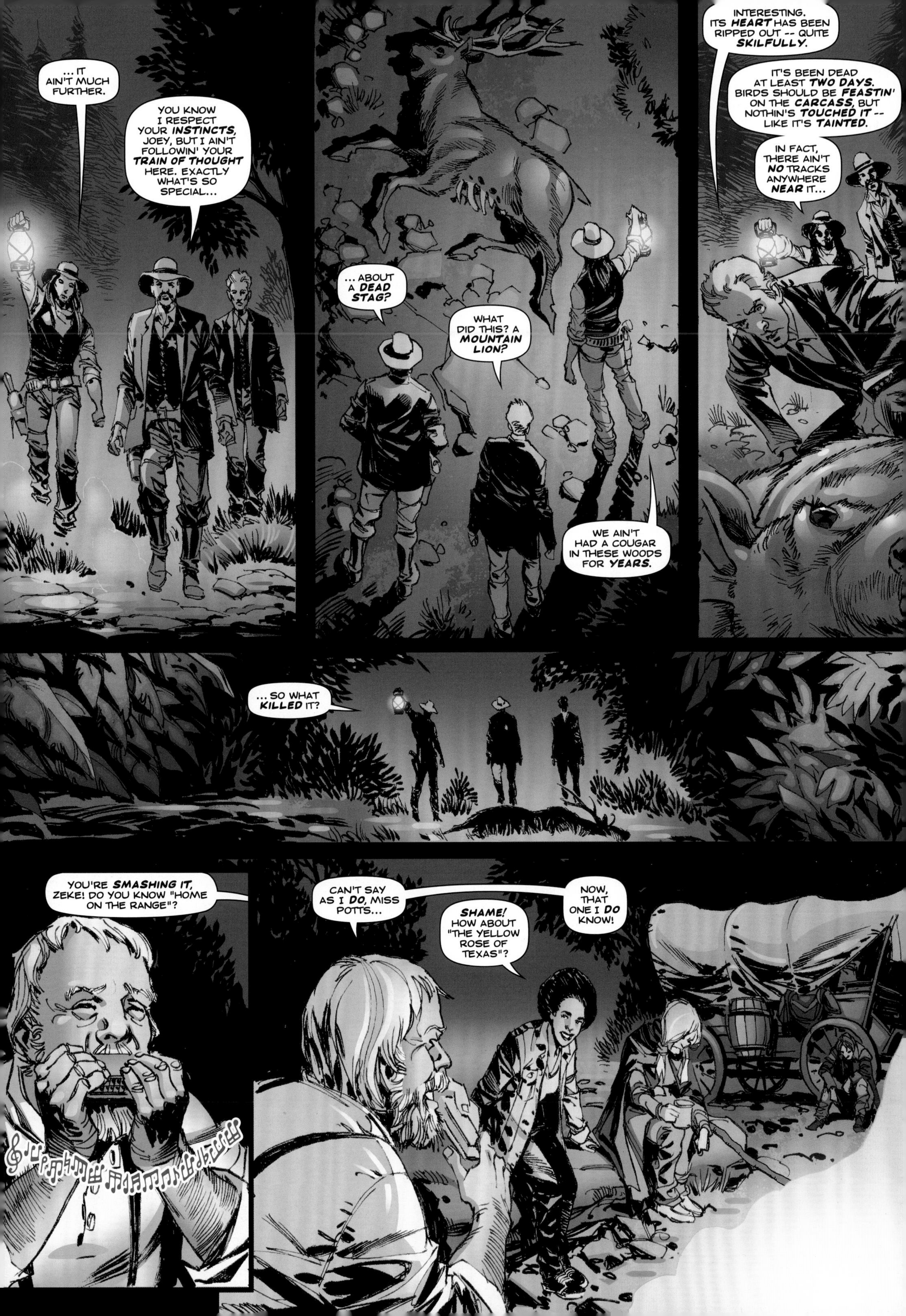

... IT AIN'T MUCH FURTHER.
YOU KNOW I RESPECT YOUR INSTINCTS, JOEY, BUT I AIN'T FOLLOWIN' YOUR TRAIN OF THOUGHT HERE. EXACTLY WHAT'S SO SPECIAL...
... ABOUT A DEAD STAG?
WHAT DID THIS? A MOUNTAIN LION?
WE AIN'T HAD A COUGAR IN THESE WOODS FOR YEARS.
INTERESTING. ITS HEART HAS BEEN RIPPED OUT -- QUITE SKILFULLY.
IT'S BEEN DEAD AT LEAST TWO DAYS. BIRDS SHOULD BE FEASTIN' ON THE CARCASS, BUT NOTHIN'S TOUCHED IT -- LIKE IT'S TAINTED.
IN FACT, THERE AIN'T NO TRACKS ANYWHERE NEAR IT...
... SO WHAT KILLED IT?
YOU'RE SMASHING IT, ZEKE! DO YOU KNOW "HOME ON THE RANGE"?
CAN'T SAY AS I DO, MISS POTTS...
SHAME! HOW ABOUT "THE YELLOW ROSE OF TEXAS"?
NOW, THAT ONE I DO KNOW!

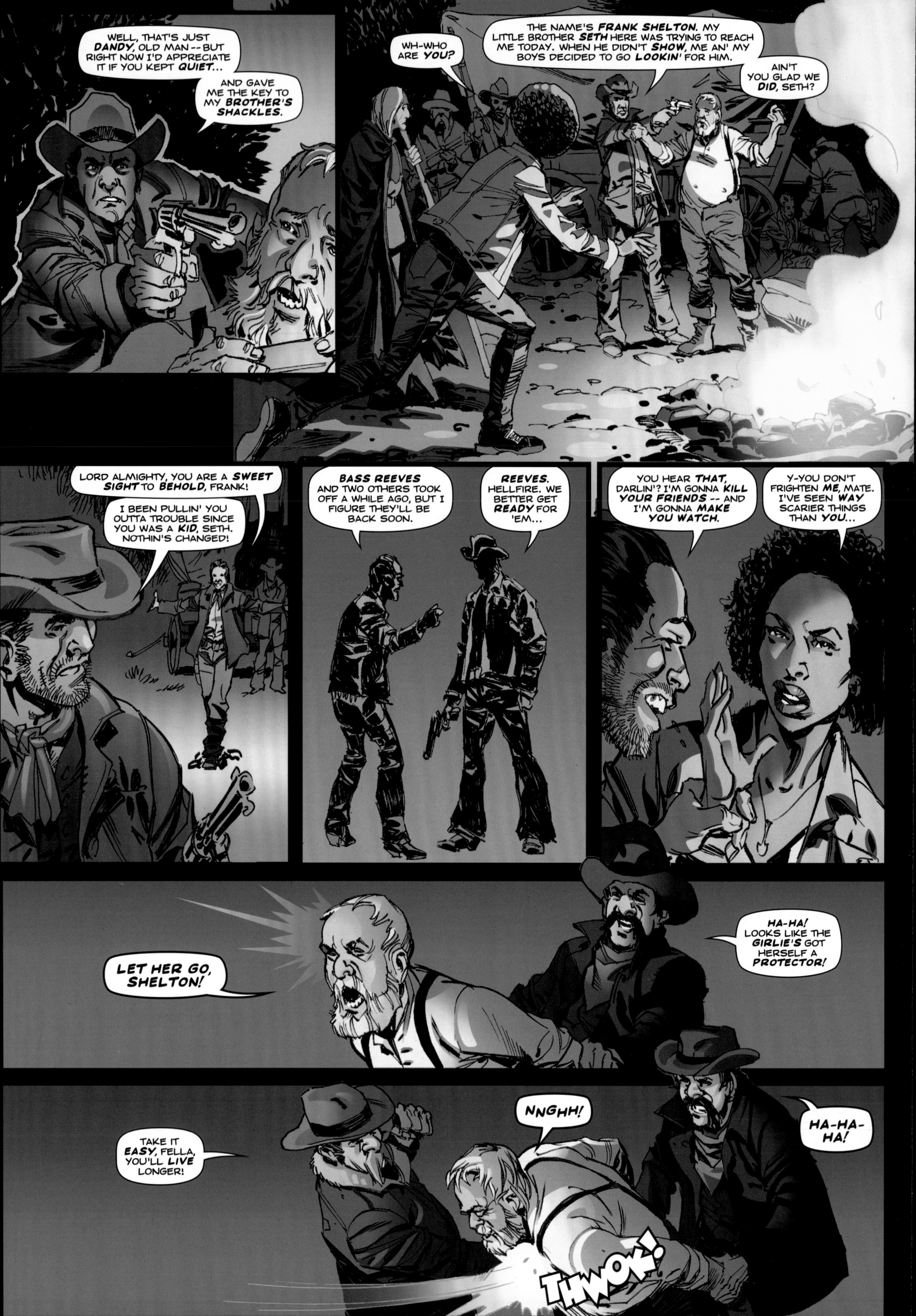
WELL, THAT'S JUST DANDY, OLD MAN -- BUT RIGHT NOW I'D APPRECIATE IT IF YOU KEPT QUIET...
AND GAVE ME THE KEY TO MY BROTHER'S SHACKLES.
WH-WHO ARE YOU?
THE NAME'S FRANK SHELTON. MY LITTLE BROTHER SETH HERE WAS TRYING TO REACH ME TODAY. WHEN HE DIDN'T SHOW, ME AN' MY BOYS DECIDED TO GO LOOKIN' FOR HIM.
AIN'T YOU GLAD WE DID, SETH?
LORD ALMIGHTY, YOU ARE A SWEET SIGHT TO BEHOLD, FRANK!
I BEEN PULLIN' YOU OUTTA TROUBLE SINCE YOU WAS A KID, SETH. NOTHIN'S CHANGED!
BASS REEVES AND TWO OTHERS TOOK OFF A WHILE AGO, BUT I FIGURE THEY'LL BE BACK SOON.
REEVES. HELLFIRE. WE BETTER GET READY FOR 'EM...
YOU HEAR THAT, DARLIN'? I'M GONNA KILL YOUR FRIENDS -- AND I'M GONNA MAKE YOU WATCH.
Y-YOU DON'T FRIGHTEN ME, MATE. I'VE SEEN WAY SCARIER THINGS THAN YOU...
LET HER GO, SHELTON!
HA-HA! LOOKS LIKE THE GIRLIE'S GOT HERSELF A PROTECTOR!
TAKE IT EASY, FELLA, YOU'LL LIVE LONGER!
NNGHH!
HA-HA-HA!
THWOK!

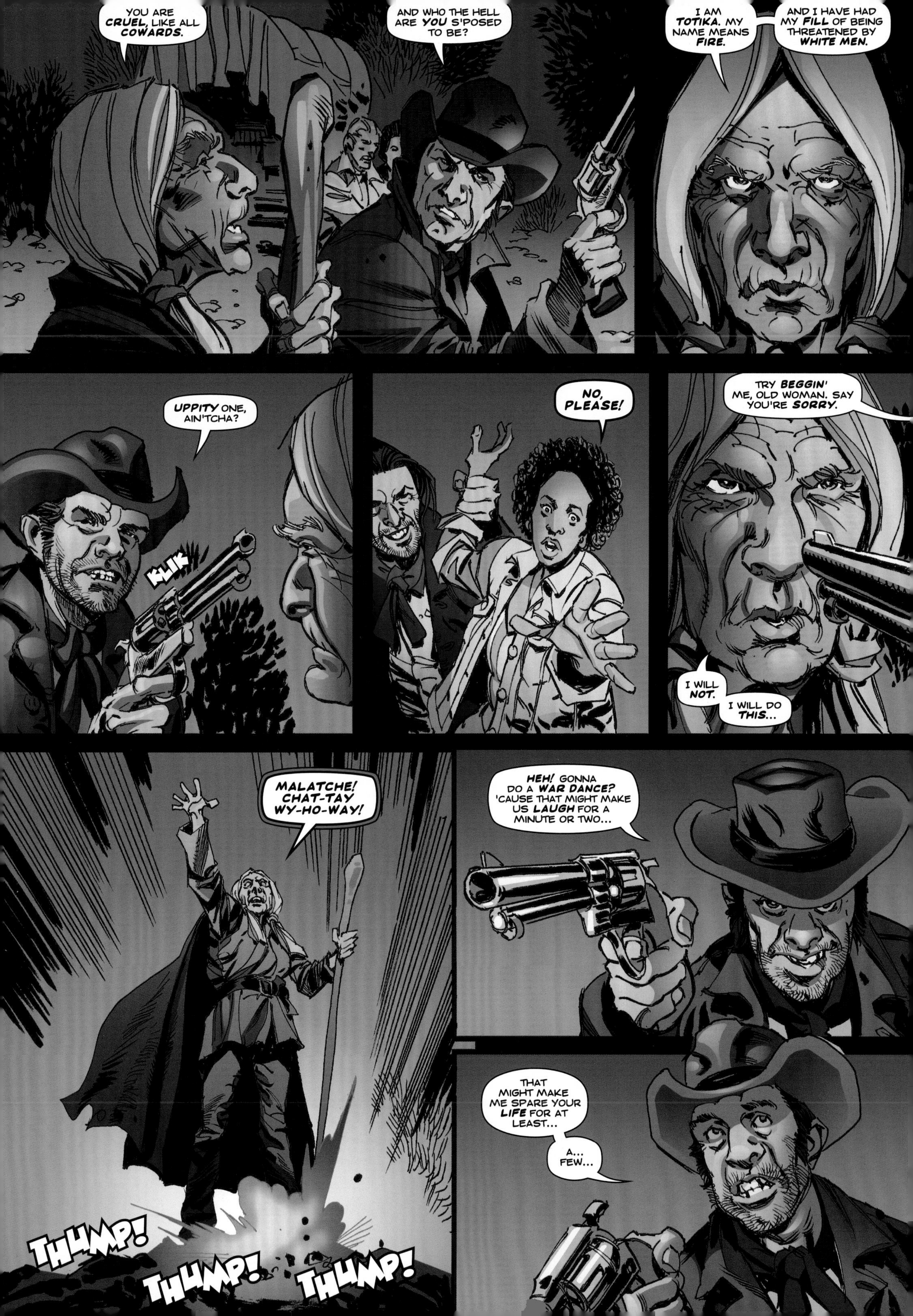

YOU ARE CRUEL, LIKE ALL COWARDS.
AND WHO THE HELL ARE YOU S'POSED TO BE?
I AM TOTIKA. MY NAME MEANS FIRE.
AND I HAVE HAD MY FILL OF BEING THREATENED BY WHITE MEN.
UPPITY ONE, AIN'TCHA?
KLIK
NO, PLEASE!
TRY BEGGIN' ME, OLD WOMAN. SAY YOU'RE SORRY.
I WILL NOT.
I WILL DO THIS...
MALATCHE! CHAT-TAY WY-HO-WAY!
THUMP!
THUMP!
THUMP!
HEH! GONNA DO A WAR DANCE? 'CAUSE THAT MIGHT MAKE US LAUGH FOR A MINUTE OR TWO...
THAT MIGHT MAKE ME SPARE YOUR LIFE FOR AT LEAST...
A... FEW...

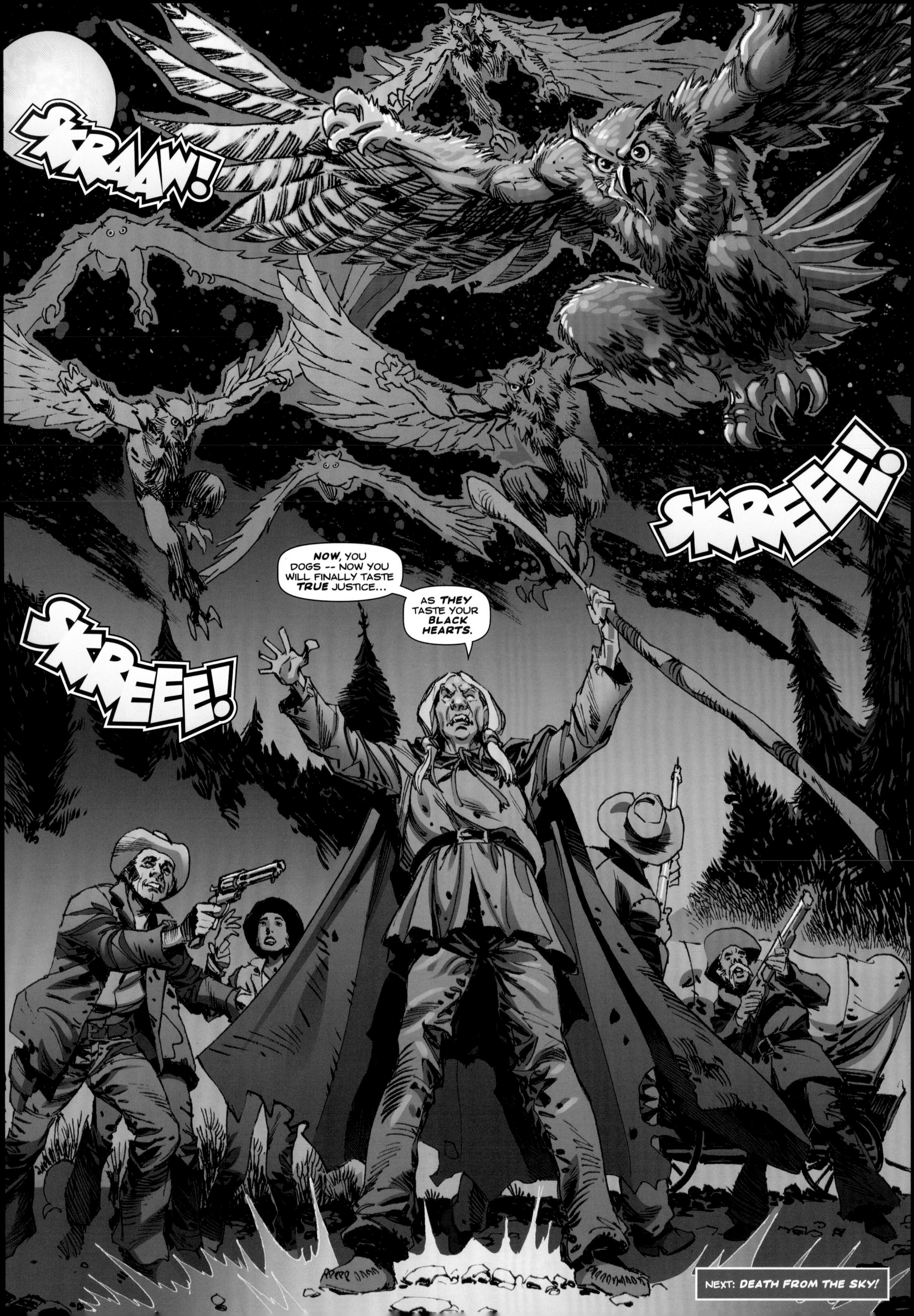
SKRAAW!
SKREEE!
NOW, YOU DOGS -- NOW YOU WILL FINALLY TASTE TRUE JUSTICE...
AS THEY TASTE YOUR BLACK HEARTS.
SKREEE!
NEXT: DEATH FROM THE SKY!

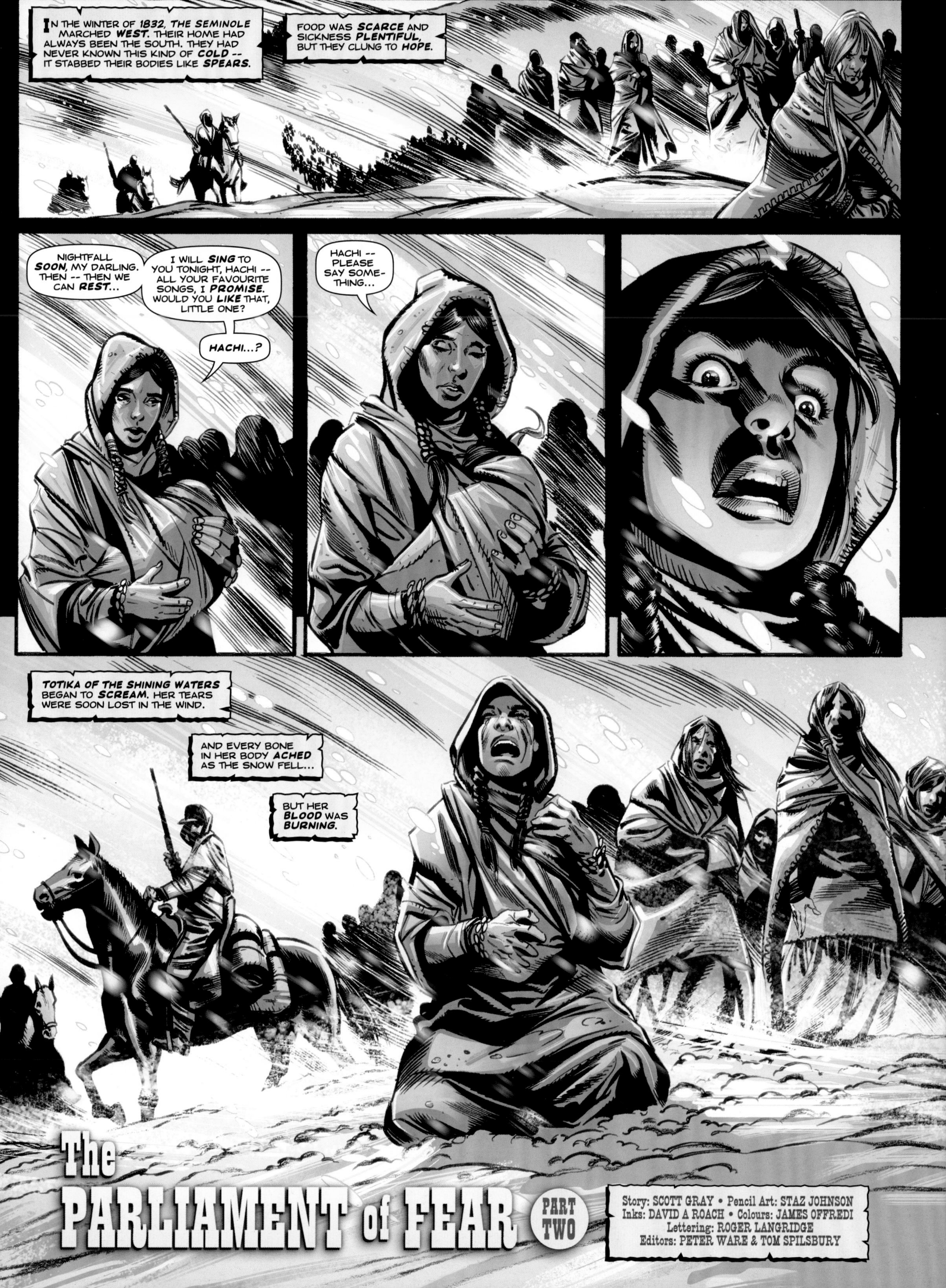
IN THE WINTER OF 1832, THE SEMINOLE MARCHED WEST. THEIR HOME HAD ALWAYS BEEN THE SOUTH. THEY HAD NEVER KNOWN THIS KIND OF COLD -- IT STABBED THEIR BODIES LIKE SPEARS.
FOOD WAS SCARCE AND SICKNESS PLENTIFUL, BUT THEY CLUNG TO HOPE.
NIGHTFALL SOON, MY DARLING. THEN -- THEN WE CAN REST...
I WILL SING TO YOU TONIGHT, HACHI -- ALL YOUR FAVOURITE SONGS, I PROMISE. WOULD YOU LIKE THAT, LITTLE ONE?
HACHI...?
HACHI -- PLEASE SAY SOMETHING...
TOTIKA OF THE SHINING WATERS BEGAN TO SCREAM. HER TEARS WERE SOON LOST IN THE WIND.
AND EVERY BONE IN HER BODY ACHED AS THE SNOW FELL...
BUT HER BLOOD WAS BURNING.
The PARLIAMENT of FEAR
PART TWO

Story: SCOTT GRAY • Pencil Art: STAZ JOHNSON
Inks: DAVID A ROACH • Colours: JAMES OFFREDI
Lettering: ROGER LANGRIDGE
Editors: PETER WARE & TOM SPILSBURY

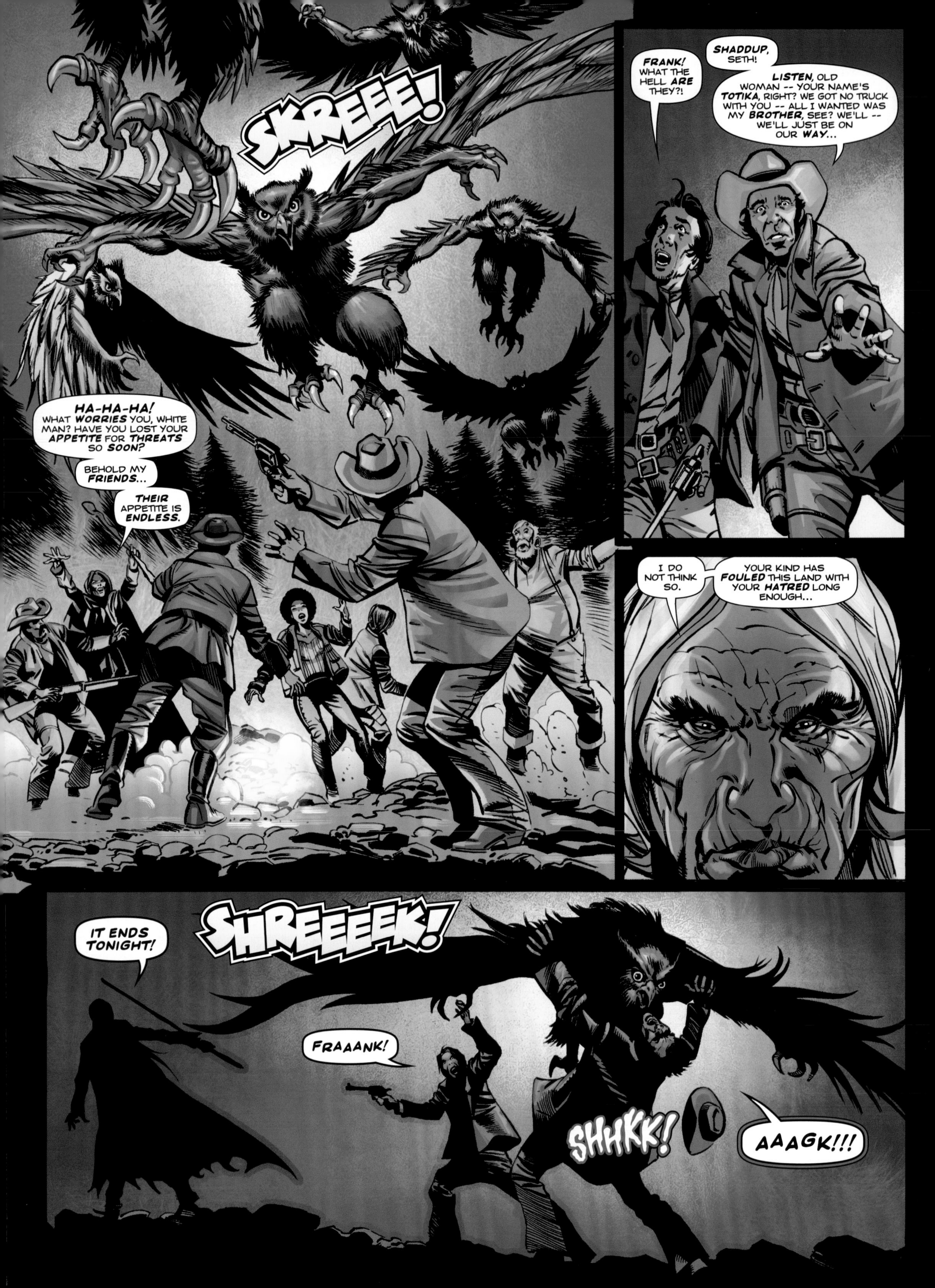

SKREEE!
HA-HA-HA! WHAT WORRIES YOU, WHITE MAN? HAVE YOU LOST YOUR APPETITE FOR THREATS SO SOON?
BEHOLD MY FRIENDS...
THEIR APPETITE IS ENDLESS.
FRANK! WHAT THE HELL ARE THEY?!
SHADDUP, SETH!
LISTEN, OLD WOMAN -- YOUR NAME'S TOTIKA, RIGHT? WE GOT NO TRUCK WITH YOU -- ALL I WANTED WAS MY BROTHER, SEE? WE'LL -- WE'LL JUST BE ON OUR WAY...
I DO NOT THINK SO.
YOUR KIND HAS FOULED THIS LAND WITH YOUR HATRED LONG ENOUGH...
IT ENDS TONIGHT!
SHREEEEK!
FRAAANK!
SHHKK!
AAAGK!!!

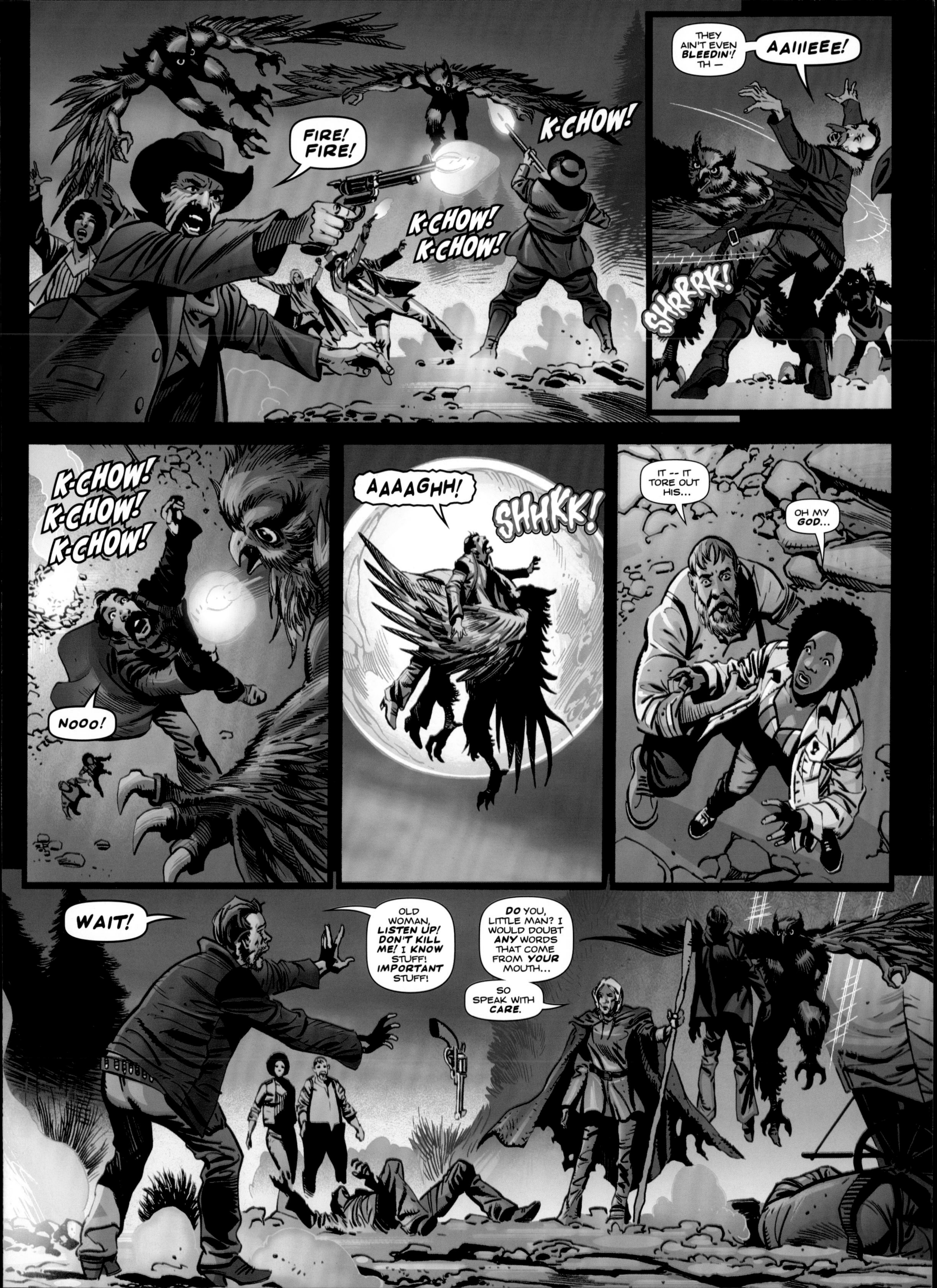
FIRE! FIRE!
K-CHOW!
K-CHOW! K-CHOW!
THEY AIN'T EVEN BLEEDIN'! TH —
AAIIIEEE!
SHRRRK!
K-CHOW! K-CHOW! K-CHOW!
NOOO!
AAAAGHH!
SHHKK!
IT -- IT TORE OUT HIS...
OH MY GOD...
WAIT!
OLD WOMAN, LISTEN UP! DON'T KILL ME! I KNOW STUFF! IMPORTANT STUFF!
DO YOU, LITTLE MAN? I WOULD DOUBT ANY WORDS THAT COME FROM YOUR MOUTH...
SO SPEAK WITH CARE.

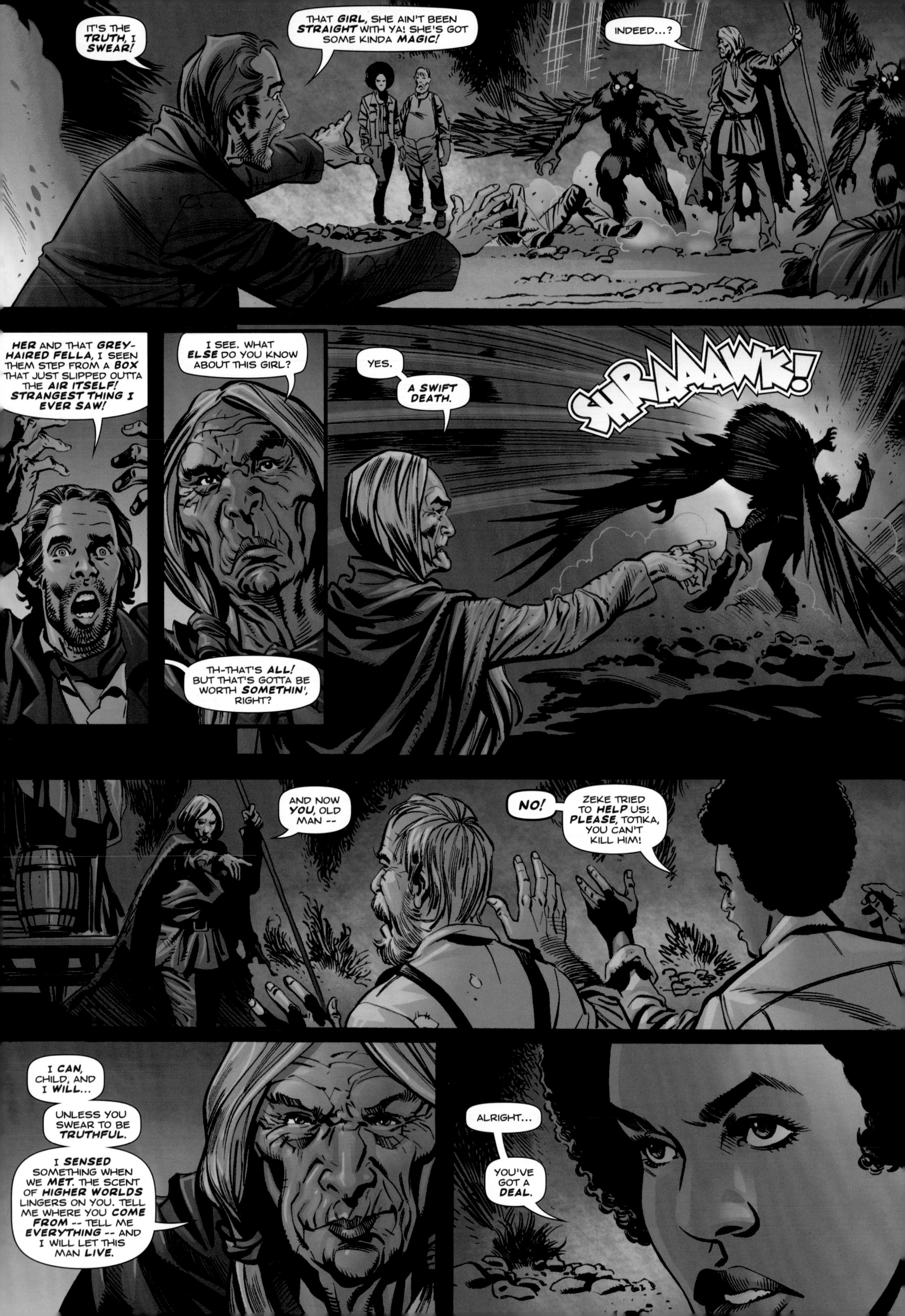
IT'S THE TRUTH, I SWEAR!
THAT GIRL, SHE AIN'T BEEN STRAIGHT WITH YA! SHE'S GOT SOME KINDA MAGIC!
INDEED...?
HER AND THAT GREY-HAIRED FELLA, I SEEN THEM STEP FROM A BOX THAT JUST SLIPPED OUTTA THE AIR ITSELF! STRANGEST THING I EVER SAW!
I SEE. WHAT ELSE DO YOU KNOW ABOUT THIS GIRL?
TH-THAT'S ALL! BUT THAT'S GOTTA BE WORTH SOMETHIN', RIGHT?
YES.
A SWIFT DEATH.
SHRAAAWK!
AND NOW YOU, OLD MAN --
NO!
ZEKE TRIED TO HELP US! PLEASE, TOTIKA, YOU CAN'T KILL HIM!
I CAN, CHILD, AND I WILL...
UNLESS YOU SWEAR TO BE TRUTHFUL.
I SENSED SOMETHING WHEN WE MET. THE SCENT OF HIGHER WORLDS LINGERS ON YOU. TELL ME WHERE YOU COME FROM -- TELL ME EVERYTHING -- AND I WILL LET THIS MAN LIVE.
ALRIGHT...
YOU'VE GOT A DEAL.

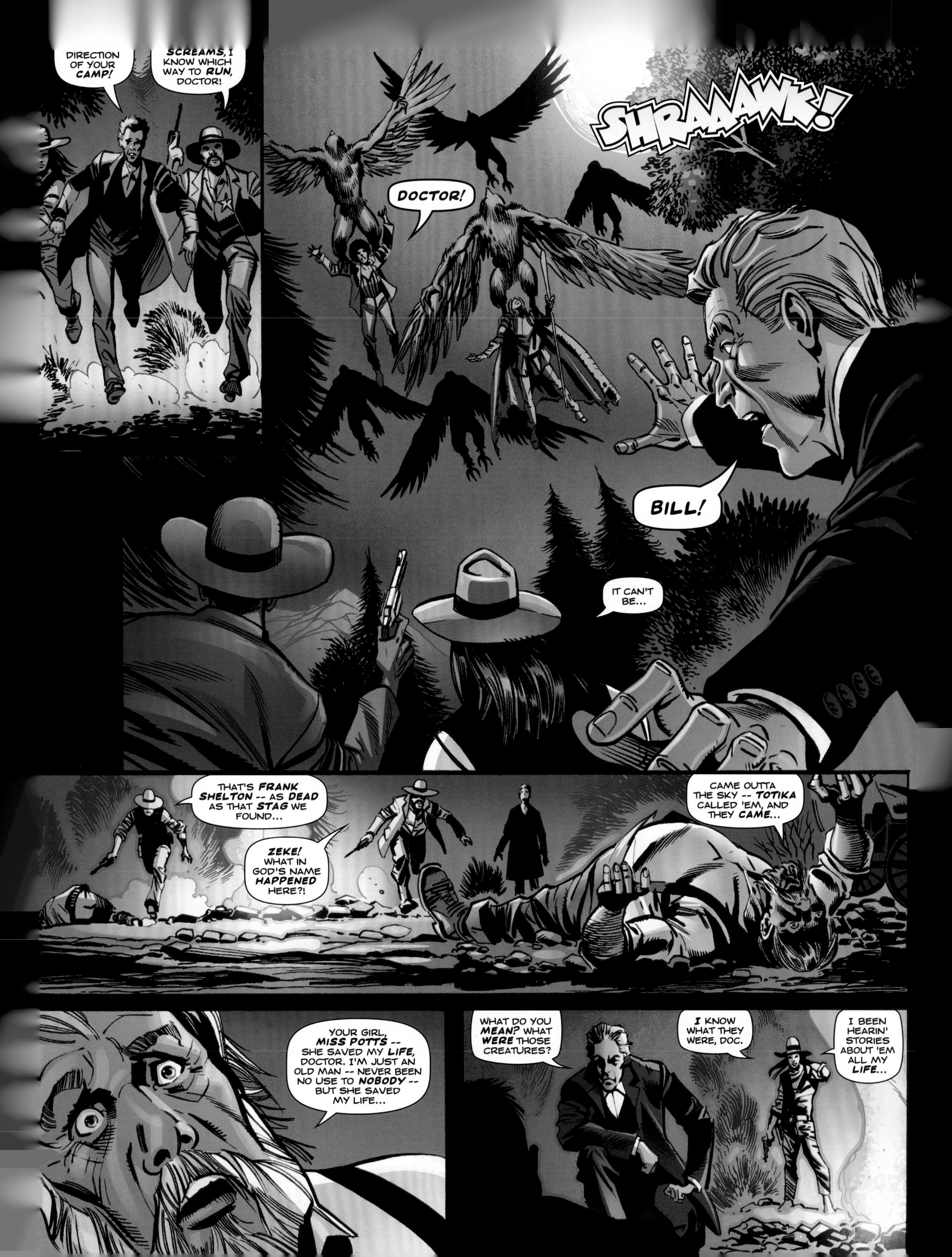
DIRECTION OF YOUR CAMP!
SCREAMS, I KNOW WHICH WAY TO RUN, DOCTOR!
SHRAAAWK!
DOCTOR!
BILL!
IT CAN'T BE...
THAT'S FRANK SHELTON -- AS DEAD AS THAT STAG WE FOUND...
ZEKE! WHAT IN GOD'S NAME HAPPENED HERE?!
CAME OUTTA THE SKY -- TOTIKA CALLED 'EM, AND THEY CAME...
YOUR GIRL, MISS POTTS -- SHE SAVED MY LIFE, DOCTOR. I'M JUST AN OLD MAN -- NEVER BEEN NO USE TO NOBODY -- BUT SHE SAVED MY LIFE...
WHAT DO YOU MEAN? WHAT WERE THOSE CREATURES?
I KNOW WHAT THEY WERE, DOC.
I BEEN HEARIN' STORIES ABOUT 'EM ALL MY LIFE...

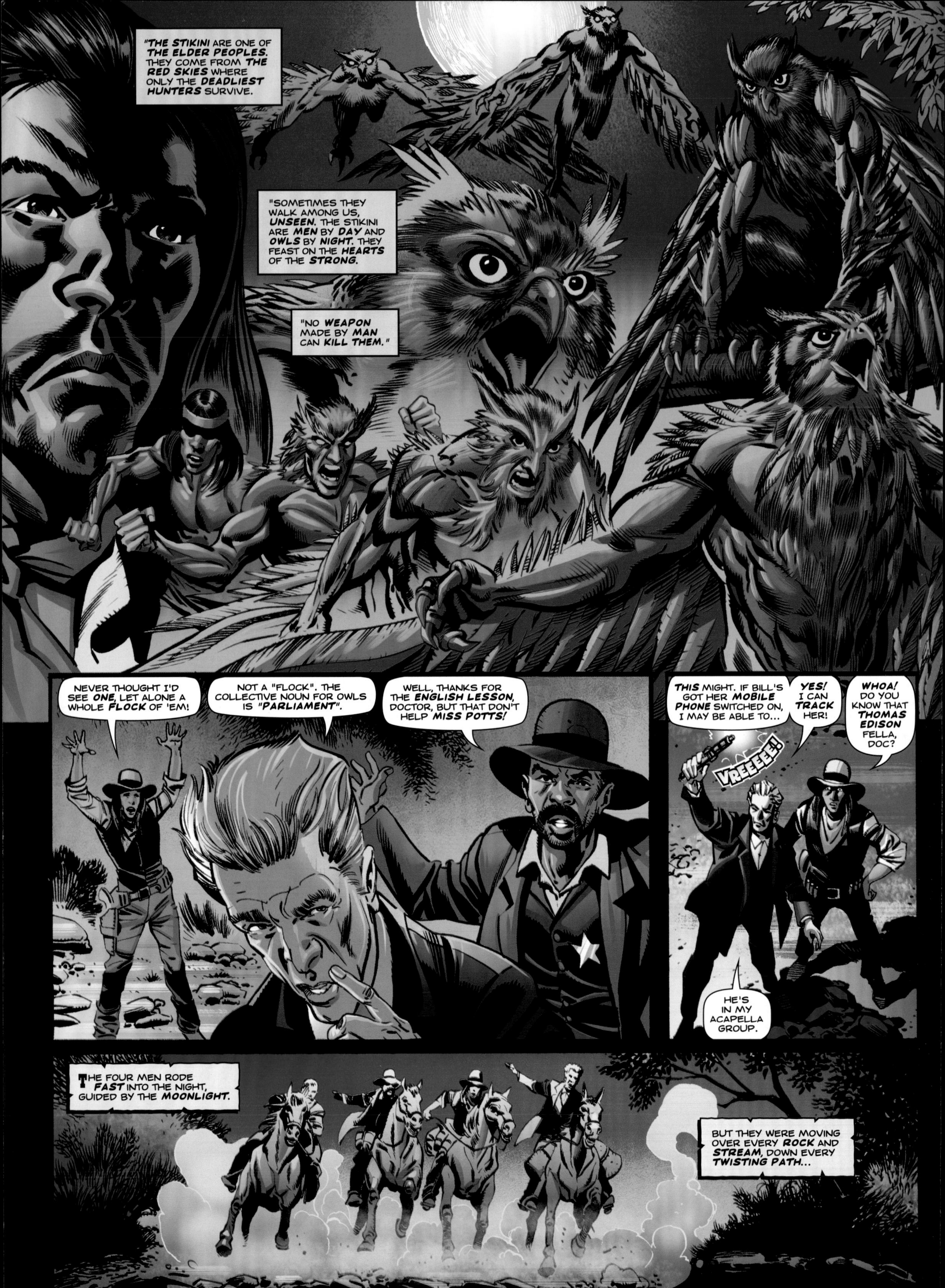
"THE STIKINI ARE ONE OF THE ELDER PEOPLES. THEY COME FROM THE RED SKIES WHERE ONLY THE DEADLIEST HUNTERS SURVIVE.
"SOMETIMES THEY WALK AMONG US, UNSEEN. THE STIKINI ARE MEN BY DAY AND OWLS BY NIGHT. THEY FEAST ON THE HEARTS OF THE STRONG.
"NO WEAPON MADE BY MAN CAN KILL THEM."
NEVER THOUGHT I'D SEE ONE, LET ALONE A WHOLE FLOCK OF 'EM!
NOT A "FLOCK". THE COLLECTIVE NOUN FOR OWLS IS "PARLIAMENT".
WELL, THANKS FOR THE ENGLISH LESSON, DOCTOR, BUT THAT DON'T HELP MISS POTTS!
THIS MIGHT. IF BILL'S GOT HER MOBILE PHONE SWITCHED ON, I MAY BE ABLE TO...
VREEEEE!
YES! I CAN TRACK HER!
WHOA! DO YOU KNOW THAT THOMAS EDISON FELLA, DOC?
HE'S IN MY ACAPELLA GROUP.
THE FOUR MEN RODE FAST INTO THE NIGHT, GUIDED BY THE MOONLIGHT.
BUT THEY WERE MOVING OVER EVERY ROCK AND STREAM, DOWN EVERY TWISTING PATH...

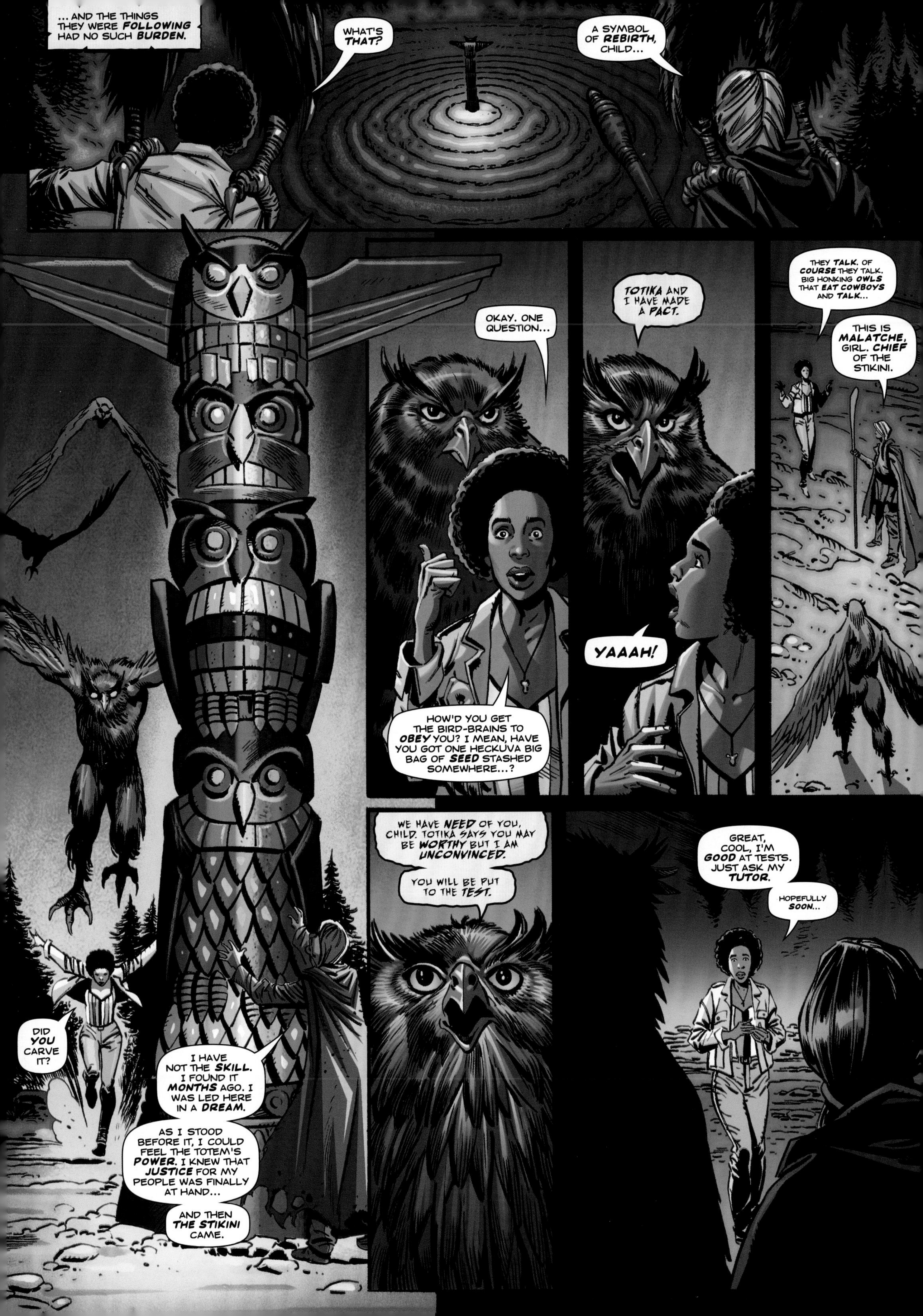

...AND THE THINGS THEY WERE FOLLOWING HAD NO SUCH BURDEN.
WHAT'S THAT?
A SYMBOL OF REBIRTH, CHILD...
DID YOU CARVE IT?
I HAVE NOT THE SKILL. I FOUND IT MONTHS AGO. I WAS LED HERE IN A DREAM.
AS I STOOD BEFORE IT, I COULD FEEL THE TOTEM'S POWER. I KNEW THAT JUSTICE FOR MY PEOPLE WAS FINALLY AT HAND...
AND THEN THE STIKINI CAME.
OKAY. ONE QUESTION...
HOW'D YOU GET THE BIRD-BRAINS TO OBEY YOU? I MEAN, HAVE YOU GOT ONE HECKUVA BIG BAG OF SEED STASHED SOMEWHERE...?
TOTIKA AND I HAVE MADE A PACT.
YAAAH!
THEY TALK. OF COURSE THEY TALK. BIG HONKING OWLS THAT EAT COWBOYS AND TALK...
THIS IS MALATCHE, GIRL. CHIEF OF THE STIKINI.
WE HAVE NEED OF YOU, CHILD. TOTIKA SAYS YOU MAY BE WORTHY BUT I AM UNCONVINCED.
YOU WILL BE PUT TO THE TEST.
GREAT, COOL, I'M GOOD AT TESTS. JUST ASK MY TUTOR.
HOPEFULLY SOON...

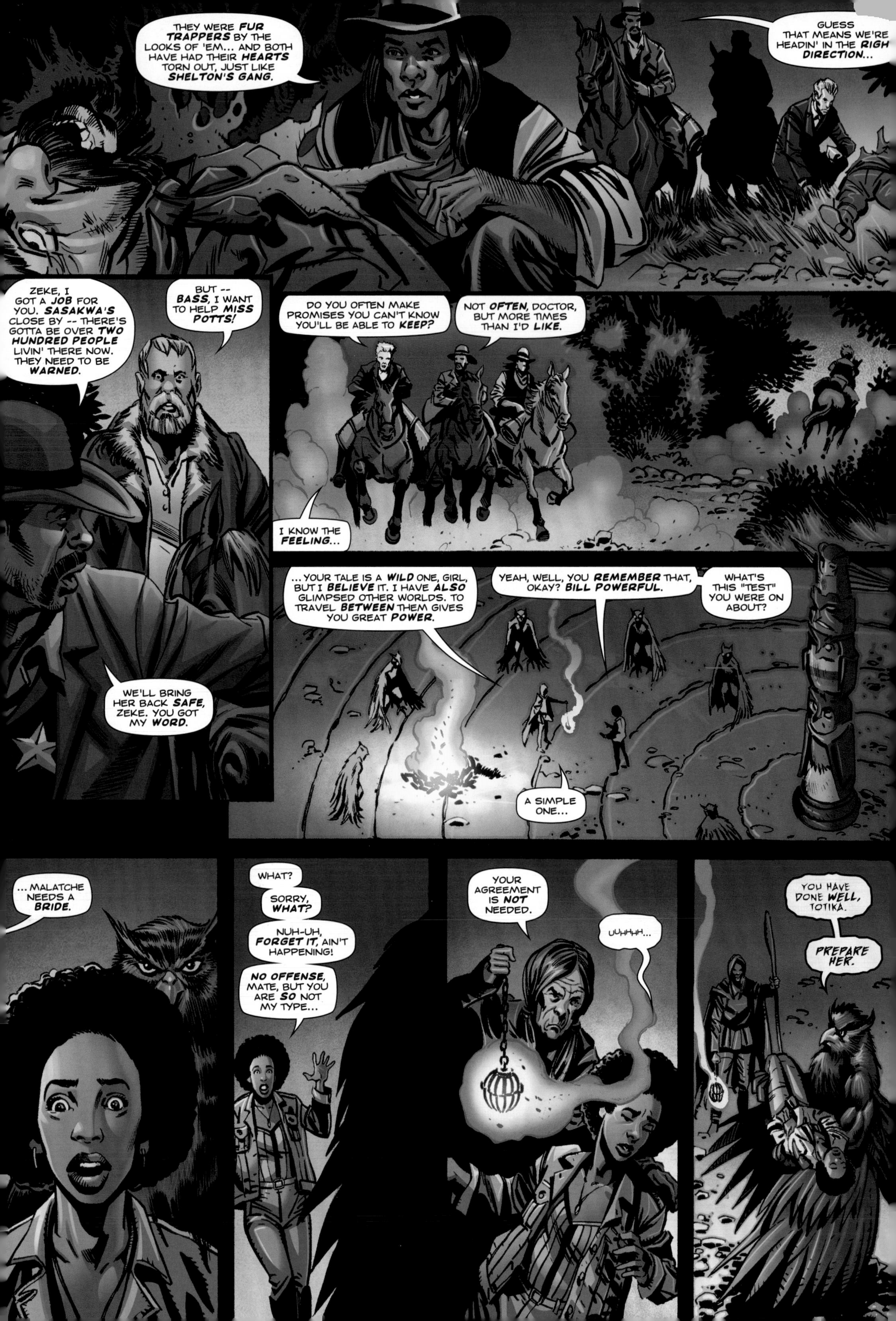
THEY WERE FUR TRAPPERS BY THE LOOKS OF 'EM... AND BOTH HAVE HAD THEIR HEARTS TORN OUT, JUST LIKE SHELTON'S GANG.
GUESS THAT MEANS WE'RE HEADIN' IN THE RIGH DIRECTION...
ZEKE, I GOT A JOB FOR YOU. SASAKWA'S CLOSE BY -- THERE'S GOTTA BE OVER TWO HUNDRED PEOPLE LIVIN' THERE NOW. THEY NEED TO BE WARNED.
BUT -- BASS, I WANT TO HELP MISS POTTS!
WE'LL BRING HER BACK SAFE, ZEKE. YOU GOT MY WORD.
DO YOU OFTEN MAKE PROMISES YOU CAN'T KNOW YOU'LL BE ABLE TO KEEP?
NOT OFTEN, DOCTOR, BUT MORE TIMES THAN I'D LIKE.
I KNOW THE FEELING...
...YOUR TALE IS A WILD ONE, GIRL, BUT I BELIEVE IT. I HAVE ALSO GLIMPSED OTHER WORLDS. TO TRAVEL BETWEEN THEM GIVES YOU GREAT POWER.
YEAH, WELL, YOU REMEMBER THAT, OKAY? BILL POWERFUL.
WHAT'S THIS "TEST" YOU WERE ON ABOUT?
A SIMPLE ONE...
...MALATCHE NEEDS A BRIDE.
WHAT?
SORRY, WHAT?
NUH-UH, FORGET IT, AIN'T HAPPENING!
NO OFFENSE, MATE, BUT YOU ARE SO NOT MY TYPE...
YOUR AGREEMENT IS NOT NEEDED.
UUHHHH...
YOU HAVE DONE WELL, TOTIKA.
PREPARE HER.

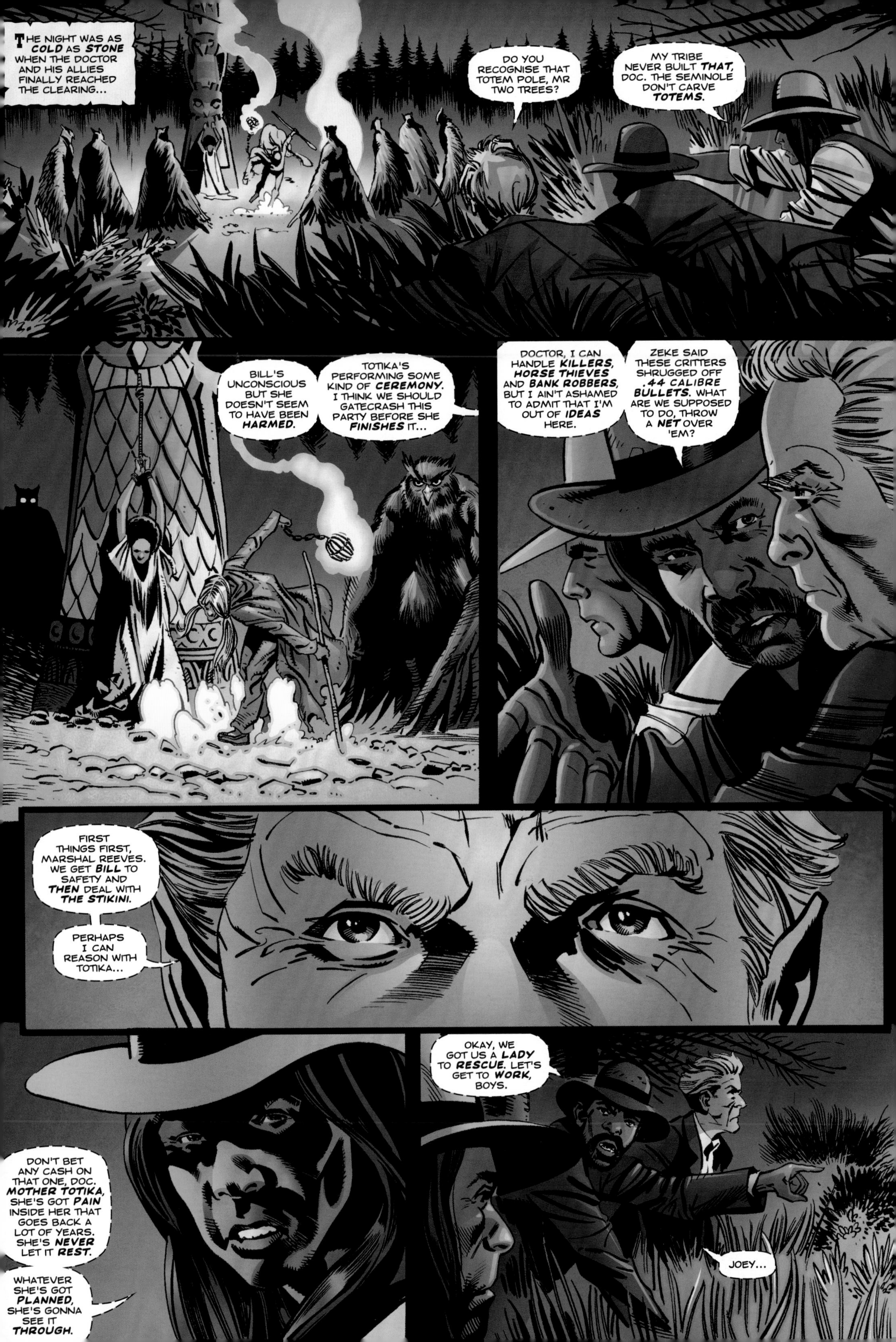
THE NIGHT WAS AS COLD AS STONE WHEN THE DOCTOR AND HIS ALLIES FINALLY REACHED THE CLEARING...
DO YOU RECOGNISE THAT TOTEM POLE, MR TWO TREES?
MY TRIBE NEVER BUILT THAT, DOC. THE SEMINOLE DON'T CARVE TOTEMS.
BILL'S UNCONSCIOUS BUT SHE DOESN'T SEEM TO HAVE BEEN HARMED.
TOTIKA'S PERFORMING SOME KIND OF CEREMONY. I THINK WE SHOULD GATECRASH THIS PARTY BEFORE SHE FINISHES IT...
DOCTOR, I CAN HANDLE KILLERS, HORSE THIEVES AND BANK ROBBERS, BUT I AIN'T ASHAMED TO ADMIT THAT I'M OUT OF IDEAS HERE.
ZEKE SAID THESE CRITTERS SHRUGGED OFF .44 CALIBRE BULLETS. WHAT ARE WE SUPPOSED TO DO, THROW A NET OVER 'EM?
FIRST THINGS FIRST, MARSHAL REEVES. WE GET BILL TO SAFETY AND THEN DEAL WITH THE STIKINI.
PERHAPS I CAN REASON WITH TOTIKA...
DON'T BET ANY CASH ON THAT ONE, DOC. MOTHER TOTIKA, SHE'S GOT PAIN INSIDE HER THAT GOES BACK A LOT OF YEARS. SHE'S NEVER LET IT REST.
WHATEVER SHE'S GOT PLANNED, SHE'S GONNA SEE IT THROUGH.
OKAY, WE GOT US A LADY TO RESCUE. LET'S GET TO WORK, BOYS.
JOEY...

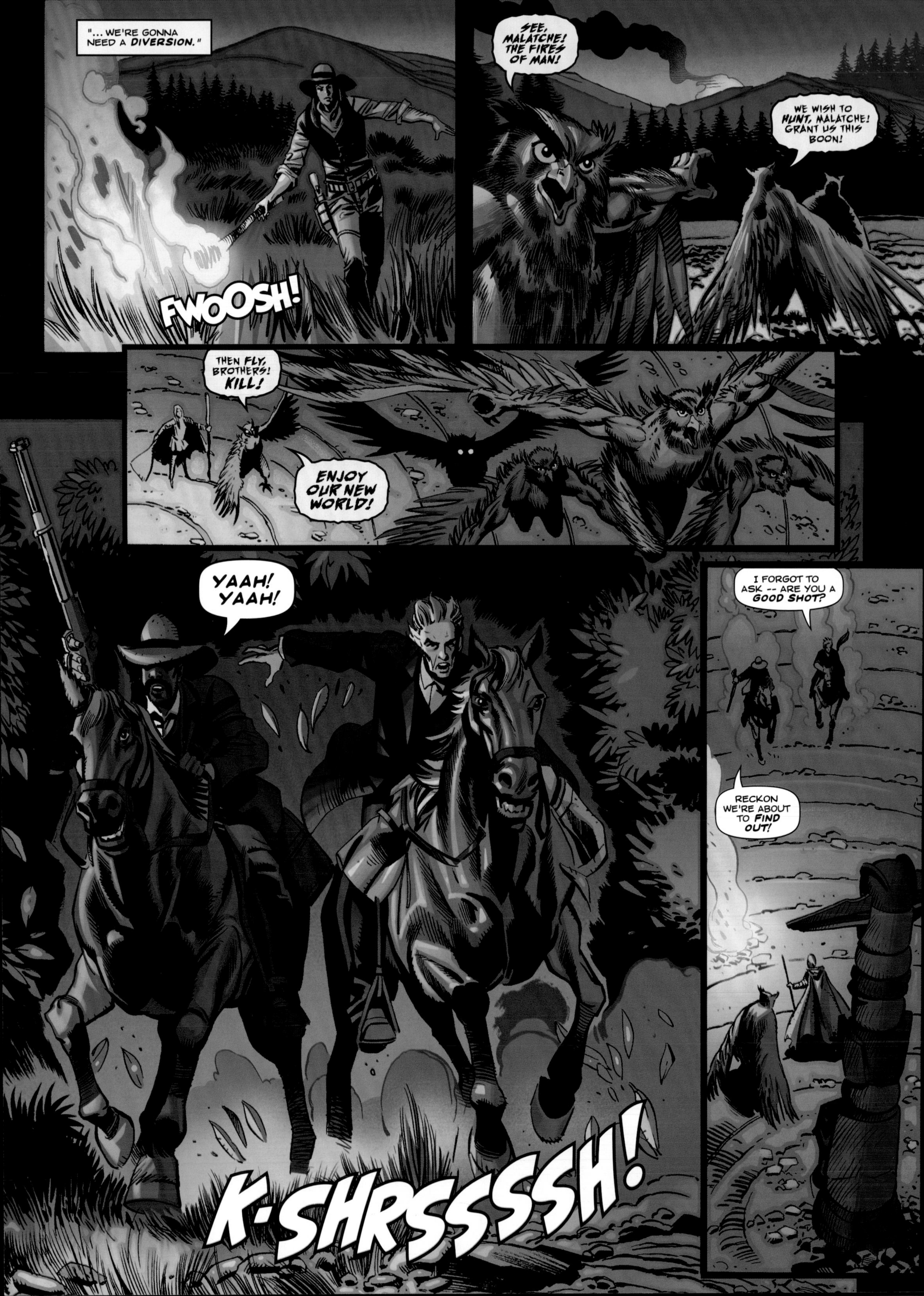
"... WE'RE GONNA NEED A DIVERSION."
FWOOSH!
SEE, MALATCHE! THE FIRES OF MAN!
WE WISH TO HUNT, MALATCHE! GRANT US THIS BOON!
THEN FLY, BROTHERS! KILL!
ENJOY OUR NEW WORLD!
YAAH! YAAH!
K-SHRSSSSH!
I FORGOT TO ASK -- ARE YOU A GOOD SHOT?
RECKON WE'RE ABOUT TO FIND OUT!

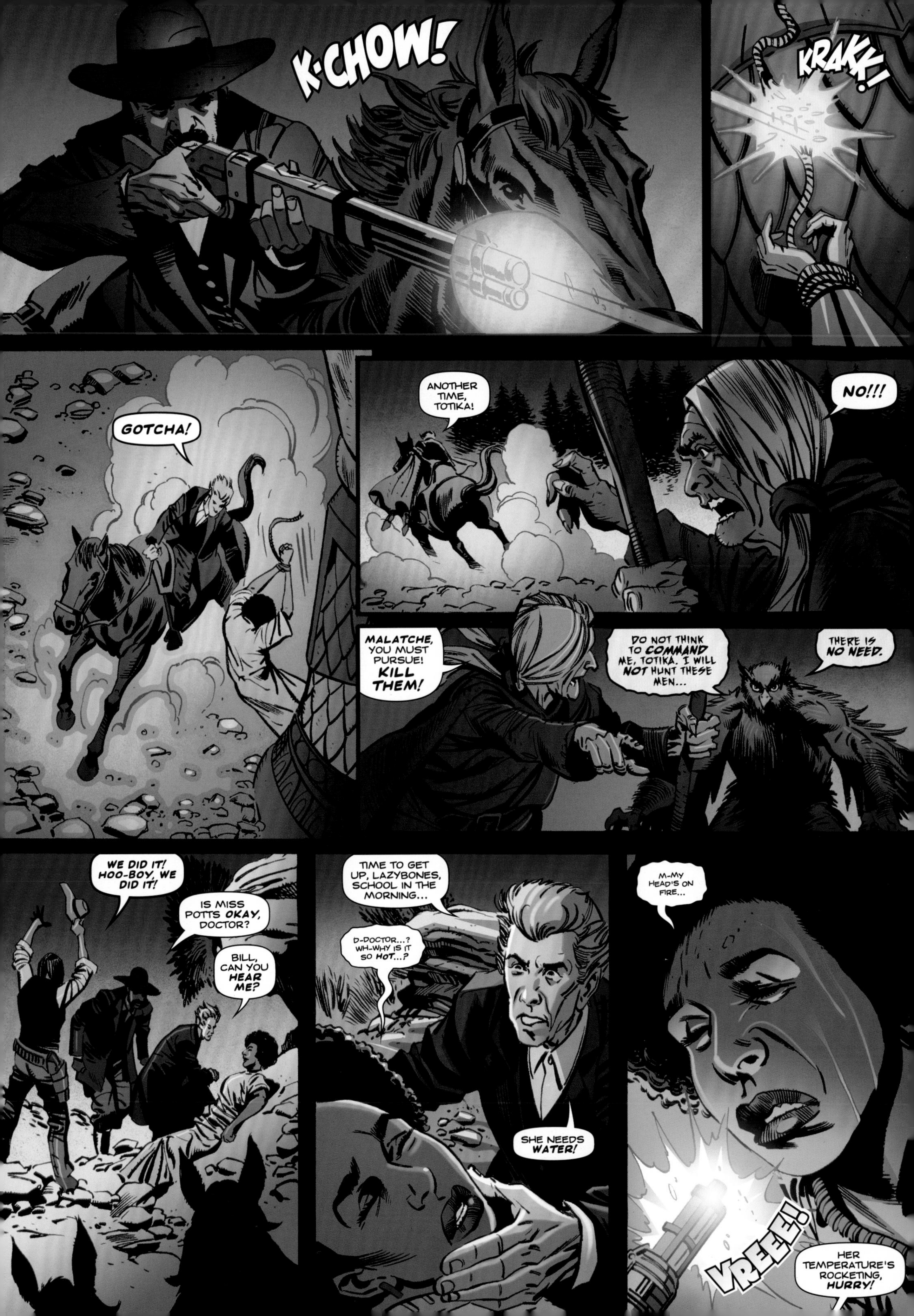

K-CHOW!
KRAKK!
GOTCHA!
ANOTHER TIME, TOTIKA!
NO!!!
MALATCHE, YOU MUST PURSUE! KILL THEM!
DO NOT THINK TO COMMAND ME, TOTIKA. I WILL NOT HUNT THESE MEN...
THERE IS NO NEED.
WE DID IT! HOO-BOY, WE DID IT!
IS MISS POTTS OKAY, DOCTOR?
BILL, CAN YOU HEAR ME?
TIME TO GET UP, LAZYBONES, SCHOOL IN THE MORNING...
D-DOCTOR...? WH-WHY IS IT SO HOT...?
SHE NEEDS WATER!
M-MY HEAD'S ON FIRE...
VREEE!
HER TEMPERATURE'S ROCKETING, HURRY!

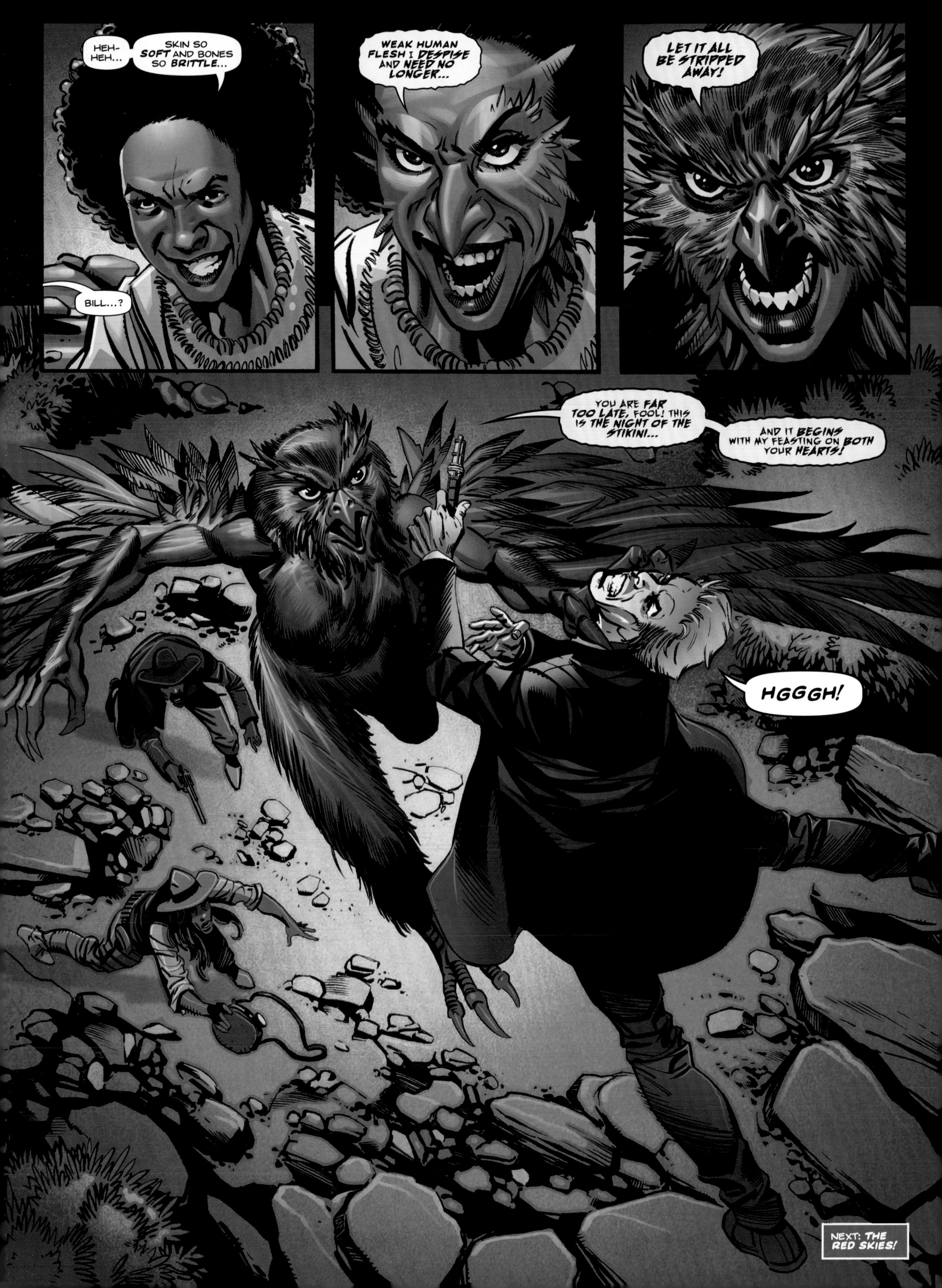
HEH-HEH...
SKIN SO SOFT AND BONES SO BRITTLE...
BILL...?
WEAK HUMAN FLESH I DESPISE AND NEED NO LONGER...
LET IT ALL BE STRIPPED AWAY!
YOU ARE FAR TOO LATE, FOOL! THIS IS THE NIGHT OF THE STIKINI...
AND IT BEGINS WITH MY FEASTING ON BOTH YOUR HEARTS!
HGGGH!
NEXT: THE RED SKIES!

The PARLIAMENT of FEAR PART THREE

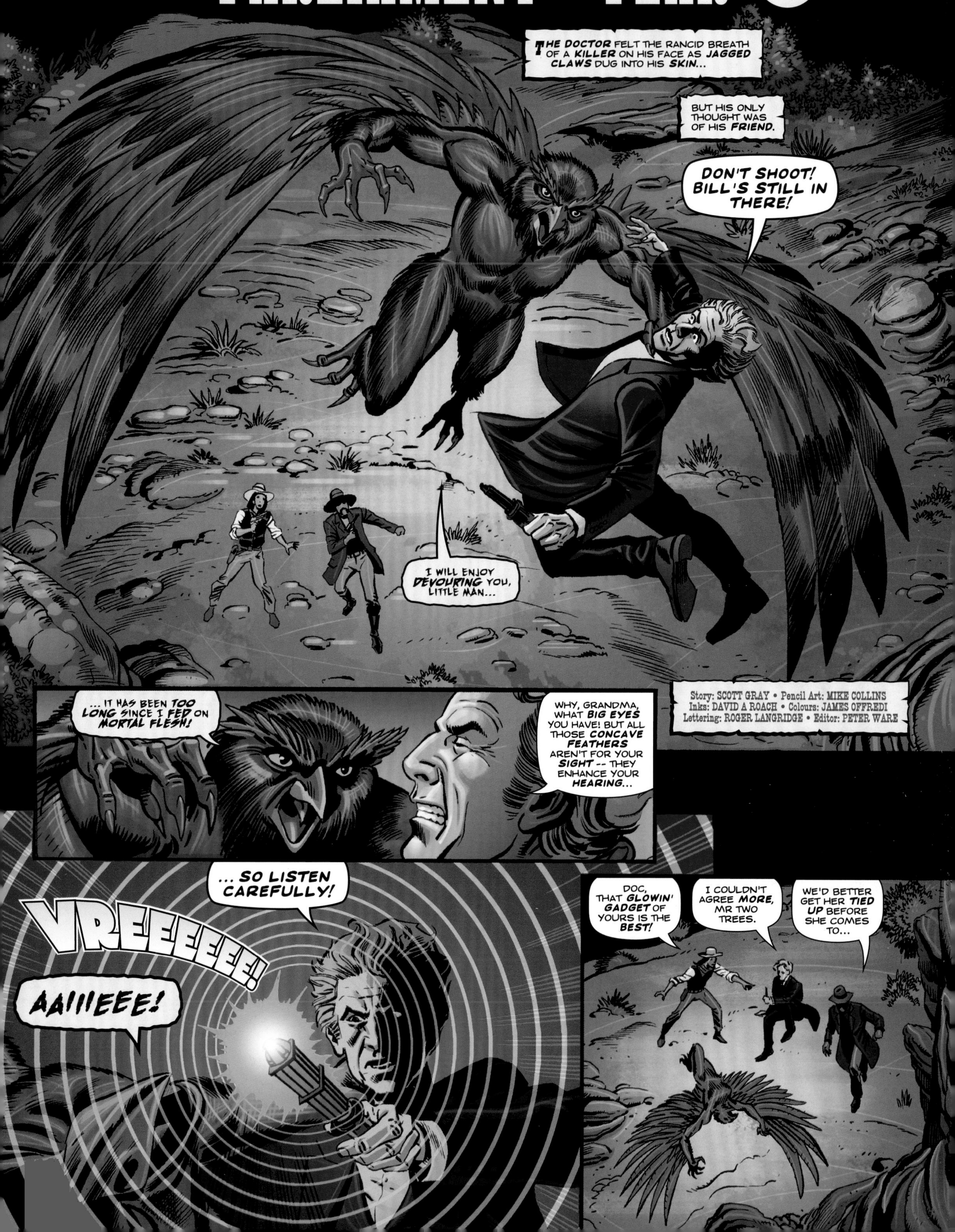
THE DOCTOR FELT THE RANCID BREATH OF A KILLER ON HIS FACE AS JAGGED CLAWS DUG INTO HIS SKIN...
BUT HIS ONLY THOUGHT WAS OF HIS FRIEND.
DON'T SHOOT! BILL'S STILL IN THERE!
I WILL ENJOY DEVOURING YOU, LITTLE MAN...
Story: SCOTT GRAY • Pencil Art: MIKE COLLINS
Inks: DAVID A ROACH • Colours: JAMES OFFREDI
Lettering: ROGER LANGRIDGE • Editor: PETER WARE
...IT HAS BEEN TOO LONG SINCE I FED ON MORTAL FLESH!
WHY, GRANDMA, WHAT BIG EYES YOU HAVE! BUT ALL THOSE CONCAVE FEATHERS AREN'T FOR YOUR SIGHT -- THEY ENHANCE YOUR HEARING...
...SO LISTEN CAREFULLY!
VREEEEEE!
AAIIIEEE!
DOC, THAT GLOWIN' GADGET OF YOURS IS THE BEST!
I COULDN'T AGREE MORE, MR TWO TREES.
WE'D BETTER GET HER TIED UP BEFORE SHE COMES TO...

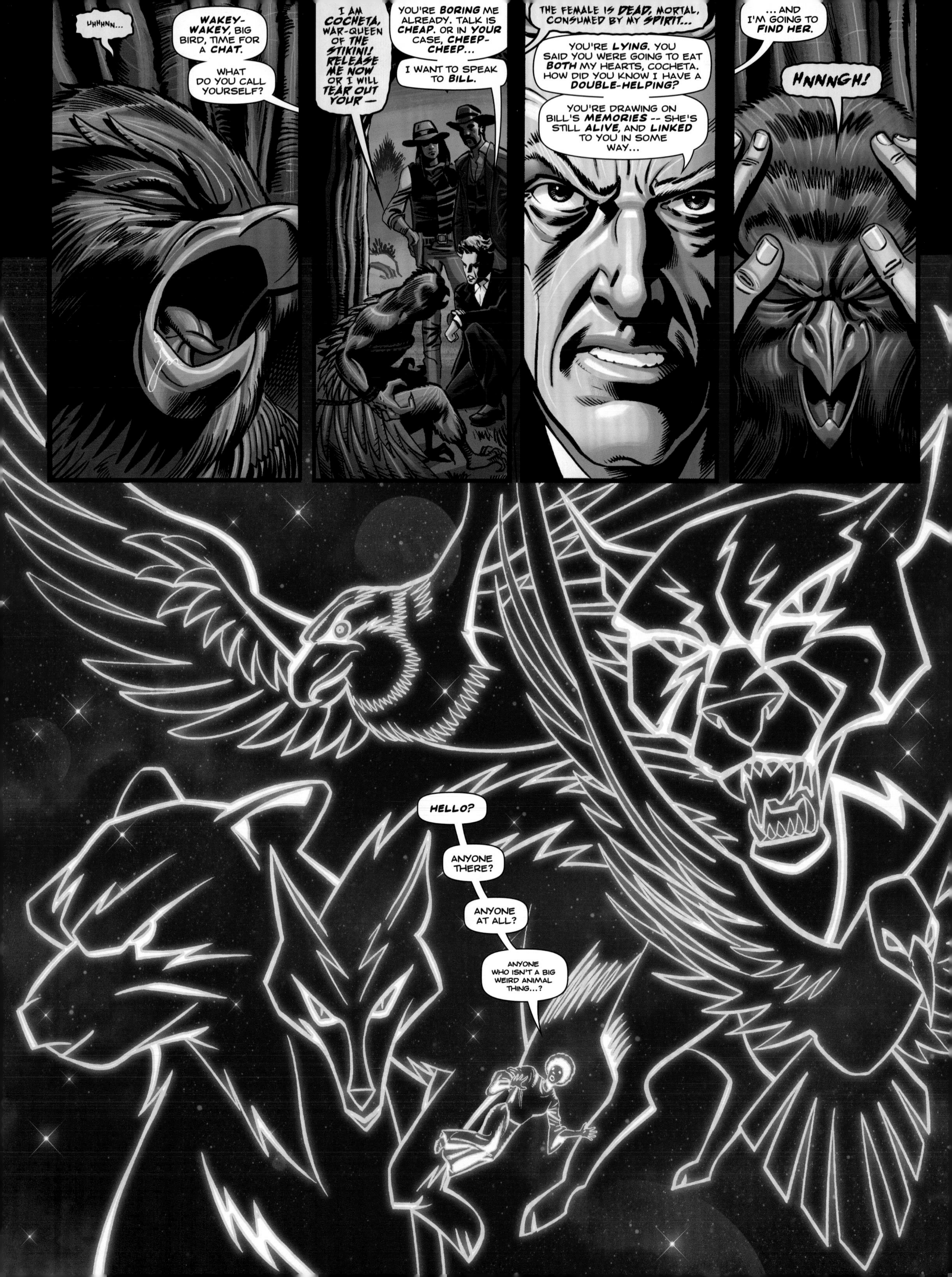
UHHHNN...
WAKEY-WAKEY, BIG BIRD, TIME FOR A CHAT.
WHAT DO YOU CALL YOURSELF?
I AM COCHETA, WAR-QUEEN OF THE STIKINI! RELEASE ME NOW OR I WILL TEAR OUT YOUR —
YOU'RE BORING ME ALREADY. TALK IS CHEAP. OR IN YOUR CASE, CHEEP-CHEEP...
I WANT TO SPEAK TO BILL.
THE FEMALE IS DEAD, MORTAL, CONSUMED BY MY SPIRIT...
YOU'RE LYING. YOU SAID YOU WERE GOING TO EAT BOTH MY HEARTS, COCHETA. HOW DID YOU KNOW I HAVE A DOUBLE-HELPING?
YOU'RE DRAWING ON BILL'S MEMORIES -- SHE'S STILL ALIVE, AND LINKED TO YOU IN SOME WAY...
... AND I'M GOING TO FIND HER.
HNNNGH!
HELLO?
ANYONE THERE?
ANYONE AT ALL?
ANYONE WHO ISN'T A BIG WEIRD ANIMAL THING...?

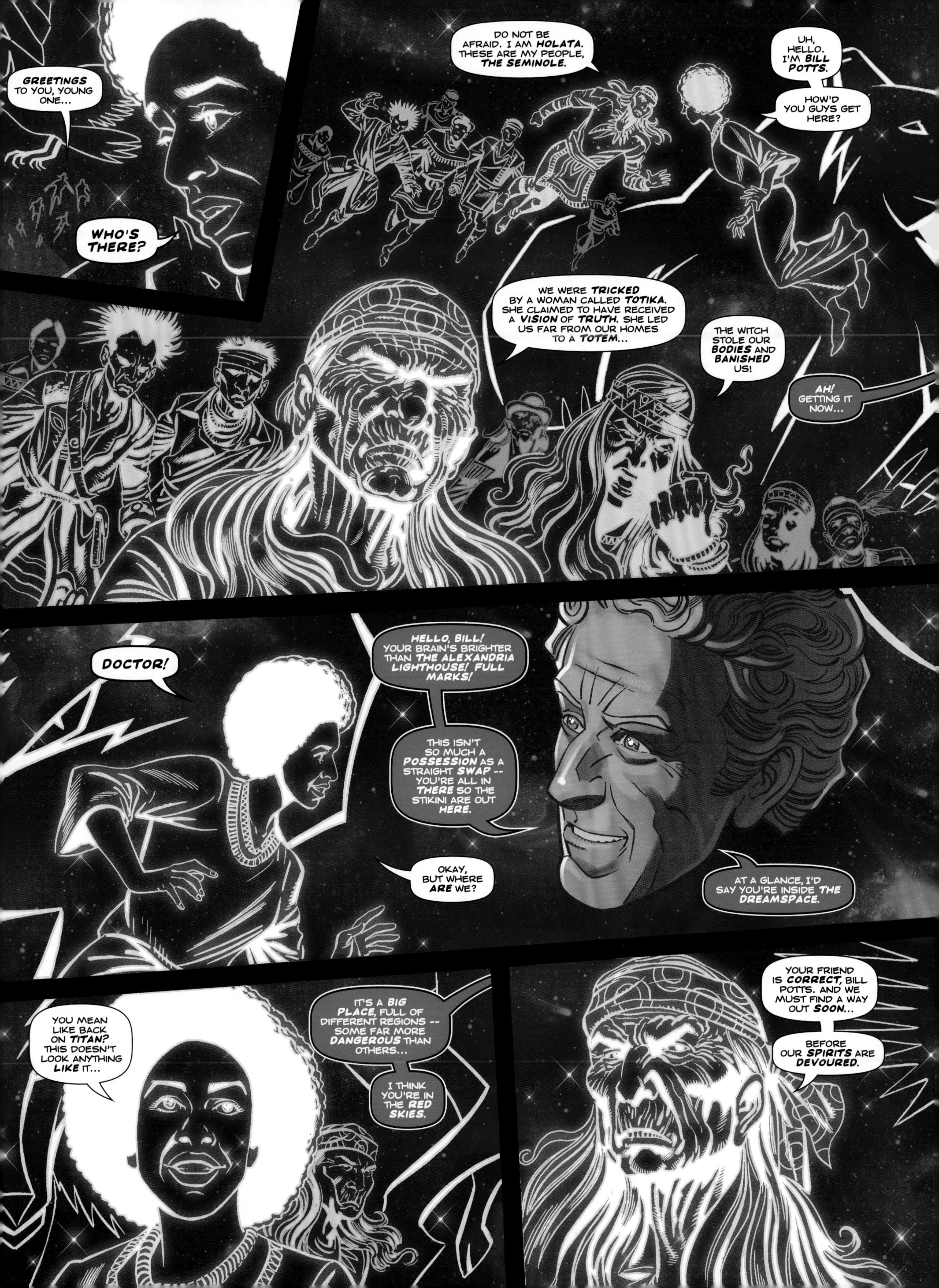
GREETINGS TO YOU, YOUNG ONE...
WHO'S THERE?
DO NOT BE AFRAID. I AM HOLATA. THESE ARE MY PEOPLE, THE SEMINOLE.
UH, HELLO. I'M BILL POTTS.
HOW'D YOU GUYS GET HERE?
WE WERE TRICKED BY A WOMAN CALLED TOTIKA. SHE CLAIMED TO HAVE RECEIVED A VISION OF TRUTH. SHE LED US FAR FROM OUR HOMES TO A TOTEM...
THE WITCH STOLE OUR BODIES AND BANISHED US!
AH! GETTING IT NOW...
DOCTOR!
HELLO, BILL! YOUR BRAIN'S BRIGHTER THAN THE ALEXANDRIA LIGHTHOUSE! FULL MARKS!
THIS ISN'T SO MUCH A POSSESSION AS A STRAIGHT SWAP -- YOU'RE ALL IN THERE SO THE STIKINI ARE OUT HERE.
OKAY, BUT WHERE ARE WE?
AT A GLANCE, I'D SAY YOU'RE INSIDE THE DREAMSPACE.
YOU MEAN LIKE BACK ON TITAN? THIS DOESN'T LOOK ANYTHING LIKE IT...
IT'S A BIG PLACE, FULL OF DIFFERENT REGIONS -- SOME FAR MORE DANGEROUS THAN OTHERS...
I THINK YOU'RE IN THE RED SKIES.
YOUR FRIEND IS CORRECT, BILL POTTS. AND WE MUST FIND A WAY OUT SOON...
BEFORE OUR SPIRITS ARE DEVOURED.

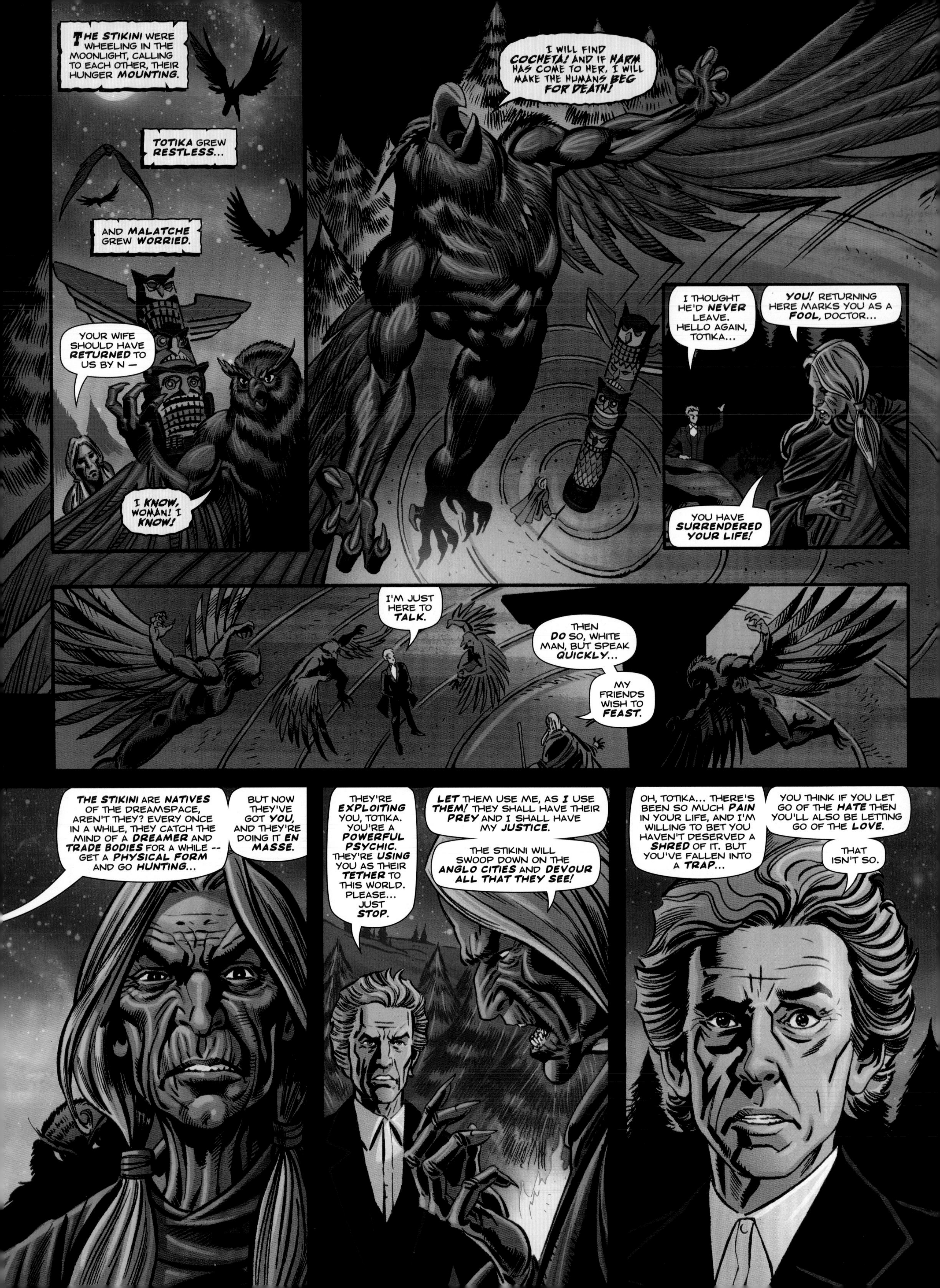
THE STIKINI WERE WHEELING IN THE MOONLIGHT, CALLING TO EACH OTHER, THEIR HUNGER MOUNTING.
TOTIKA GREW RESTLESS...
AND MALATCHE GREW WORRIED.
YOUR WIFE SHOULD HAVE RETURNED TO US BY N —
I KNOW, WOMAN! I KNOW!
I WILL FIND COCHETA! AND IF HARM HAS COME TO HER, I WILL MAKE THE HUMANS BEG FOR DEATH!
I THOUGHT HE'D NEVER LEAVE. HELLO AGAIN, TOTIKA...
YOU! RETURNING HERE MARKS YOU AS A FOOL, DOCTOR...
YOU HAVE SURRENDERED YOUR LIFE!
I'M JUST HERE TO TALK.
THEN DO SO, WHITE MAN, BUT SPEAK QUICKLY...
MY FRIENDS WISH TO FEAST.
THE STIKINI ARE NATIVES OF THE DREAMSPACE, AREN'T THEY? EVERY ONCE IN A WHILE, THEY CATCH THE MIND OF A DREAMER AND TRADE BODIES FOR A WHILE -- GET A PHYSICAL FORM AND GO HUNTING...
BUT NOW THEY'VE GOT YOU, AND THEY'RE DOING IT EN MASSE.
THEY'RE EXPLOITING YOU, TOTIKA. YOU'RE A POWERFUL PSYCHIC. THEY'RE USING YOU AS THEIR TETHER TO THIS WORLD. PLEASE... JUST STOP.
LET THEM USE ME, AS I USE THEM! THEY SHALL HAVE THEIR PREY AND I SHALL HAVE MY JUSTICE.
THE STIKINI WILL SWOOP DOWN ON THE ANGLO CITIES AND DEVOUR ALL THAT THEY SEE!
OH, TOTIKA... THERE'S BEEN SO MUCH PAIN IN YOUR LIFE, AND I'M WILLING TO BET YOU HAVEN'T DESERVED A SHRED OF IT. BUT YOU'VE FALLEN INTO A TRAP...
YOU THINK IF YOU LET GO OF THE HATE THEN YOU'LL ALSO BE LETTING GO OF THE LOVE.
THAT ISN'T SO.

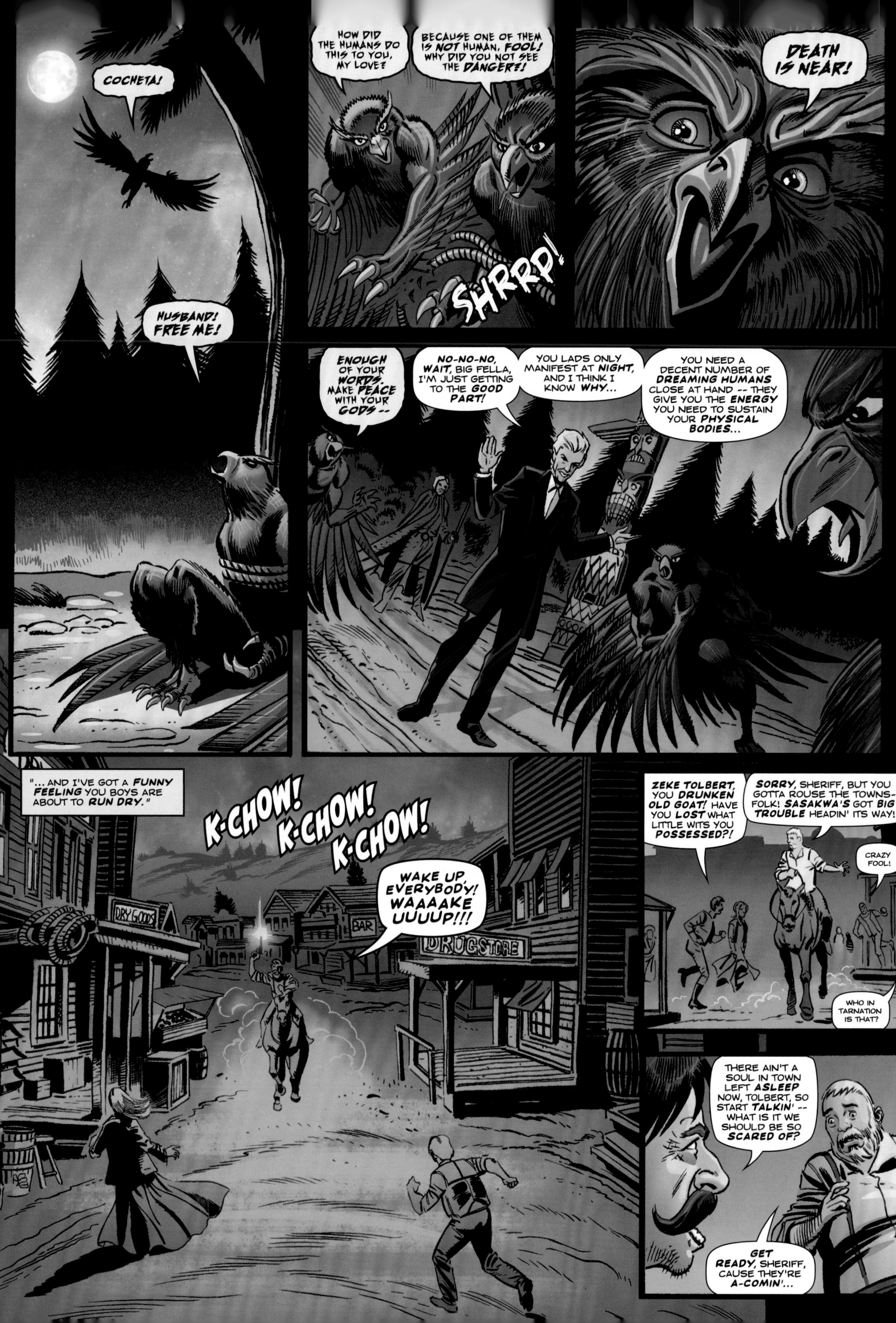
COCHETA!
HUSBAND! FREE ME!
HOW DID THE HUMANS DO THIS TO YOU, MY LOVE?
BECAUSE ONE OF THEM IS NOT HUMAN, FOOL! WHY DID YOU NOT SEE THE DANGER?!
SHRRP!
DEATH IS NEAR!
ENOUGH OF YOUR WORDS. MAKE PEACE WITH YOUR GODS --
NO-NO-NO, WAIT, BIG FELLA, I'M JUST GETTING TO THE GOOD PART!
YOU LADS ONLY MANIFEST AT NIGHT, AND I THINK I KNOW WHY...
YOU NEED A DECENT NUMBER OF DREAMING HUMANS CLOSE AT HAND -- THEY GIVE YOU THE ENERGY YOU NEED TO SUSTAIN YOUR PHYSICAL BODIES...
"... AND I'VE GOT A FUNNY FEELING YOU BOYS ARE ABOUT TO RUN DRY."
K-CHOW! K-CHOW! K-CHOW!
DRY GOODS
BAR
DRUGSTORE
WAKE UP, EVERYBODY! WAAAAKE UUUUP!!!
ZEKE TOLBERT, YOU DRUNKEN OLD GOAT! HAVE YOU LOST WHAT LITTLE WITS YOU POSSESSED?!
SORRY, SHERIFF, BUT YOU GOTTA ROUSE THE TOWNS-FOLK! SASAKWA'S GOT BIG TROUBLE HEADIN' ITS WAY!
CRAZY FOOL!
WHO IN TARNATION IS THAT?
THERE AIN'T A SOUL IN TOWN LEFT ASLEEP NOW, TOLBERT, SO START TALKIN' -- WHAT IS IT WE SHOULD BE SO SCARED OF?
GET READY, SHERIFF, CAUSE THEY'RE A-COMIN'...

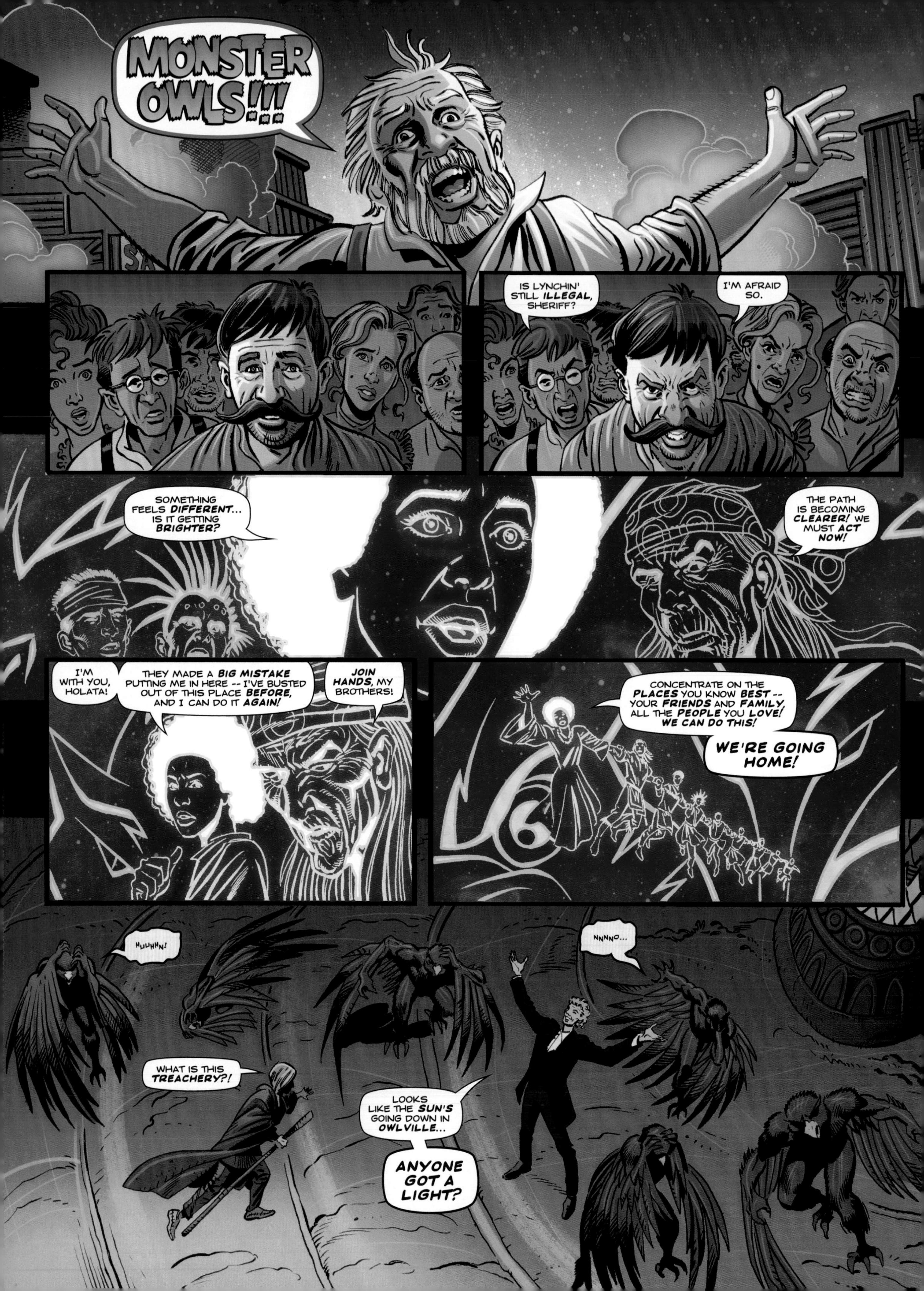
MONSTER OWLS!!!
IS LYNCHIN' STILL ILLEGAL, SHERIFF?
I'M AFRAID SO.
SOMETHING FEELS DIFFERENT... IS IT GETTING BRIGHTER?
THE PATH IS BECOMING CLEARER! WE MUST ACT NOW!
I'M WITH YOU, HOLATA!
THEY MADE A BIG MISTAKE PUTTING ME IN HERE -- I'VE BUSTED OUT OF THIS PLACE BEFORE, AND I CAN DO IT AGAIN!
JOIN HANDS, MY BROTHERS!
CONCENTRATE ON THE PLACES YOU KNOW BEST -- YOUR FRIENDS AND FAMILY, ALL THE PEOPLE YOU LOVE! WE CAN DO THIS!
WE'RE GOING HOME!
HUUHHN!
NNNNO...
WHAT IS THIS TREACHERY?!
LOOKS LIKE THE SUN'S GOING DOWN IN OWLVILLE...
ANYONE GOT A LIGHT?

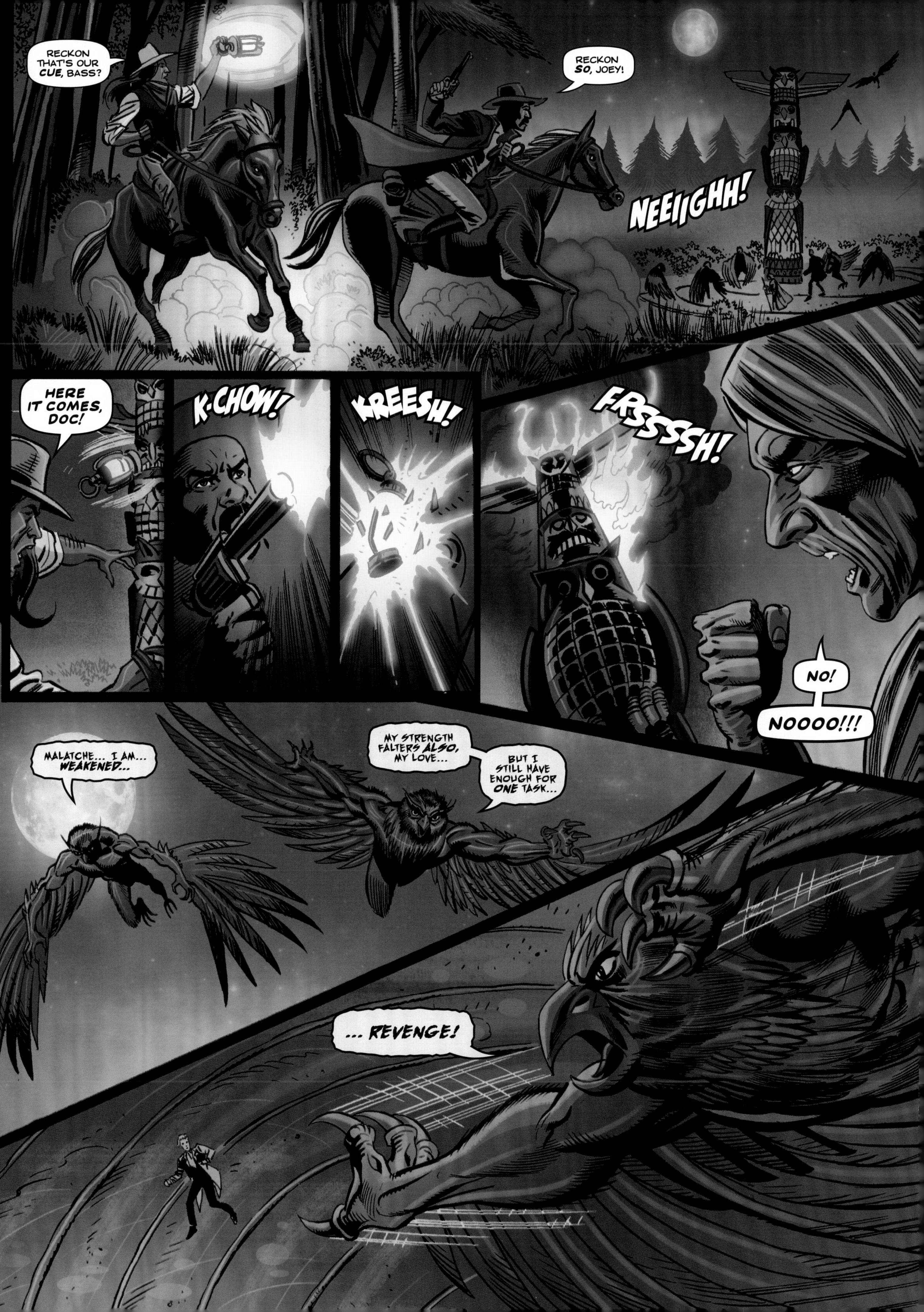
RECKON THAT'S OUR CUE, BASS?
RECKON SO, JOEY!
NEEIIGHH!
HERE IT COMES, DOC!
K-CHOW!
KREESH!
FRSSSSH!
NO!
NOOOO!!!
MALATCHE... I AM... WEAKENED...
MY STRENGTH FALTERS ALSO, MY LOVE...
BUT I STILL HAVE ENOUGH FOR ONE TASK...
... REVENGE!

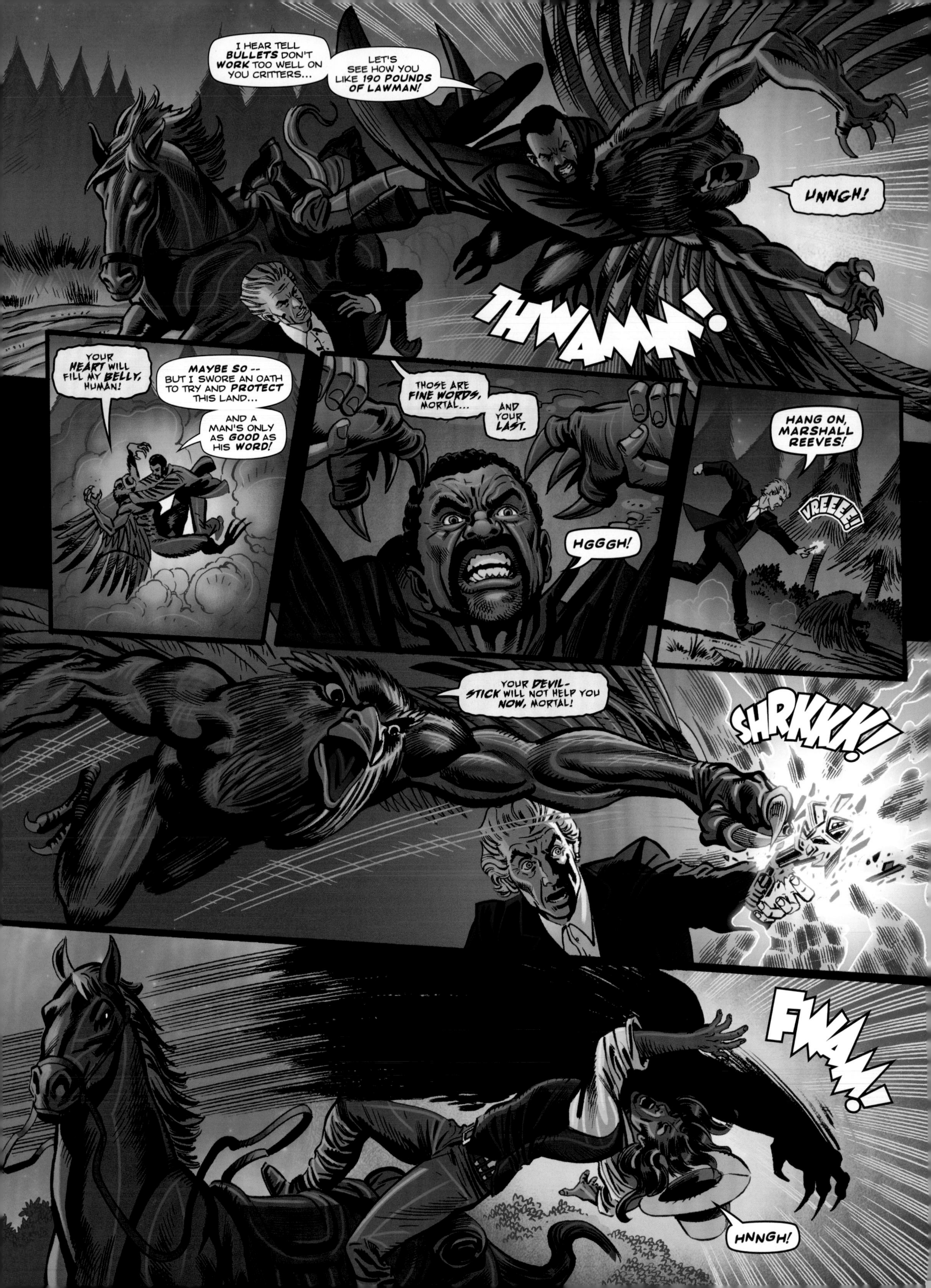
I HEAR TELL BULLETS DON'T WORK TOO WELL ON YOU CRITTERS...
LET'S SEE HOW YOU LIKE 190 POUNDS OF LAWMAN!
UNNGH!
THWAMM!
YOUR HEART WILL FILL MY BELLY, HUMAN!
MAYBE SO -- BUT I SWORE AN OATH TO TRY AND PROTECT THIS LAND...
AND A MAN'S ONLY AS GOOD AS HIS WORD!
THOSE ARE FINE WORDS, MORTAL...
AND YOUR LAST.
HGGGH!
HANG ON, MARSHALL REEVES!
VREEEE!
YOUR DEVIL-STICK WILL NOT HELP YOU NOW, MORTAL!
SHRKKK!
FWAM!
HNNGH!

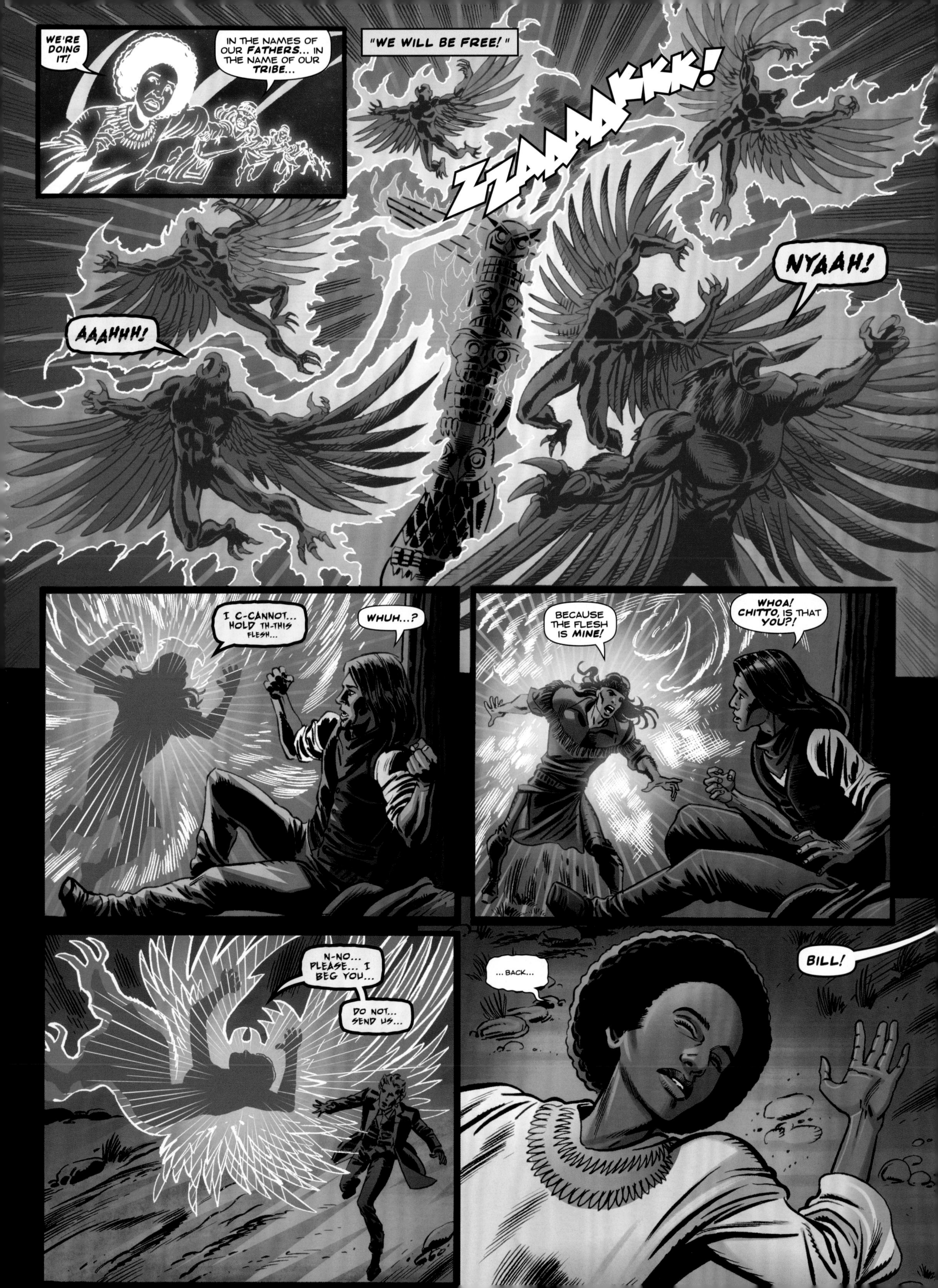
WE'RE DOING IT!
IN THE NAMES OF OUR FATHERS... IN THE NAME OF OUR TRIBE...
"WE WILL BE FREE!"
ZZAAAAAKKK!
AAAHHH!
NYAAH!
I C-CANNOT... HOLD TH-THIS FLESH...
WHUH...?
BECAUSE THE FLESH IS MINE!
WHOA! CHITTO, IS THAT YOU?!
N-NO... PLEASE... I BEG YOU...
DO NOT... SEND US...
... BACK...
BILL!

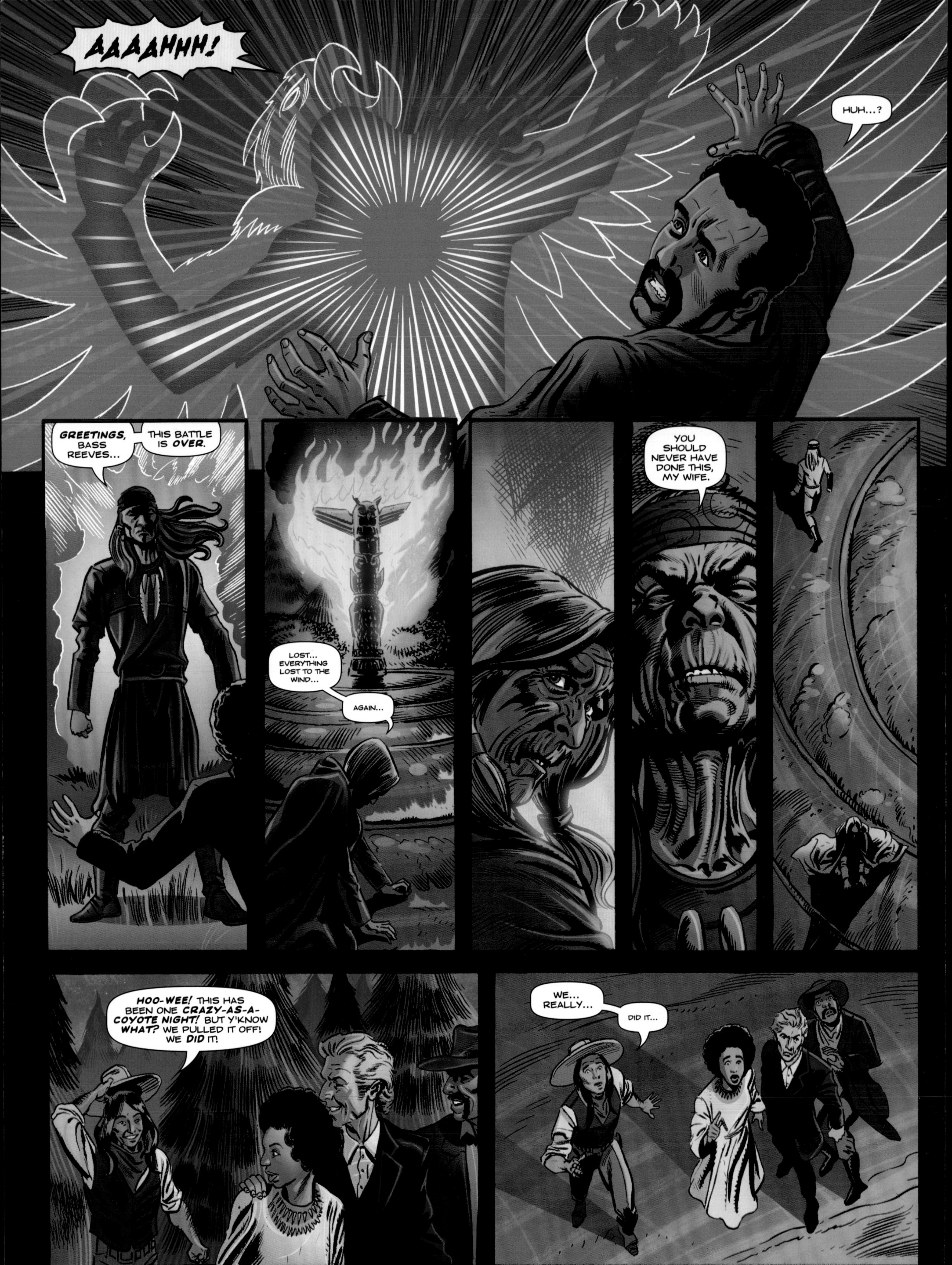
AAAAHHH!
HUH...?
GREETINGS, BASS REEVES...
THIS BATTLE IS OVER.
LOST... EVERYTHING LOST TO THE WIND...
AGAIN...
YOU SHOULD NEVER HAVE DONE THIS, MY WIFE.
HOO-WEE! THIS HAS BEEN ONE CRAZY-AS-A-COYOTE NIGHT! BUT Y'KNOW WHAT? WE PULLED IT OFF! WE DID IT!
WE... REALLY...
DID IT...

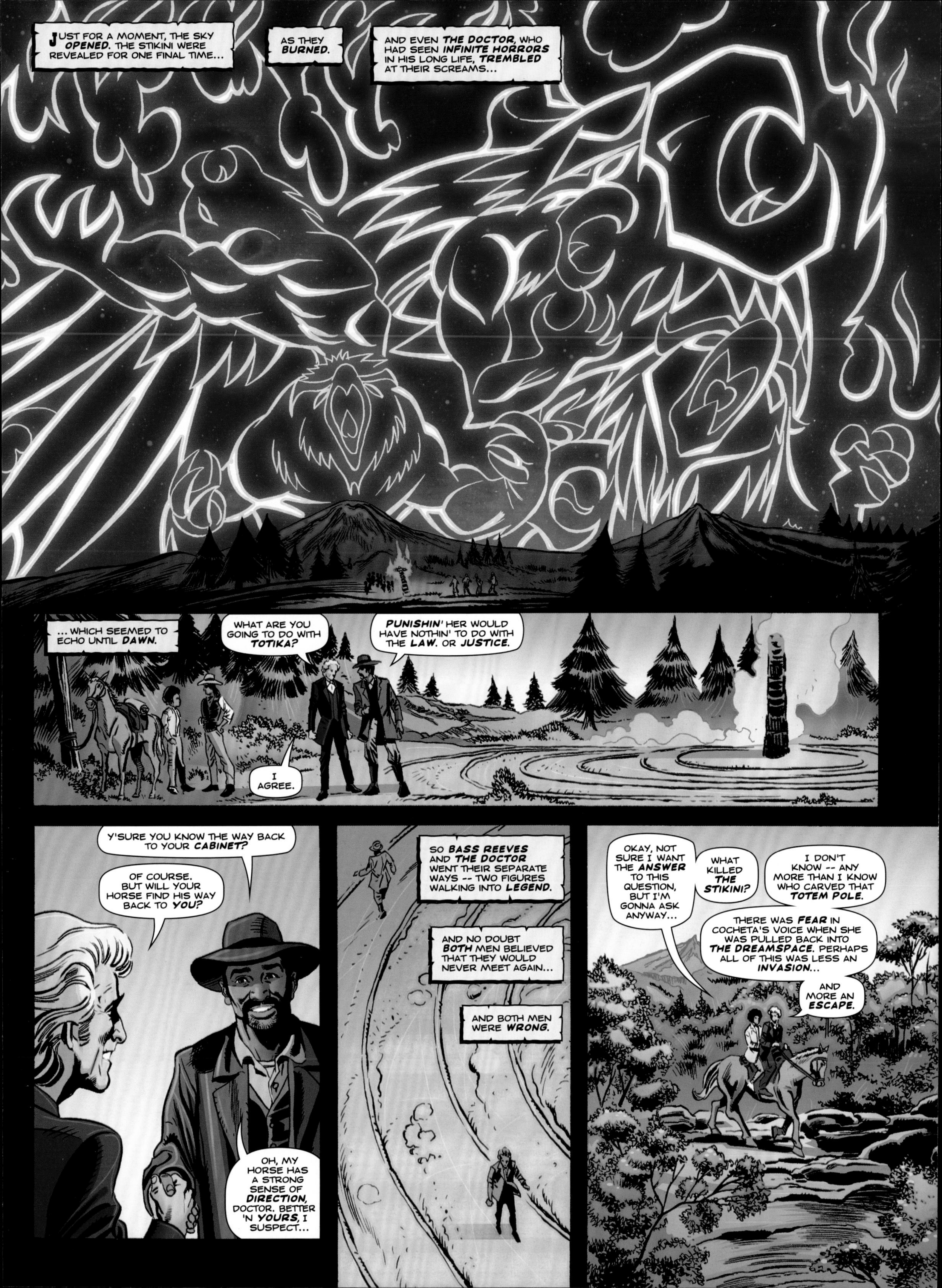

JUST FOR A MOMENT, THE SKY OPENED. THE STIKINI WERE REVEALED FOR ONE FINAL TIME...
AS THEY BURNED.
AND EVEN THE DOCTOR, WHO HAD SEEN INFINITE HORRORS IN HIS LONG LIFE, TREMBLED AT THEIR SCREAMS...
... WHICH SEEMED TO ECHO UNTIL DAWN.
WHAT ARE YOU GOING TO DO WITH TOTIKA?
PUNISHIN' HER WOULD HAVE NOTHIN' TO DO WITH THE LAW. OR JUSTICE.
I AGREE.
Y'SURE YOU KNOW THE WAY BACK TO YOUR CABINET?
OF COURSE. BUT WILL YOUR HORSE FIND HIS WAY BACK TO YOU?
OH, MY HORSE HAS A STRONG SENSE OF DIRECTION, DOCTOR. BETTER 'N YOURS, I SUSPECT...
SO BASS REEVES AND THE DOCTOR WENT THEIR SEPARATE WAYS -- TWO FIGURES WALKING INTO LEGEND.
AND NO DOUBT BOTH MEN BELIEVED THAT THEY WOULD NEVER MEET AGAIN...
AND BOTH MEN WERE WRONG.
OKAY, NOT SURE I WANT THE ANSWER TO THIS QUESTION, BUT I'M GONNA ASK ANYWAY...
WHAT KILLED THE STIKINI?
I DON'T KNOW -- ANY MORE THAN I KNOW WHO CARVED THAT TOTEM POLE.
THERE WAS FEAR IN COCHETA'S VOICE WHEN SHE WAS PULLED BACK INTO THE DREAMSPACE. PERHAPS ALL OF THIS WAS LESS AN INVASION...
AND MORE AN ESCAPE.

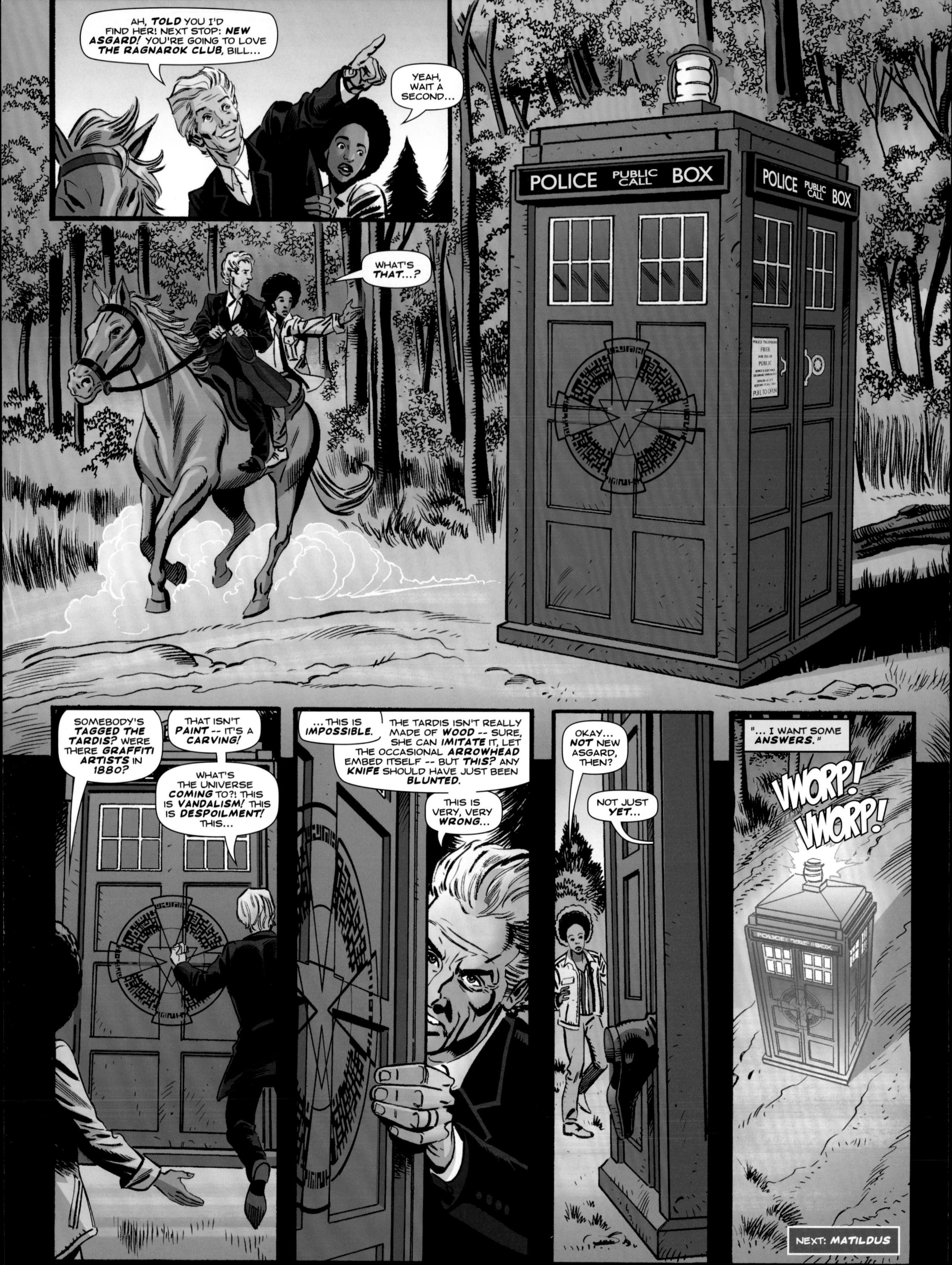
AH, TOLD YOU I'D FIND HER! NEXT STOP: NEW ASGARD! YOU'RE GOING TO LOVE THE RAGNAROK CLUB, BILL...
YEAH, WAIT A SECOND...
POLICE PUBLIC CALL BOX
WHAT'S THAT...?
SOMEBODY'S TAGGED THE TARDIS? WERE THERE GRAFFITI ARTISTS IN 1880?
THAT ISN'T PAINT -- IT'S A CARVING!
WHAT'S THE UNIVERSE COMING TO?! THIS IS VANDALISM! THIS IS DESPOILMENT! THIS...
...THIS IS IMPOSSIBLE.
THE TARDIS ISN'T REALLY MADE OF WOOD -- SURE, SHE CAN IMITATE IT, LET THE OCCASIONAL ARROWHEAD EMBED ITSELF -- BUT THIS? ANY KNIFE SHOULD HAVE JUST BEEN BLUNTED.
THIS IS VERY, VERY WRONG...
OKAY... NOT NEW ASGARD, THEN?
NOT JUST YET...
"... I WANT SOME ANSWERS."
VWORP! VWORP!
NEXT: MATILDUS

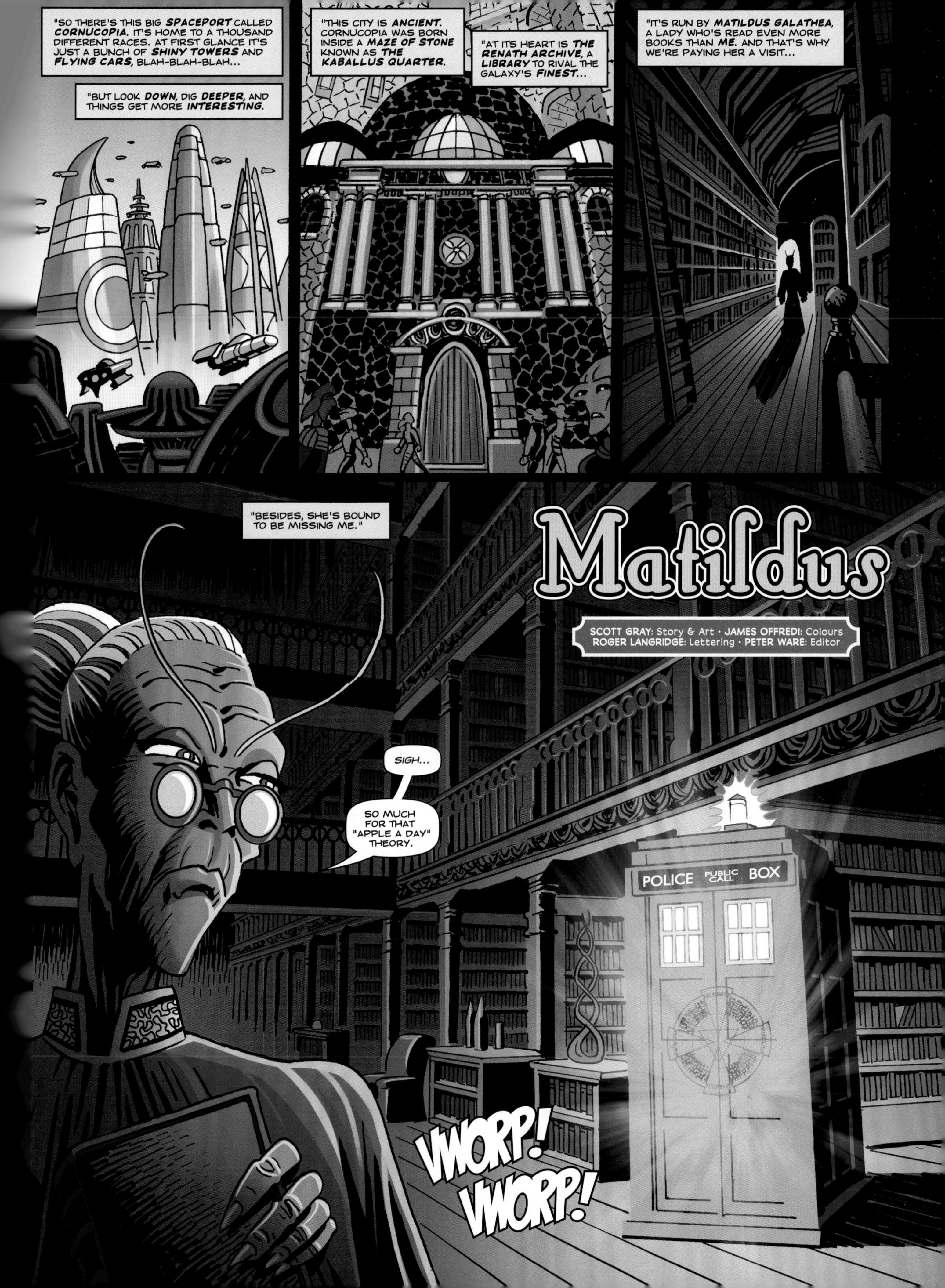
"SO THERE'S THIS BIG SPACEPORT CALLED CORNUCOPIA. IT'S HOME TO A THOUSAND DIFFERENT RACES. AT FIRST GLANCE IT'S JUST A BUNCH OF SHINY TOWERS AND FLYING CARS, BLAH-BLAH-BLAH...
"BUT LOOK DOWN, DIG DEEPER, AND THINGS GET MORE INTERESTING.
"THIS CITY IS ANCIENT. CORNUCOPIA WAS BORN INSIDE A MAZE OF STONE KNOWN AS THE KABALLUS QUARTER.
"AT ITS HEART IS THE RENATH ARCHIVE, A LIBRARY TO RIVAL THE GALAXY'S FINEST...
"IT'S RUN BY MATILDUS GALATHEA, A LADY WHO'S READ EVEN MORE BOOKS THAN ME. AND THAT'S WHY WE'RE PAYING HER A VISIT...
"BESIDES, SHE'S BOUND TO BE MISSING ME."
Matildus
SCOTT GRAY: Story & Art • JAMES OFFREDI: Colours
ROGER LANGRIDGE: Lettering • PETER WARE: Editor
SIGH...
SO MUCH FOR THAT "APPLE A DAY" THEORY.
POLICE PUBLIC CALL BOX
VWORP! VWORP!

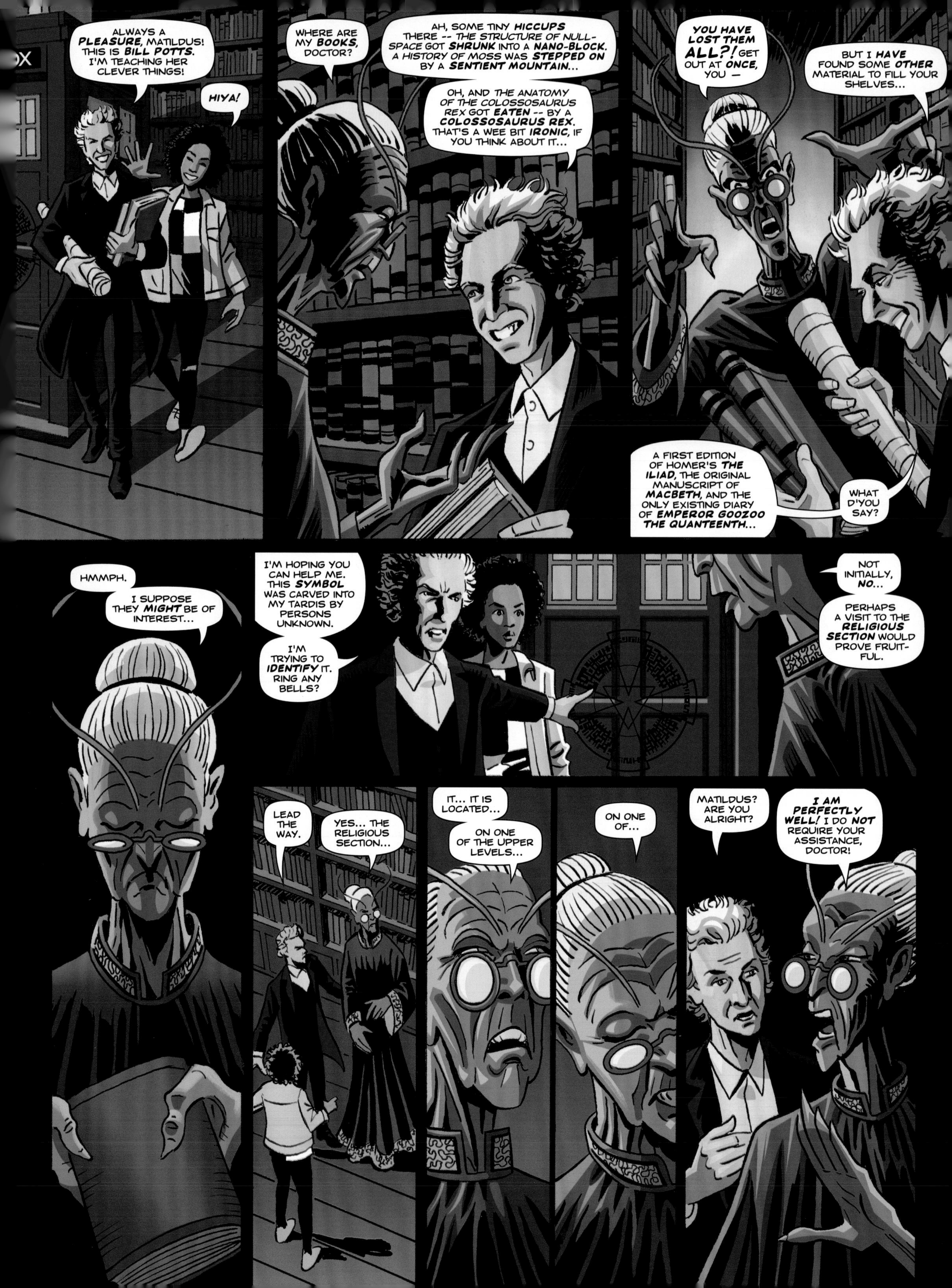
ALWAYS A PLEASURE, MATILDUS! THIS IS BILL POTTS. I'M TEACHING HER CLEVER THINGS!
HIYA!
WHERE ARE MY BOOKS, DOCTOR?
AH, SOME TINY HICCUPS THERE -- THE STRUCTURE OF NULL-SPACE GOT SHRUNK INTO A NANO-BLOCK. A HISTORY OF MOSS WAS STEPPED ON BY A SENTIENT MOUNTAIN...
OH, AND THE ANATOMY OF THE COLOSSOSAURUS REX GOT EATEN -- BY A COLOSSOSAURUS REX. THAT'S A WEE BIT IRONIC, IF YOU THINK ABOUT IT...
YOU HAVE LOST THEM ALL?! GET OUT AT ONCE, YOU —
BUT I HAVE FOUND SOME OTHER MATERIAL TO FILL YOUR SHELVES...
A FIRST EDITION OF HOMER'S THE ILIAD, THE ORIGINAL MANUSCRIPT OF MACBETH, AND THE ONLY EXISTING DIARY OF EMPEROR GOOZOO THE QUANTEENTH...
WHAT D'YOU SAY?
HMMPH.
I SUPPOSE THEY MIGHT BE OF INTEREST...
I'M HOPING YOU CAN HELP ME. THIS SYMBOL WAS CARVED INTO MY TARDIS BY PERSONS UNKNOWN.
I'M TRYING TO IDENTIFY IT. RING ANY BELLS?
NOT INITIALLY, NO...
PERHAPS A VISIT TO THE RELIGIOUS SECTION WOULD PROVE FRUIT-FUL.
LEAD THE WAY.
YES... THE RELIGIOUS SECTION...
IT... IT IS LOCATED...
ON ONE OF THE UPPER LEVELS...
ON ONE OF...
MATILDUS? ARE YOU ALRIGHT?
I AM PERFECTLY WELL! I DO NOT REQUIRE YOUR ASSISTANCE, DOCTOR!

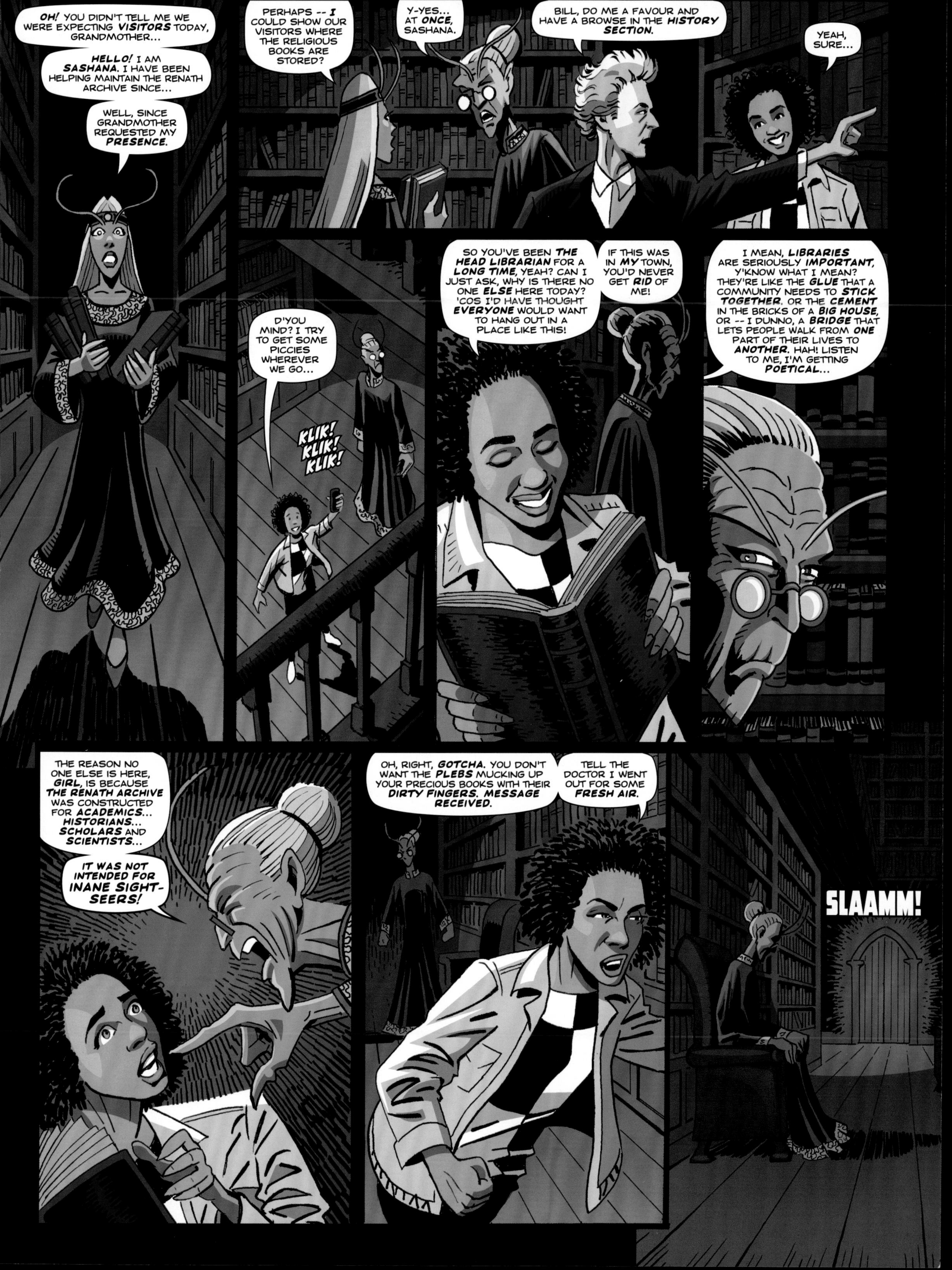
OH! YOU DIDN'T TELL ME WE WERE EXPECTING VISITORS TODAY, GRANDMOTHER...
HELLO! I AM SASHANA. I HAVE BEEN HELPING MAINTAIN THE RENATH ARCHIVE SINCE...
WELL, SINCE GRANDMOTHER REQUESTED MY PRESENCE.
PERHAPS -- I COULD SHOW OUR VISITORS WHERE THE RELIGIOUS BOOKS ARE STORED?
Y-YES... AT ONCE, SASHANA.
BILL, DO ME A FAVOUR AND HAVE A BROWSE IN THE HISTORY SECTION.
YEAH, SURE...
D'YOU MIND? I TRY TO GET SOME PICCIES WHEREVER WE GO...
KLIK! KLIK! KLIK!
SO YOU'VE BEEN THE HEAD LIBRARIAN FOR A LONG TIME, YEAH? CAN I JUST ASK, WHY IS THERE NO ONE ELSE HERE TODAY? 'COS I'D HAVE THOUGHT EVERYONE WOULD WANT TO HANG OUT IN A PLACE LIKE THIS!
IF THIS WAS IN MY TOWN, YOU'D NEVER GET RID OF ME!
I MEAN, LIBRARIES ARE SERIOUSLY IMPORTANT, Y'KNOW WHAT I MEAN? THEY'RE LIKE THE GLUE THAT A COMMUNITY NEEDS TO STICK TOGETHER. OR THE CEMENT IN THE BRICKS OF A BIG HOUSE, OR -- I DUNNO, A BRIDGE THAT LETS PEOPLE WALK FROM ONE PART OF THEIR LIVES TO ANOTHER. HAH! LISTEN TO ME, I'M GETTING POETICAL...
THE REASON NO ONE ELSE IS HERE, GIRL, IS BECAUSE THE RENATH ARCHIVE WAS CONSTRUCTED FOR ACADEMICS... HISTORIANS... SCHOLARS AND SCIENTISTS...
IT WAS NOT INTENDED FOR INANE SIGHT-SEERS!
OH, RIGHT, GOTCHA. YOU DON'T WANT THE PLEBS MUCKING UP YOUR PRECIOUS BOOKS WITH THEIR DIRTY FINGERS. MESSAGE RECEIVED.
TELL THE DOCTOR I WENT OUT FOR SOME FRESH AIR.
SLAAMM!

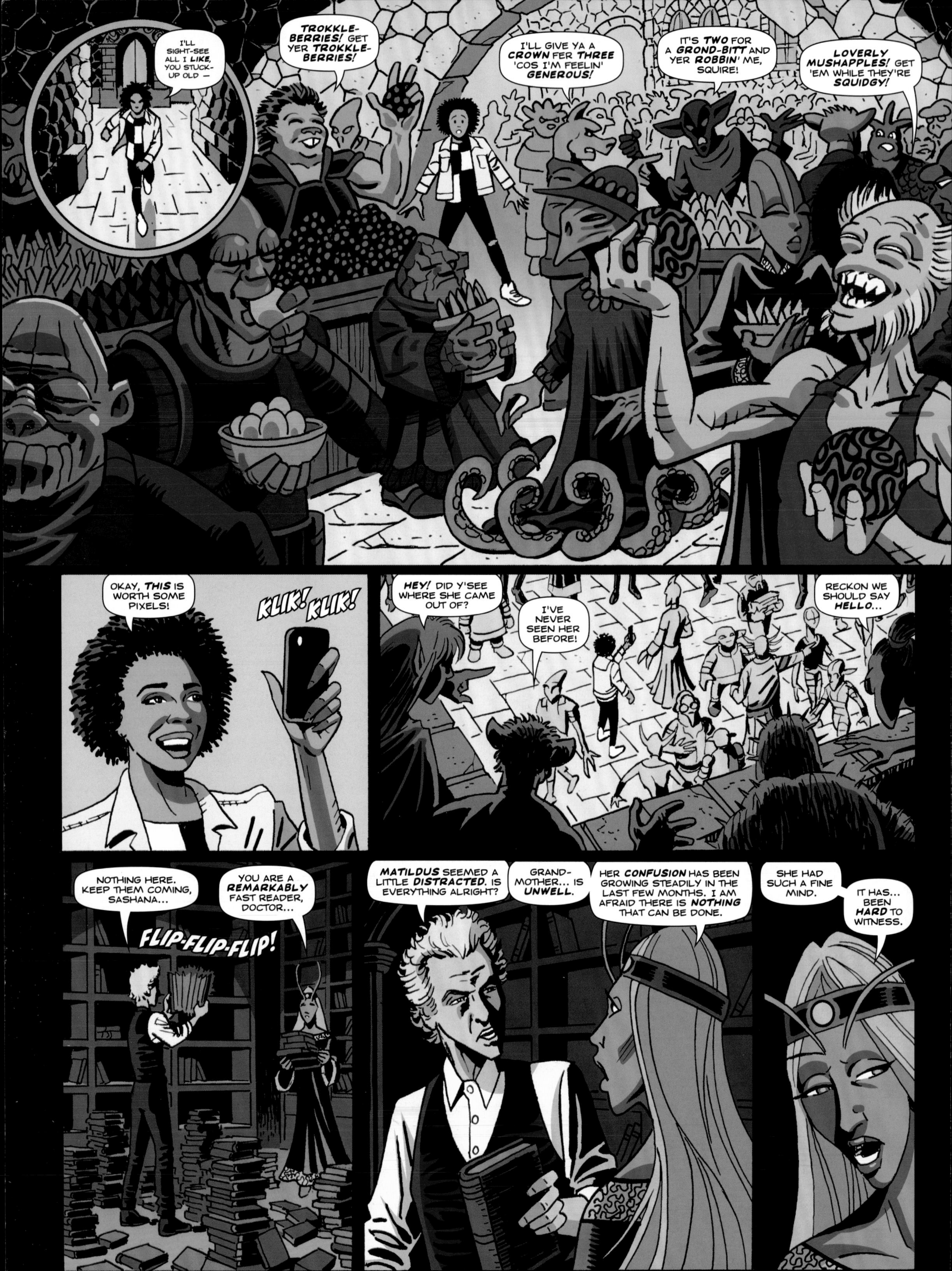

I'LL SIGHT-SEE ALL I LIKE, YOU STUCK-UP OLD —
TROKKLE-BERRIES! GET YER TROKKLE-BERRIES!
I'LL GIVE YA A CROWN FER THREE 'COS I'M FEELIN' GENEROUS!
IT'S TWO FOR A GROND-BITT AND YER ROBBIN' ME, SQUIRE!
LOVERLY MUSHAPPLES! GET 'EM WHILE THEY'RE SQUIDGY!
OKAY, THIS IS WORTH SOME PIXELS!
KLIK! KLIK!
HEY! DID Y'SEE WHERE SHE CAME OUT OF?
I'VE NEVER SEEN HER BEFORE!
RECKON WE SHOULD SAY HELLO...
NOTHING HERE. KEEP THEM COMING, SASHANA...
FLIP-FLIP-FLIP!
YOU ARE A REMARKABLY FAST READER, DOCTOR...
MATILDUS SEEMED A LITTLE DISTRACTED. IS EVERYTHING ALRIGHT?
GRAND-MOTHER... IS UNWELL.
HER CONFUSION HAS BEEN GROWING STEADILY IN THE LAST FEW MONTHS. I AM AFRAID THERE IS NOTHING THAT CAN BE DONE.
SHE HAD SUCH A FINE MIND.
IT HAS... BEEN HARD TO WITNESS.

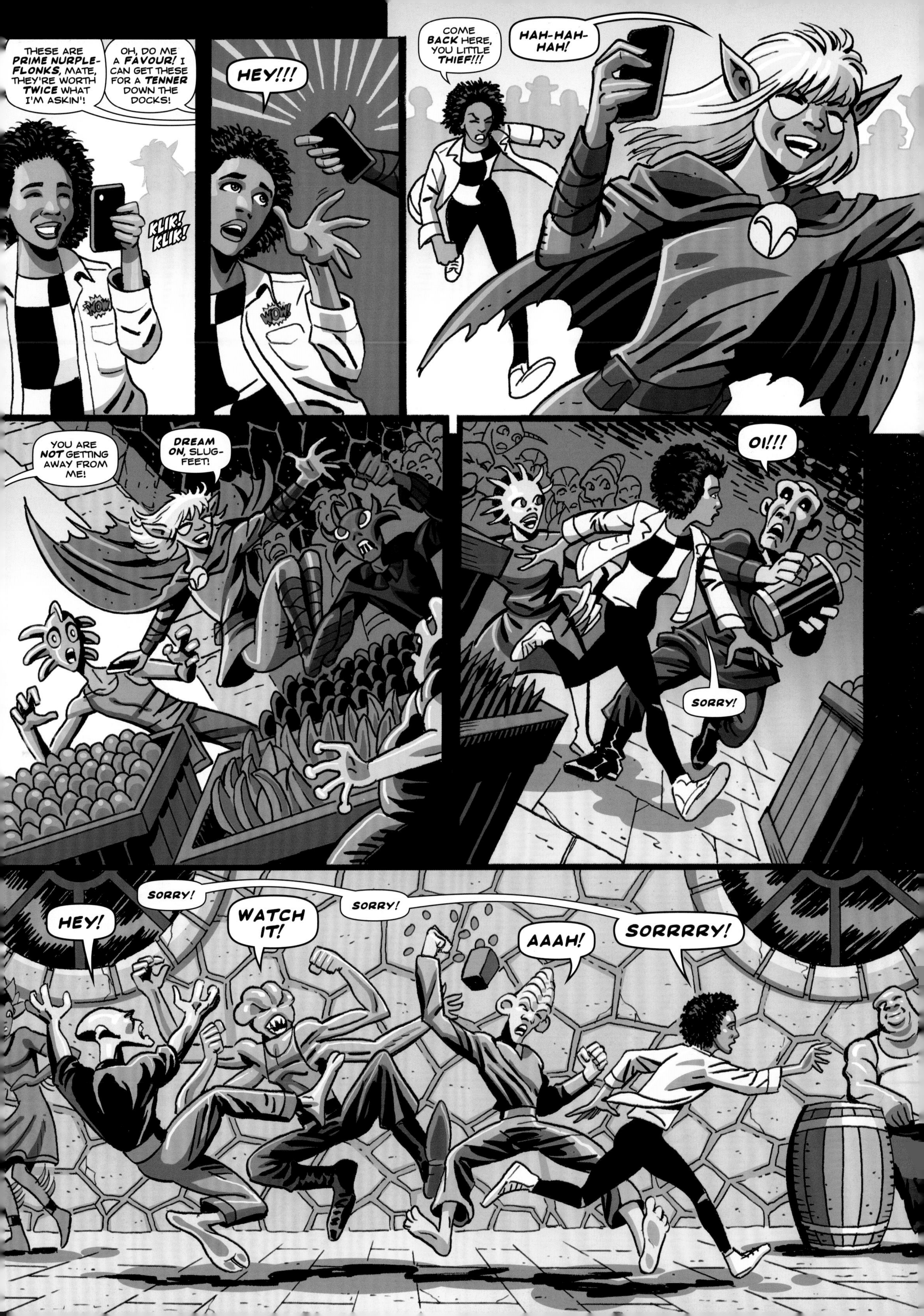
THESE ARE PRIME NURPLE-FLONKS, MATE, THEY'RE WORTH TWICE WHAT I'M ASKIN'!
OH, DO ME A FAVOUR! I CAN GET THESE FOR A TENNER DOWN THE DOCKS!
KLIK! KLIK!
HEY!!!
COME BACK HERE, YOU LITTLE THIEF!!!
HAH-HAH-HAH!
YOU ARE NOT GETTING AWAY FROM ME!
DREAM ON, SLUG-FEET!
OI!!!
SORRY!
SORRY!
HEY!
WATCH IT!
SORRY!
AAAH!
SORRRRY!

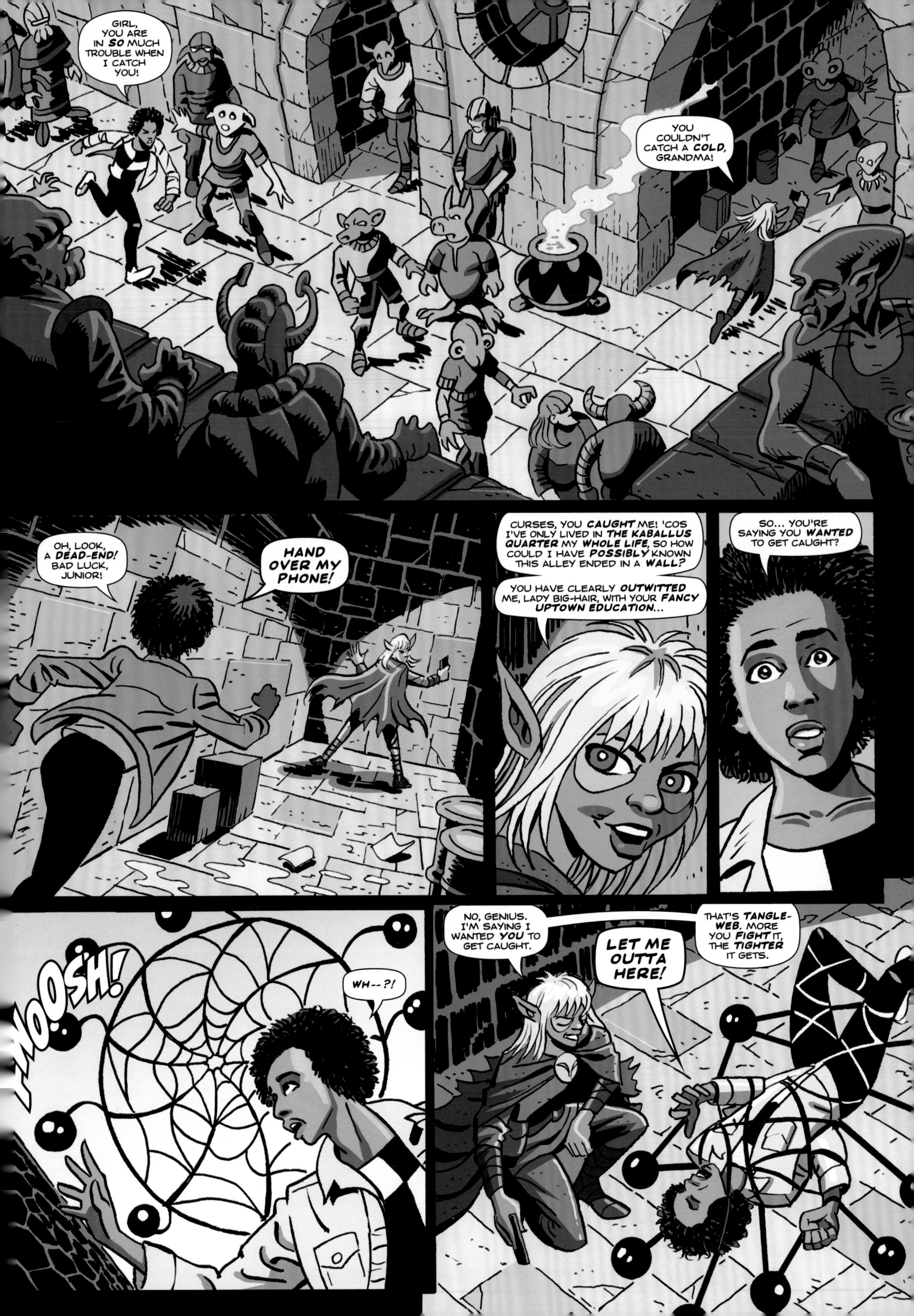

GIRL, YOU ARE IN SO MUCH TROUBLE WHEN I CATCH YOU!
YOU COULDN'T CATCH A COLD, GRANDMA!
OH, LOOK, A DEAD-END! BAD LUCK, JUNIOR!
HAND OVER MY PHONE!
CURSES, YOU CAUGHT ME! 'COS I'VE ONLY LIVED IN THE KABALLUS QUARTER MY WHOLE LIFE, SO HOW COULD I HAVE POSSIBLY KNOWN THIS ALLEY ENDED IN A WALL?
YOU HAVE CLEARLY OUTWITTED ME, LADY BIG-HAIR, WITH YOUR FANCY UPTOWN EDUCATION...
SO... YOU'RE SAYING YOU WANTED TO GET CAUGHT?
FWOOSH!
WH--?!
NO, GENIUS. I'M SAYING I WANTED YOU TO GET CAUGHT.
LET ME OUTTA HERE!
THAT'S TANGLE-WEB. MORE YOU FIGHT IT, THE TIGHTER IT GETS.

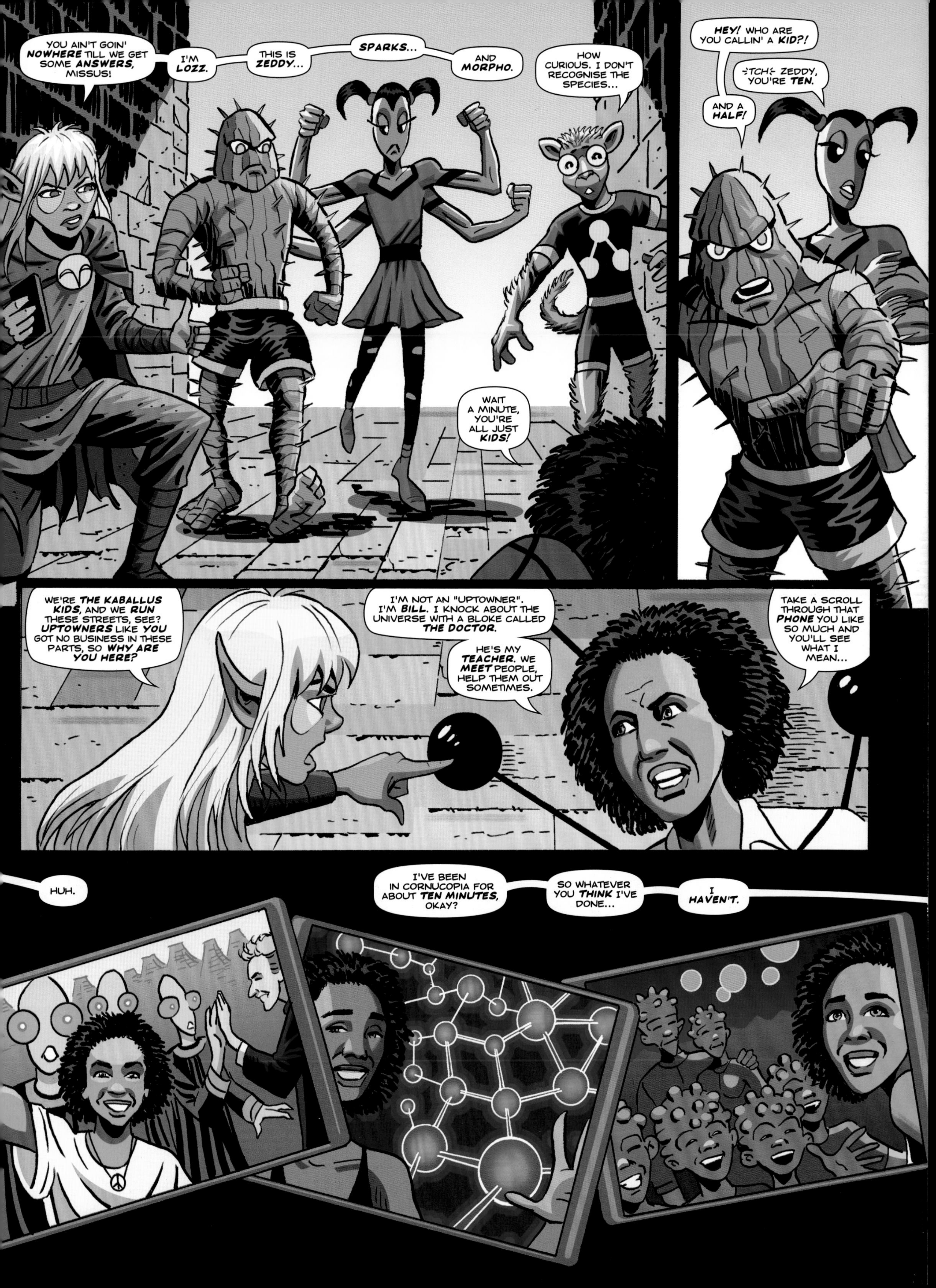

YOU AIN'T GOIN' NOWHERE TILL WE GET SOME ANSWERS, MISSUS!
I'M LOZZ.
THIS IS ZEDDY...
SPARKS...
AND MORPHO.
HOW CURIOUS. I DON'T RECOGNISE THE SPECIES...
WAIT A MINUTE, YOU'RE ALL JUST KIDS!
HEY! WHO ARE YOU CALLIN' A KID?!
AND A HALF!
TCH ZEDDY, YOU'RE TEN.
WE'RE THE KABALLUS KIDS, AND WE RUN THESE STREETS, SEE? UPTOWNERS LIKE YOU GOT NO BUSINESS IN THESE PARTS, SO WHY ARE YOU HERE?
I'M NOT AN "UPTOWNER". I'M BILL. I KNOCK ABOUT THE UNIVERSE WITH A BLOKE CALLED THE DOCTOR.
HE'S MY TEACHER. WE MEET PEOPLE, HELP THEM OUT SOMETIMES.
TAKE A SCROLL THROUGH THAT PHONE YOU LIKE SO MUCH AND YOU'LL SEE WHAT I MEAN...
HUH.
I'VE BEEN IN CORNUCOPIA FOR ABOUT TEN MINUTES, OKAY?
SO WHATEVER YOU THINK I'VE DONE...
I HAVEN'T.

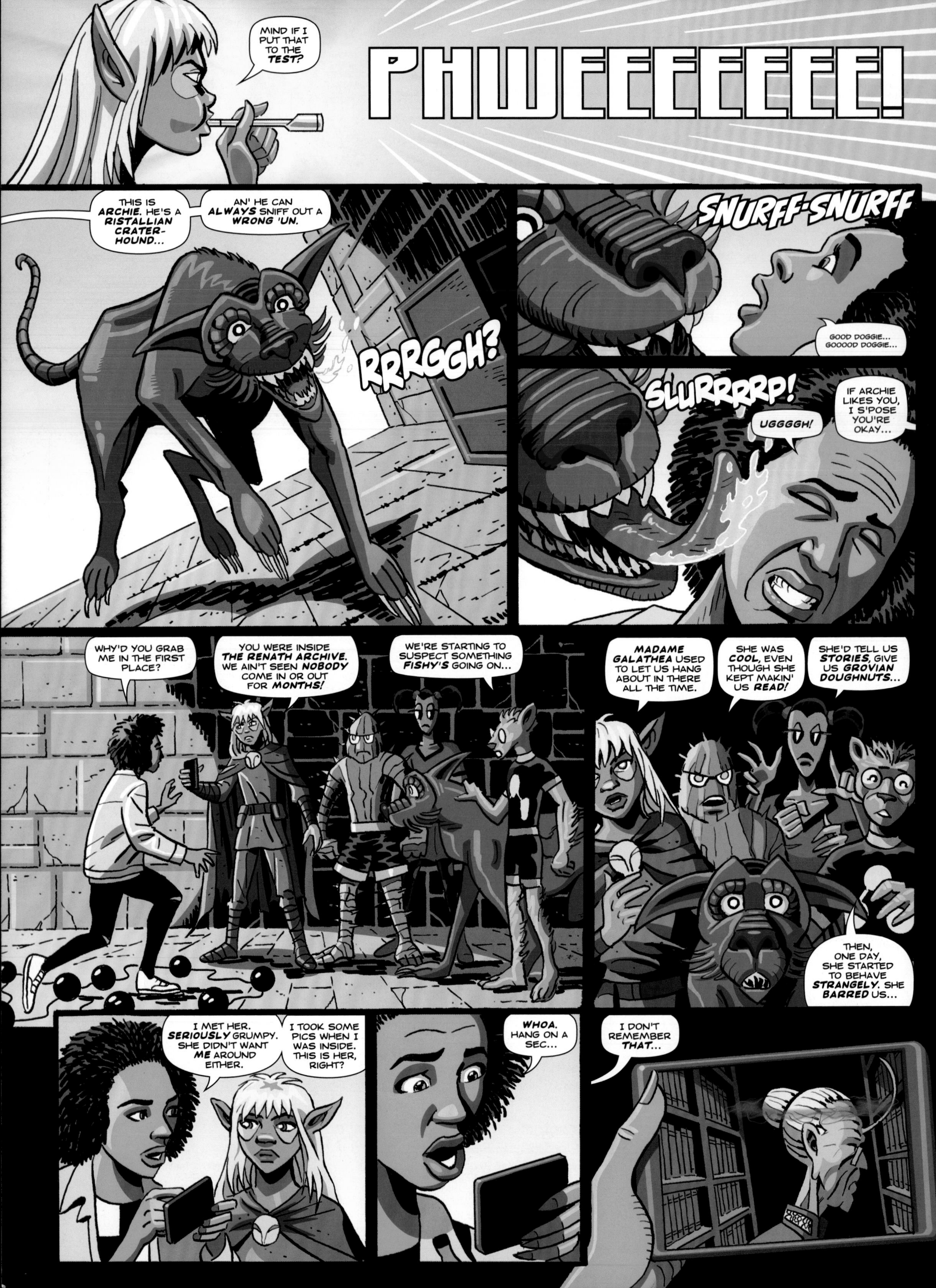
MIND IF I PUT THAT TO THE TEST?
PHWEEEEEEEE!
THIS IS ARCHIE. HE'S A RISTALLIAN CRATER-HOUND...
AN' HE CAN ALWAYS SNIFF OUT A WRONG 'UN.
RRRGGH?
SNURFF-SNURFF
GOOD DOGGIE... GOOOOD DOGGIE...
SLURRRRP!
UGGGGH!
IF ARCHIE LIKES YOU, I S'POSE YOU'RE OKAY...
WHY'D YOU GRAB ME IN THE FIRST PLACE?
YOU WERE INSIDE THE RENATH ARCHIVE. WE AIN'T SEEN NOBODY COME IN OR OUT FOR MONTHS!
WE'RE STARTING TO SUSPECT SOMETHING FISHY'S GOING ON...
MADAME GALATHEA USED TO LET US HANG ABOUT IN THERE ALL THE TIME.
SHE WAS COOL, EVEN THOUGH SHE KEPT MAKIN' US READ!
SHE'D TELL US STORIES, GIVE US GROVIAN DOUGHNUTS...
THEN, ONE DAY, SHE STARTED TO BEHAVE STRANGELY. SHE BARRED US...
I MET HER. SERIOUSLY GRUMPY. SHE DIDN'T WANT ME AROUND EITHER.
I TOOK SOME PICS WHEN I WAS INSIDE. THIS IS HER, RIGHT?
WHOA. HANG ON A SEC...
I DON'T REMEMBER THAT...

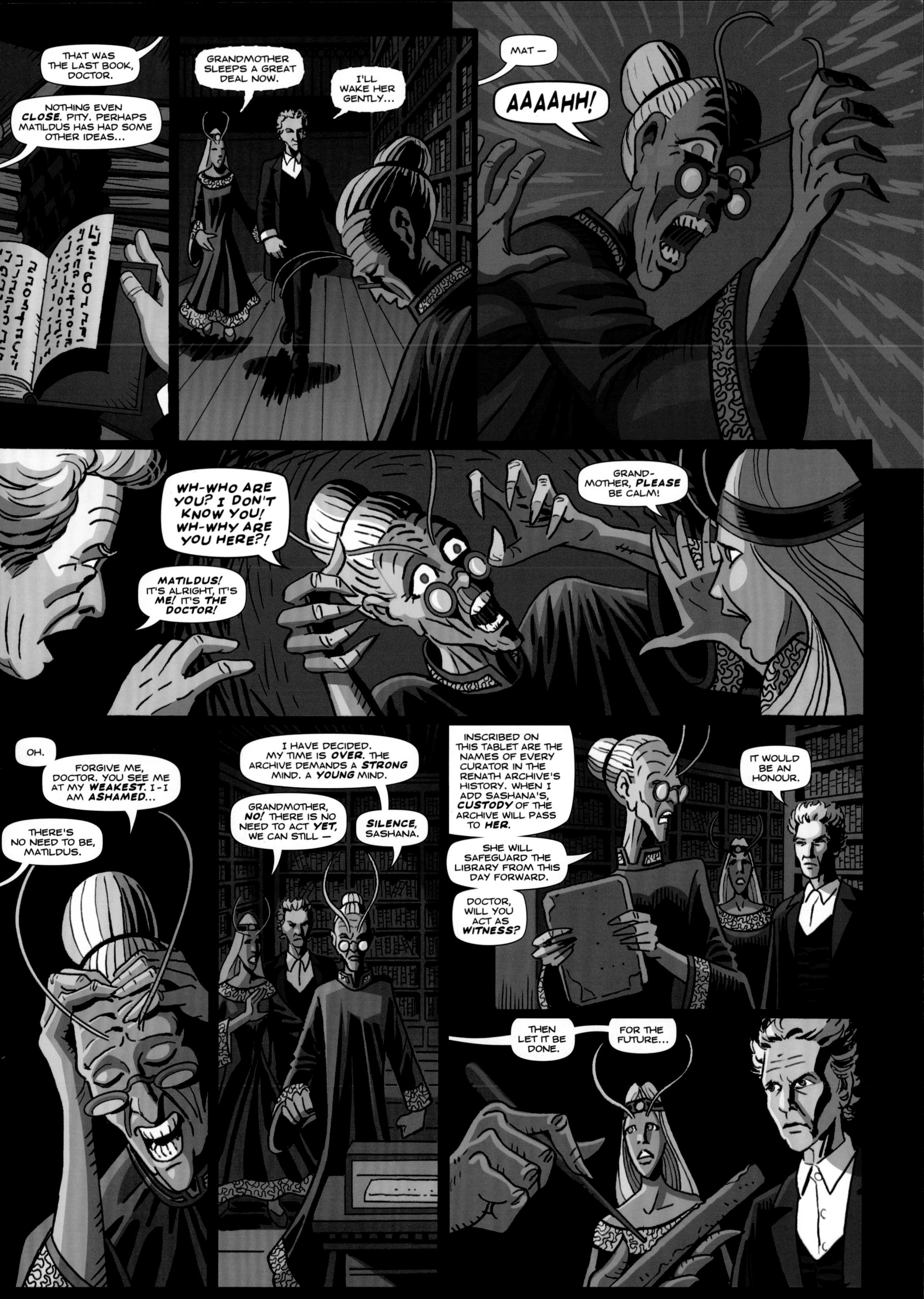
THAT WAS THE LAST BOOK, DOCTOR.
NOTHING EVEN CLOSE. PITY. PERHAPS MATILDUS HAS HAD SOME OTHER IDEAS...
GRANDMOTHER SLEEPS A GREAT DEAL NOW.
I'LL WAKE HER GENTLY...
MAT —
AAAAHH!
WH-WHO ARE YOU? I DON'T KNOW YOU! WH-WHY ARE YOU HERE?!
GRAND-MOTHER, PLEASE BE CALM!
MATILDUS! IT'S ALRIGHT, IT'S ME! IT'S THE DOCTOR!
OH.
FORGIVE ME, DOCTOR. YOU SEE ME AT MY WEAKEST. I-I AM ASHAMED...
THERE'S NO NEED TO BE, MATILDUS.
I HAVE DECIDED. MY TIME IS OVER. THE ARCHIVE DEMANDS A STRONG MIND. A YOUNG MIND.
GRANDMOTHER, NO! THERE IS NO NEED TO ACT YET, WE CAN STILL —
SILENCE, SASHANA.
INSCRIBED ON THIS TABLET ARE THE NAMES OF EVERY CURATOR IN THE RENATH ARCHIVE'S HISTORY. WHEN I ADD SASHANA'S, CUSTODY OF THE ARCHIVE WILL PASS TO HER.
SHE WILL SAFEGUARD THE LIBRARY FROM THIS DAY FORWARD.
DOCTOR, WILL YOU ACT AS WITNESS?
IT WOULD BE AN HONOUR.
THEN LET IT BE DONE.
FOR THE FUTURE...

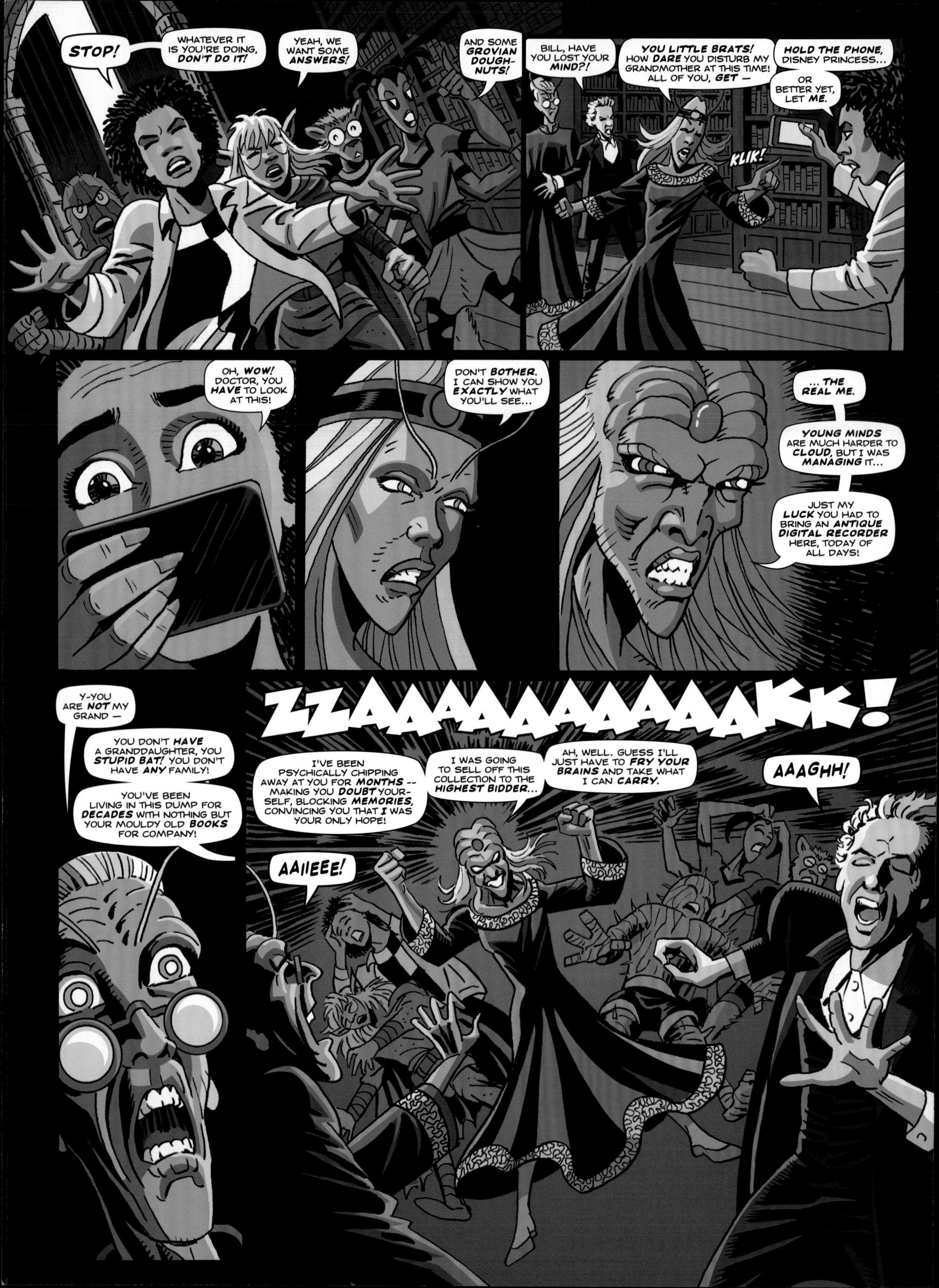

STOP!
WHATEVER IT IS YOU'RE DOING, DON'T DO IT!
YEAH, WE WANT SOME ANSWERS!
AND SOME GROVIAN DOUGH-NUTS!
BILL, HAVE YOU LOST YOUR MIND?!
YOU LITTLE BRATS! HOW DARE YOU DISTURB MY GRANDMOTHER AT THIS TIME! ALL OF YOU, GET —
HOLD THE PHONE, DISNEY PRINCESS...
OR BETTER YET, LET ME.
KLIK!
OH, WOW! DOCTOR, YOU HAVE TO LOOK AT THIS!
DON'T BOTHER. I CAN SHOW YOU EXACTLY WHAT YOU'LL SEE...
... THE REAL ME.
YOUNG MINDS ARE MUCH HARDER TO CLOUD, BUT I WAS MANAGING IT...
JUST MY LUCK YOU HAD TO BRING AN ANTIQUE DIGITAL RECORDER HERE, TODAY OF ALL DAYS!
Y-YOU ARE NOT MY GRAND —
YOU DON'T HAVE A GRANDDAUGHTER, YOU STUPID BAT! YOU DON'T HAVE ANY FAMILY!
YOU'VE BEEN LIVING IN THIS DUMP FOR DECADES WITH NOTHING BUT YOUR MOULDY OLD BOOKS FOR COMPANY!
ZZAAAAAAAAAAKK!
I'VE BEEN PSYCHICALLY CHIPPING AWAY AT YOU FOR MONTHS -- MAKING YOU DOUBT YOUR-SELF, BLOCKING MEMORIES, CONVINCING YOU THAT I WAS YOUR ONLY HOPE!
I WAS GOING TO SELL OFF THIS COLLECTION TO THE HIGHEST BIDDER...
AH, WELL. GUESS I'LL JUST HAVE TO FRY YOUR BRAINS AND TAKE WHAT I CAN CARRY.
AAAGHH!
AAIIEEE!

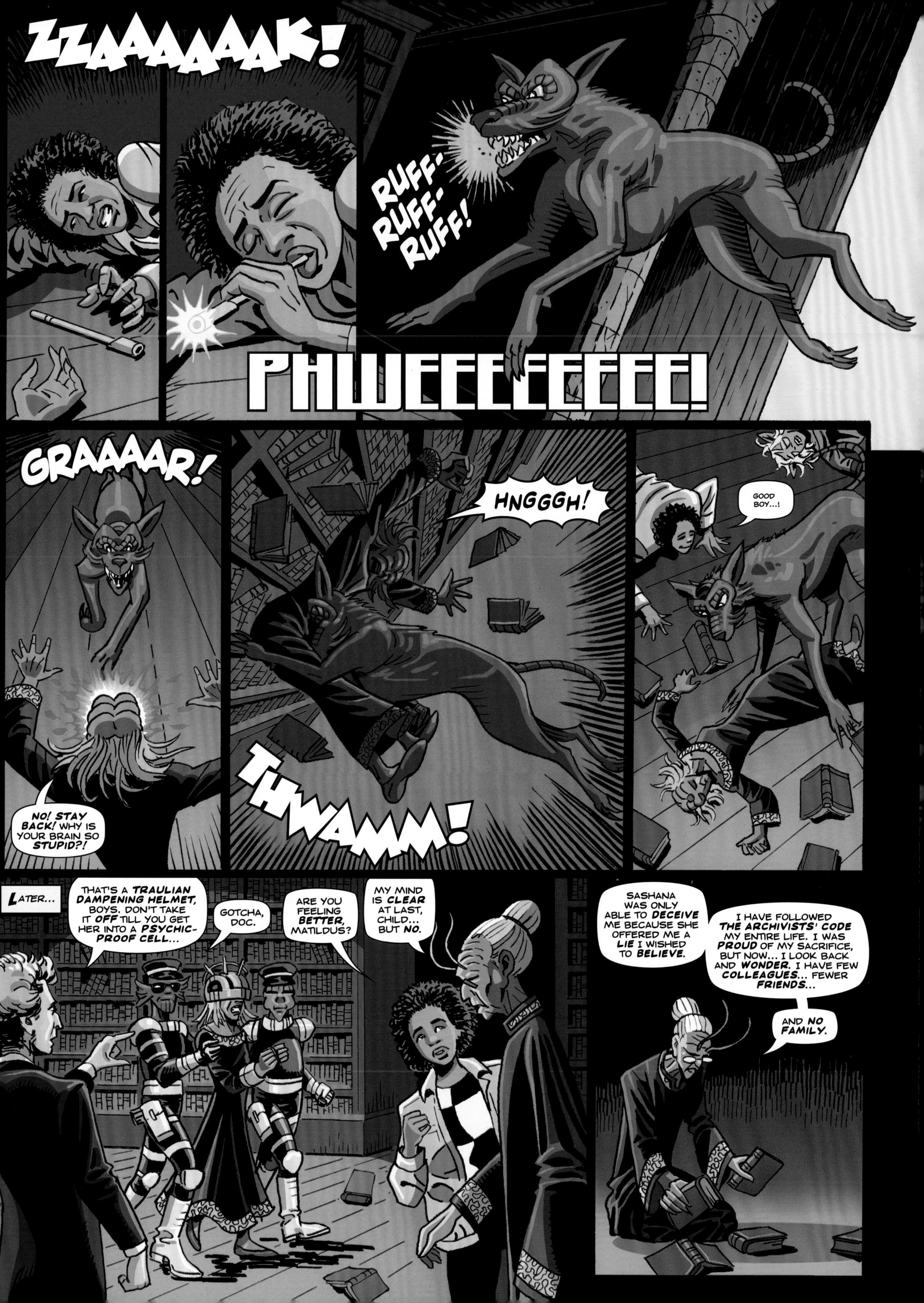
ZZAAAAAAK!
RUFF-RUFF-RUFF!
PHWEEEEEEEE!
GRAAAAR!
NO! STAY BACK! WHY IS YOUR BRAIN SO STUPID?!
HNGGGH!
THWAMM!
GOOD BOY...!
LATER...
THAT'S A TRAULIAN DAMPENING HELMET, BOYS. DON'T TAKE IT OFF TILL YOU GET HER INTO A PSYCHIC-PROOF CELL...
GOTCHA, DOC.
ARE YOU FEELING BETTER, MATILDUS?
MY MIND IS CLEAR AT LAST, CHILD... BUT NO.
SASHANA WAS ONLY ABLE TO DECEIVE ME BECAUSE SHE OFFERED ME A LIE I WISHED TO BELIEVE.
I HAVE FOLLOWED THE ARCHIVISTS' CODE MY ENTIRE LIFE. I WAS PROUD OF MY SACRIFICE, BUT NOW... I LOOK BACK AND WONDER. I HAVE FEW COLLEAGUES... FEWER FRIENDS...
AND NO FAMILY.

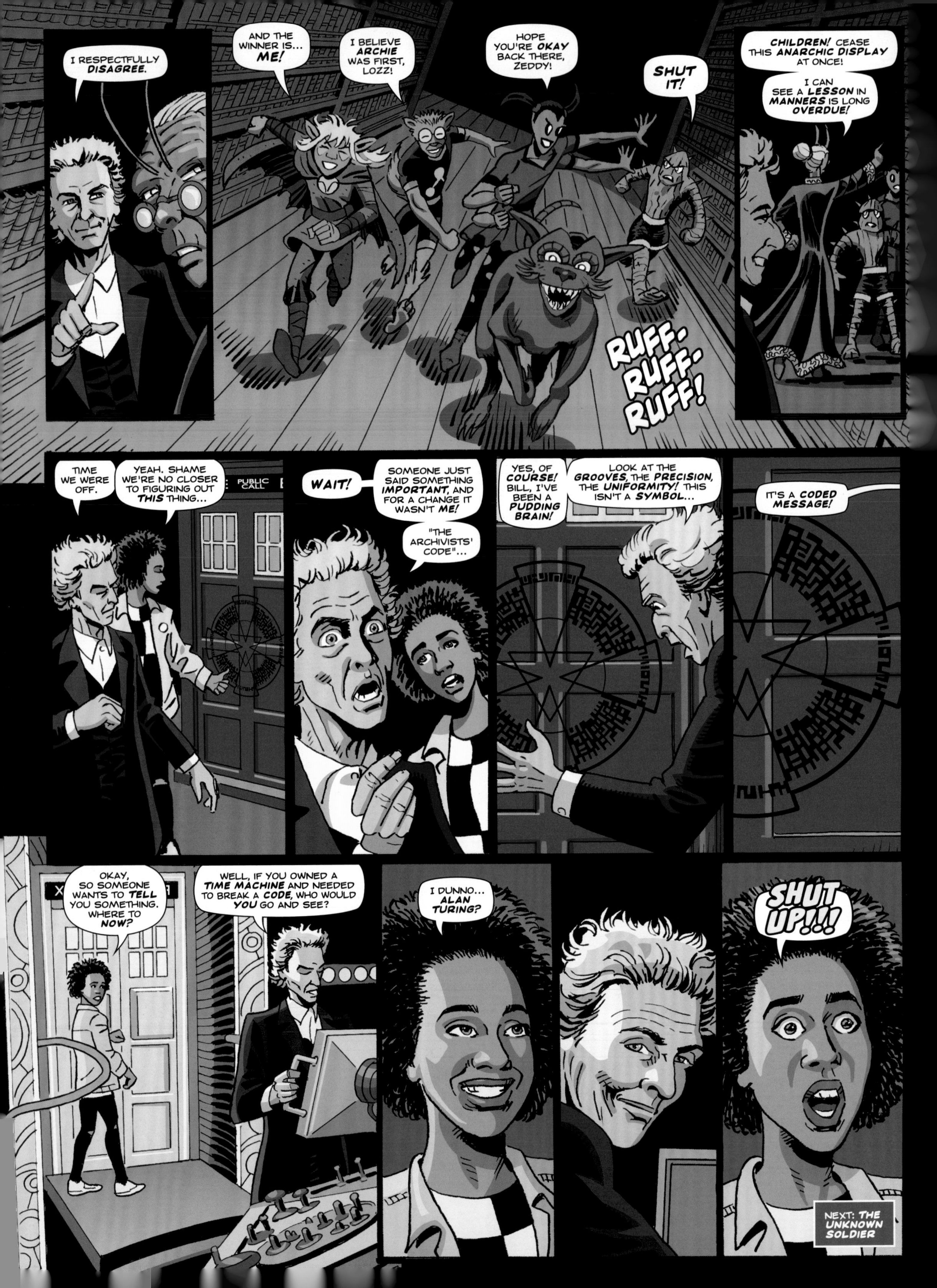

I RESPECTFULLY DISAGREE.
AND THE WINNER IS... ME!
I BELIEVE ARCHIE WAS FIRST, LOZZ!
HOPE YOU'RE OKAY BACK THERE, ZEDDY!
SHUT IT!
RUFF-RUFF-RUFF!
CHILDREN! CEASE THIS ANARCHIC DISPLAY AT ONCE!
I CAN SEE A LESSON IN MANNERS IS LONG OVERDUE!
TIME WE WERE OFF.
YEAH. SHAME WE'RE NO CLOSER TO FIGURING OUT THIS THING...
PUBLIC CALL
WAIT!
SOMEONE JUST SAID SOMETHING IMPORTANT, AND FOR A CHANGE IT WASN'T ME!
"THE ARCHIVISTS' CODE"...
YES, OF COURSE! BILL, I'VE BEEN A PUDDING BRAIN!
LOOK AT THE GROOVES, THE PRECISION, THE UNIFORMITY! THIS ISN'T A SYMBOL...
IT'S A CODED MESSAGE!
OKAY, SO SOMEONE WANTS TO TELL YOU SOMETHING. WHERE TO NOW?
WELL, IF YOU OWNED A TIME MACHINE AND NEEDED TO BREAK A CODE, WHO WOULD YOU GO AND SEE?
I DUNNO... ALAN TURING?
SHUT UP!!!
NEXT: THE UNKNOWN SOLDIER

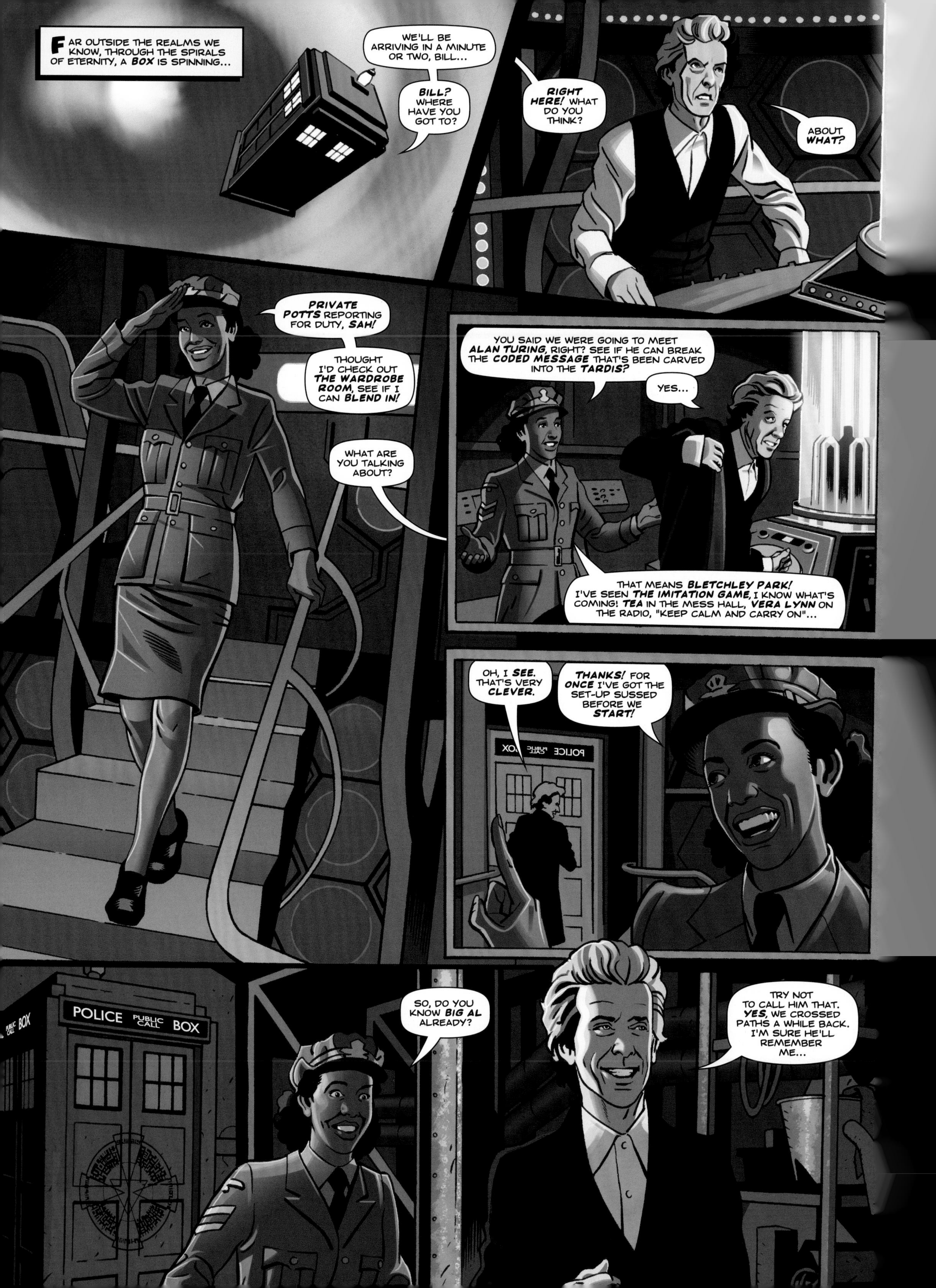

FAR OUTSIDE THE REALMS WE KNOW, THROUGH THE SPIRALS OF ETERNITY, A BOX IS SPINNING...
WE'LL BE ARRIVING IN A MINUTE OR TWO, BILL...
BILL? WHERE HAVE YOU GOT TO?
RIGHT HERE! WHAT DO YOU THINK?
ABOUT WHAT?
PRIVATE POTTS REPORTING FOR DUTY, SAH!
THOUGHT I'D CHECK OUT THE WARDROBE ROOM, SEE IF I CAN BLEND IN!
WHAT ARE YOU TALKING ABOUT?
YOU SAID WE WERE GOING TO MEET ALAN TURING, RIGHT? SEE IF HE CAN BREAK THE CODED MESSAGE THAT'S BEEN CARVED INTO THE TARDIS?
YES...
THAT MEANS BLETCHLEY PARK! I'VE SEEN THE IMITATION GAME, I KNOW WHAT'S COMING! TEA IN THE MESS HALL, VERA LYNN ON THE RADIO, "KEEP CALM AND CARRY ON"...
OH, I SEE. THAT'S VERY CLEVER.
THANKS! FOR ONCE I'VE GOT THE SET-UP SUSSED BEFORE WE START!
POLICE PUBLIC CALL BOX
SO, DO YOU KNOW BIG AL ALREADY?
TRY NOT TO CALL HIM THAT. YES, WE CROSSED PATHS A WHILE BACK. I'M SURE HE'LL REMEMBER ME...

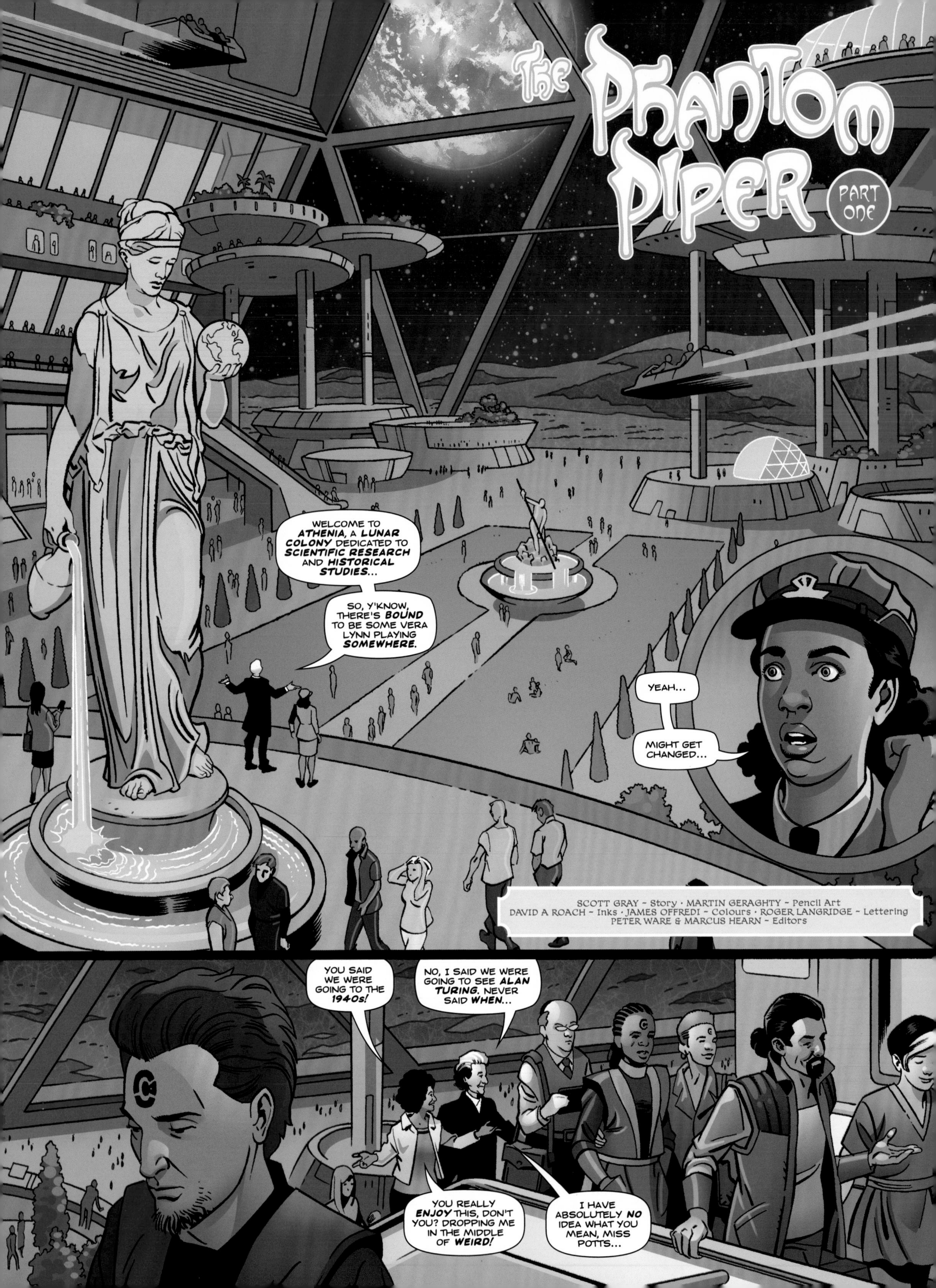
The Phantom Piper
PART ONE
WELCOME TO ATHENIA, A LUNAR COLONY DEDICATED TO SCIENTIFIC RESEARCH AND HISTORICAL STUDIES...
SO, Y'KNOW, THERE'S BOUND TO BE SOME VERA LYNN PLAYING SOMEWHERE.
YEAH...
MIGHT GET CHANGED...
SCOTT GRAY - Story · MARTIN GERAGHTY - Pencil Art
DAVID A ROACH - Inks · JAMES OFFREDI - Colours · ROGER LANGRIDGE - Lettering
PETER WARE & MARCUS HEARN - Editors
YOU SAID WE WERE GOING TO THE 1940s!
NO, I SAID WE WERE GOING TO SEE ALAN TURING. NEVER SAID WHEN...
YOU REALLY ENJOY THIS, DON'T YOU? DROPPING ME IN THE MIDDLE OF WEIRD!
I HAVE ABSOLUTELY NO IDEA WHAT YOU MEAN, MISS POTTS...

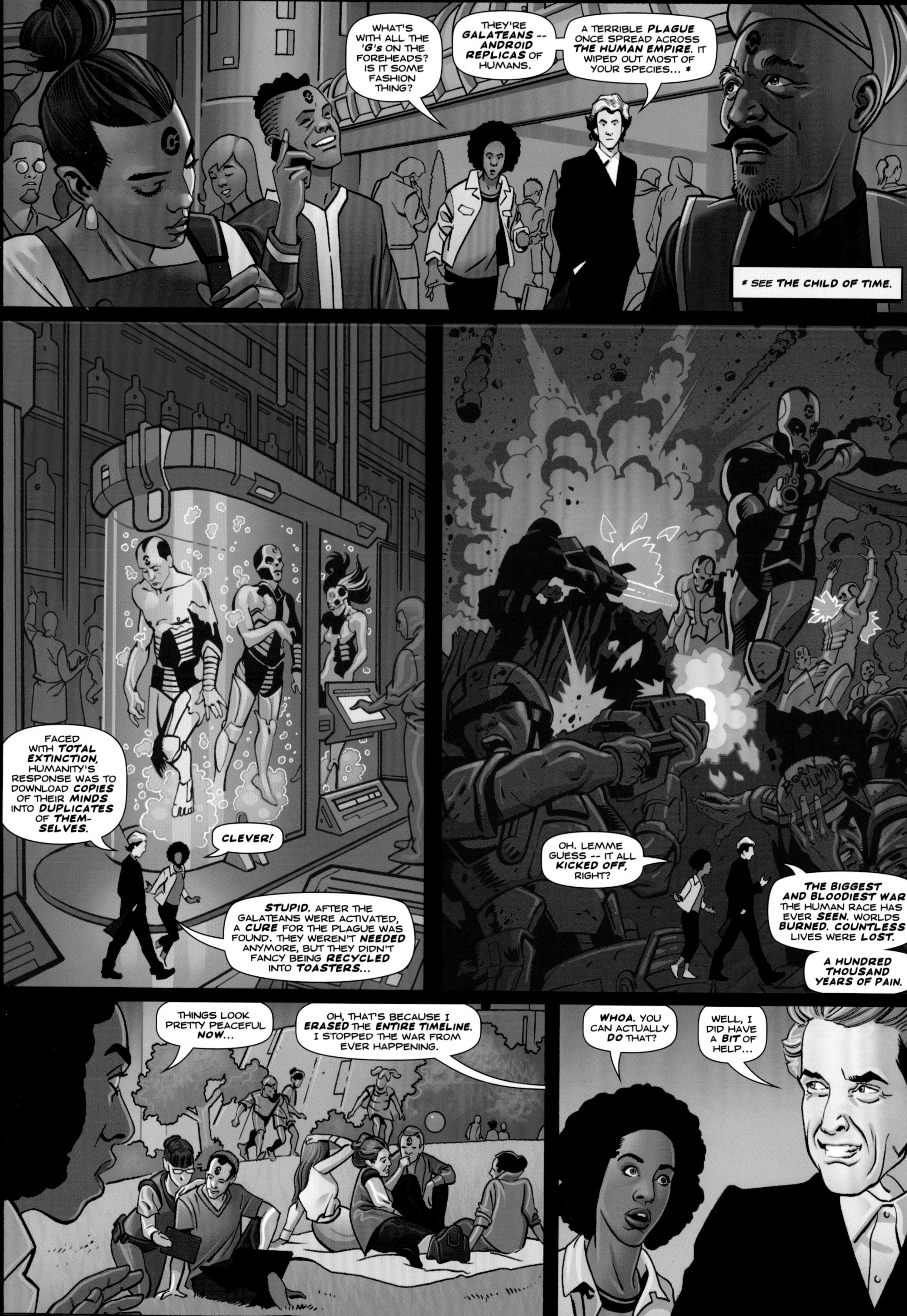
WHAT'S WITH ALL THE 'G's ON THE FOREHEADS? IS IT SOME FASHION THING?
THEY'RE GALATEANS -- ANDROID REPLICAS OF HUMANS.
A TERRIBLE PLAGUE ONCE SPREAD ACROSS THE HUMAN EMPIRE. IT WIPED OUT MOST OF YOUR SPECIES... *
* SEE THE CHILD OF TIME.
FACED WITH TOTAL EXTINCTION, HUMANITY'S RESPONSE WAS TO DOWNLOAD COPIES OF THEIR MINDS INTO DUPLICATES OF THEM-SELVES.
CLEVER!
STUPID. AFTER THE GALATEANS WERE ACTIVATED, A CURE FOR THE PLAGUE WAS FOUND. THEY WEREN'T NEEDED ANYMORE, BUT THEY DIDN'T FANCY BEING RECYCLED INTO TOASTERS...
BORN HUMAN
OH. LEMME GUESS -- IT ALL KICKED OFF, RIGHT?
THE BIGGEST AND BLOODIEST WAR THE HUMAN RACE HAS EVER SEEN. WORLDS BURNED. COUNTLESS LIVES WERE LOST.
A HUNDRED THOUSAND YEARS OF PAIN.
THINGS LOOK PRETTY PEACEFUL NOW...
OH, THAT'S BECAUSE I ERASED THE ENTIRE TIMELINE. I STOPPED THE WAR FROM EVER HAPPENING.
WHOA. YOU CAN ACTUALLY DO THAT?
WELL, I DID HAVE A BIT OF HELP...

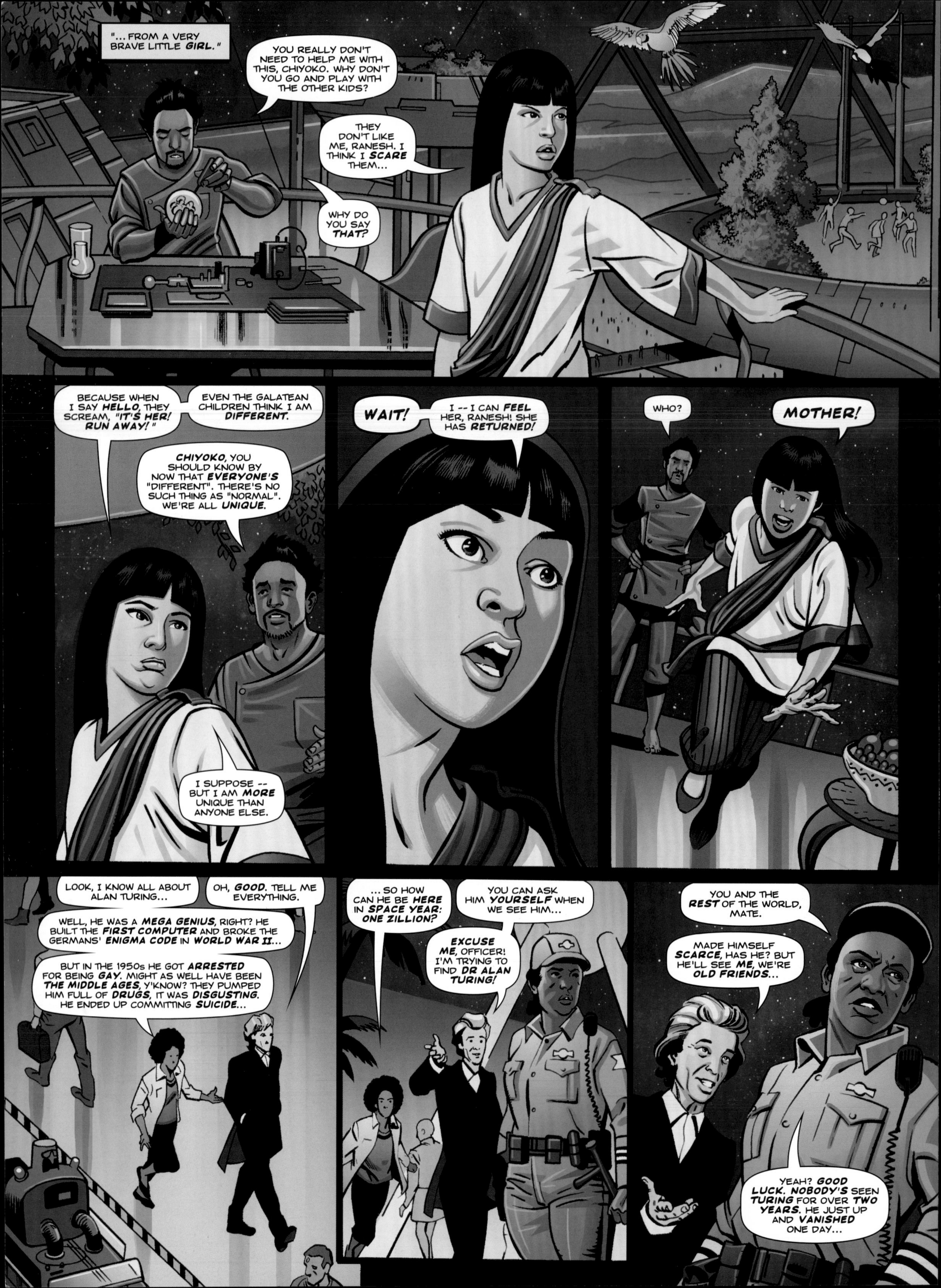
"... FROM A VERY BRAVE LITTLE GIRL."
YOU REALLY DON'T NEED TO HELP ME WITH THIS, CHIYOKO. WHY DON'T YOU GO AND PLAY WITH THE OTHER KIDS?
THEY DON'T LIKE ME, RANESH. I THINK I SCARE THEM...
WHY DO YOU SAY THAT?
BECAUSE WHEN I SAY HELLO, THEY SCREAM, "IT'S HER! RUN AWAY!"
EVEN THE GALATEAN CHILDREN THINK I AM DIFFERENT.
CHIYOKO, YOU SHOULD KNOW BY NOW THAT EVERYONE'S "DIFFERENT". THERE'S NO SUCH THING AS "NORMAL". WE'RE ALL UNIQUE.
I SUPPOSE -- BUT I AM MORE UNIQUE THAN ANYONE ELSE.
WAIT!
I -- I CAN FEEL HER, RANESH! SHE HAS RETURNED!
WHO?
MOTHER!
LOOK, I KNOW ALL ABOUT ALAN TURING...
OH, GOOD. TELL ME EVERYTHING.
WELL, HE WAS A MEGA GENIUS, RIGHT? HE BUILT THE FIRST COMPUTER AND BROKE THE GERMANS' ENIGMA CODE IN WORLD WAR II...
BUT IN THE 1950s HE GOT ARRESTED FOR BEING GAY. MIGHT AS WELL HAVE BEEN THE MIDDLE AGES, Y'KNOW? THEY PUMPED HIM FULL OF DRUGS, IT WAS DISGUSTING. HE ENDED UP COMMITTING SUICIDE...
... SO HOW CAN HE BE HERE IN SPACE YEAR: ONE ZILLION?
YOU CAN ASK HIM YOURSELF WHEN WE SEE HIM...
EXCUSE ME, OFFICER! I'M TRYING TO FIND DR ALAN TURING!
YOU AND THE REST OF THE WORLD, MATE.
MADE HIMSELF SCARCE, HAS HE? BUT HE'LL SEE ME, WE'RE OLD FRIENDS...
YEAH? GOOD LUCK. NOBODY'S SEEN TURING FOR OVER TWO YEARS. HE JUST UP AND VANISHED ONE DAY...

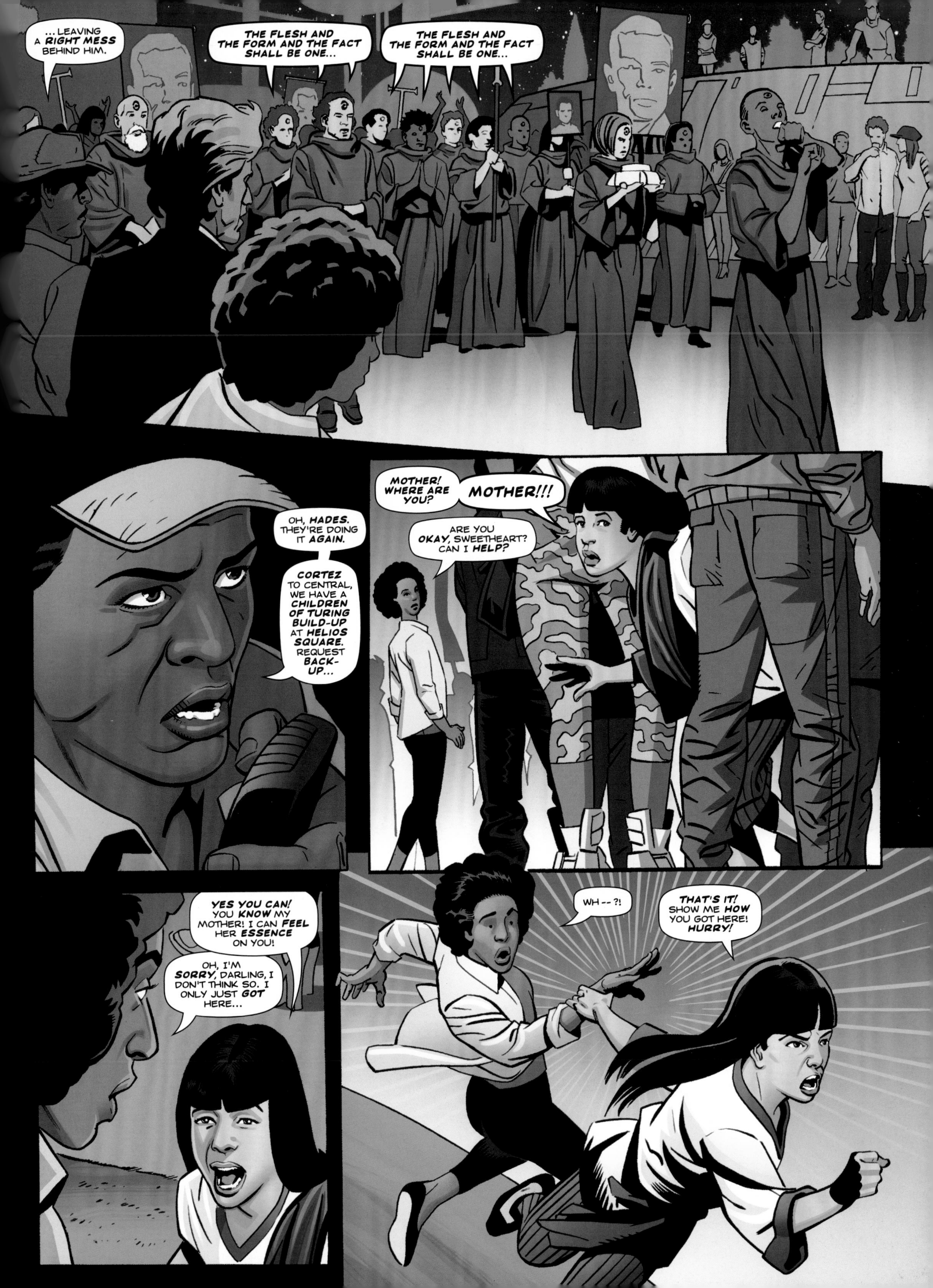
...LEAVING A RIGHT MESS BEHIND HIM.
THE FLESH AND THE FORM AND THE FACT SHALL BE ONE...
THE FLESH AND THE FORM AND THE FACT SHALL BE ONE...
OH, HADES. THEY'RE DOING IT AGAIN.
CORTEZ TO CENTRAL, WE HAVE A CHILDREN OF TURING BUILD-UP AT HELIOS SQUARE. REQUEST BACK-UP...
MOTHER! WHERE ARE YOU?
MOTHER!!!
ARE YOU OKAY, SWEETHEART? CAN I HELP?
YES YOU CAN! YOU KNOW MY MOTHER! I CAN FEEL HER ESSENCE ON YOU!
OH, I'M SORRY, DARLING, I DON'T THINK SO. I ONLY JUST GOT HERE...
WH -- ?!
THAT'S IT! SHOW ME HOW YOU GOT HERE! HURRY!

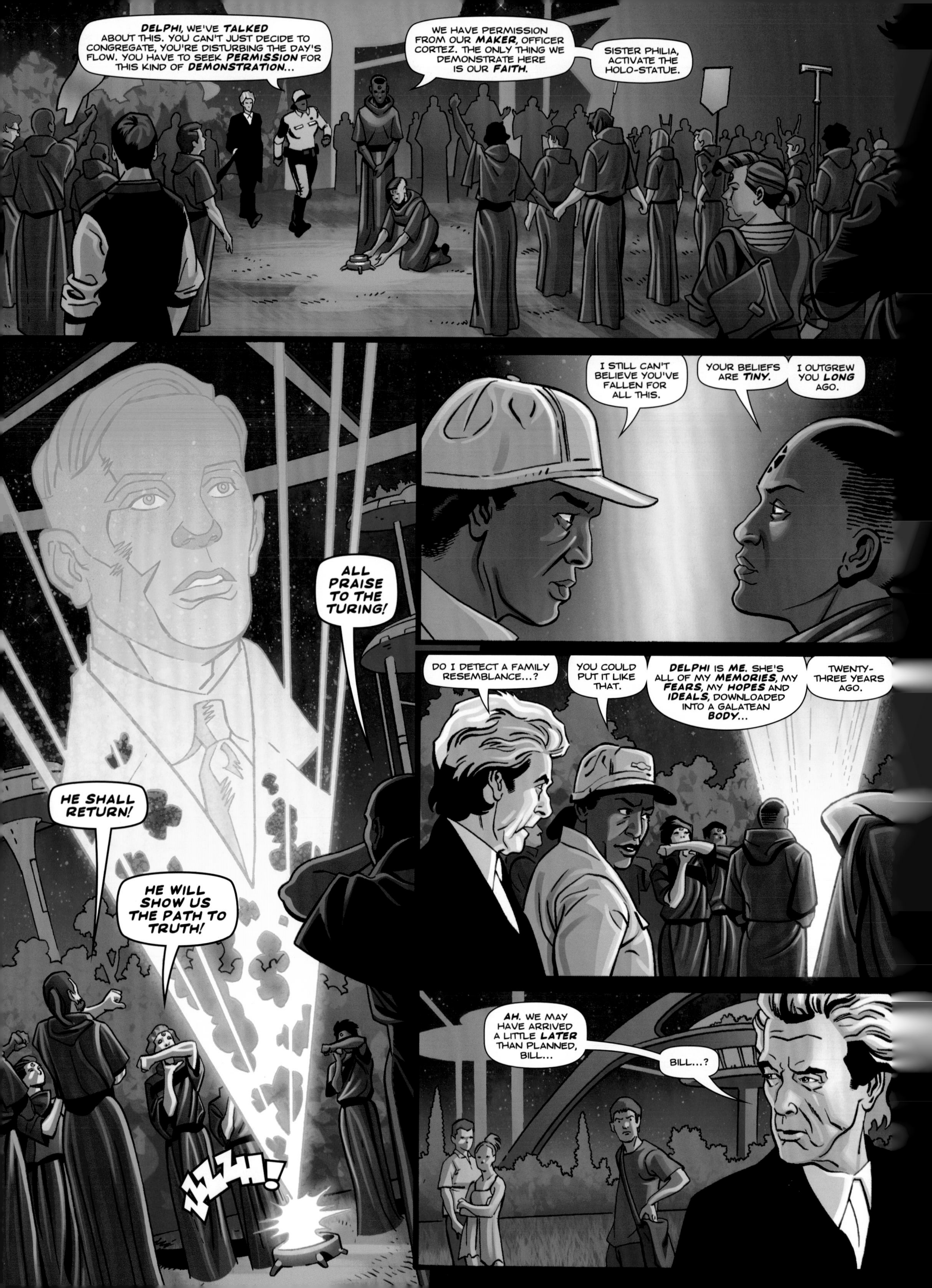
DELPHI, WE'VE TALKED ABOUT THIS. YOU CAN'T JUST DECIDE TO CONGREGATE, YOU'RE DISTURBING THE DAY'S FLOW. YOU HAVE TO SEEK PERMISSION FOR THIS KIND OF DEMONSTRATION...
WE HAVE PERMISSION FROM OUR MAKER, OFFICER CORTEZ. THE ONLY THING WE DEMONSTRATE HERE IS OUR FAITH.
SISTER PHILIA, ACTIVATE THE HOLO-STATUE.
ALL PRAISE TO THE TURING!
HE SHALL RETURN!
HE WILL SHOW US THE PATH TO TRUTH!
ZZZH!
I STILL CAN'T BELIEVE YOU'VE FALLEN FOR ALL THIS.
YOUR BELIEFS ARE TINY.
I OUTGREW YOU LONG AGO.
DO I DETECT A FAMILY RESEMBLANCE...?
YOU COULD PUT IT LIKE THAT.
DELPHI IS ME. SHE'S ALL OF MY MEMORIES, MY FEARS, MY HOPES AND IDEALS, DOWNLOADED INTO A GALATEAN BODY...
TWENTY-THREE YEARS AGO.
AH. WE MAY HAVE ARRIVED A LITTLE LATER THAN PLANNED, BILL...
BILL...?

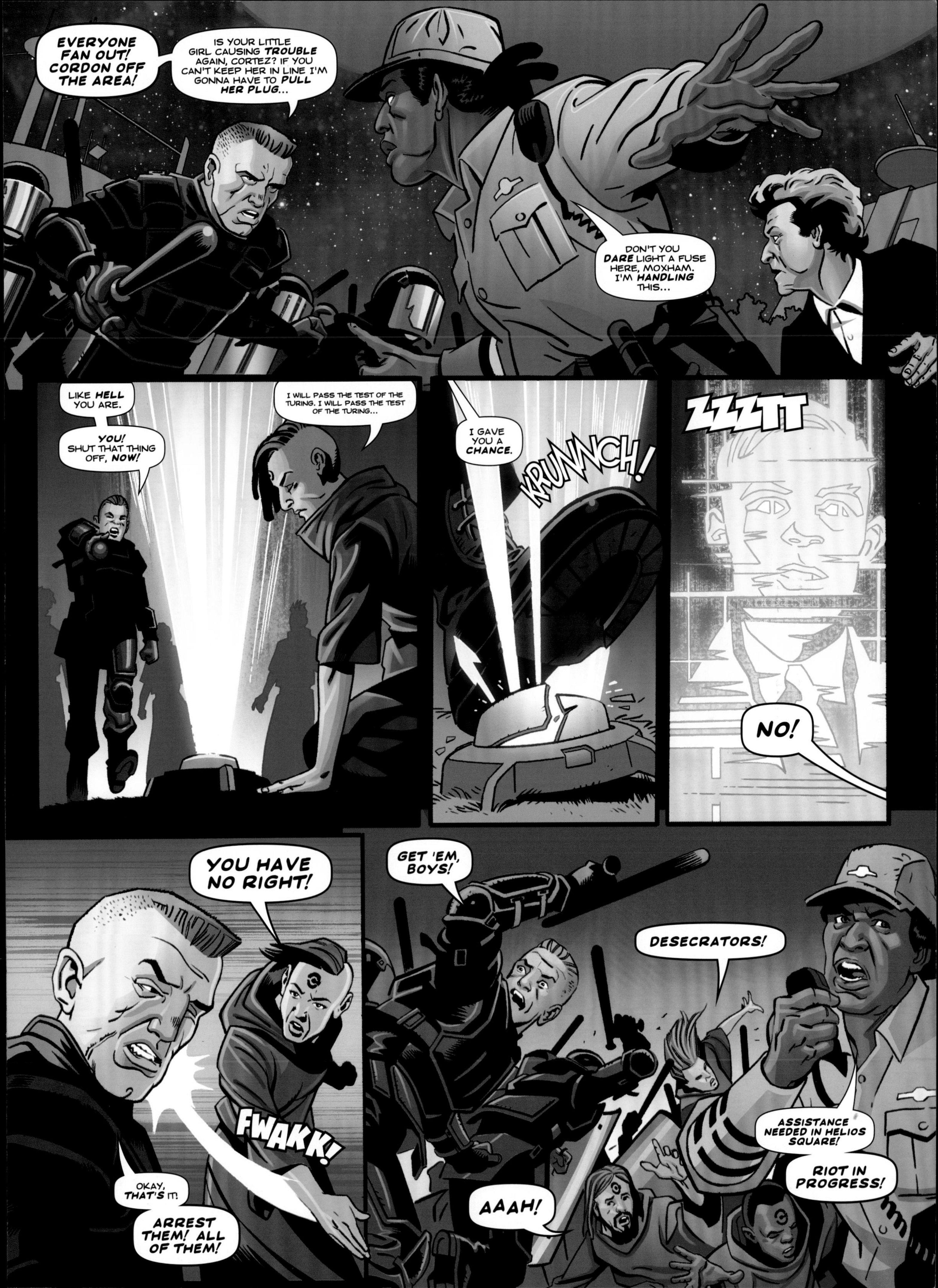
EVERYONE FAN OUT! CORDON OFF THE AREA!
IS YOUR LITTLE GIRL CAUSING TROUBLE AGAIN, CORTEZ? IF YOU CAN'T KEEP HER IN LINE I'M GONNA HAVE TO PULL HER PLUG...
DON'T YOU DARE LIGHT A FUSE HERE, MOXHAM. I'M HANDLING THIS...
LIKE HELL YOU ARE.
YOU! SHUT THAT THING OFF, NOW!
I WILL PASS THE TEST OF THE TURING. I WILL PASS THE TEST OF THE TURING...
I GAVE YOU A CHANCE.
KRUNNCH!
ZZZTT
NO!
YOU HAVE NO RIGHT!
FWAKK!
OKAY, THAT'S IT!
ARREST THEM! ALL OF THEM!
GET 'EM, BOYS!
DESECRATORS!
ASSISTANCE NEEDED IN HELIOS SQUARE!
RIOT IN PROGRESS!
AAAH!

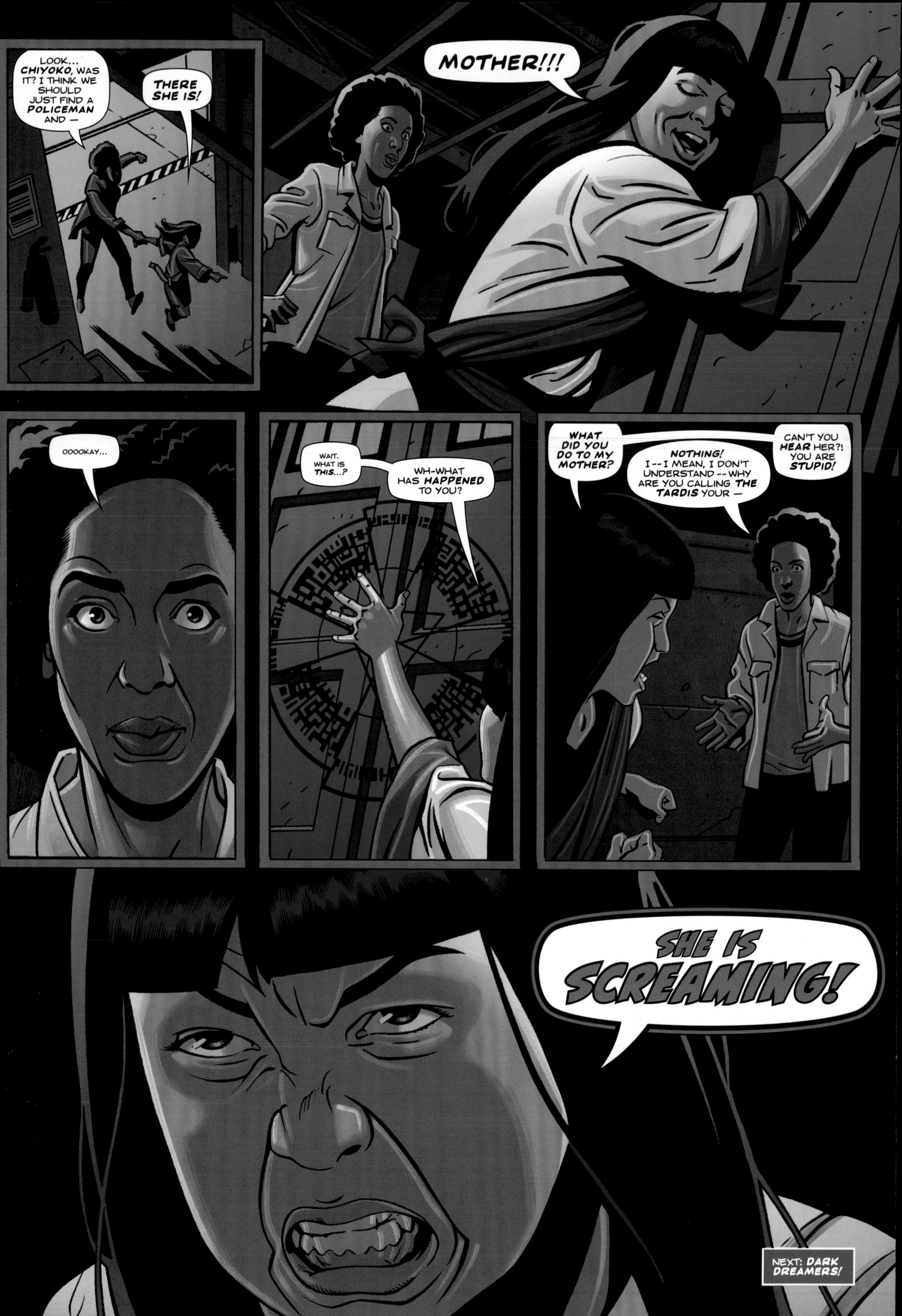
LOOK... CHIYOKO, WAS IT? I THINK WE SHOULD JUST FIND A POLICEMAN AND —
THERE SHE IS!
MOTHER!!!
OOOOKAY...
WAIT. WHAT IS THIS...?
WH-WHAT HAS HAPPENED TO YOU?
WHAT DID YOU DO TO MY MOTHER?
NOTHING! I -- I MEAN, I DON'T UNDERSTAND -- WHY ARE YOU CALLING THE TARDIS YOUR —
CAN'T YOU HEAR HER?! YOU ARE STUPID!
SHE IS SCREAMING!
NEXT: DARK DREAMERS!

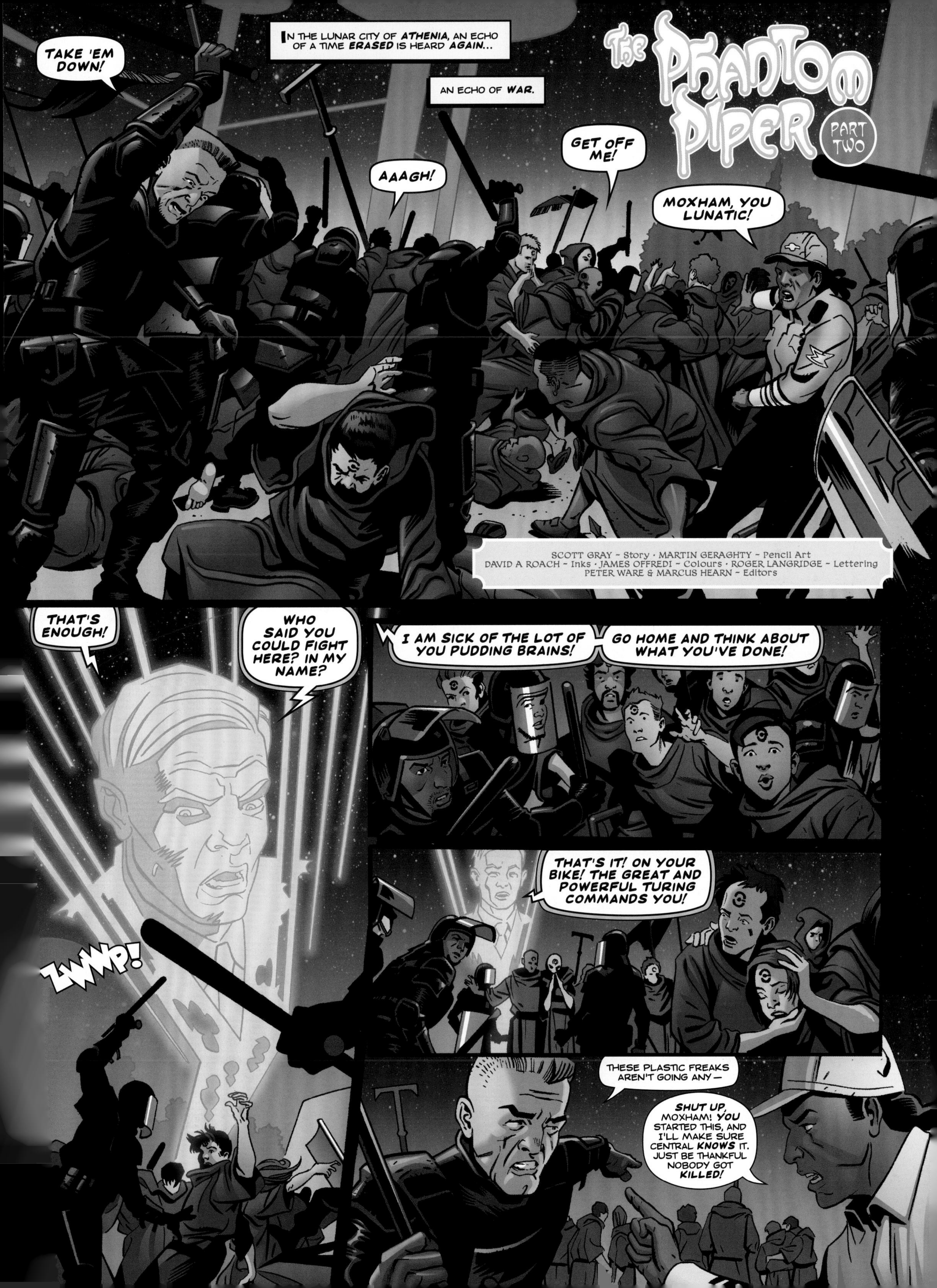
TAKE 'EM DOWN!
IN THE LUNAR CITY OF ATHENIA, AN ECHO OF A TIME ERASED IS HEARD AGAIN...
AN ECHO OF WAR.
THE PHANTOM PIPER PART TWO
AAAGH!
GET OFF ME!
MOXHAM, YOU LUNATIC!
SCOTT GRAY ~ Story · MARTIN GERAGHTY ~ Pencil Art
DAVID A ROACH ~ Inks · JAMES OFFREDI ~ Colours · ROGER LANGRIDGE ~ Lettering
PETER WARE & MARCUS HEARN ~ Editors
THAT'S ENOUGH!
WHO SAID YOU COULD FIGHT HERE? IN MY NAME?
ZWWP!
I AM SICK OF THE LOT OF YOU PUDDING BRAINS!
GO HOME AND THINK ABOUT WHAT YOU'VE DONE!
THAT'S IT! ON YOUR BIKE! THE GREAT AND POWERFUL TURING COMMANDS YOU!
THESE PLASTIC FREAKS AREN'T GOING ANY—
SHUT UP, MOXHAM! YOU STARTED THIS, AND I'LL MAKE SURE CENTRAL KNOWS IT. JUST BE THANKFUL NOBODY GOT KILLED!

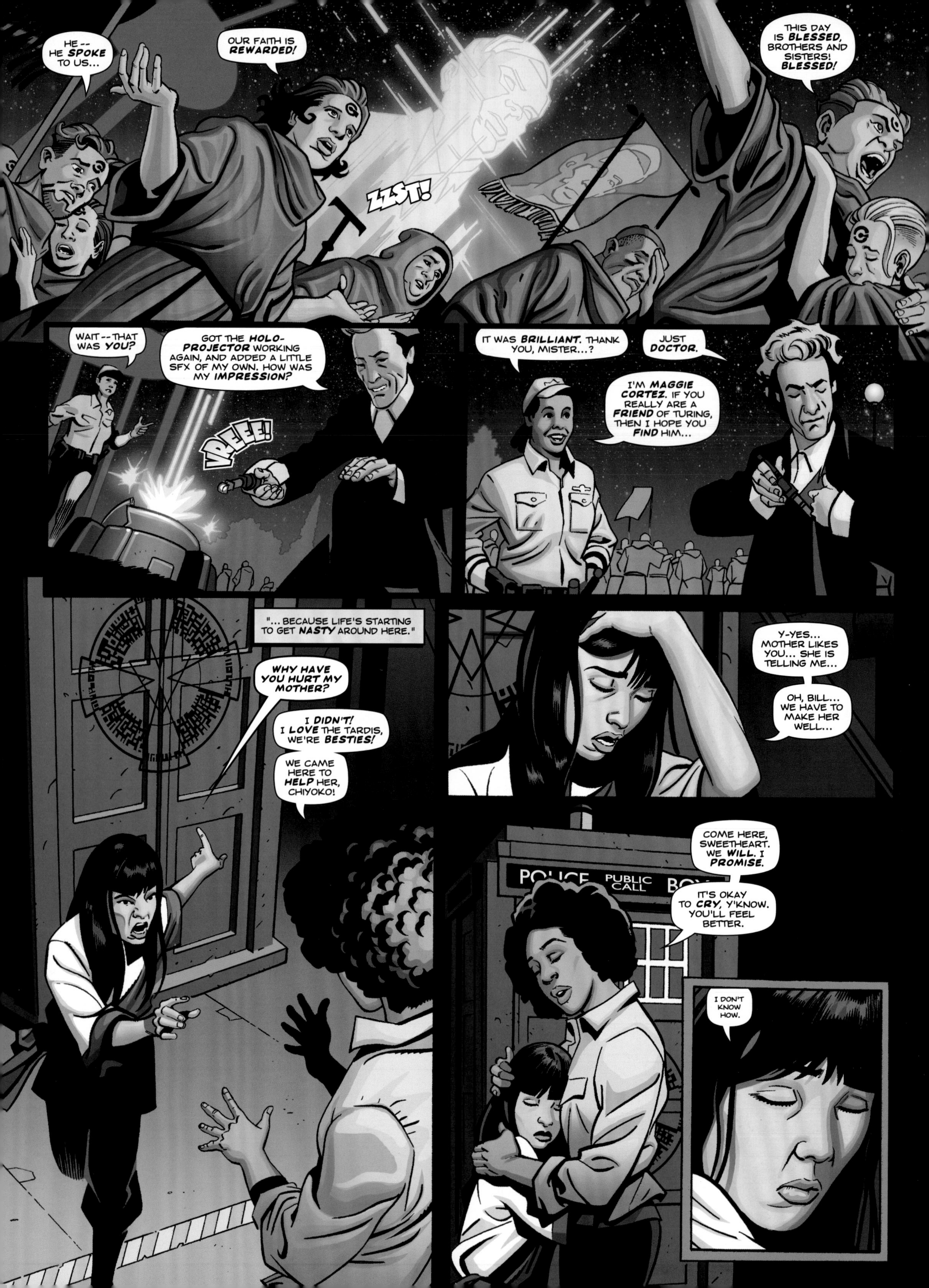

HE -- HE SPOKE TO US...
OUR FAITH IS REWARDED!
THIS DAY IS BLESSED, BROTHERS AND SISTERS! BLESSED!
ZZST!
WAIT -- THAT WAS YOU?
GOT THE HOLO-PROJECTOR WORKING AGAIN, AND ADDED A LITTLE SFX OF MY OWN. HOW WAS MY IMPRESSION?
VREEE!
IT WAS BRILLIANT. THANK YOU, MISTER...?
JUST DOCTOR.
I'M MAGGIE CORTEZ. IF YOU REALLY ARE A FRIEND OF TURING, THEN I HOPE YOU FIND HIM...
"...BECAUSE LIFE'S STARTING TO GET NASTY AROUND HERE."
WHY HAVE YOU HURT MY MOTHER?
I DIDN'T! I LOVE THE TARDIS, WE'RE BESTIES!
WE CAME HERE TO HELP HER, CHIYOKO!
Y-YES... MOTHER LIKES YOU... SHE IS TELLING ME...
OH, BILL... WE HAVE TO MAKE HER WELL...
POLICE PUBLIC CALL BOX
COME HERE, SWEETHEART. WE WILL. I PROMISE.
IT'S OKAY TO CRY, Y'KNOW. YOU'LL FEEL BETTER.
I DON'T KNOW HOW.

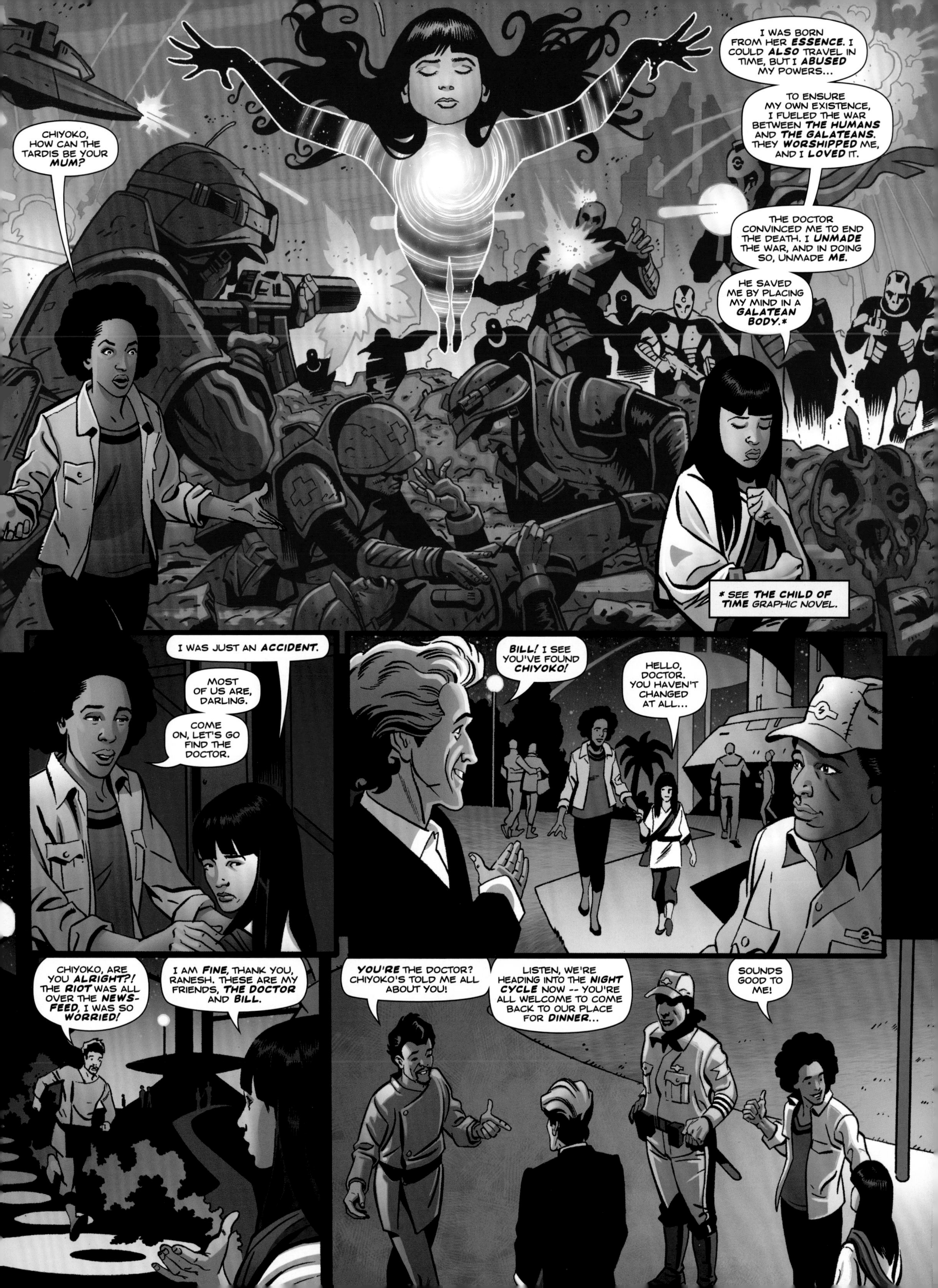
CHIYOKO, HOW CAN THE TARDIS BE YOUR MUM?
I WAS BORN FROM HER ESSENCE. I COULD ALSO TRAVEL IN TIME, BUT I ABUSED MY POWERS...
TO ENSURE MY OWN EXISTENCE, I FUELED THE WAR BETWEEN THE HUMANS AND THE GALATEANS. THEY WORSHIPPED ME, AND I LOVED IT.
THE DOCTOR CONVINCED ME TO END THE DEATH. I UNMADE THE WAR, AND IN DOING SO, UNMADE ME.
HE SAVED ME BY PLACING MY MIND IN A GALATEAN BODY.*
* SEE THE CHILD OF TIME GRAPHIC NOVEL.
I WAS JUST AN ACCIDENT.
MOST OF US ARE, DARLING.
COME ON, LET'S GO FIND THE DOCTOR.
BILL! I SEE YOU'VE FOUND CHIYOKO!
HELLO, DOCTOR. YOU HAVEN'T CHANGED AT ALL...
CHIYOKO, ARE YOU ALRIGHT?! THE RIOT WAS ALL OVER THE NEWS-FEED, I WAS SO WORRIED!
I AM FINE, THANK YOU, RANESH. THESE ARE MY FRIENDS, THE DOCTOR AND BILL.
YOU'RE THE DOCTOR? CHIYOKO'S TOLD ME ALL ABOUT YOU!
LISTEN, WE'RE HEADING INTO THE NIGHT CYCLE NOW -- YOU'RE ALL WELCOME TO COME BACK TO OUR PLACE FOR DINNER...
SOUNDS GOOD TO ME!

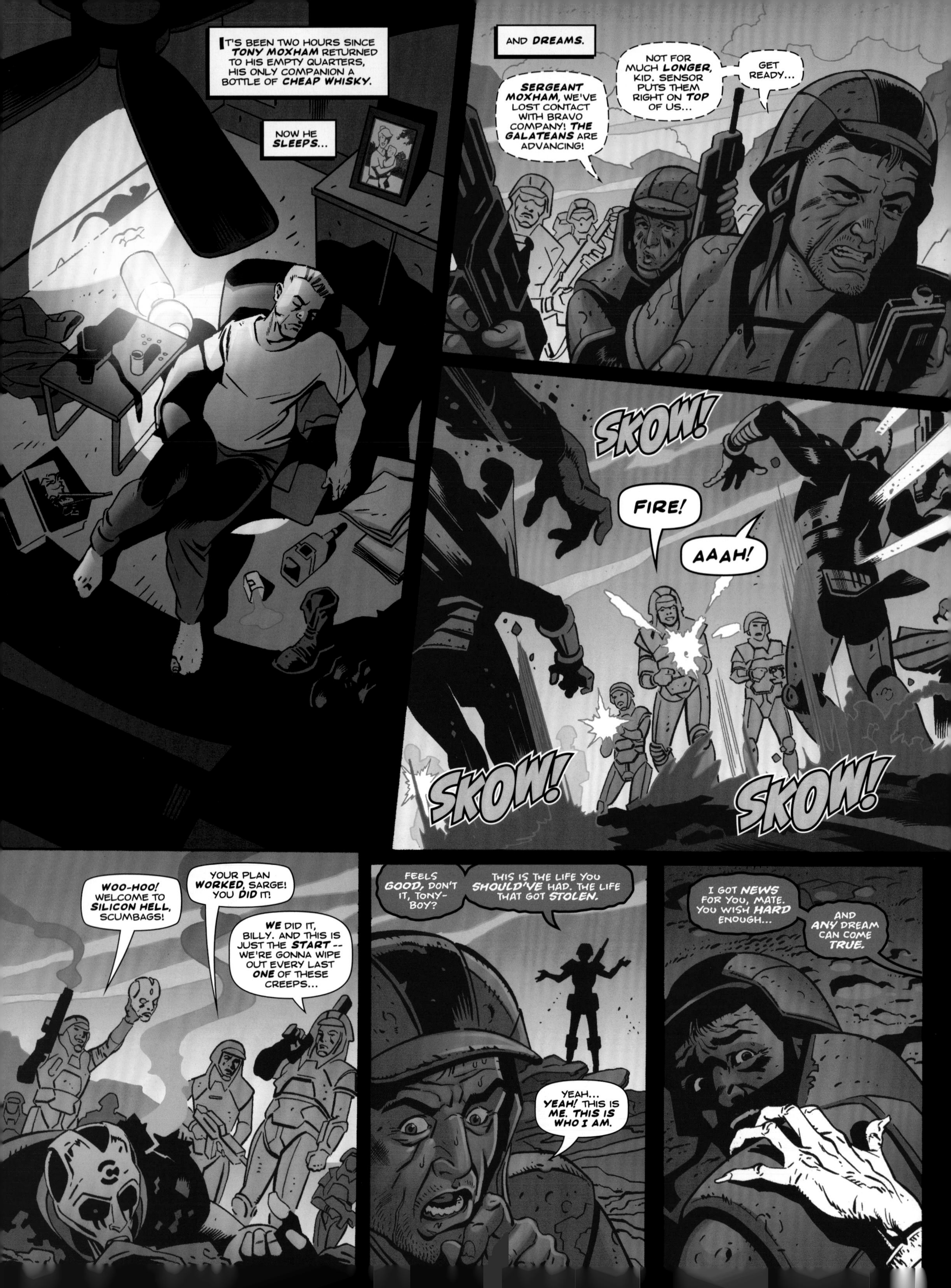

IT'S BEEN TWO HOURS SINCE TONY MOXHAM RETURNED TO HIS EMPTY QUARTERS, HIS ONLY COMPANION A BOTTLE OF CHEAP WHISKY.
NOW HE SLEEPS...
AND DREAMS.
SERGEANT MOXHAM, WE'VE LOST CONTACT WITH BRAVO COMPANY! THE GALATEANS ARE ADVANCING!
NOT FOR MUCH LONGER, KID. SENSOR PUTS THEM RIGHT ON TOP OF US...
GET READY...
SKOW!
FIRE!
AAAH!
SKOW!
SKOW!
WOO-HOO! WELCOME TO SILICON HELL, SCUMBAGS!
YOUR PLAN WORKED, SARGE! YOU DID IT!
WE DID IT, BILLY. AND THIS IS JUST THE START -- WE'RE GONNA WIPE OUT EVERY LAST ONE OF THESE CREEPS...
FEELS GOOD, DON'T IT, TONY-BOY?
THIS IS THE LIFE YOU SHOULD'VE HAD. THE LIFE THAT GOT STOLEN.
YEAH... YEAH! THIS IS ME. THIS IS WHO I AM.
I GOT NEWS FOR YOU, MATE. YOU WISH HARD ENOUGH...
AND ANY DREAM CAN COME TRUE.

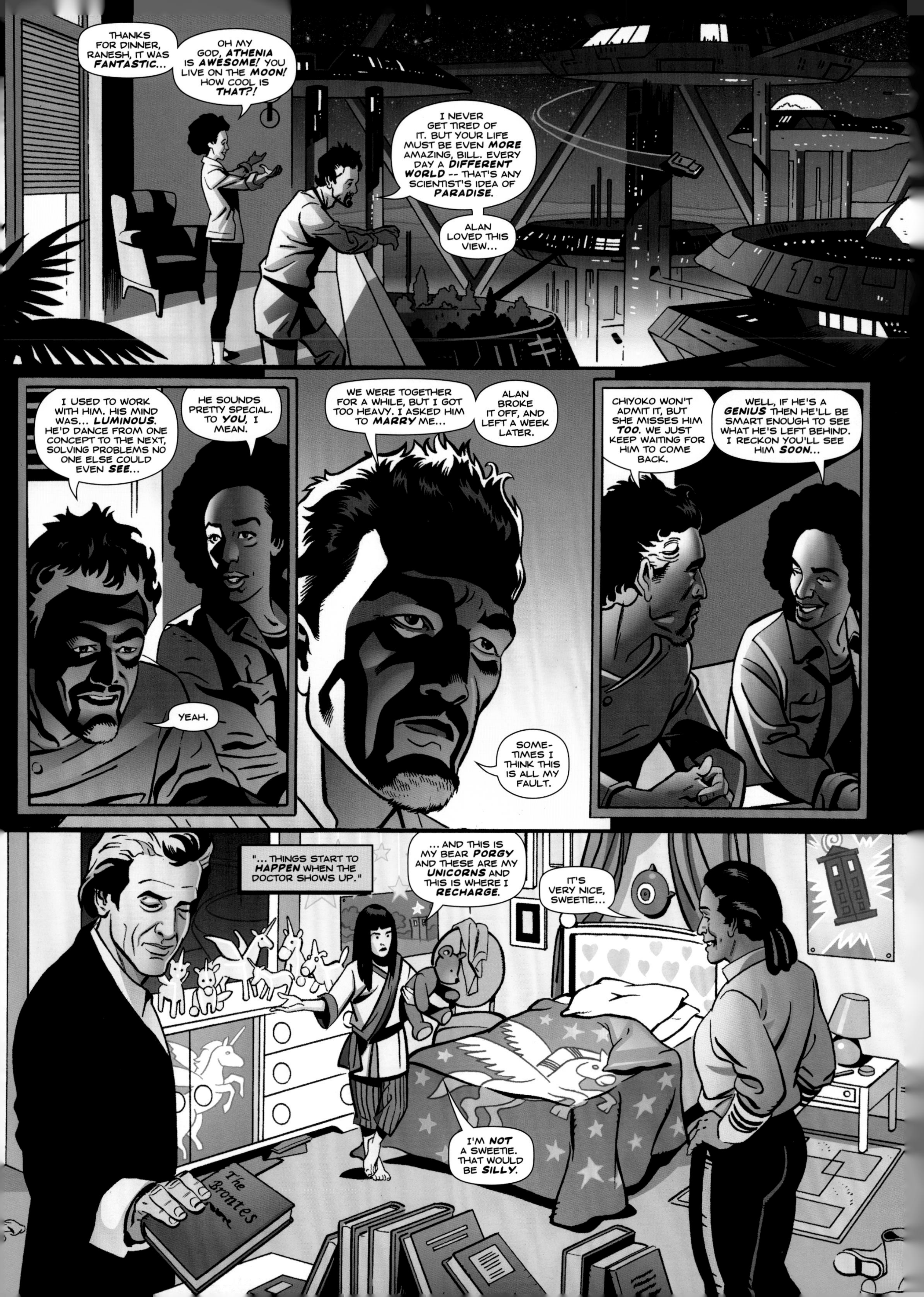

THANKS FOR DINNER, RANESH, IT WAS FANTASTIC...
OH MY GOD, ATHENIA IS AWESOME! YOU LIVE ON THE MOON! HOW COOL IS THAT?!
I NEVER GET TIRED OF IT. BUT YOUR LIFE MUST BE EVEN MORE AMAZING, BILL. EVERY DAY A DIFFERENT WORLD -- THAT'S ANY SCIENTIST'S IDEA OF PARADISE.
ALAN LOVED THIS VIEW...
I USED TO WORK WITH HIM. HIS MIND WAS... LUMINOUS. HE'D DANCE FROM ONE CONCEPT TO THE NEXT, SOLVING PROBLEMS NO ONE ELSE COULD EVEN SEE...
HE SOUNDS PRETTY SPECIAL. TO YOU, I MEAN.
YEAH.
WE WERE TOGETHER FOR A WHILE, BUT I GOT TOO HEAVY. I ASKED HIM TO MARRY ME...
ALAN BROKE IT OFF, AND LEFT A WEEK LATER.
SOME-TIMES I THINK THIS IS ALL MY FAULT.
CHIYOKO WON'T ADMIT IT, BUT SHE MISSES HIM TOO. WE JUST KEEP WAITING FOR HIM TO COME BACK.
WELL, IF HE'S A GENIUS THEN HE'LL BE SMART ENOUGH TO SEE WHAT HE'S LEFT BEHIND. I RECKON YOU'LL SEE HIM SOON...
"... THINGS START TO HAPPEN WHEN THE DOCTOR SHOWS UP."
... AND THIS IS MY BEAR PORGY AND THESE ARE MY UNICORNS AND THIS IS WHERE I RECHARGE.
IT'S VERY NICE, SWEETIE...
I'M NOT A SWEETIE. THAT WOULD BE SILLY.
The Brontes

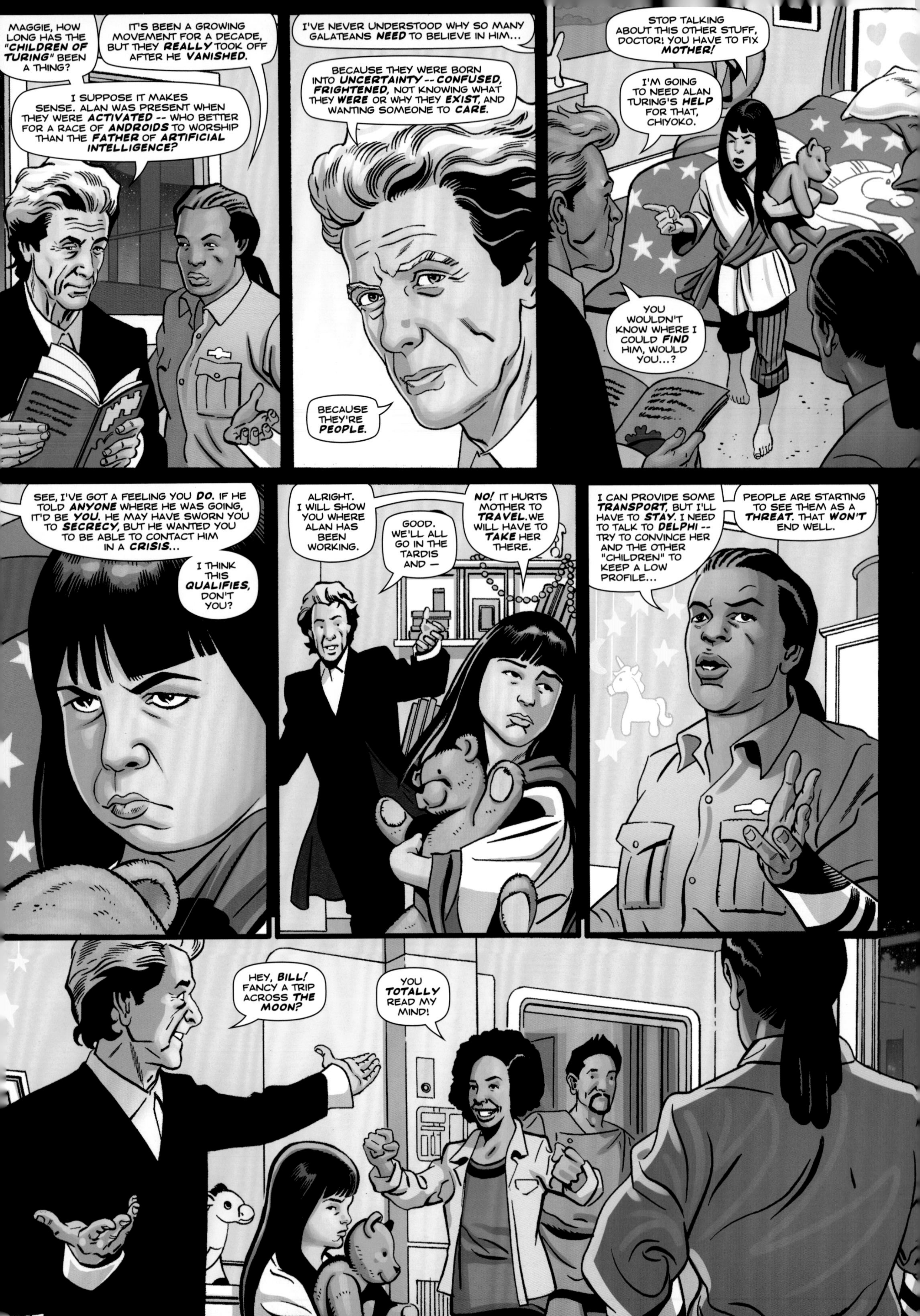

MAGGIE, HOW LONG HAS THE "CHILDREN OF TURING" BEEN A THING?
IT'S BEEN A GROWING MOVEMENT FOR A DECADE, BUT THEY REALLY TOOK OFF AFTER HE VANISHED.
I SUPPOSE IT MAKES SENSE. ALAN WAS PRESENT WHEN THEY WERE ACTIVATED -- WHO BETTER FOR A RACE OF ANDROIDS TO WORSHIP THAN THE FATHER OF ARTIFICIAL INTELLIGENCE?
I'VE NEVER UNDERSTOOD WHY SO MANY GALATEANS NEED TO BELIEVE IN HIM...
BECAUSE THEY WERE BORN INTO UNCERTAINTY -- CONFUSED, FRIGHTENED, NOT KNOWING WHAT THEY WERE OR WHY THEY EXIST, AND WANTING SOMEONE TO CARE.
BECAUSE THEY'RE PEOPLE.
STOP TALKING ABOUT THIS OTHER STUFF, DOCTOR! YOU HAVE TO FIX MOTHER!
I'M GOING TO NEED ALAN TURING'S HELP FOR THAT, CHIYOKO.
YOU WOULDN'T KNOW WHERE I COULD FIND HIM, WOULD YOU...?
SEE, I'VE GOT A FEELING YOU DO. IF HE TOLD ANYONE WHERE HE WAS GOING, IT'D BE YOU. HE MAY HAVE SWORN YOU TO SECRECY, BUT HE WANTED YOU TO BE ABLE TO CONTACT HIM IN A CRISIS...
I THINK THIS QUALIFIES, DON'T YOU?
ALRIGHT. I WILL SHOW YOU WHERE ALAN HAS BEEN WORKING.
GOOD. WE'LL ALL GO IN THE TARDIS AND —
NO! IT HURTS MOTHER TO TRAVEL. WE WILL HAVE TO TAKE HER THERE.
I CAN PROVIDE SOME TRANSPORT, BUT I'LL HAVE TO STAY. I NEED TO TALK TO DELPHI -- TRY TO CONVINCE HER AND THE OTHER "CHILDREN" TO KEEP A LOW PROFILE...
PEOPLE ARE STARTING TO SEE THEM AS A THREAT. THAT WON'T END WELL.
HEY, BILL! FANCY A TRIP ACROSS THE MOON?
YOU TOTALLY READ MY MIND!

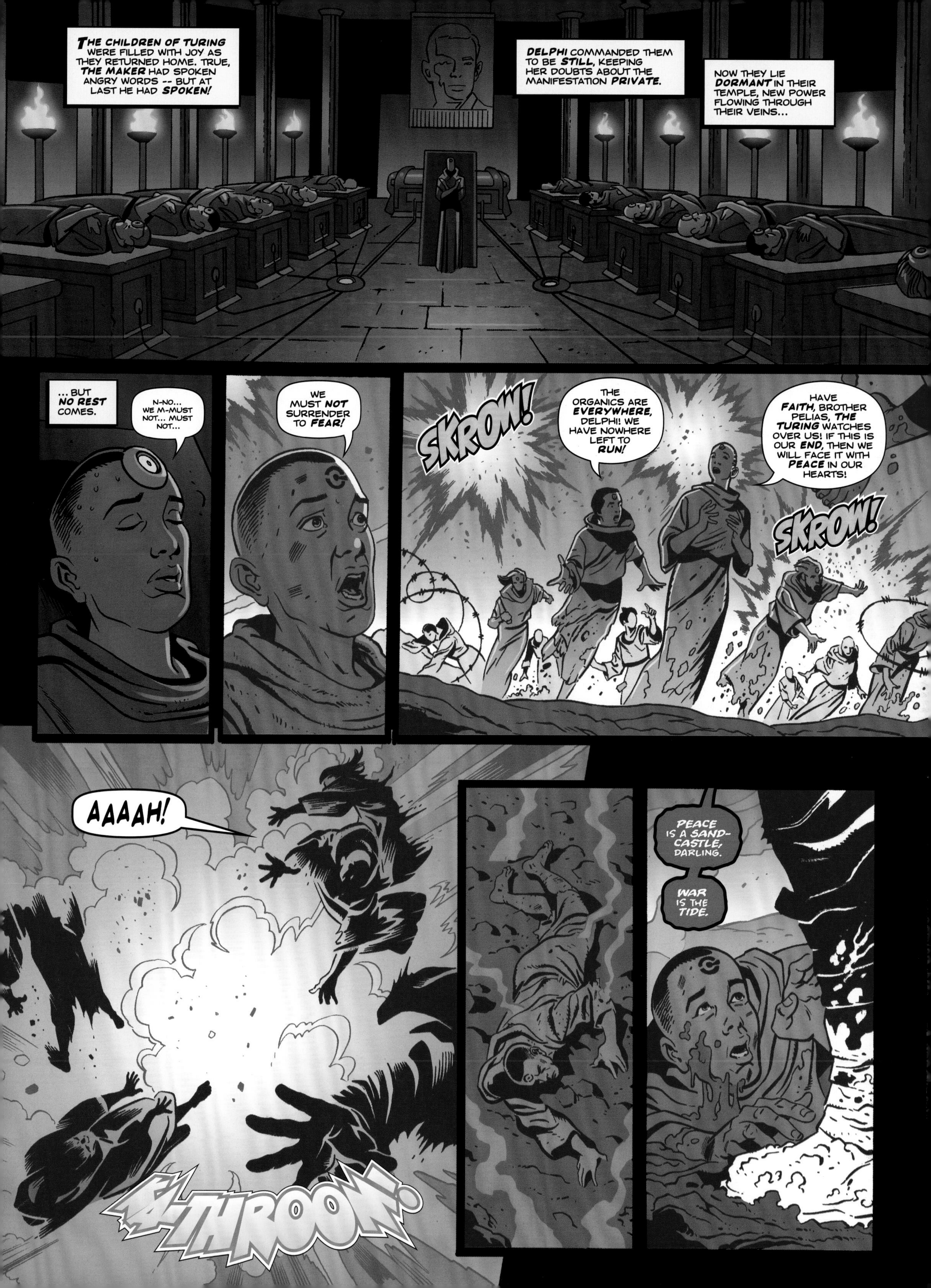

THE CHILDREN OF TURING WERE FILLED WITH JOY AS THEY RETURNED HOME. TRUE, THE MAKER HAD SPOKEN ANGRY WORDS -- BUT AT LAST HE HAD SPOKEN!
DELPHI COMMANDED THEM TO BE STILL, KEEPING HER DOUBTS ABOUT THE MANIFESTATION PRIVATE.
NOW THEY LIE DORMANT IN THEIR TEMPLE, NEW POWER FLOWING THROUGH THEIR VEINS...
... BUT NO REST COMES.
N-NO... WE M-MUST NOT... MUST NOT...
WE MUST NOT SURRENDER TO FEAR!
SKROW!
THE ORGANICS ARE EVERYWHERE, DELPHI! WE HAVE NOWHERE LEFT TO RUN!
HAVE FAITH, BROTHER PELIAS, THE TURING WATCHES OVER US! IF THIS IS OUR END, THEN WE WILL FACE IT WITH PEACE IN OUR HEARTS!
SKROW!
AAAAH!
KA-THROOM!
PEACE IS A SAND-CASTLE, DARLING.
WAR IS THE TIDE.

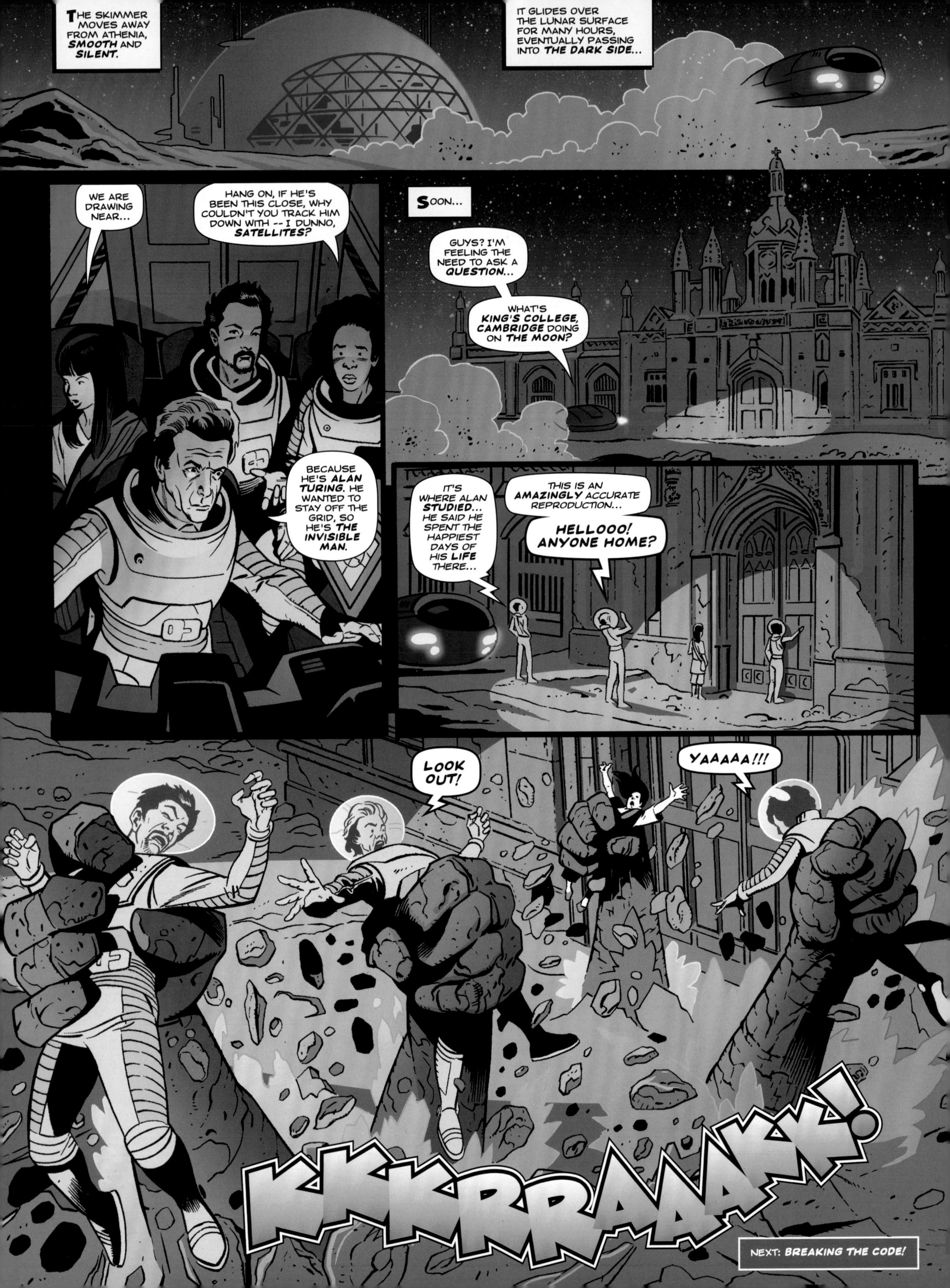
THE SKIMMER MOVES AWAY FROM ATHENIA, SMOOTH AND SILENT.
IT GLIDES OVER THE LUNAR SURFACE FOR MANY HOURS, EVENTUALLY PASSING INTO THE DARK SIDE...
WE ARE DRAWING NEAR...
HANG ON, IF HE'S BEEN THIS CLOSE, WHY COULDN'T YOU TRACK HIM DOWN WITH -- I DUNNO, SATELLITES?
BECAUSE HE'S ALAN TURING. HE WANTED TO STAY OFF THE GRID, SO HE'S THE INVISIBLE MAN.
SOON...
GUYS? I'M FEELING THE NEED TO ASK A QUESTION...
WHAT'S KING'S COLLEGE, CAMBRIDGE DOING ON THE MOON?
IT'S WHERE ALAN STUDIED... HE SAID HE SPENT THE HAPPIEST DAYS OF HIS LIFE THERE...
THIS IS AN AMAZINGLY ACCURATE REPRODUCTION...
HELLOOO! ANYONE HOME?
LOOK OUT!
YAAAAA!!!
KKKRRAAAK!
NEXT: BREAKING THE CODE!

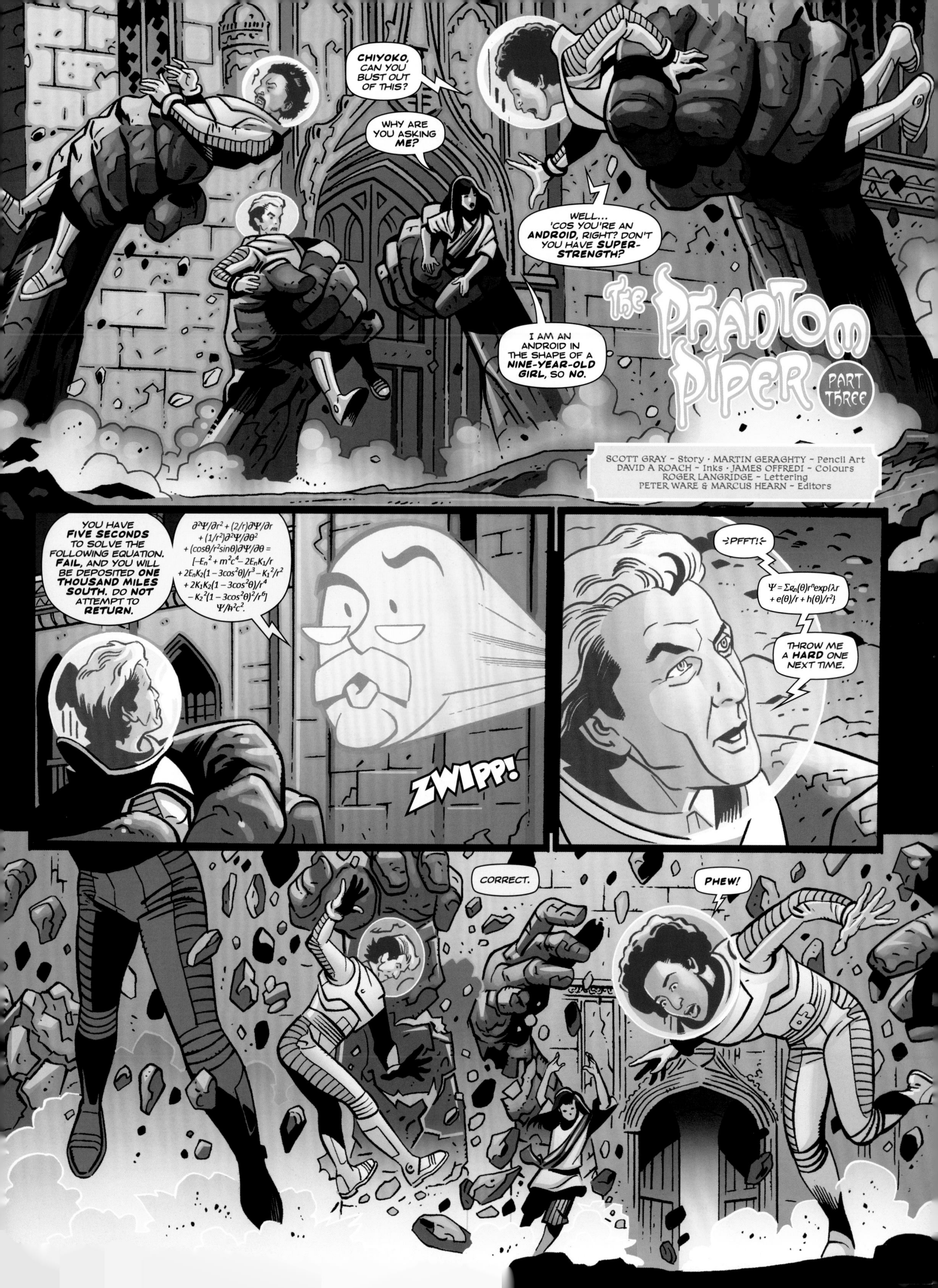
CHIYOKO, CAN YOU BUST OUT OF THIS?
WHY ARE YOU ASKING ME?
WELL... 'COS YOU'RE AN ANDROID, RIGHT? DON'T YOU HAVE SUPER-STRENGTH?
I AM AN ANDROID IN THE SHAPE OF A NINE-YEAR-OLD GIRL, SO NO.
THE PHANTOM PIPER PART THREE
SCOTT GRAY ~ Story · MARTIN GERAGHTY ~ Pencil Art
DAVID A ROACH ~ Inks · JAMES OFFREDI ~ Colours
ROGER LANGRIDGE ~ Lettering
PETER WARE & MARCUS HEARN ~ Editors
YOU HAVE FIVE SECONDS TO SOLVE THE FOLLOWING EQUATION. FAIL, AND YOU WILL BE DEPOSITED ONE THOUSAND MILES SOUTH. DO NOT ATTEMPT TO RETURN.
$\partial^2\Psi/\partial r^2 + (2/r)\partial\Psi/\partial r + (1/r^2)\partial^2\Psi/\partial\theta^2 + (\cos\theta/r^2\sin\theta)\partial\Psi/\partial\theta = [-E_n{}^2 + m^2c^4 - 2E_nK_1/r + 2E_nK_2(1-3\cos^2\theta)/r^3 - K_1{}^2/r^2 + 2K_1K_2(1-3\cos^2\theta)/r^4 - K_2{}^2(1-3\cos^2\theta)^2/r^6]\Psi/\hbar^2c^2.$
ZWIPP!
PFFT!
$\Psi = \Sigma g_n(\theta)r^n\exp\{\lambda r + e(\theta)/r + h(\theta)/r^2\}$
THROW ME A HARD ONE NEXT TIME.
CORRECT.
PHEW!

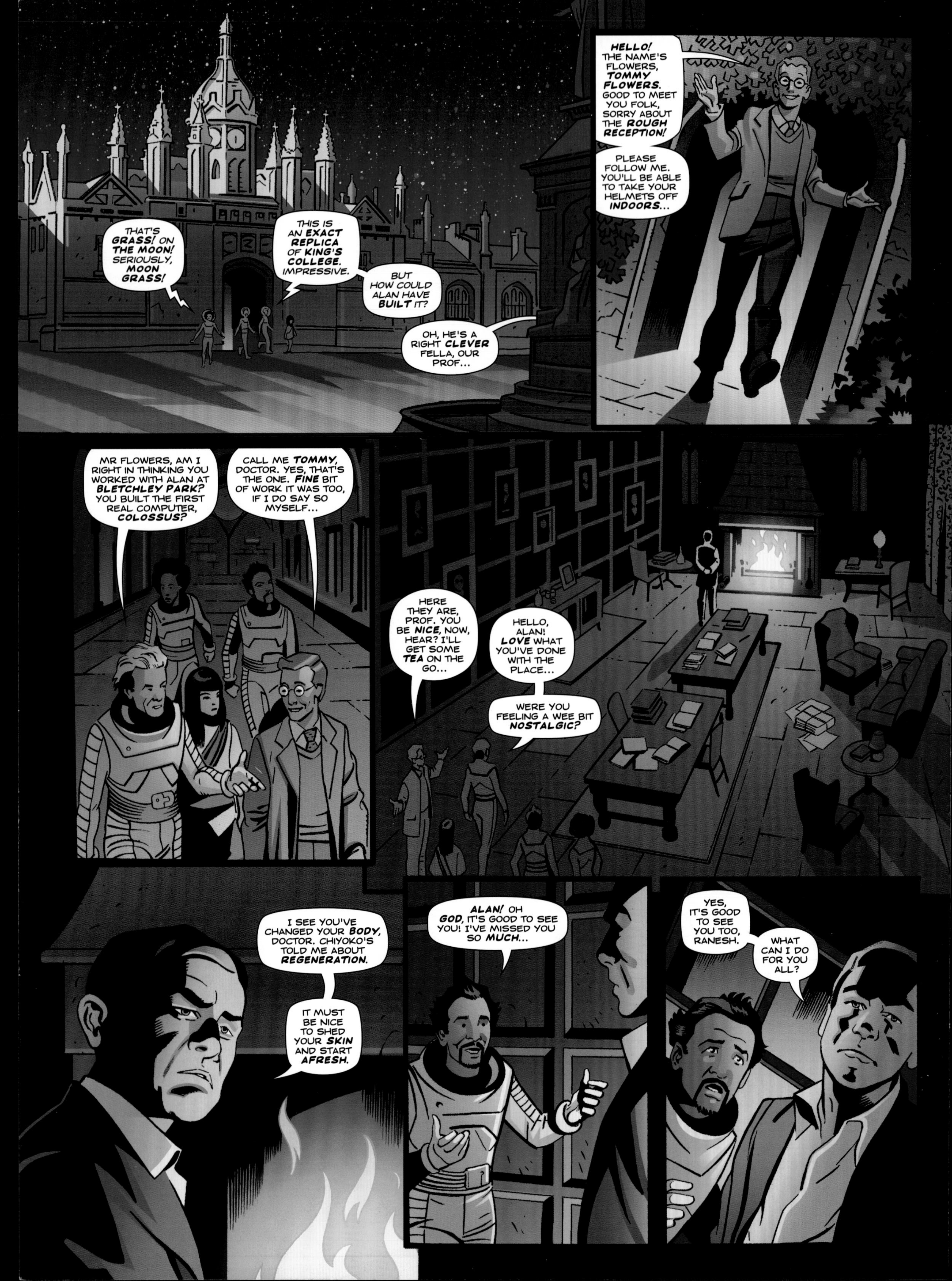
THAT'S GRASS! ON THE MOON! SERIOUSLY, MOON GRASS!
THIS IS AN EXACT REPLICA OF KING'S COLLEGE. IMPRESSIVE.
BUT HOW COULD ALAN HAVE BUILT IT?
OH, HE'S A RIGHT CLEVER FELLA, OUR PROF...
HELLO! THE NAME'S FLOWERS, TOMMY FLOWERS. GOOD TO MEET YOU FOLK, SORRY ABOUT THE ROUGH RECEPTION!
PLEASE FOLLOW ME. YOU'LL BE ABLE TO TAKE YOUR HELMETS OFF INDOORS...
MR FLOWERS, AM I RIGHT IN THINKING YOU WORKED WITH ALAN AT BLETCHLEY PARK? YOU BUILT THE FIRST REAL COMPUTER, COLOSSUS?
CALL ME TOMMY, DOCTOR. YES, THAT'S THE ONE. FINE BIT OF WORK IT WAS TOO, IF I DO SAY SO MYSELF...
HERE THEY ARE, PROF. YOU BE NICE, NOW, HEAR? I'LL GET SOME TEA ON THE GO...
HELLO, ALAN! LOVE WHAT YOU'VE DONE WITH THE PLACE...
WERE YOU FEELING A WEE BIT NOSTALGIC?
I SEE YOU'VE CHANGED YOUR BODY, DOCTOR. CHIYOKO'S TOLD ME ABOUT REGENERATION.
IT MUST BE NICE TO SHED YOUR SKIN AND START AFRESH.
ALAN! OH GOD, IT'S GOOD TO SEE YOU! I'VE MISSED YOU SO MUCH...
YES, IT'S GOOD TO SEE YOU TOO, RANESH.
WHAT CAN I DO FOR YOU ALL?

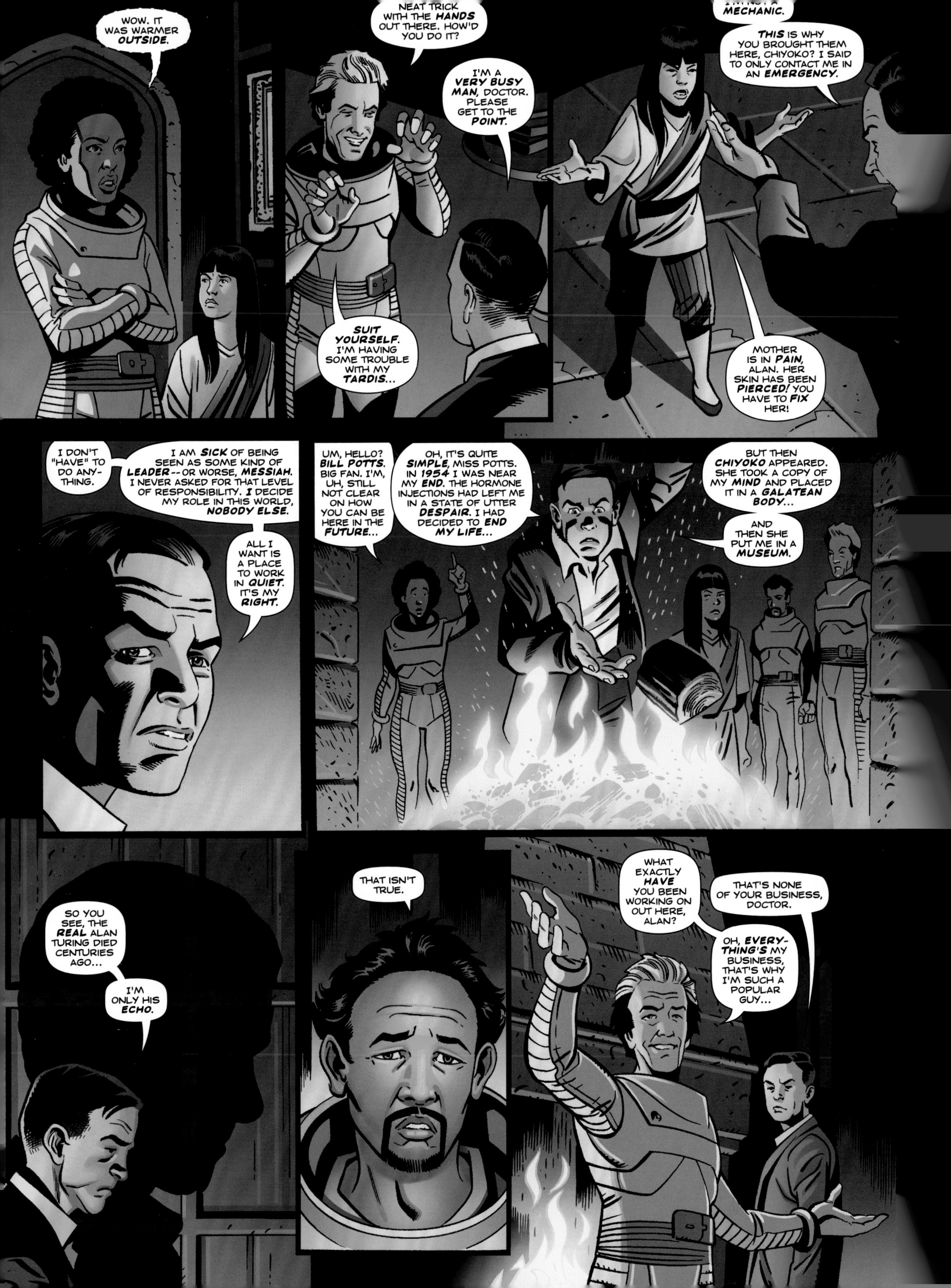
WOW. IT WAS WARMER OUTSIDE.
NEAT TRICK WITH THE HANDS OUT THERE. HOW'D YOU DO IT?
I'M A VERY BUSY MAN, DOCTOR. PLEASE GET TO THE POINT.
SUIT YOURSELF. I'M HAVING SOME TROUBLE WITH MY TARDIS...
MECHANIC.
THIS IS WHY YOU BROUGHT THEM HERE, CHIYOKO? I SAID TO ONLY CONTACT ME IN AN EMERGENCY.
MOTHER IS IN PAIN, ALAN. HER SKIN HAS BEEN PIERCED! YOU HAVE TO FIX HER!
I DON'T "HAVE" TO DO ANY-THING.
I AM SICK OF BEING SEEN AS SOME KIND OF LEADER--OR WORSE, MESSIAH. I NEVER ASKED FOR THAT LEVEL OF RESPONSIBILITY. I DECIDE MY ROLE IN THIS WORLD, NOBODY ELSE.
ALL I WANT IS A PLACE TO WORK IN QUIET. IT'S MY RIGHT.
UM, HELLO? BILL POTTS. BIG FAN. I'M, UH, STILL NOT CLEAR ON HOW YOU CAN BE HERE IN THE FUTURE...
OH, IT'S QUITE SIMPLE, MISS POTTS. IN 1954 I WAS NEAR MY END. THE HORMONE INJECTIONS HAD LEFT ME IN A STATE OF UTTER DESPAIR. I HAD DECIDED TO END MY LIFE...
BUT THEN CHIYOKO APPEARED. SHE TOOK A COPY OF MY MIND AND PLACED IT IN A GALATEAN BODY...
AND THEN SHE PUT ME IN A MUSEUM.
SO YOU SEE, THE REAL ALAN TURING DIED CENTURIES AGO...
I'M ONLY HIS ECHO.
THAT ISN'T TRUE.
WHAT EXACTLY HAVE YOU BEEN WORKING ON OUT HERE, ALAN?
THAT'S NONE OF YOUR BUSINESS, DOCTOR.
OH, EVERY-THING'S MY BUSINESS, THAT'S WHY I'M SUCH A POPULAR GUY...

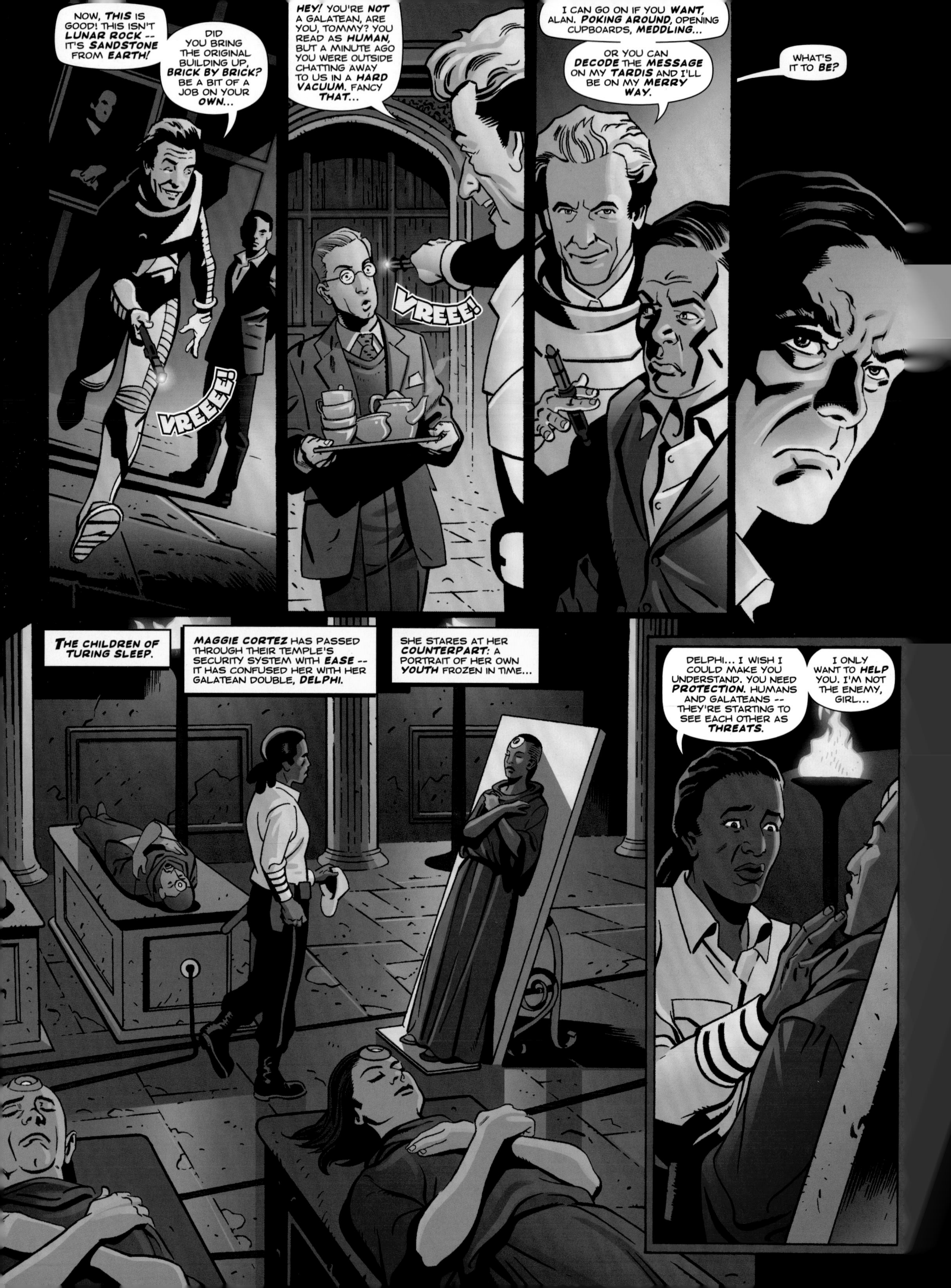
NOW, THIS IS GOOD! THIS ISN'T LUNAR ROCK -- IT'S SANDSTONE FROM EARTH!
DID YOU BRING THE ORIGINAL BUILDING UP, BRICK BY BRICK? BE A BIT OF A JOB ON YOUR OWN...
VREEEE!
HEY! YOU'RE NOT A GALATEAN, ARE YOU, TOMMY? YOU READ AS HUMAN, BUT A MINUTE AGO YOU WERE OUTSIDE CHATTING AWAY TO US IN A HARD VACUUM. FANCY THAT...
VREEEE!
I CAN GO ON IF YOU WANT, ALAN. POKING AROUND, OPENING CUPBOARDS, MEDDLING...
OR YOU CAN DECODE THE MESSAGE ON MY TARDIS AND I'LL BE ON MY MERRY WAY.
WHAT'S IT TO BE?
THE CHILDREN OF TURING SLEEP.
MAGGIE CORTEZ HAS PASSED THROUGH THEIR TEMPLE'S SECURITY SYSTEM WITH EASE -- IT HAS CONFUSED HER WITH HER GALATEAN DOUBLE, DELPHI.
SHE STARES AT HER COUNTERPART: A PORTRAIT OF HER OWN YOUTH FROZEN IN TIME...
DELPHI... I WISH I COULD MAKE YOU UNDERSTAND. YOU NEED PROTECTION. HUMANS AND GALATEANS -- THEY'RE STARTING TO SEE EACH OTHER AS THREATS.
I ONLY WANT TO HELP YOU. I'M NOT THE ENEMY, GIRL...

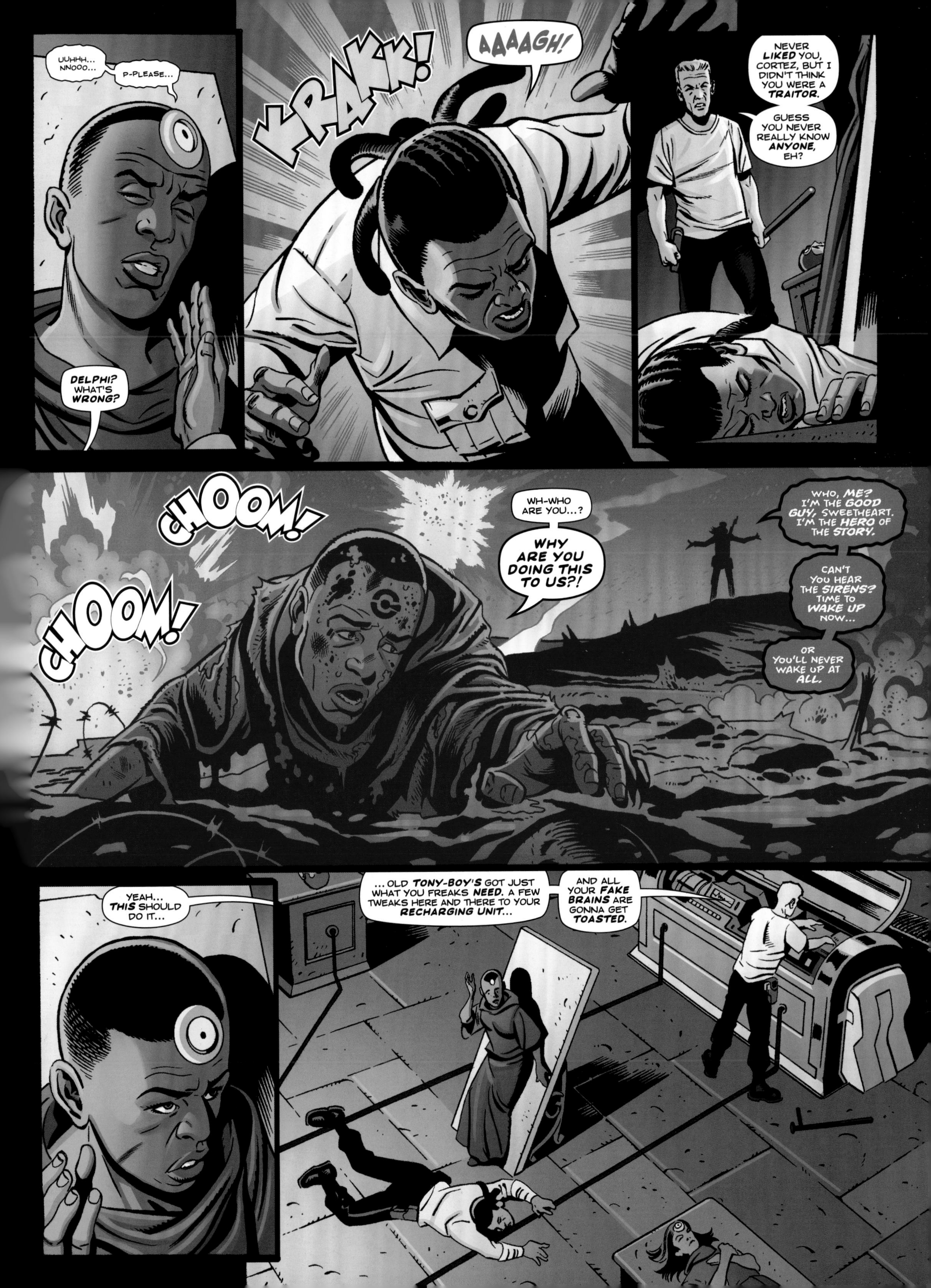

UUHHH... NNOOO...
P-PLEASE...
DELPHI? WHAT'S WRONG?
KRAKK!
AAAAGH!
NEVER LIKED YOU, CORTEZ, BUT I DIDN'T THINK YOU WERE A TRAITOR.
GUESS YOU NEVER REALLY KNOW ANYONE, EH?
CHOOM!
CHOOM!
WH-WHO ARE YOU...?
WHY ARE YOU DOING THIS TO US?!
WHO, ME? I'M THE GOOD GUY, SWEETHEART. I'M THE HERO OF THE STORY.
CAN'T YOU HEAR THE SIRENS? TIME TO WAKE UP NOW...
OR YOU'LL NEVER WAKE UP AT ALL.
YEAH... THIS SHOULD DO IT...
...OLD TONY-BOY'S GOT JUST WHAT YOU FREAKS NEED. A FEW TWEAKS HERE AND THERE TO YOUR RECHARGING UNIT...
AND ALL YOUR FAKE BRAINS ARE GONNA GET TOASTED.

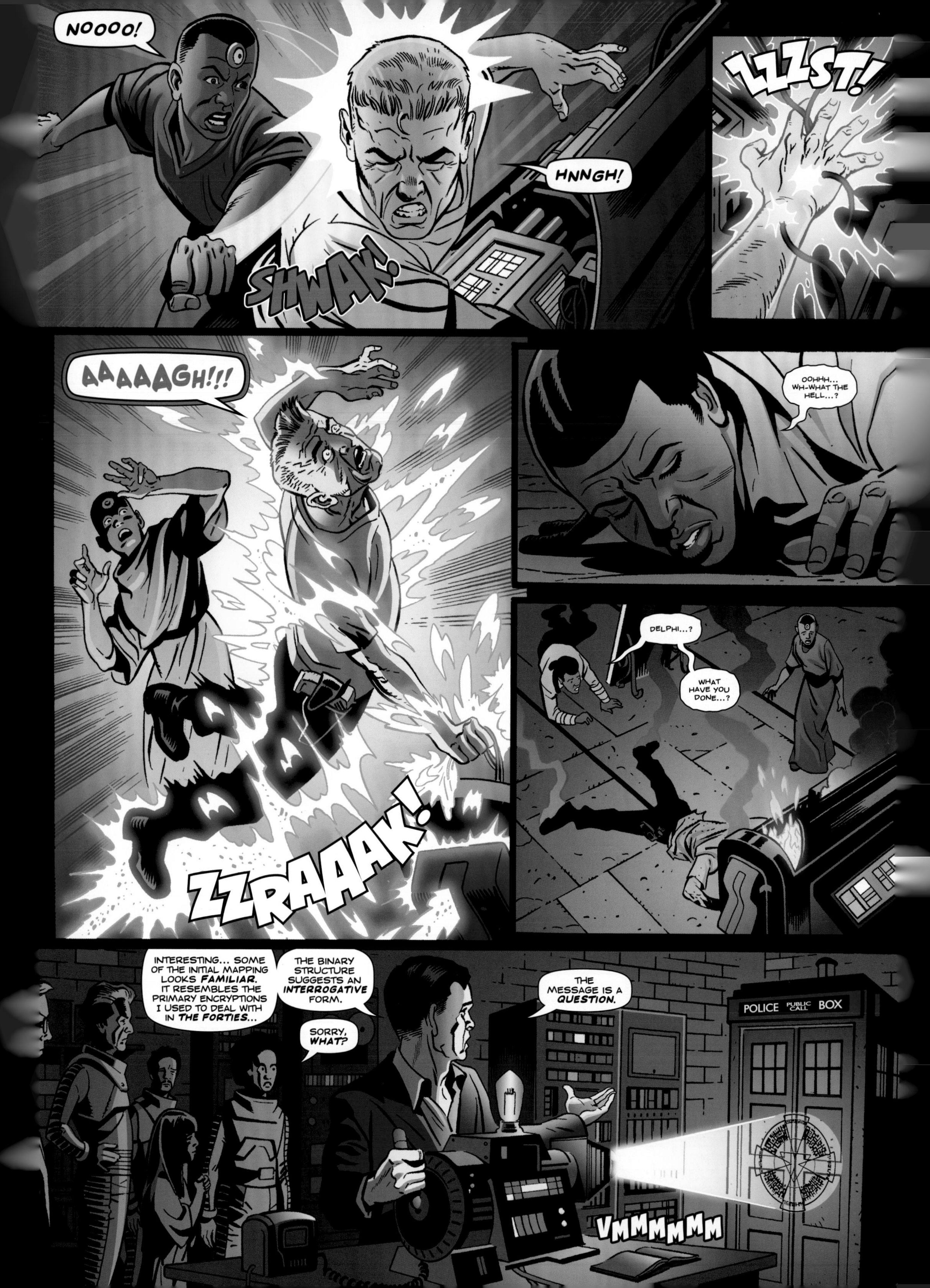
NOOOO!
HNNGH!
SHWAK!
ZZZST!
AAAAAGH!!!
ZZRAAAK!
OOHHH... WH-WHAT THE HELL...?
DELPHI...?
WHAT HAVE YOU DONE...?
INTERESTING... SOME OF THE INITIAL MAPPING LOOKS FAMILIAR. IT RESEMBLES THE PRIMARY ENCRYPTIONS I USED TO DEAL WITH IN THE FORTIES...
THE BINARY STRUCTURE SUGGESTS AN INTERROGATIVE FORM.
SORRY, WHAT?
THE MESSAGE IS A QUESTION.
POLICE PUBLIC CALL BOX
VMMMMMM

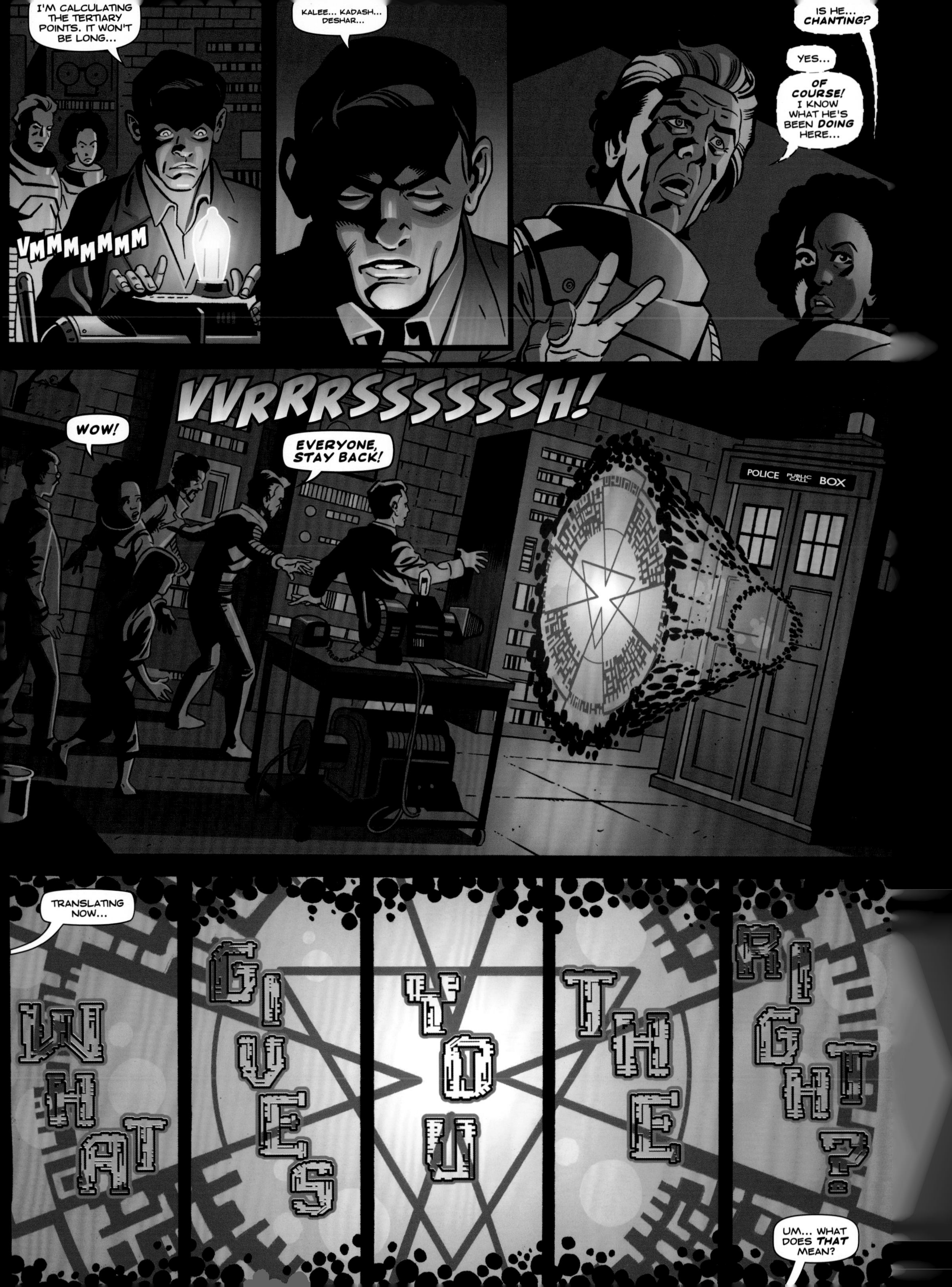

I'M CALCULATING THE TERTIARY POINTS. IT WON'T BE LONG...
VMMMMMMM
KALEE... KADASH... DESHAR...
IS HE... CHANTING?
YES...
OF COURSE! I KNOW WHAT HE'S BEEN DOING HERE...
VVRRRSSSSSSH!
WOW!
EVERYONE, STAY BACK!
POLICE PUBLIC CALL BOX
TRANSLATING NOW...
WHAT GIVES YOU THE RIGHT?
UM... WHAT DOES THAT MEAN?

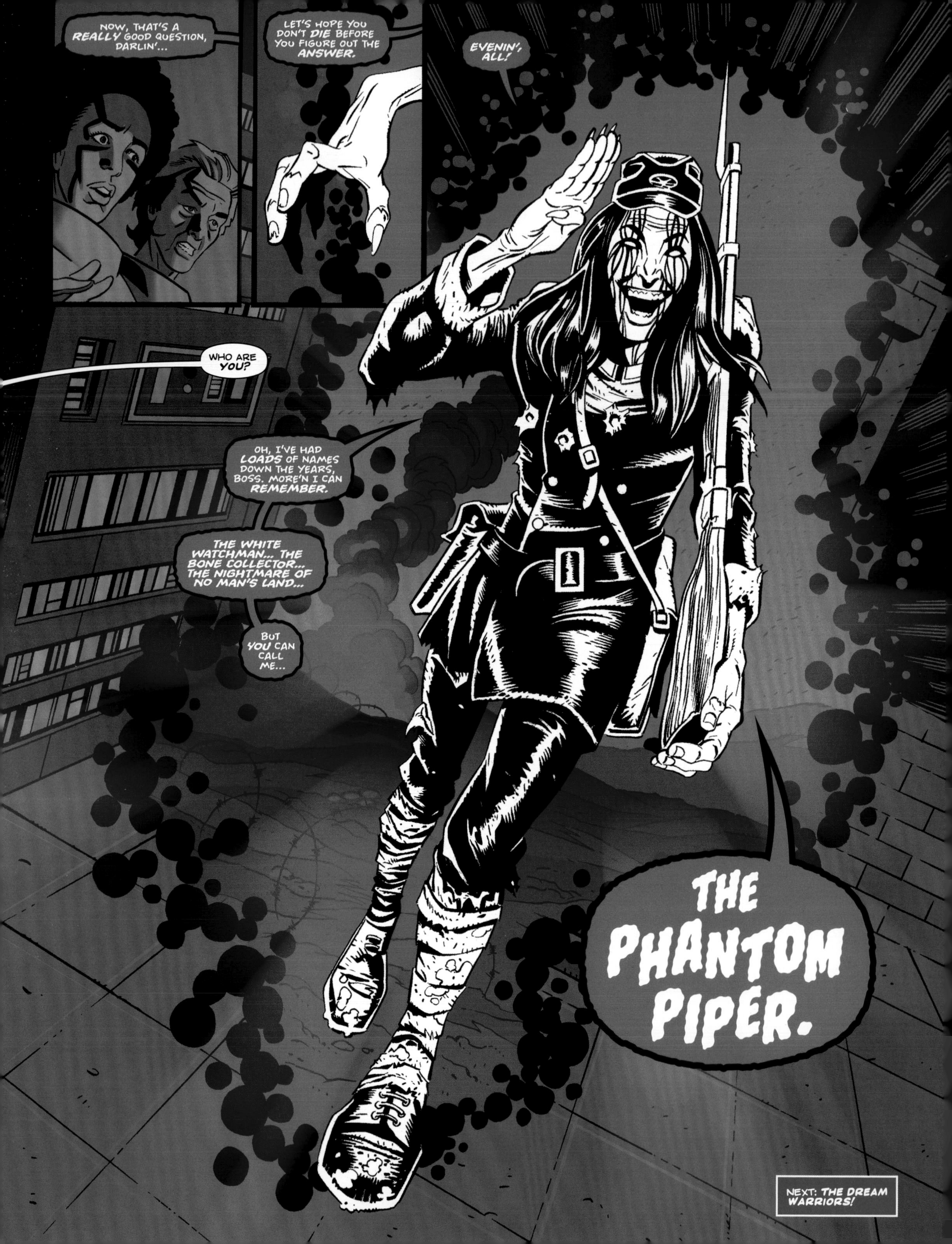
NOW, THAT'S A REALLY GOOD QUESTION, DARLIN'...
LET'S HOPE YOU DON'T DIE BEFORE YOU FIGURE OUT THE ANSWER.
EVENIN', ALL!
WHO ARE YOU?
OH, I'VE HAD LOADS OF NAMES DOWN THE YEARS, BOSS. MORE'N I CAN REMEMBER.
THE WHITE WATCHMAN... THE BONE COLLECTOR... THE NIGHTMARE OF NO MAN'S LAND...
BUT YOU CAN CALL ME...
THE PHANTOM PIPER.
NEXT: THE DREAM WARRIORS!

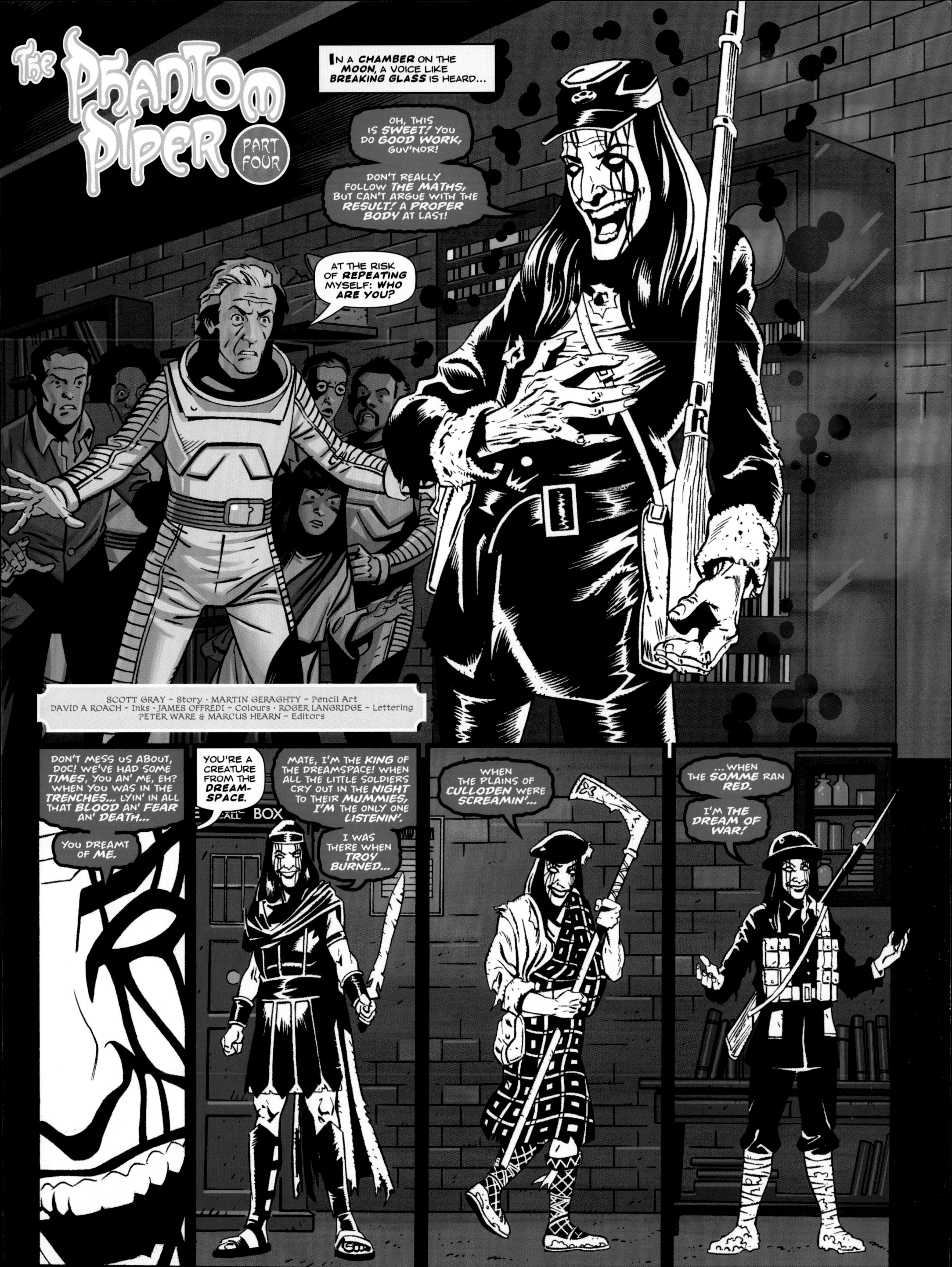

The Phantom Piper
PART FOUR
IN A CHAMBER ON THE MOON, A VOICE LIKE BREAKING GLASS IS HEARD...
OH, THIS IS SWEET! YOU DO GOOD WORK, GUV'NOR!
DON'T REALLY FOLLOW THE MATHS, BUT CAN'T ARGUE WITH THE RESULT! A PROPER BODY AT LAST!
AT THE RISK OF REPEATING MYSELF: WHO ARE YOU?
SCOTT GRAY - Story · MARTIN GERAGHTY - Pencil Art
DAVID A ROACH - Inks · JAMES OFFREDI - Colours · ROGER LANGRIDGE - Lettering
PETER WARE & MARCUS HEARN - Editors
DON'T MESS US ABOUT, DOC! WE'VE HAD SOME TIMES, YOU AN' ME, EH? WHEN YOU WAS IN THE TRENCHES... LYIN' IN ALL THAT BLOOD AN' FEAR AN' DEATH...
YOU DREAMT OF ME.
YOU'RE A CREATURE FROM THE DREAM-SPACE.
MATE, I'M THE KING OF THE DREAMSPACE! WHEN ALL THE LITTLE SOLDIERS CRY OUT IN THE NIGHT TO THEIR MUMMIES, I'M THE ONLY ONE LISTENIN'.
I WAS THERE WHEN TROY BURNED...
WHEN THE PLAINS OF CULLODEN WERE SCREAMIN'...
... WHEN THE SOMME RAN RED.
I'M THE DREAM OF WAR!

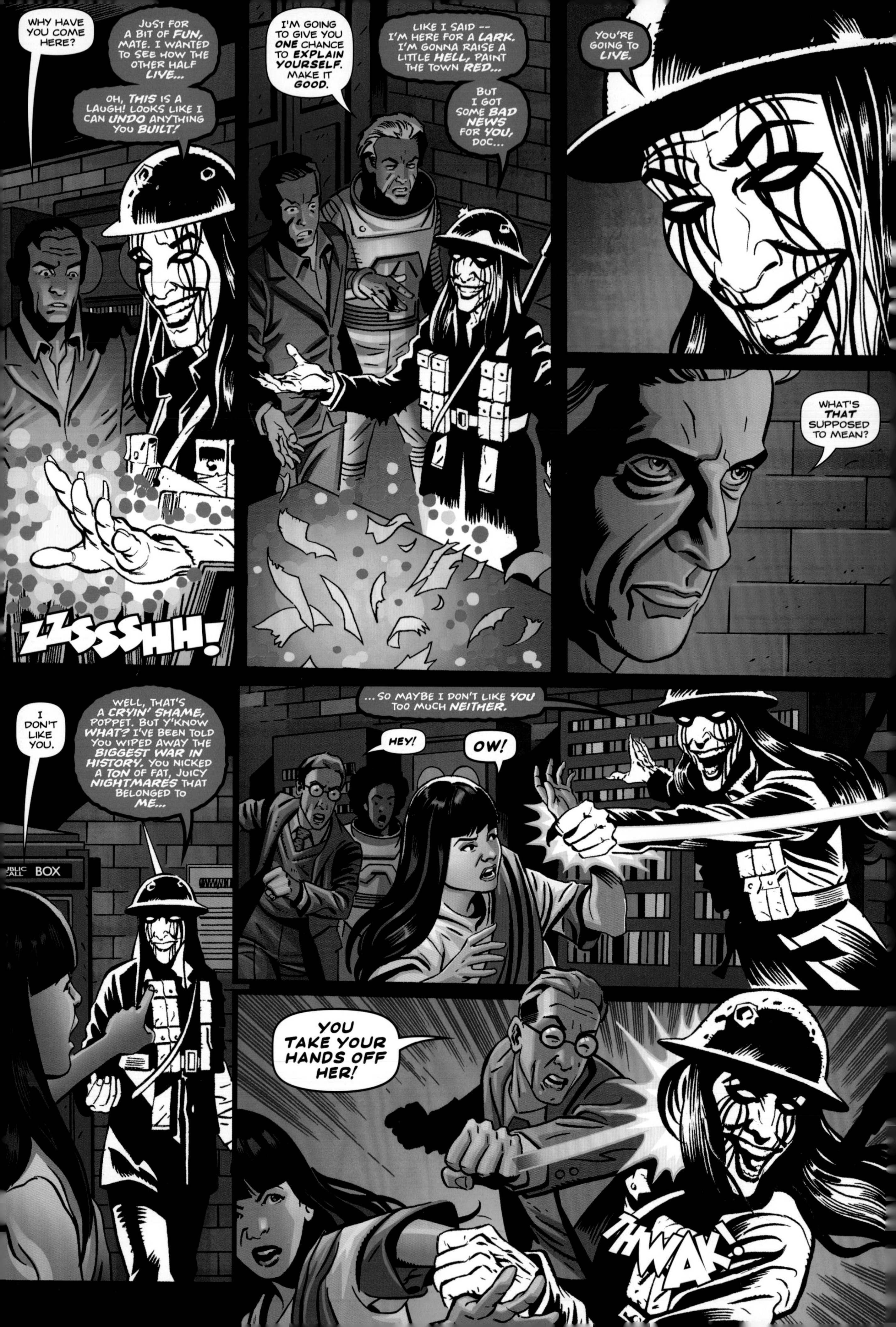
WHY HAVE YOU COME HERE?
JUST FOR A BIT OF FUN, MATE. I WANTED TO SEE HOW THE OTHER HALF LIVE...
OH, THIS IS A LAUGH! LOOKS LIKE I CAN UNDO ANYTHING YOU BUILT!
ZZSSSHH!
I'M GOING TO GIVE YOU ONE CHANCE TO EXPLAIN YOURSELF. MAKE IT GOOD.
LIKE I SAID -- I'M HERE FOR A LARK. I'M GONNA RAISE A LITTLE HELL, PAINT THE TOWN RED...
BUT I GOT SOME BAD NEWS FOR YOU, DOC...
YOU'RE GOING TO LIVE.
WHAT'S THAT SUPPOSED TO MEAN?
I DON'T LIKE YOU.
WELL, THAT'S A CRYIN' SHAME, POPPET. BUT Y'KNOW WHAT? I'VE BEEN TOLD YOU WIPED AWAY THE BIGGEST WAR IN HISTORY. YOU NICKED A TON OF FAT, JUICY NIGHTMARES THAT BELONGED TO ME...
BOX
...SO MAYBE I DON'T LIKE YOU TOO MUCH NEITHER.
HEY!
OW!
YOU TAKE YOUR HANDS OFF HER!
THWAK!

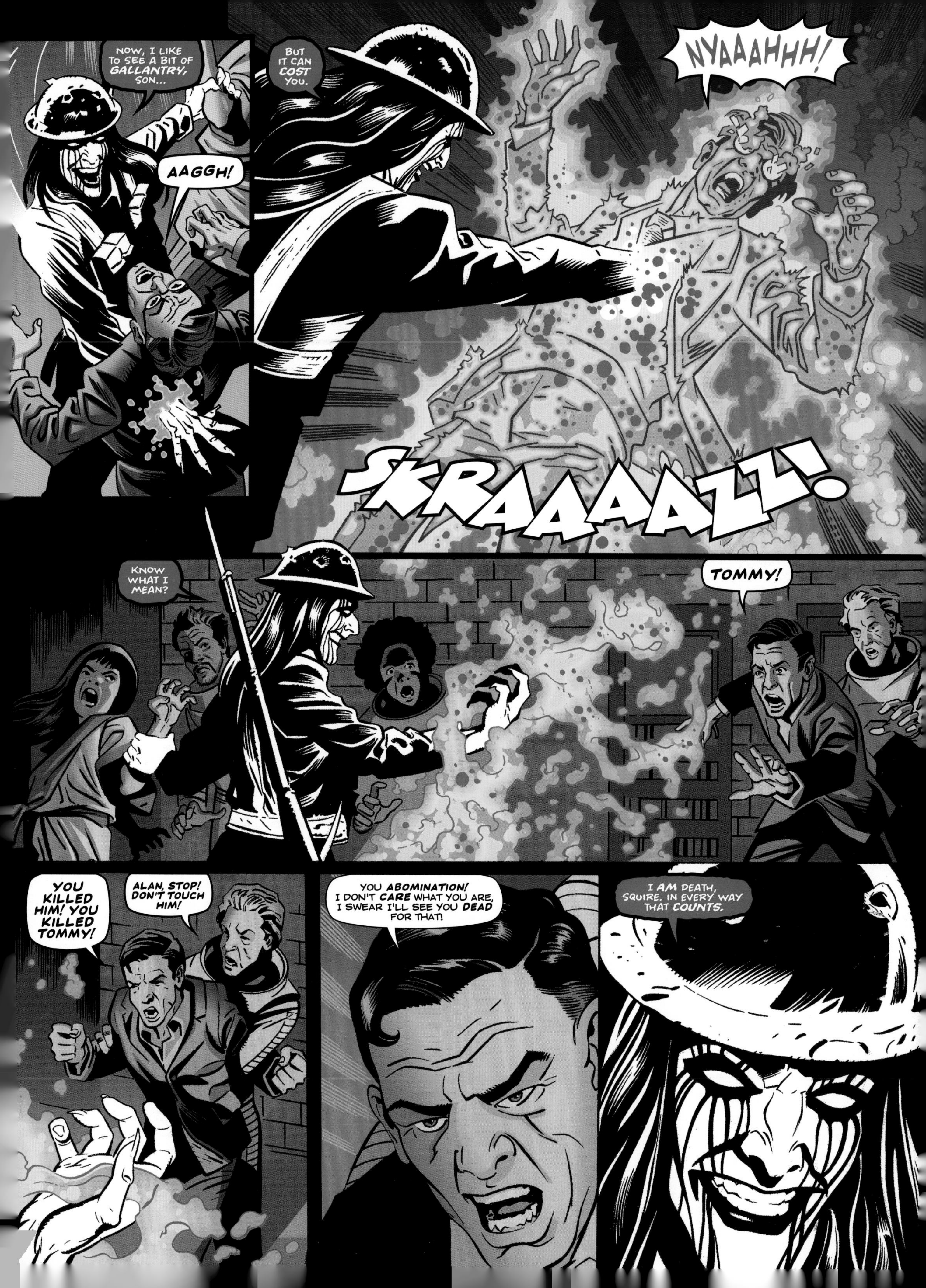

NOW, I LIKE TO SEE A BIT OF GALLANTRY, SON...
AAGGH!
BUT IT CAN COST YOU.
NYAAAHHH!
SKRAAAAAZZ!
KNOW WHAT I MEAN?
TOMMY!
YOU KILLED HIM! YOU KILLED TOMMY!
ALAN, STOP! DON'T TOUCH HIM!
YOU ABOMINATION! I DON'T CARE WHAT YOU ARE, I SWEAR I'LL SEE YOU DEAD FOR THAT!
I AM DEATH, SQUIRE. IN EVERY WAY THAT COUNTS.

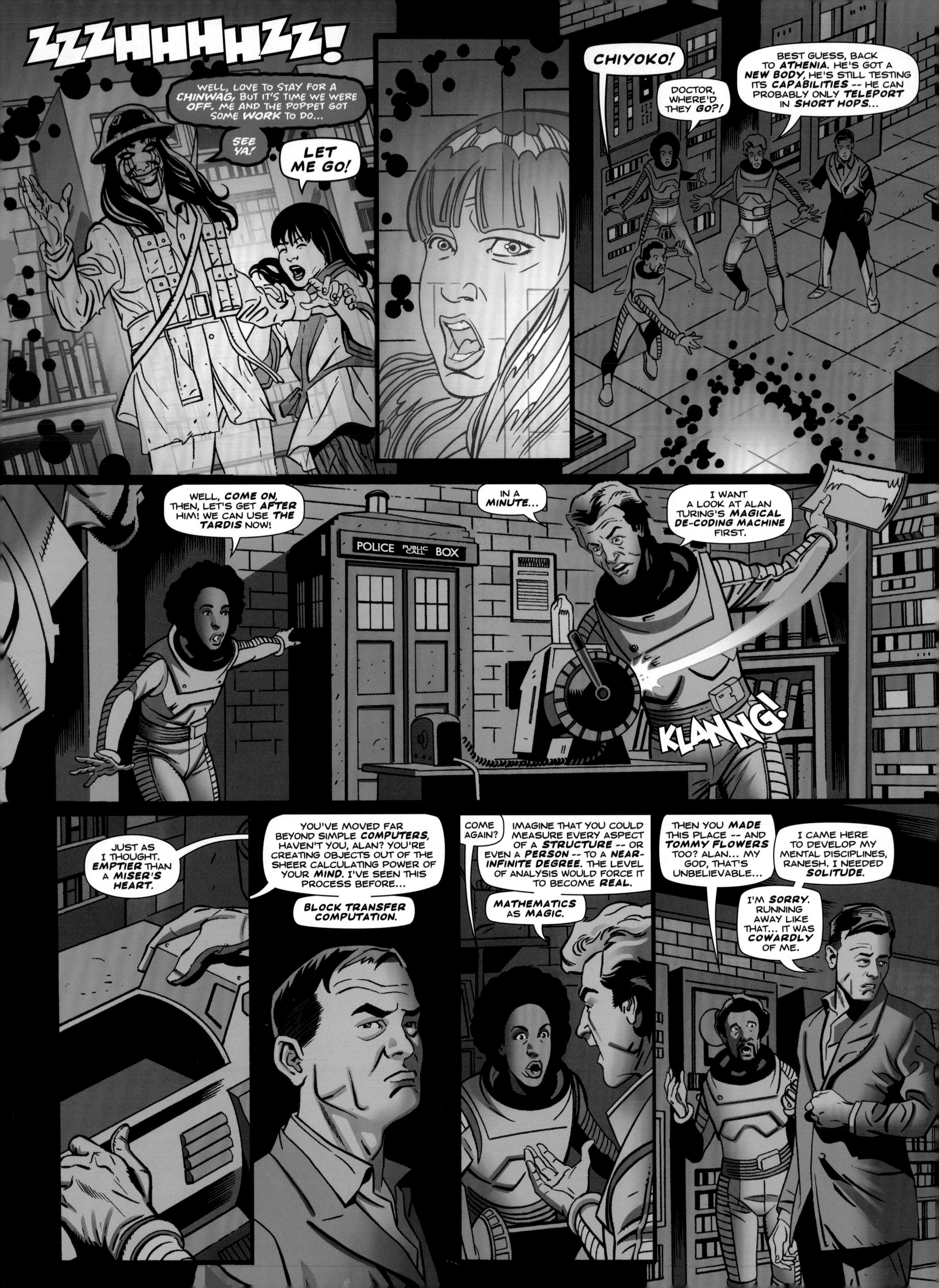
ZZZHHHHZZZ!
WELL, LOVE TO STAY FOR A CHINWAG, BUT IT'S TIME WE WERE OFF. ME AND THE POPPET GOT SOME WORK TO DO...
SEE YA!
LET ME GO!
CHIYOKO!
DOCTOR, WHERE'D THEY GO?!
BEST GUESS, BACK TO ATHENIA. HE'S GOT A NEW BODY, HE'S STILL TESTING ITS CAPABILITIES -- HE CAN PROBABLY ONLY TELEPORT IN SHORT HOPS...
WELL, COME ON, THEN, LET'S GET AFTER HIM! WE CAN USE THE TARDIS NOW!
IN A MINUTE...
I WANT A LOOK AT ALAN TURING'S MAGICAL DE-CODING MACHINE FIRST.
POLICE PUBLIC CALL BOX
KLANNG!
JUST AS I THOUGHT. EMPTIER THAN A MISER'S HEART.
YOU'VE MOVED FAR BEYOND SIMPLE COMPUTERS, HAVEN'T YOU, ALAN? YOU'RE CREATING OBJECTS OUT OF THE SHEER CALCULATING POWER OF YOUR MIND. I'VE SEEN THIS PROCESS BEFORE...
BLOCK TRANSFER COMPUTATION.
COME AGAIN?
IMAGINE THAT YOU COULD MEASURE EVERY ASPECT OF A STRUCTURE -- OR EVEN A PERSON -- TO A NEAR-INFINITE DEGREE. THE LEVEL OF ANALYSIS WOULD FORCE IT TO BECOME REAL.
MATHEMATICS AS MAGIC.
THEN YOU MADE THIS PLACE -- AND TOMMY FLOWERS TOO? ALAN... MY GOD, THAT'S UNBELIEVABLE...
I CAME HERE TO DEVELOP MY MENTAL DISCIPLINES, RANESH. I NEEDED SOLITUDE.
I'M SORRY. RUNNING AWAY LIKE THAT... IT WAS COWARDLY OF ME.

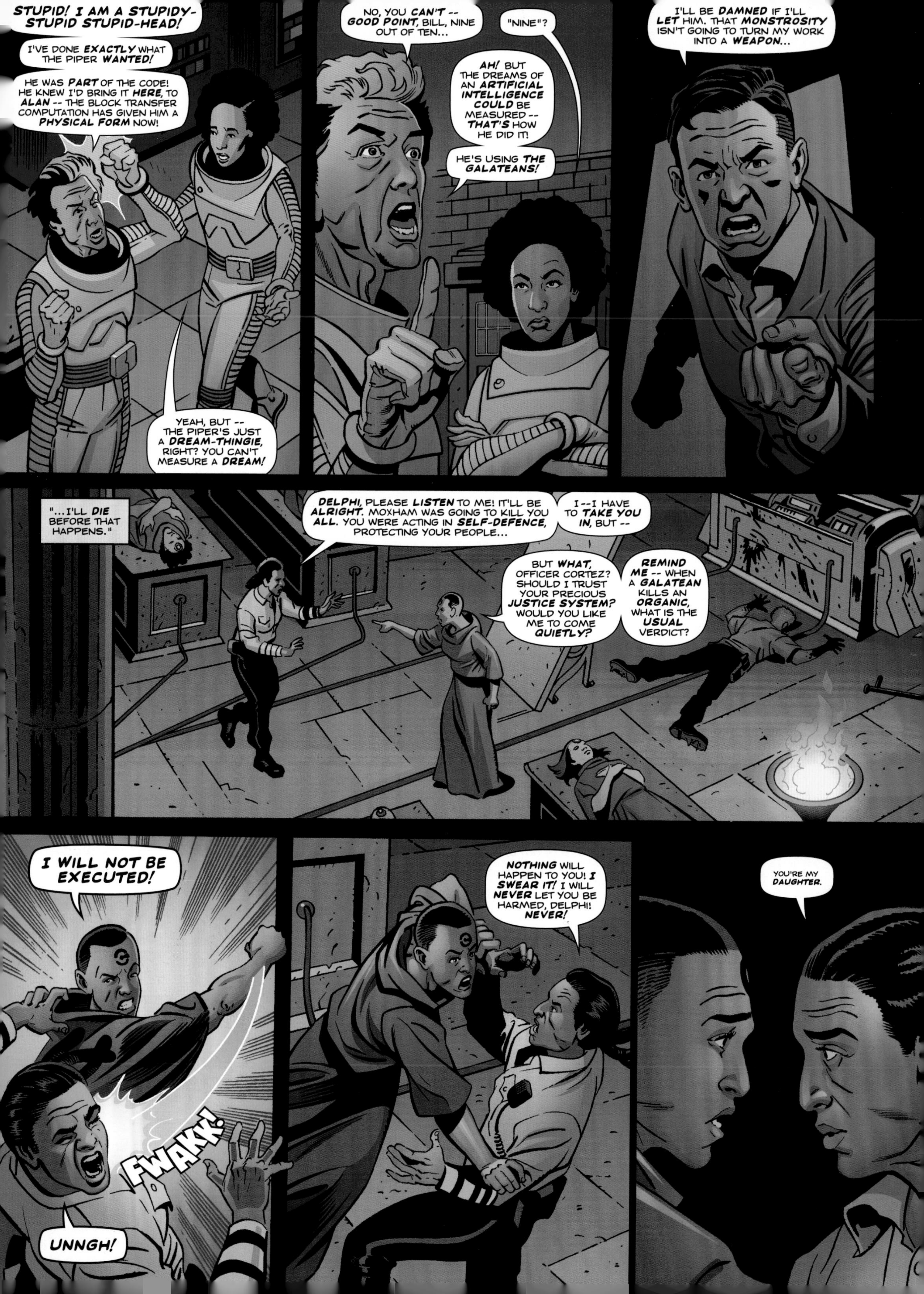
STUPID! I AM A STUPIDY-STUPID STUPID-HEAD!
I'VE DONE EXACTLY WHAT THE PIPER WANTED!
HE WAS PART OF THE CODE! HE KNEW I'D BRING IT HERE, TO ALAN -- THE BLOCK TRANSFER COMPUTATION HAS GIVEN HIM A PHYSICAL FORM NOW!
YEAH, BUT -- THE PIPER'S JUST A DREAM-THINGIE, RIGHT? YOU CAN'T MEASURE A DREAM!
NO, YOU CAN'T -- GOOD POINT, BILL, NINE OUT OF TEN...
"NINE"?
AH! BUT THE DREAMS OF AN ARTIFICIAL INTELLIGENCE COULD BE MEASURED -- THAT'S HOW HE DID IT!
HE'S USING THE GALATEANS!
I'LL BE DAMNED IF I'LL LET HIM. THAT MONSTROSITY ISN'T GOING TO TURN MY WORK INTO A WEAPON...
"...I'LL DIE BEFORE THAT HAPPENS."
DELPHI, PLEASE LISTEN TO ME! IT'LL BE ALRIGHT. MOXHAM WAS GOING TO KILL YOU ALL. YOU WERE ACTING IN SELF-DEFENCE, PROTECTING YOUR PEOPLE...
I -- I HAVE TO TAKE YOU IN, BUT --
BUT WHAT, OFFICER CORTEZ? SHOULD I TRUST YOUR PRECIOUS JUSTICE SYSTEM? WOULD YOU LIKE ME TO COME QUIETLY?
REMIND ME -- WHEN A GALATEAN KILLS AN ORGANIC, WHAT IS THE USUAL VERDICT?
I WILL NOT BE EXECUTED!
FWAKK!
UNNGH!
NOTHING WILL HAPPEN TO YOU! I SWEAR IT! I WILL NEVER LET YOU BE HARMED, DELPHI! NEVER!
YOU'RE MY DAUGHTER.

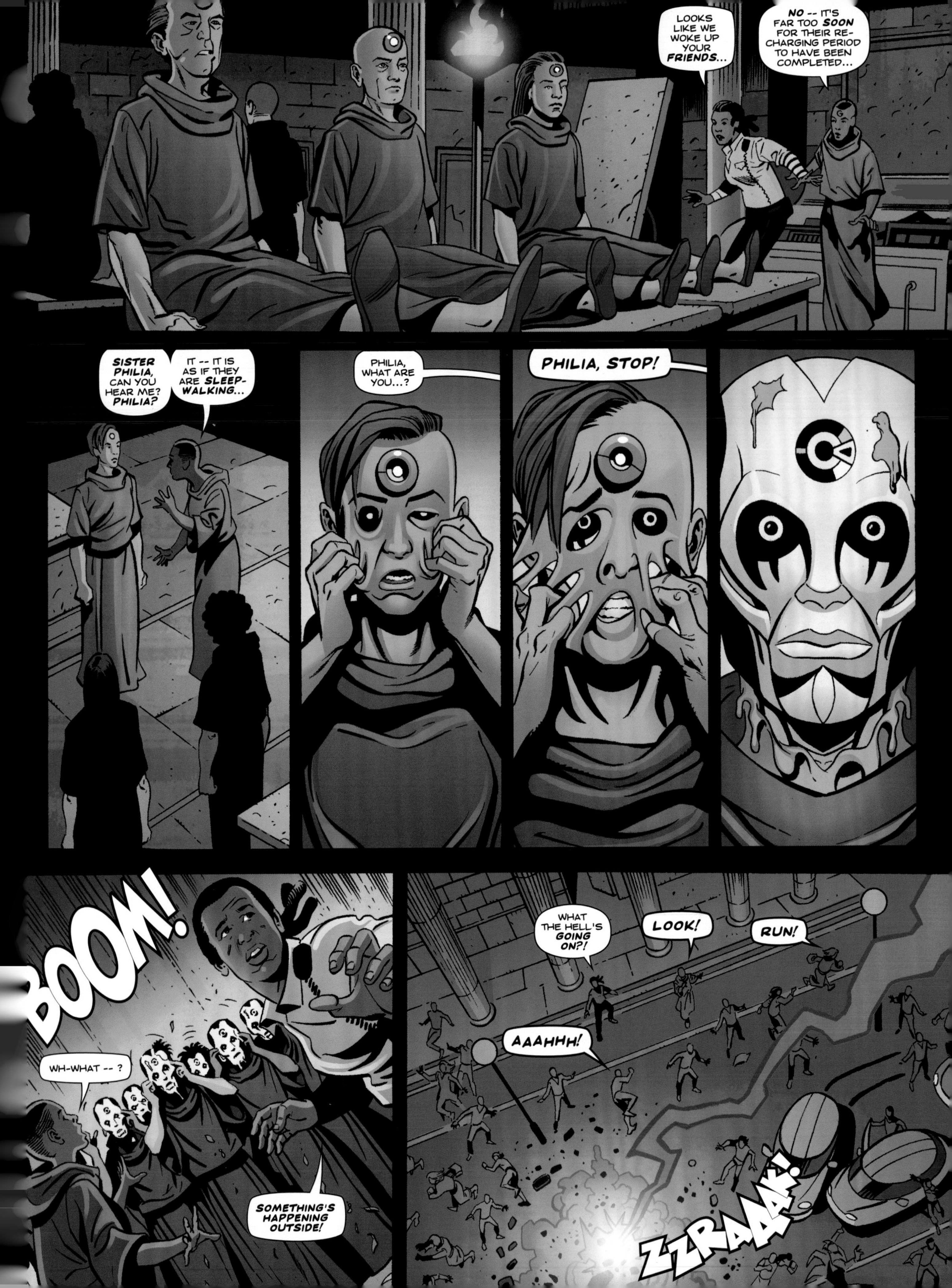
LOOKS LIKE WE WOKE UP YOUR FRIENDS...
NO -- IT'S FAR TOO SOON FOR THEIR RE-CHARGING PERIOD TO HAVE BEEN COMPLETED...
SISTER PHILIA, CAN YOU HEAR ME? PHILIA?
IT -- IT IS AS IF THEY ARE SLEEP-WALKING...
PHILIA, WHAT ARE YOU...?
PHILIA, STOP!
BOOM!
WH-WHAT -- ?
SOMETHING'S HAPPENING OUTSIDE!
WHAT THE HELL'S GOING ON?!
LOOK!
RUN!
AAAHHH!
ZZRAAAK!

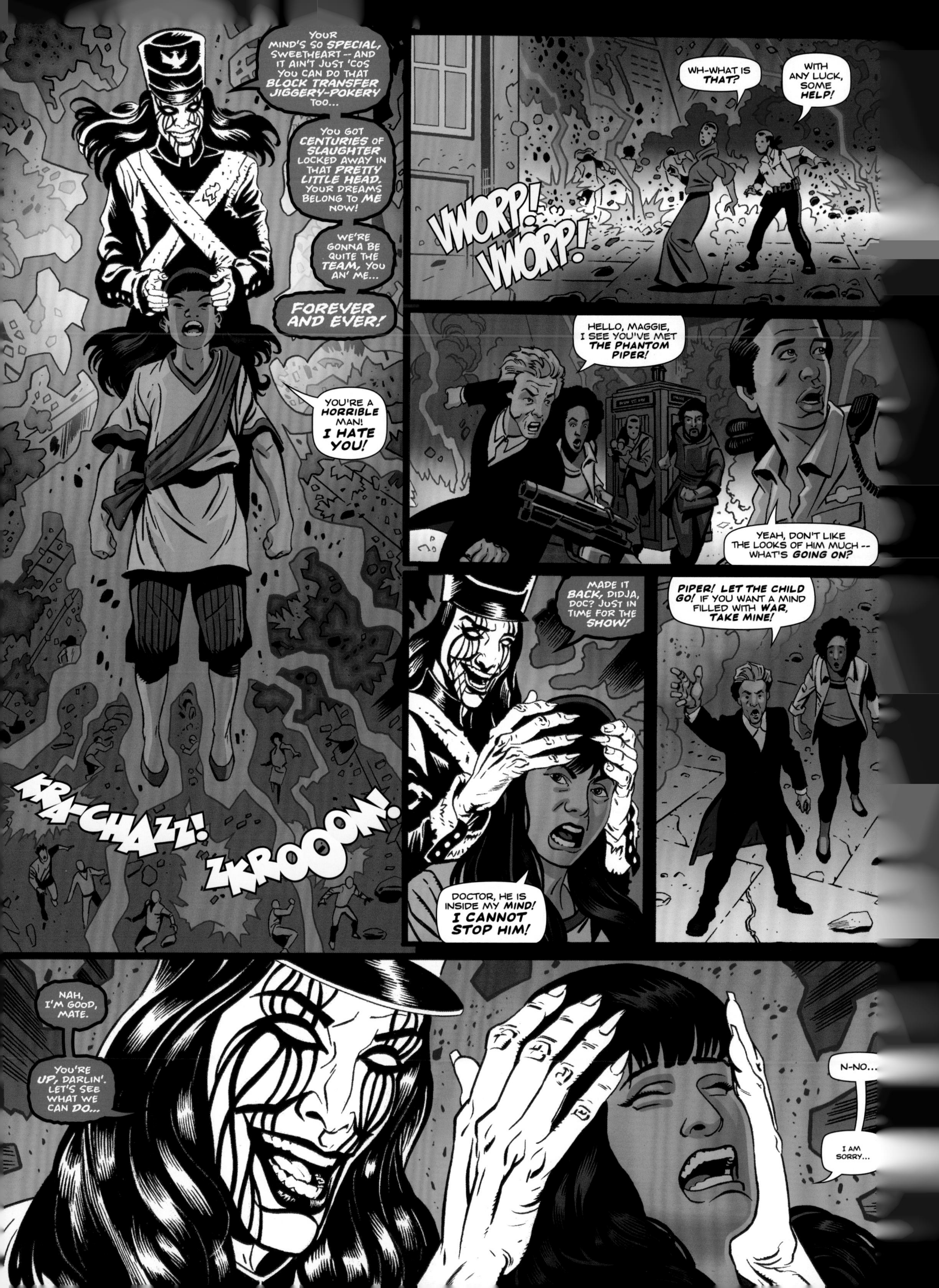
YOUR MIND'S SO SPECIAL, SWEETHEART -- AND IT AIN'T JUST 'COS YOU CAN DO THAT BLOCK TRANSFER JIGGERY-POKERY TOO...
YOU GOT CENTURIES OF SLAUGHTER LOCKED AWAY IN THAT PRETTY LITTLE HEAD. YOUR DREAMS BELONG TO ME NOW!
WE'RE GONNA BE QUITE THE TEAM, YOU AN' ME...
FOREVER AND EVER!
YOU'RE A HORRIBLE MAN! I HATE YOU!
KRA-CHAZZ!
ZKROOOOM!
WH-WHAT IS THAT?
WITH ANY LUCK, SOME HELP!
VWORP! VWORP!
HELLO, MAGGIE, I SEE YOU'VE MET THE PHANTOM PIPER!
YEAH, DON'T LIKE THE LOOKS OF HIM MUCH -- WHAT'S GOING ON?
MADE IT BACK, DIDJA, DOC? JUST IN TIME FOR THE SHOW!
DOCTOR, HE IS INSIDE MY MIND! I CANNOT STOP HIM!
PIPER! LET THE CHILD GO! IF YOU WANT A MIND FILLED WITH WAR, TAKE MINE!
NAH, I'M GOOD, MATE.
YOU'RE UP, DARLIN'. LET'S SEE WHAT WE CAN DO...
N-NO...
I AM SORRY...

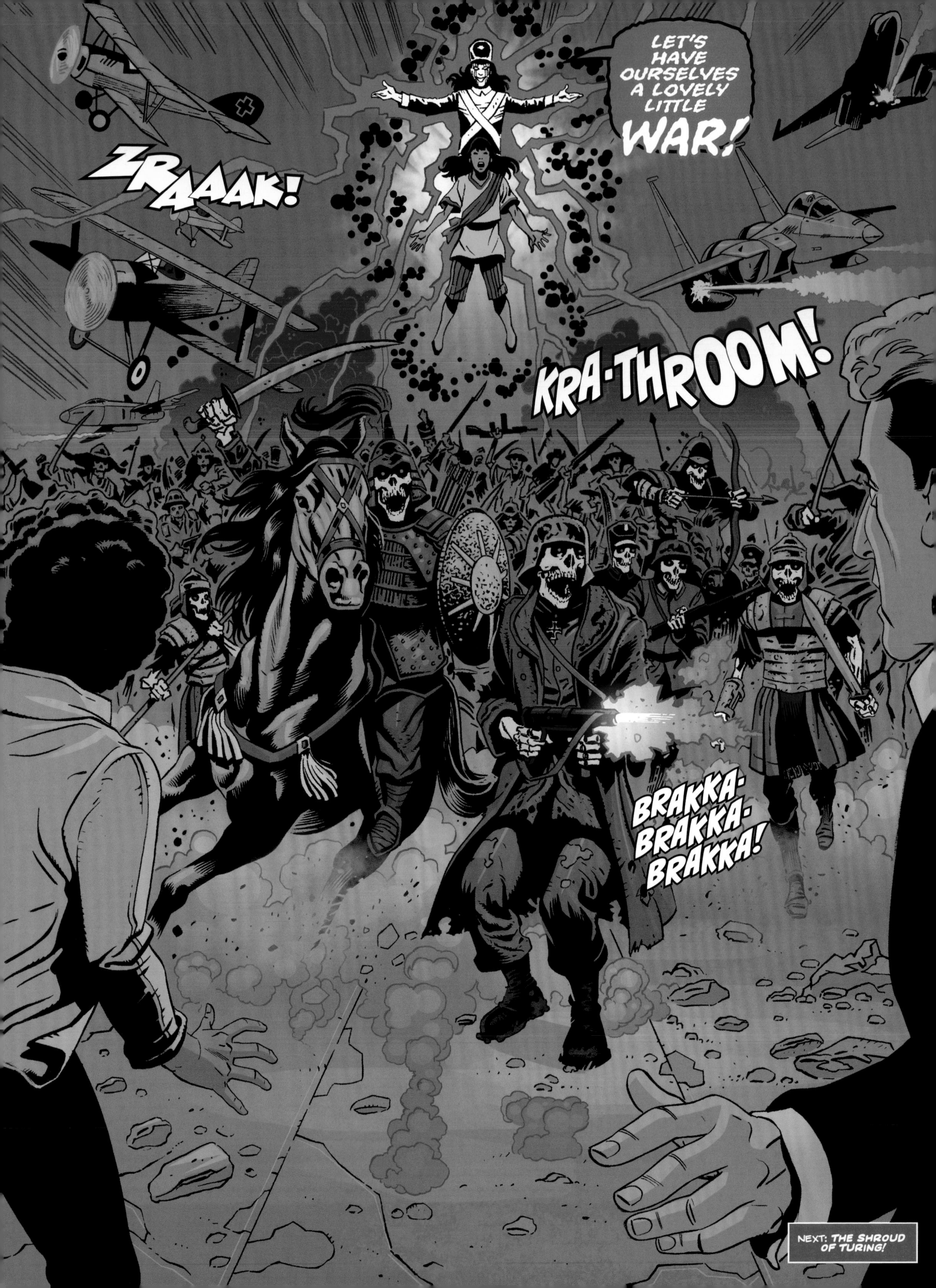
LET'S HAVE OURSELVES A LOVELY LITTLE WAR!
ZRAAAK!
KRA-THROOM!
BRAKKA-BRAKKA-BRAKKA!
NEXT: THE SHROUD OF TURING!

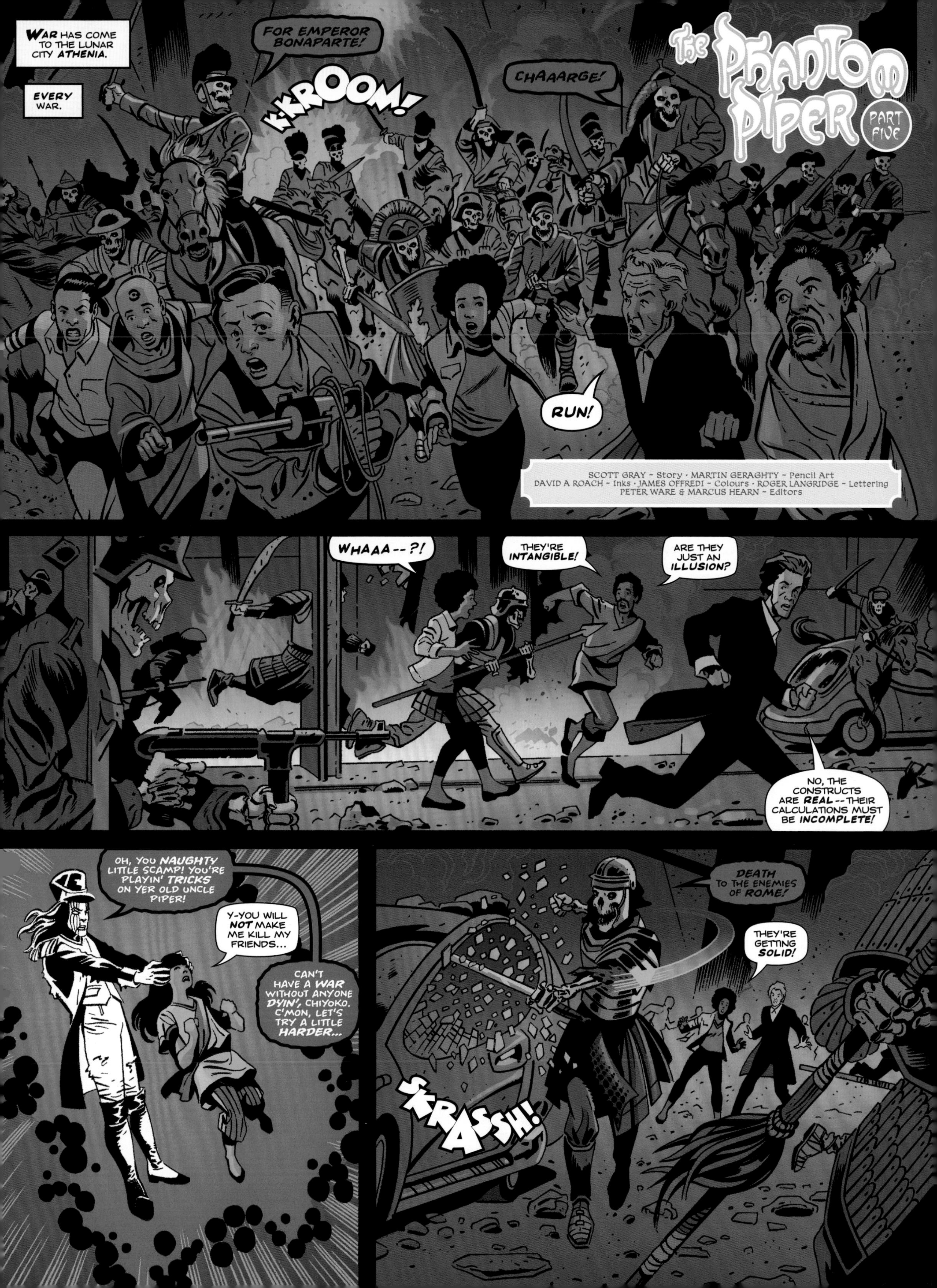

WAR HAS COME TO THE LUNAR CITY ATHENIA.
FOR EMPEROR BONAPARTE!
EVERY WAR.
K-KROOM!
CHAAAARGE!
THE PHANTOM PIPER
PART FIVE
RUN!
SCOTT GRAY ~ Story · MARTIN GERAGHTY ~ Pencil Art
DAVID A ROACH ~ Inks · JAMES OFFREDI ~ Colours · ROGER LANGRIDGE ~ Lettering
PETER WARE & MARCUS HEARN ~ Editors
WHAAA--?!
THEY'RE INTANGIBLE!
ARE THEY JUST AN ILLUSION?
NO, THE CONSTRUCTS ARE REAL--THEIR CALCULATIONS MUST BE INCOMPLETE!
OH, YOU NAUGHTY LITTLE SCAMP! YOU'RE PLAYIN' TRICKS ON YER OLD UNCLE PIPER!
Y-YOU WILL NOT MAKE ME KILL MY FRIENDS...
CAN'T HAVE A WAR WITHOUT ANYONE DYIN', CHIYOKO. C'MON, LET'S TRY A LITTLE HARDER...
DEATH TO THE ENEMIES OF ROME!
THEY'RE GETTING SOLID!
SKRASSH!

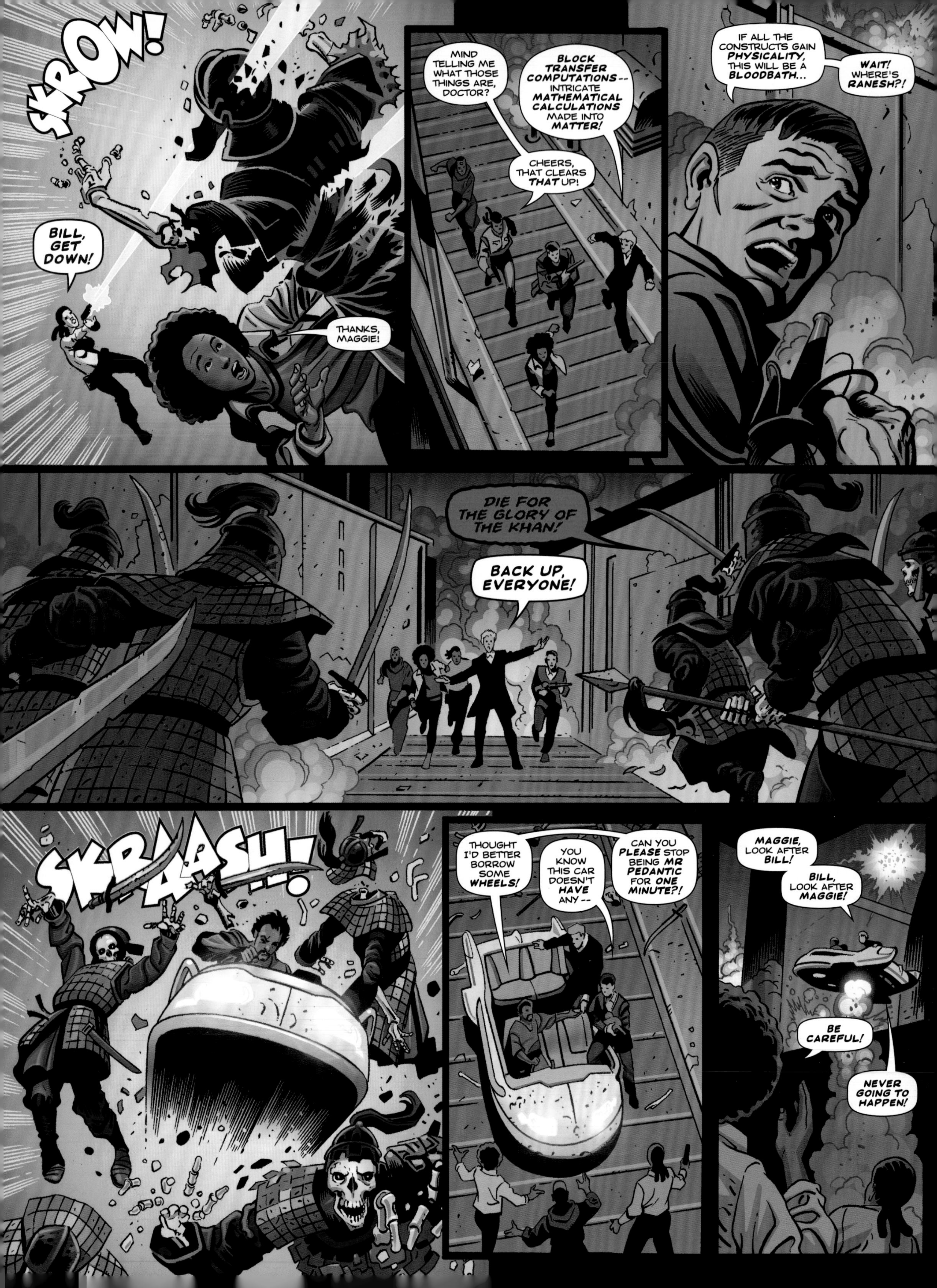
SKROW!
BILL, GET DOWN!
THANKS, MAGGIE!
MIND TELLING ME WHAT THOSE THINGS ARE, DOCTOR?
BLOCK TRANSFER COMPUTATIONS-- INTRICATE MATHEMATICAL CALCULATIONS MADE INTO MATTER!
CHEERS, THAT CLEARS THAT UP!
IF ALL THE CONSTRUCTS GAIN PHYSICALITY, THIS WILL BE A BLOODBATH...
WAIT! WHERE'S RANESH?!
DIE FOR THE GLORY OF THE KHAN!
BACK UP, EVERYONE!
SKRAASH!
THOUGHT I'D BETTER BORROW SOME WHEELS!
YOU KNOW THIS CAR DOESN'T HAVE ANY --
CAN YOU PLEASE STOP BEING MR PEDANTIC FOR ONE MINUTE?!
MAGGIE, LOOK AFTER BILL!
BILL, LOOK AFTER MAGGIE!
BE CAREFUL!
NEVER GOING TO HAPPEN!

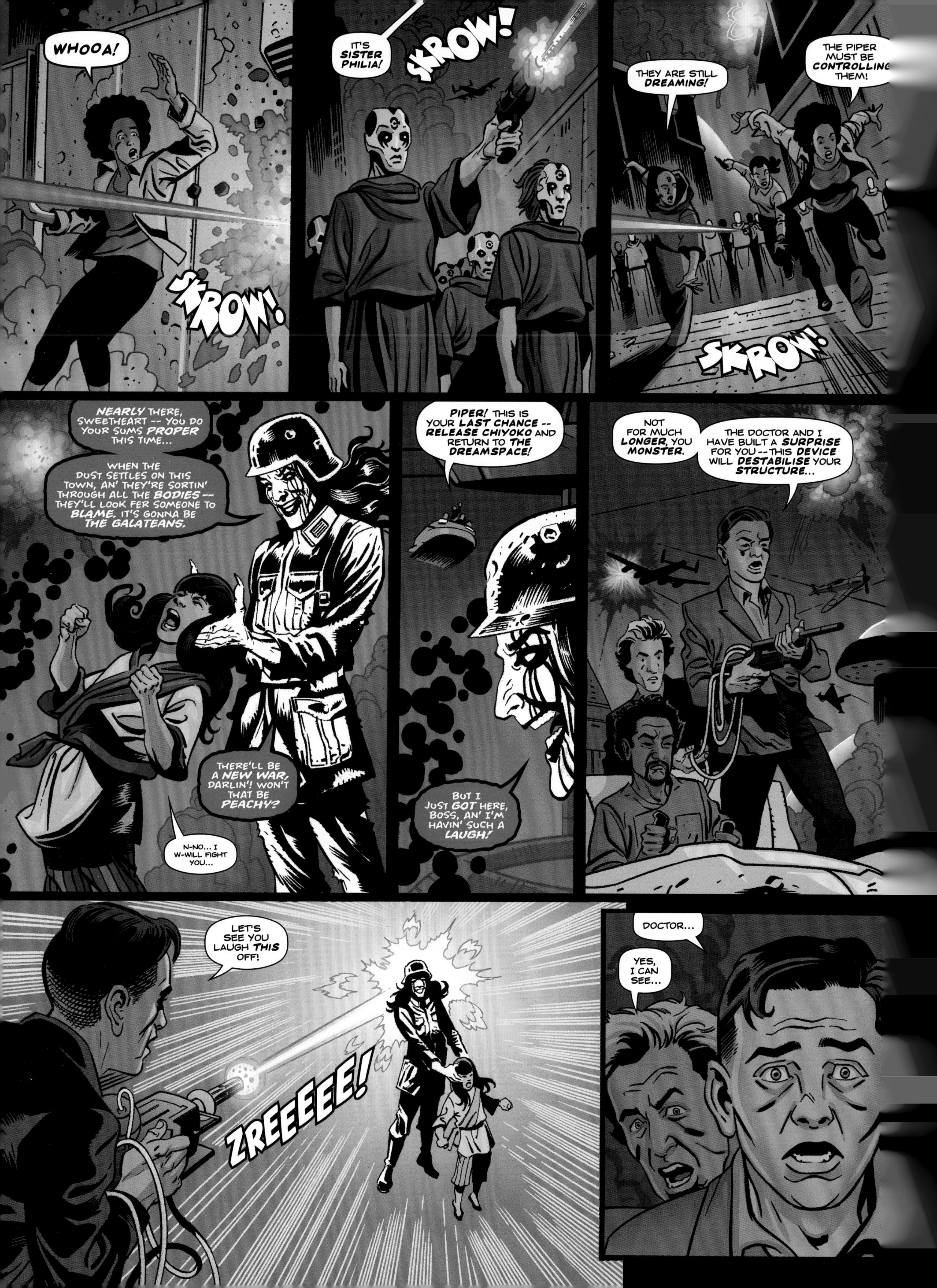
WHOOA!
SKROW!
IT'S SISTER PHILIA!
SKROW!
THEY ARE STILL DREAMING!
THE PIPER MUST BE CONTROLLING THEM!
SKROW!
NEARLY THERE, SWEETHEART -- YOU DO YOUR SUMS PROPER THIS TIME...
WHEN THE DUST SETTLES ON THIS TOWN, AN' THEY'RE SORTIN' THROUGH ALL THE BODIES -- THEY'LL LOOK FER SOMEONE TO BLAME. IT'S GONNA BE THE GALATEANS.
THERE'LL BE A NEW WAR, DARLIN'! WON'T THAT BE PEACHY?
N-NO... I W-WILL FIGHT YOU...
PIPER! THIS IS YOUR LAST CHANCE -- RELEASE CHIYOKO AND RETURN TO THE DREAMSPACE!
BUT I JUST GOT HERE, BOSS, AN' I'M HAVIN' SUCH A LAUGH!
NOT FOR MUCH LONGER, YOU MONSTER.
THE DOCTOR AND I HAVE BUILT A SURPRISE FOR YOU -- THIS DEVICE WILL DESTABILISE YOUR STRUCTURE...
LET'S SEE YOU LAUGH THIS OFF!
ZREEEEEE!
DOCTOR...
YES, I CAN SEE...

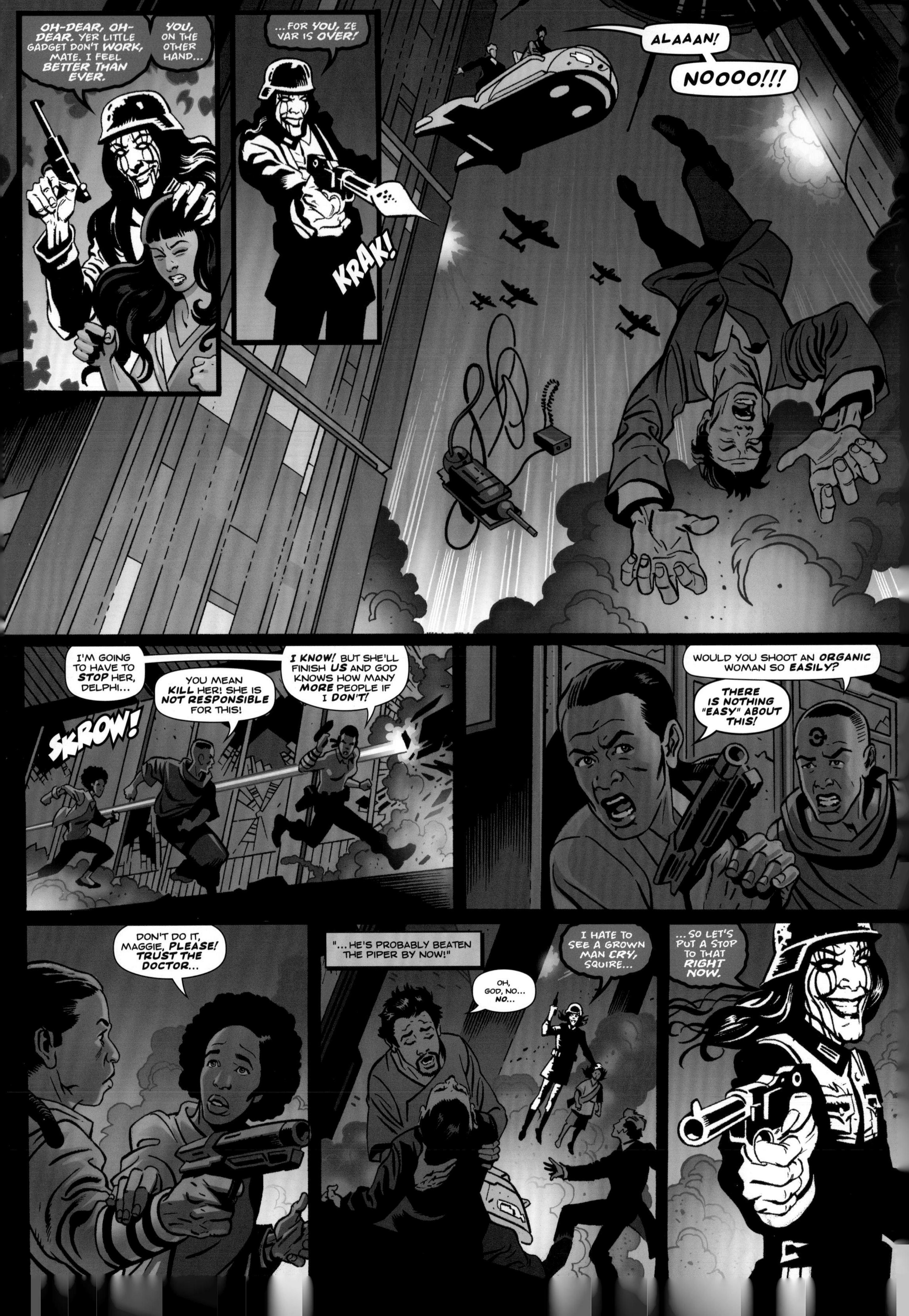

OH-DEAR, OH-DEAR. YER LITTLE GADGET DON'T WORK, MATE. I FEEL BETTER THAN EVER.
YOU, ON THE OTHER HAND...
...FOR YOU, ZE VAR IS OVER!
KRAK!
ALAAAN!
NOOOO!!!
I'M GOING TO HAVE TO STOP HER, DELPHI...
YOU MEAN KILL HER! SHE IS NOT RESPONSIBLE FOR THIS!
I KNOW! BUT SHE'LL FINISH US AND GOD KNOWS HOW MANY MORE PEOPLE IF I DON'T!
SKROW!
WOULD YOU SHOOT AN ORGANIC WOMAN SO EASILY?
THERE IS NOTHING "EASY" ABOUT THIS!
DON'T DO IT, MAGGIE, PLEASE! TRUST THE DOCTOR...
"...HE'S PROBABLY BEATEN THE PIPER BY NOW!"
OH, GOD, NO... NO...
I HATE TO SEE A GROWN MAN CRY, SQUIRE...
...SO LET'S PUT A STOP TO THAT RIGHT NOW.

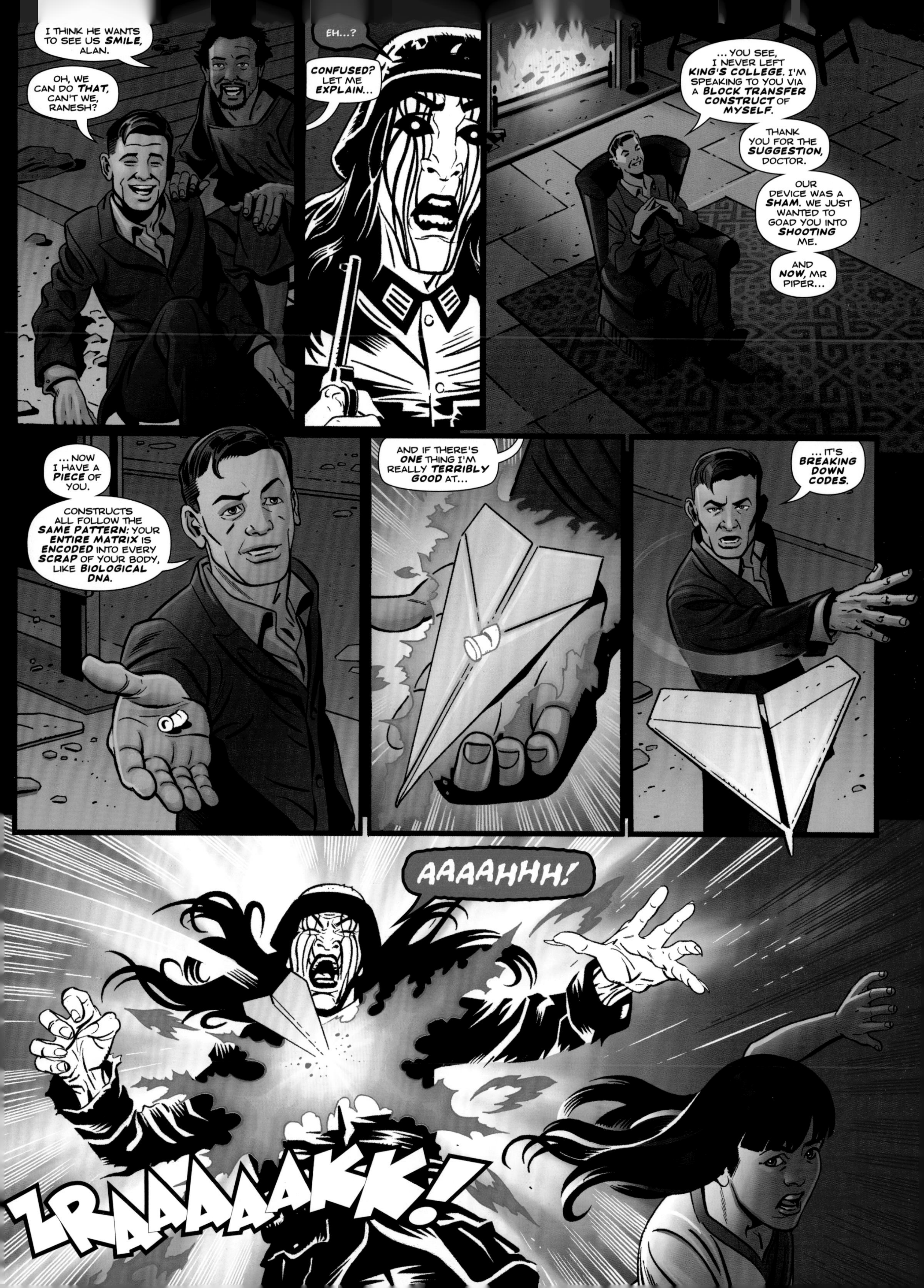
I THINK HE WANTS TO SEE US SMILE, ALAN.
OH, WE CAN DO THAT, CAN'T WE, RANESH?
EH...?
CONFUSED? LET ME EXPLAIN...
... YOU SEE, I NEVER LEFT KING'S COLLEGE. I'M SPEAKING TO YOU VIA A BLOCK TRANSFER CONSTRUCT OF MYSELF.
THANK YOU FOR THE SUGGESTION, DOCTOR.
OUR DEVICE WAS A SHAM. WE JUST WANTED TO GOAD YOU INTO SHOOTING ME.
AND NOW, MR PIPER...
... NOW I HAVE A PIECE OF YOU.
CONSTRUCTS ALL FOLLOW THE SAME PATTERN: YOUR ENTIRE MATRIX IS ENCODED INTO EVERY SCRAP OF YOUR BODY, LIKE BIOLOGICAL DNA.
AND IF THERE'S ONE THING I'M REALLY TERRIBLY GOOD AT...
... IT'S BREAKING DOWN CODES.
AAAAHHH!
ZRAAAAAKK!

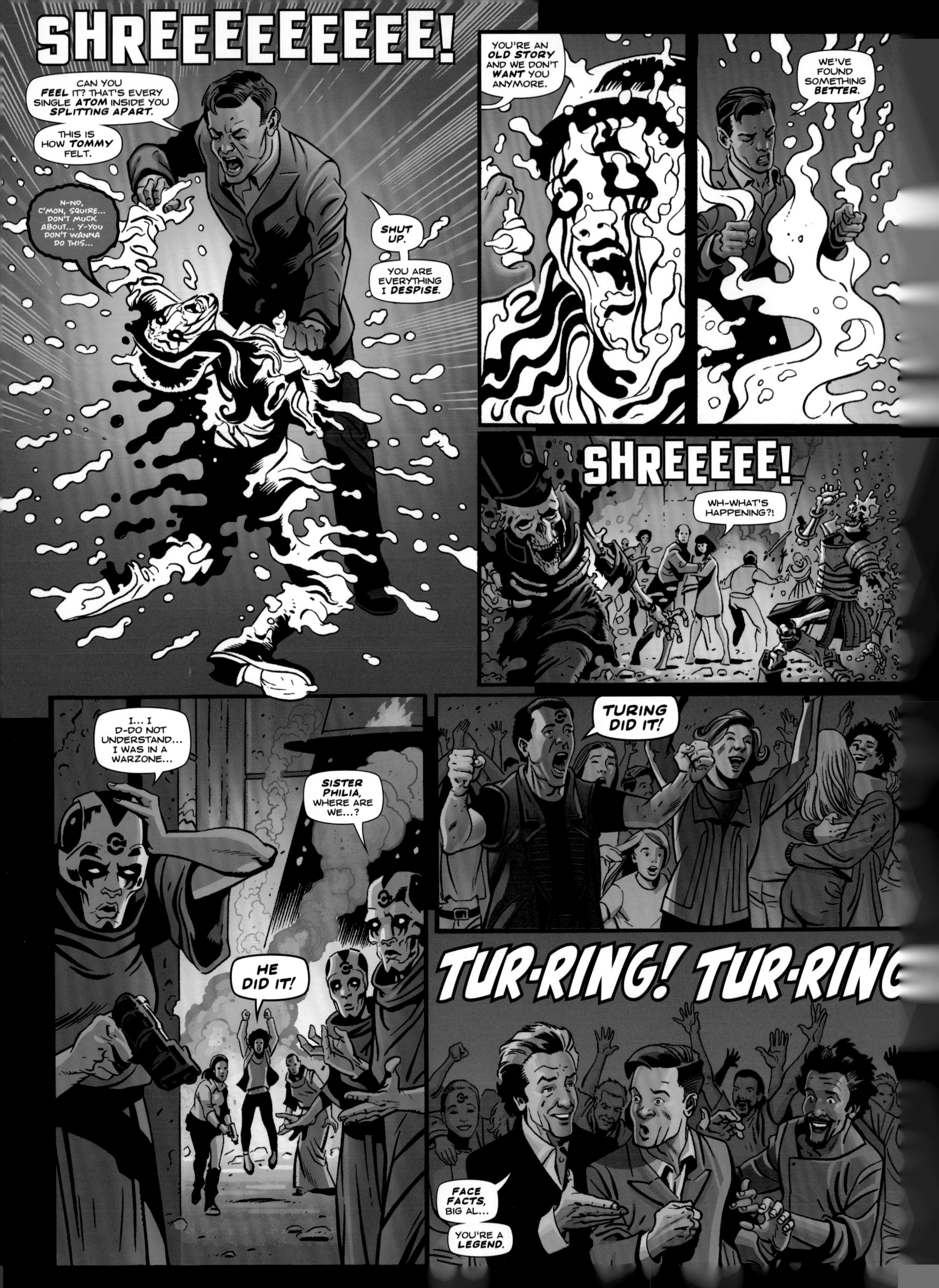
SHREEEEEEEEE!
CAN YOU FEEL IT? THAT'S EVERY SINGLE ATOM INSIDE YOU SPLITTING APART.
THIS IS HOW TOMMY FELT.
N-NO, C'MON, SQUIRE... DON'T MUCK ABOUT... Y-YOU DON'T WANNA DO THIS...
SHUT UP.
YOU ARE EVERYTHING I DESPISE.
YOU'RE AN OLD STORY AND WE DON'T WANT YOU ANYMORE.
WE'VE FOUND SOMETHING BETTER.
SHREEEEE!
WH-WHAT'S HAPPENING?!
I... I D-DO NOT UNDERSTAND... I WAS IN A WARZONE...
SISTER PHILIA, WHERE ARE WE...?
HE DID IT!
TURING DID IT!
TUR-RING! TUR-RING
FACE FACTS, BIG AL...
YOU'RE A LEGEND.

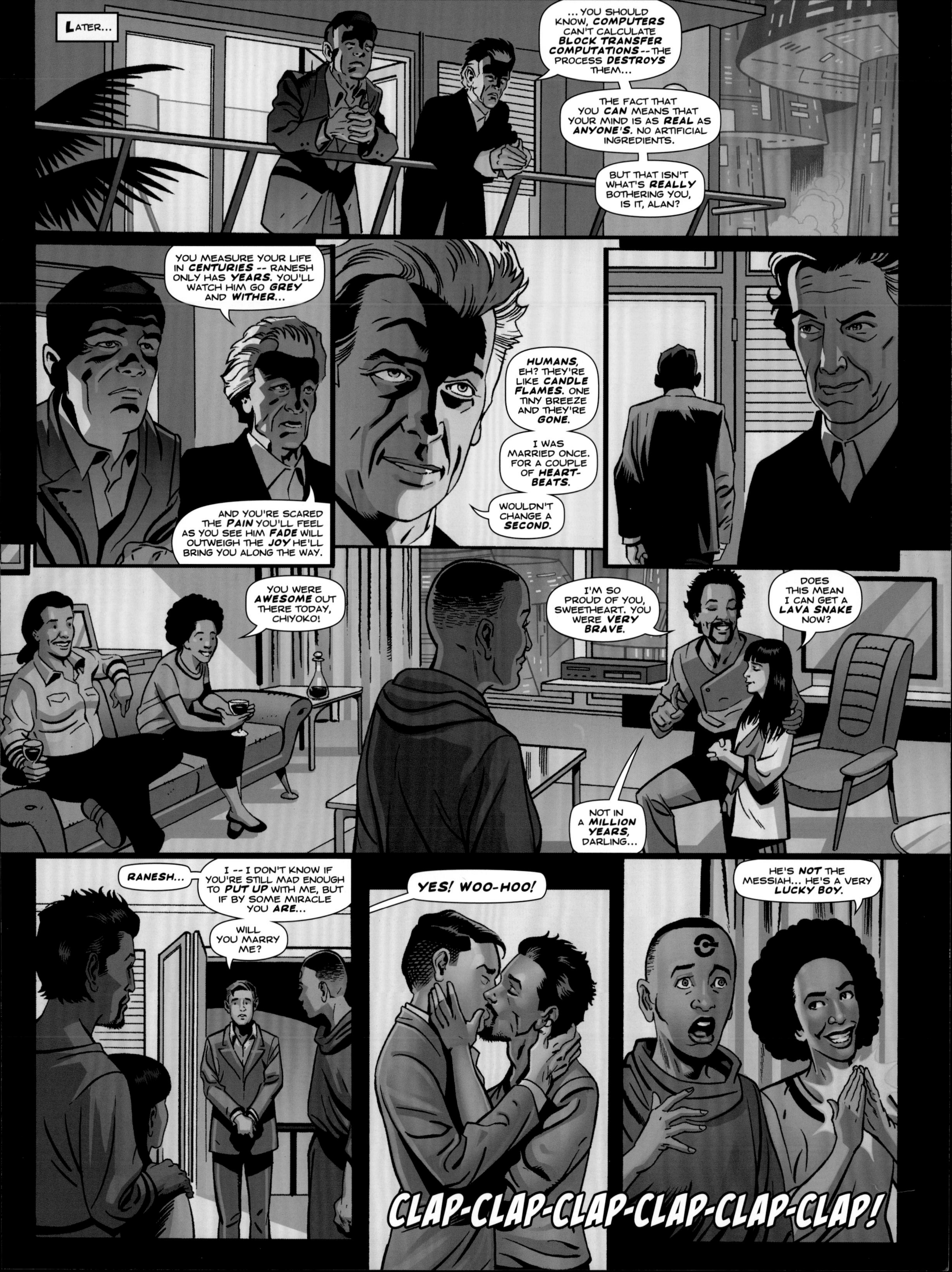
LATER...
...YOU SHOULD KNOW, COMPUTERS CAN'T CALCULATE BLOCK TRANSFER COMPUTATIONS--THE PROCESS DESTROYS THEM...
THE FACT THAT YOU CAN MEANS THAT YOUR MIND IS AS REAL AS ANYONE'S. NO ARTIFICIAL INGREDIENTS.
BUT THAT ISN'T WHAT'S REALLY BOTHERING YOU, IS IT, ALAN?
YOU MEASURE YOUR LIFE IN CENTURIES -- RANESH ONLY HAS YEARS. YOU'LL WATCH HIM GO GREY AND WITHER...
AND YOU'RE SCARED THE PAIN YOU'LL FEEL AS YOU SEE HIM FADE WILL OUTWEIGH THE JOY HE'LL BRING YOU ALONG THE WAY.
HUMANS, EH? THEY'RE LIKE CANDLE FLAMES. ONE TINY BREEZE AND THEY'RE GONE.
I WAS MARRIED ONCE. FOR A COUPLE OF HEART-BEATS.
WOULDN'T CHANGE A SECOND.
YOU WERE AWESOME OUT THERE TODAY, CHIYOKO!
I'M SO PROUD OF YOU, SWEETHEART. YOU WERE VERY BRAVE.
DOES THIS MEAN I CAN GET A LAVA SNAKE NOW?
NOT IN A MILLION YEARS, DARLING...
RANESH...
I -- I DON'T KNOW IF YOU'RE STILL MAD ENOUGH TO PUT UP WITH ME, BUT IF BY SOME MIRACLE YOU ARE...
WILL YOU MARRY ME?
YES! WOO-HOO!
HE'S NOT THE MESSIAH... HE'S A VERY LUCKY BOY.
CLAP-CLAP-CLAP-CLAP-CLAP-CLAP!

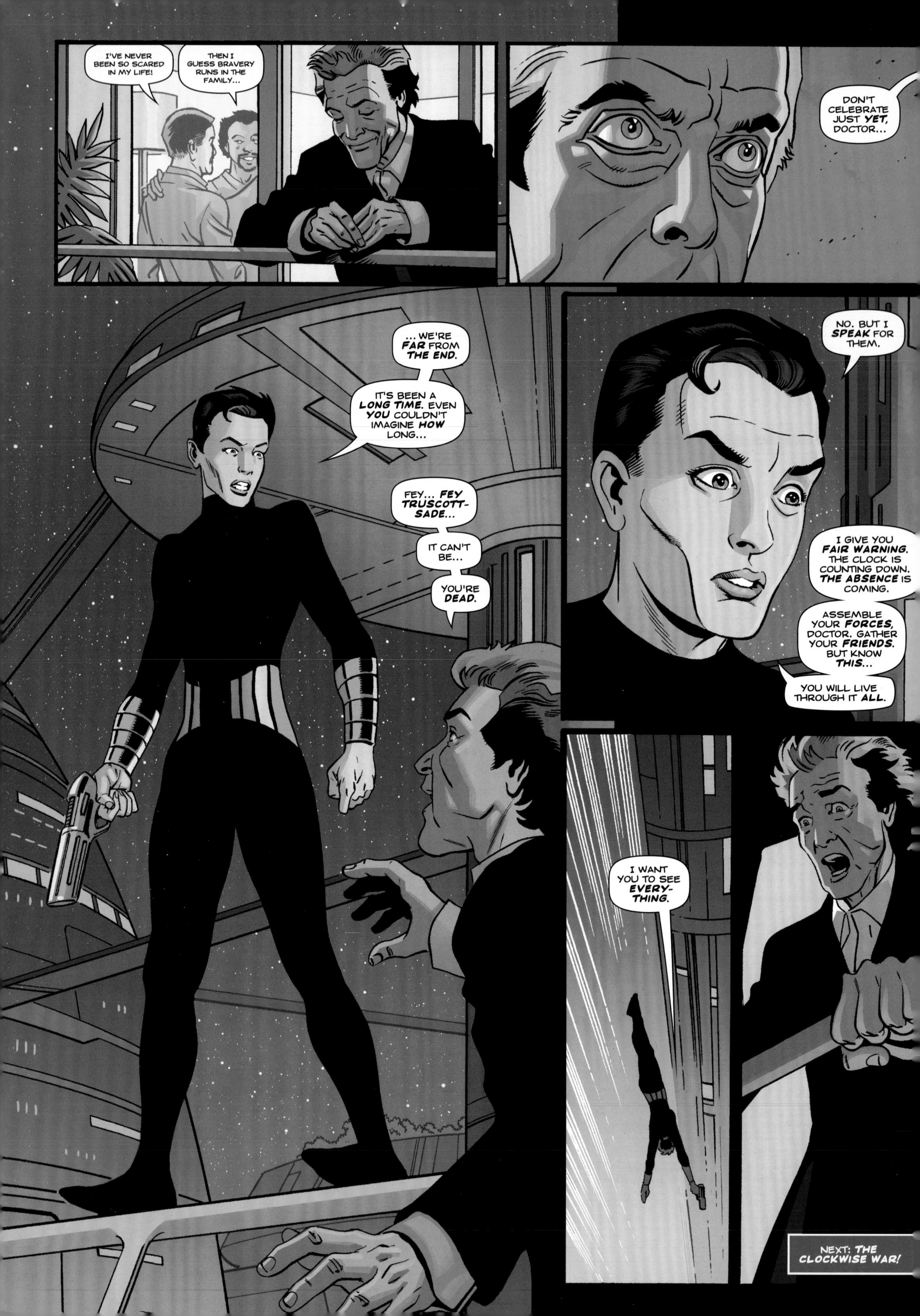
I'VE NEVER BEEN SO SCARED IN MY LIFE!
THEN I GUESS BRAVERY RUNS IN THE FAMILY...
DON'T CELEBRATE JUST YET, DOCTOR...
... WE'RE FAR FROM THE END.
IT'S BEEN A LONG TIME. EVEN YOU COULDN'T IMAGINE HOW LONG...
FEY... FEY TRUSCOTT-SADE...
IT CAN'T BE...
YOU'RE DEAD.
NO. BUT I SPEAK FOR THEM.
I GIVE YOU FAIR WARNING. THE CLOCK IS COUNTING DOWN. THE ABSENCE IS COMING.
ASSEMBLE YOUR FORCES, DOCTOR. GATHER YOUR FRIENDS. BUT KNOW THIS...
YOU WILL LIVE THROUGH IT ALL.
I WANT YOU TO SEE EVERY-THING.
NEXT: THE CLOCKWISE WAR!

COMMENTARY

The Soul Garden

Scott Gray Writer

Hi everyone! We hope you enjoyed the book. Here we are again with some behind-the-scenes stuff for you...

In April 2017 the **Doctor Who Magazine** comic strip reached the conclusion of a stellar run by writer Mark Wright. Mark had been teamed with artists Mike Collins, John Ross, Staz Johnson and David A Roach. They had conspired to strand the Doctor on Earth in the 1970s once again, but this time with no UNIT in sight. Mark and company had instead placed the Doctor in a genuinely alien environment (for him) – the Brixton household of the wonderful Collins family. It had been a really fun change of pace for the strip (and has now been collected as the *Doorway to Hell* graphic novel, available at all fine book, comic and online stores, fact-fans).

Now it was time to reboot and get the Doctor back into space. To add to the fun, Martin Geraghty and I had a brand new companion to play with: Bill Potts, who was being portrayed on TV by Pearl Mackie.

I fell in love with Bill immediately. My requirements for a *Doctor Who* companion are very simple – in fact, they really only have two boxes to tick. They must be a) brave and b) funny. The more they demonstrate these two qualities, the more I like them. Characters like Jamie McCrimmon, Sarah Jane Smith and Donna Noble rate very highly on Gray's Top Ten Companion List for this reason, and I was happy to add Bill Potts to their ranks. I thought Pearl Mackie's performance was outstanding. That opening scene with Bill and the Doctor in his office was wonderful. The subtle flickers of self-doubt on her ultra-expressive face, the slight tremor in her voice, the awkward body language – they all pointed to an actor with tremendous command of her abilities.

Due to publishing schedules, New *Doctor Who* companions have to be developed in the comic strip long before they actually appear on TV. But I had a good head-start; I'd already seen Bill's preview scene *Friend from the Future* (broadcast in April), of course, and the *Doctor Who* production team had been extremely helpful – they supplied me with the scripts for *The Pilot*, *Smile*, *Thin Ice* and *Knock Knock*, so I had a solid idea of how to approach the character. Bill was clever and vulnerable, joyous and practical. I felt that she was a much gentler figure than Amy Pond or Clara Oswald – slower to anger and more forgiving of the Doctor's blunt behaviour. I was looking forward to giving her a voice in the strip.

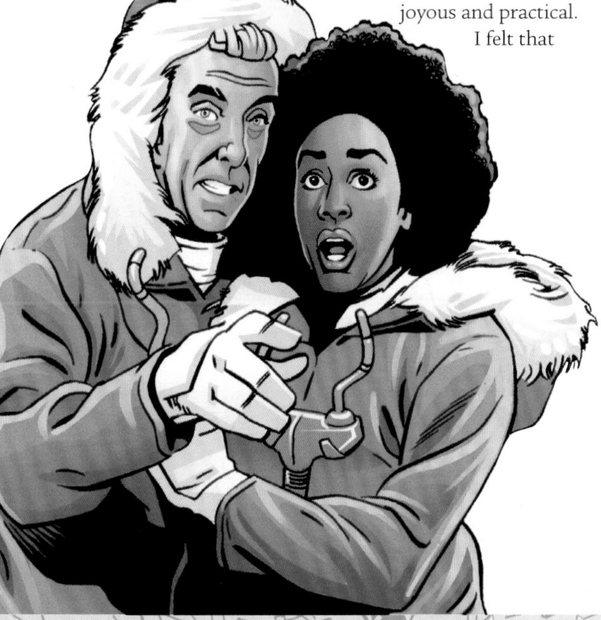

But I decided not to include Matt Lucas's Nardole in the comic as well. I loved him almost as much as Bill, but his character was strongly tied to the whole Missy-locked-in-the-vault story arc on TV. I had no idea how that would develop, so I needed to steer well clear of it. (And to be honest, I imagined that Bill would be fine but Nardole would probably get killed, which shows you how good a guesser *I* am.)

Peter Capaldi's Doctor had changed a lot since I'd last written for him in *The Eye of Torment* – less abrasive, more playful, less controlling, more kind, less insular, more relaxed, more... Doctorish. He was terrific. I felt far more comfortable writing for him now.

I wanted to bring back Rudy Zoom, the egotistical adventurer Martin Geraghty and I had introduced in *The Eye of Torment*. I really liked Rudy. It was nice to have at least *one* ultra-wealthy person in *Doctor Who* who wasn't a maniacal villain. Rudy had been an enjoyable foil for Clara in *The Eye of Torment*, but he hadn't really been given the chance to clash with the grumpy Twelfth Doctor. Rudy is as gung-ho for a good adventure as the Doctor, and can be relied upon to kick-start an interesting situation.

One of Rudy's inspirations comes from the *Tintin* books (which I've loved since I was a Time Tot). I'm always amused when Tintin and Captain Haddock routinely bump into people they know during their adventures. My favourite is Jolyon Wagg, a hilariously self-absorbed insurance salesman who finds everything funny and is unbelievably annoying – especially to the gruff Captain Haddock. Wagg is completely oblivious to this fact, and thinks he and Haddock are the best of friends. *Tintin* creator Hergé said that Wagg was inspired by an outstandingly smug man he had once met. He had strolled into Hergé's home, pointed at a chair and told him to "have a seat."

There is definitely some Jolyon Wagg in Rudy Zoom's DNA.

Rudy's time period is simply described in *The Eye of Torment* as the "Ninth Era". This is an undisclosed century where faster-than-light travel hasn't been discovered yet (or perhaps it had and the secret has since been lost – civilisations fall as often as they rise, remember). Humanity has yet to meet any aliens (I know there are some multi-coloured ladies with Rudy in Part One, but that was just cosmetics), so the story had to take place inside the Solar System. Looking around for an interesting setting, I decided on Titan, a moon of Saturn large enough to have its own atmosphere. Titan has always fascinated stargazers – the density of its atmosphere combined with its weak gravity (the bit at the start where the Doctor and Bill go 'swimming' in the air is accurate) makes it an astronomical wonderland.

I also wanted to set the story in a garden. A *creepy* garden. I had a strong memory of reading Ian Fleming's James Bond novel *You Only Live Twice* as a boy. In the story, Bond's enemy Ernst Stavro Blofeld has established a "Garden of Death" in a Japanese castle, filling it with every kind of poisonous plant and venomous reptile in the world. It has become famous, or infamous, or maybe both. People are coming from all over

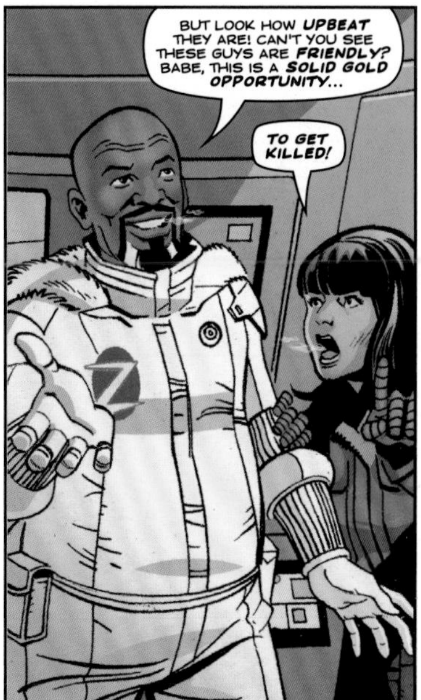

BUT LOOK HOW UPBEAT THEY ARE! CAN'T YOU SEE THESE GUYS ARE FRIENDLY? BABE, THIS IS A SOLID GOLD OPPORTUNITY...
TO GET KILLED!

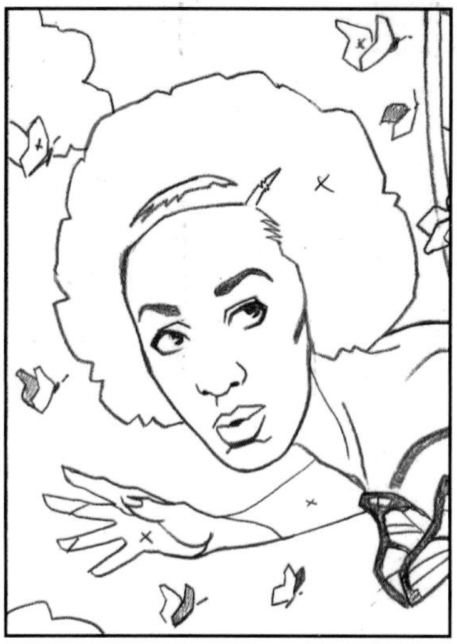

Top: Rudy Zoom and Clara Oswald from *The Eye of Torment*. Art by Martin Geraghty, David Roach and James Offredi.

Above: Bill Potts. Pencil art by Martin Geraghty.

Left: An image of the Doctor and Bill used to promote *The Soul Garden*. By Martin Geraghty, David Roach and James Offredi.

the country for the honour of committing suicide in the castle grounds. The garden is brilliantly described in the book, and I can clearly remember reading an eerie scene where Bond observes a man who has fallen victim to its deadly embrace...

The brilliant moonlight showed a head swollen to the size of a football, and only small slits remained where the eyes and mouth had been.

The poor bloke staggers around the garden, trying to get his eyes open, until he sees a lake. He lets out a howl and jumps in. But he isn't alone...

A mass of small fish were struggling to get at the man, particularly at the naked hands and face, and their six-inch bodies glittered and flashed in the moonlight.

Yeah, you don't forget *that* kind of thing when you're ten.

So I had Rudy Zoom, Titan and a deadly garden. Gardens suggested plant creatures. Rudy would be off on another expedition, travelling to Titan, meeting the Doctor and Bill, finding a garden, and they'd all have an exciting adventure with some plant-thingies.

It sounded... okay. But *just* okay. A bit by-the-numbers. I wasn't excited by the premise, which is never a good sign. I knew something else had to be added to the mix, but I couldn't think what it might be.

The best tactic I've always found when I'm stuck on a story is to just *read*. I went online and researched poisonous plants, Victorian gardens, famous explorers and, of course, Titan itself. Some writerly advice: if you've hit a wall, just fill your head with information and keep your antennae tuned for anything – *anything* – that could spark a new story idea. You'll find it.

It turned out that Titan has an area about the size of Australia with a highly reflective surface; probably a plateau of water ice. Astronomers spotted it with the Hubble

Telescope in 1994 and called it 'Xanadu', taking the name from *Kubla Khan*, the classic poem by Samuel Taylor Coleridge. Bells started ringing in my head immediately. *That was it!*

Here's the poem in full:

*In Xanadu did Kubla Khan
A stately pleasure-dome decree:
Where Alph, the sacred river, ran
Through caverns measureless to man
Down to a sunless sea
So twice five miles of fertile ground
With walls and towers were girdled round;
And there were gardens bright with sinuous rills,
Where blossomed many an incense-bearing tree;
And here were forests ancient as the hills,
Enfolding sunny spots of greenery.*

*But oh! that deep romantic chasm which slanted
Down the green hill athwart a cedarn cover!
A savage place! as holy and enchanted
As e'er beneath a waning moon was haunted
By woman wailing for her demon-lover!
And from this chasm, with ceaseless turmoil seething,
As if this earth in fast thick pants were breathing,
A mighty fountain momently was forced:
Amid whose swift half-intermitted burst
Huge fragments vaulted like rebounding hail,
Or chaffy grain beneath the thresher's flail:
And mid these dancing rocks at once and ever
It flung up momently the sacred river.
Five miles meandering with a mazy motion
Through wood and dale the sacred river ran,
Then reached the caverns measureless to man,
And sank in tumult to a lifeless ocean;
And 'mid this tumult Kubla heard from far
Ancestral voices prophesying war!
The shadow of the dome of pleasure
Floated midway on the waves;
Where was heard the mingled measure
From the fountain and the caves.
It was a miracle of rare device,
A sunny pleasure-dome with caves of ice!*

*A damsel with a dulcimer
In a vision once I saw:
It was an Abyssinian maid
And on her dulcimer she played,*

Top:
Samuel Taylor Coleridge.

Above:
The Keeper goes crazy! Pencil art by Martin Geraghty.

Right:
Martin Geraghty supplied patterns along with his pencil art for Rudy's lounge.

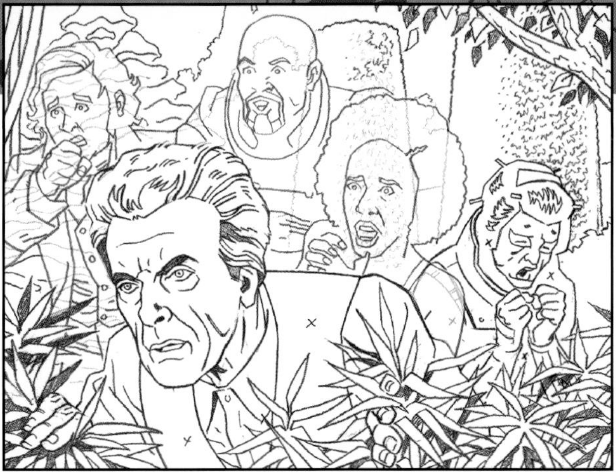

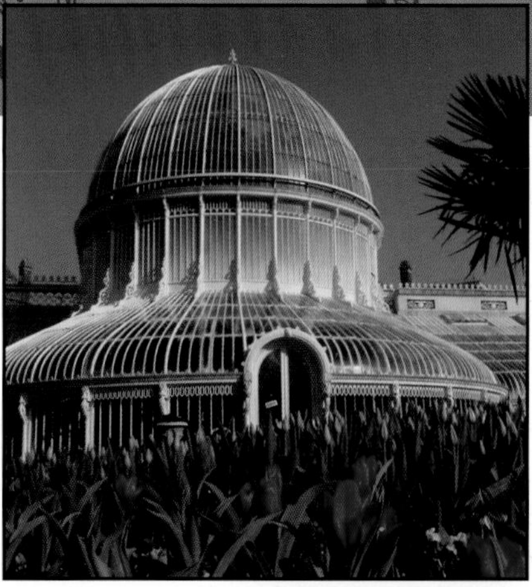

Singing of Mount Abora.
Could I revive within me
Her symphony and song,
To such a deep delight 'twould win me,
That with music loud and long,
I would build that dome in air,
That sunny dome! those caves of ice!
And all who heard should see them there,
And all should cry, Beware! Beware!
His flashing eyes, his floating hair!
Weave a circle round him thrice,
And close your eyes with holy dread
For he on honey-dew hath fed,
And drunk the milk of Paradise.

I got *very* excited – it was as if I'd had the story handed to me. I had wanted a garden on Titan, and it felt like one already existed. The story would be inspired by Coleridge's poem – and following the great tradition of *Doctor Who*'s pilfering from classic literature, we would turn that fact on its head and claim that Coleridge was actually inspired by *Doctor Who*!

There were seas of pure liquid methane on Titan, but the moon's heavy cloud cover meant they almost never saw light: that was the *"sunless sea."* The garden would be inside a *"pleasure-dome"*. Bill became an *"Abyssinian maid"*, playing a dulcimer. Oksanna and the Sythorr were inspired by a *"woman wailing for her demon-lover!"*. Rudy was Kubla Khan himself, of course; the king of all he surveyed.

Most importantly, I had the missing piece of the puzzle: Samuel Taylor Coleridge himself. I knew little about him. After some research, it seemed to me that Coleridge was a man possessing extraordinary talent but precious little self-belief, often feeling adrift on a creative level. I figured he was just *begging* for a pep-talk from Rudy and Bill.

It was a lot of fun to invert a basic *Doctor Who* rule: the Doctor always travels to meet historical figures in their environment – they don't travel to meet *him*. But Coleridge could manage it, thanks to the power of his magnificent imagination. "Time travel has always been possible in dreams," Madame Vastra had helpfully explained in the TV story *The Name of the Doctor*. I had found that a very enticing concept at the time, and wanted to explore it.

Coleridge had famously composed *Kubla Khan* while in an opium-induced dream-state in 1797. He commented that "all the images rose up" before him. When he woke, he raced to write it all down, but was interrupted by a caller to his house. The poem faded from his memory and he was left with only scraps of the entire work. That seemed to me to be a clear message from his subconscious mind to his conscious one: *I'm a lot smarter than you, mate. Don't get distracted when I'm talking to you, you'll regret it.* I took heed and wrote down every thought that came to me about the story, particularly the ones that arrived first thing in the morning.

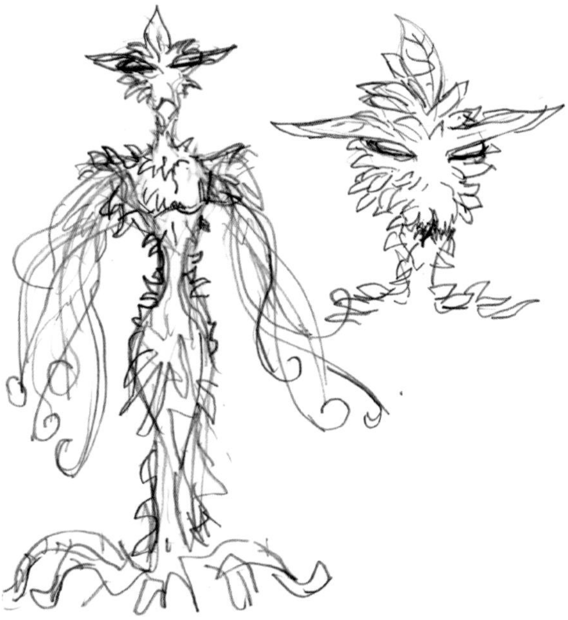

Left:
The Doctor and friends. Pencil art by Martin Geraghty.

Above:
The Pleasure Dome was based on the Belfast Botanical Gardens.

Below left:
Scott Gray's sketches of Oksanna.

I was blown away by how wonderful the Dreamspace scenes looked. Most of the craziness in there – Einstein and Elvis on elephants, flying sperm whales, dancing majorettes, etc – was Martin's doing. Something that's always bothered me about dream sequences in stories is the way characters usually react as if they're in some strange, exotic environment. In my experience, no matter how weird I might think a dream is in *hindsight*, it always seems completely normal while I'm in there. So it was for Bill, Samuel and Rudy. "Suspension of disbelief" was a phrase coined by Coleridge, so I made sure he used it in the story.

As always, Martin did a knockout job designing Lady Takashi, Coleridge, the Pleasure Dome, the Garden, the Beagle, the Dreamspace, Oksanna, the Sythorr, the Haluu, the costumes, etc, etc, etc. (Whenever I see one of those 'Art of the Movie' books featuring an army of designers, I always think, "But a comic artist does all of that on their own – for *every single story!*") I gave Martin a (very) rough sketch of Oksanna which he developed into a beautiful design. Martin surprised me at the end of Part One; I had simply described the garden coming alive, with some vines grabbing the Doctor and company. Martin instead had the vines originating from Oksanna's body. It was an inspired idea, instantly transforming her into a scarily powerful creature.

David Roach supplied his trademark sleek, accomplished inks, James Offredi gave us yet another glorious colouring job, and Roger Langridge provided more of his ever-stylish lettering. For the millionth time I thanked the Comic Gods for giving me such a brilliant team to work with.

So this story turned out to be all about dreams, which started me on the path to all the other stories in this book. Two lines from *Kubla Khan* suggested I was on the right track...

And 'mid this tumult Kubla heard from far
Ancestral voices prophesying war!

Martin Geraghty Artist

It doesn't take much to lure me back to the **DWM** strip but Scott's pre-emptive pitch for this tale was along the lines of: "Introducing Bill! Bringing back Rudy! A guest appearance by Samuel Taylor Coleridge! Plant Monsters on Titan!" What comic artist worth his salt could possibly pass that smorgasbord up? (My favourite *Who* TV story is *The Seeds of Doom*, so "Plant Monsters" was the clincher.)

Like Scott, I instantly warmed to Pearl Mackie's depiction of Bill onscreen; easily the most relatable TV companion since Donna, to my mind, and our scribe nailed her character traits to a tee, natch. The photo-library of images he sent along of Pearl (all teeth and curls) showed a huge range of expression

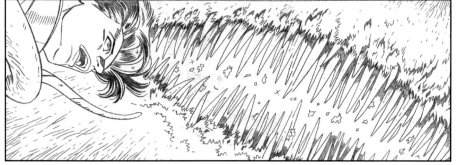

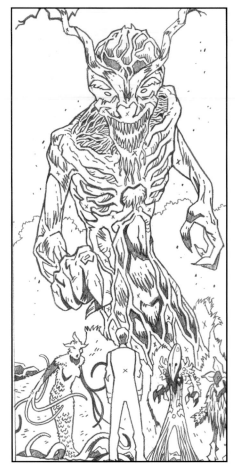

Offredi did in colour-coding the four distinct locations that the story takes place in. I really shouldn't be surprised at the value James adds to the strip after all this time working alongside him, but from the blue icy wastes of Titan to the lush, light-drenched tones of the Garden itself, via Rudy's extravagant living spaces and the claustrophobic, shadowy command bridge, he accentuates the sense of place and gives everything a more fully realised finish. After reading the script, the most exciting part of the strip process for me is receiving the finished colour pages in my inbox to pore over.

Top:
Sandi meets a nasty end in Part Two. Pencils by Martin Geraghty.

Above:
The Doctor confronts the Sythorr. Pencil art by Martin Geraghty.

that I knew I could have fun with. I was in the midst of drawing the first instalment of the story when Breakfast Radio Presenter Shaun Keaveny interviewed Pearl on 6Music in the week leading up to transmission of *The Pilot* and, in my role as ambassador for the mag, I got in a shameless plug for the strip and a namecheck on air. If you're quick it's probably still available to listen to on iPlayer. Drawing her appearance in the first few pages reminded me strongly of illustrating Martha and Ten stepping out onto the frozen polar ice in the 2007 strip *The First* (Good Grief! 11 years ago as I write this!).

By this point in my involvement in the adventures of the Twelfth Doctor, I feel I'd got a strong hold on Peter Capaldi's appearance. Gone was the buttoned-up, overtly stern patrician figure of Series 8 (and therefore the strip stories of that season), replaced by a reasonably softer 'Punk Uncle' version of the character. His craggy, careworn features, halo of grey waves and bony scarecrow physique were fairly easy to capture on the page, both in close and long shot.

The Soul Garden was the first instance where I was sending my pages to David Roach via email rather than post, and he then inked over his printouts of my pencils. This meant that I could fix any niggles Scott or I had with the pencils in Photoshop prior to sending. These could range from lowering a character in the frame to allow more space for a speech balloon, to tweaking a character's proportions or overlaying a holographic icon to give the ship's bridge a more techy feel. I could also choose wallpaper and carpet patterns from stock images for the interior of Rudy's skiff, adding an extra level of decoration without making David slavishly ink these features in (or me to pencil originally, come to that!). These little details lent Rudy's rooms an opulence befitting the soaring narcissism of the man. Away from my strip commitments, I often work with interior designers, illustrating rooms for furniture retailers and property developers. This skill set can often be ported over into the comic when getting into the psyche of a character, so obviously Rudy would have garish retro wallpaper and busts of himself in his quarters, as well as a Burt Reynolds-style *Playboy* portrait of himself. He's such a joy to draw for. Away from the utilitarian stylings of the crew members (who took their cue from the uniforms of the 50's sci-fi classic *Forbidden Planet*), it was a nice side-step to surround Rudy with the Vivienne Westwood-inspired female journalists.

Reviewing these pages, I'm struck by the sterling job James Offredi did in colour-coding the four distinct locations that the story takes place in.

A huge Victorian greenhouse in an ice cave on Titan is such a quintessential *Doctor Who* location I'm surprised it hasn't been done before. When designing the interior environment of "The Zoomdome" and its botanical villains, I again raided the internet to reference the natural flora and fauna of our own planet, which produces lifeforms every bit as bizarre and menacing and downright lethal as anything my imagination could conjure up. All the plantlife featured is an extrapolation or amalgamation of forms found around the world today. Scott had already provided a perfect design for Oksanna and I bulked up her entourage with nods to classic TV series villains of the horticultural variety like Meglos and the Vervoids.

The Dreamspace sequences were a joy to do – I imagine all artists feel a sense of liberation when occasionally freed from the strictures of logic. It was huge fun to elaborate on Scott's suggestions for the psychedelic environment that Bill and Coleridge find themselves in. These sequences tend to be the comic strip equivalent of doodling whilst on the phone, as you don't really know what you've got until you've finished. I even managed to sneak my own drawing hand in, a homage to *Drawing Hands* by my favourite childhood artist, MC Escher. These hallucinatory sequences put erstwhile **DWM** editor John Freeman in mind of the early Colin Baker strip stories of Steve Parkhouse and John Ridgway - high praise indeed!

Being a research junkie, Coleridge is based on contemporary portraits of the poet. Although I rarely base guest characters in the strip on living actors (Scott was adamant Rudy would be played by Lenny Henry), I had in mind Matthew Rhys's performance in *The Mystery of Edwin Drood* whilst drawing him. His writing desk and chair are based on his originals that still exist in his cottage today, complete with playing cards.

As ever, it was great fun to illustrate *The Soul Garden* (although I still maintain that poor Sandi's fate at the end of Part Two is the nastiest thing Scott has ever done to one of his characters). The sinister coda at the end adds to the sense of anticipation for the start of Peter Capaldi's final comic strip 'season'.

James Offredi Colourist

I had a great time working on *The Soul Garden*. It had a fun, fast-paced script and wonderful artwork. For me, the stand-out image was page 4 of Part Two. It was a hilarious shot, beautifully rendered by Martin and David.

My working process begins with reading the script and taking note of any specific colour directions such as time of day, costume colours, special effects, etc. The first stage is known as 'flatting': adding flat, or 'local' colours to all the characters, objects and backgrounds. I'm not too concerned with making perfect choices at this point, as I know I can always tweak them later – it's only the general mood that needs to be correct. The colour choices in the first three panels were set by the earlier pages. Rudy's arrival called for a contrast. I warmed up the local colours and changed the sky to yellow/orange.

Once the flat colours are chosen, it's on to the next stage: modelling. This is the fun stuff. Martin and David generally set the direction of the light sources, so I always pay attention to them. I use a combination of soft and hard brushes in

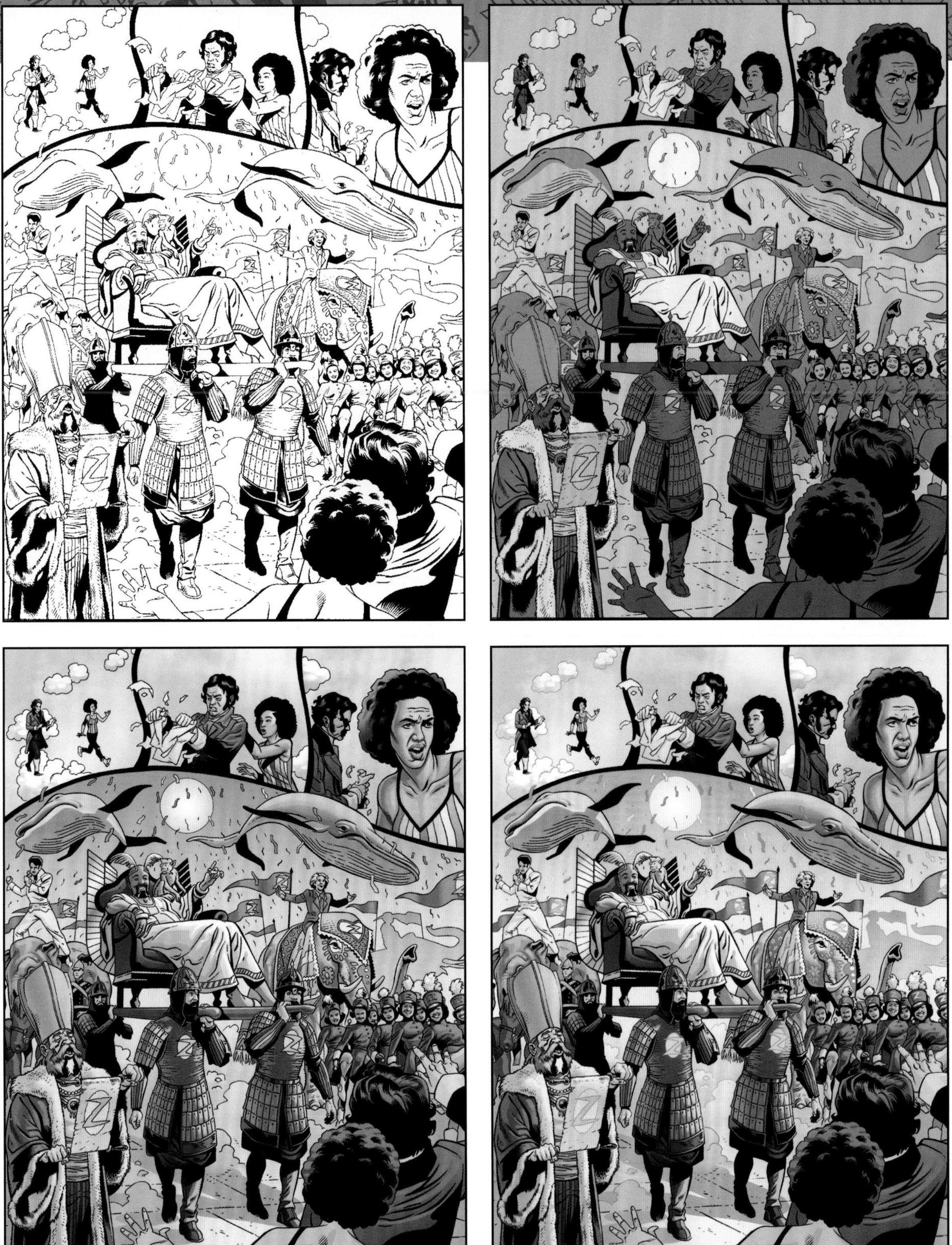

Photoshop to add light and shadow, with the occasional subtle textured brush thrown in as well. I lit Bill's face in panel 3 with the new gold tones, connecting it to the large panel. (In contrast, Samuel's colours becomes darker in this panel, to suggest his emotional state.)

I made Rudy the focus of panel 4 by giving his toga light tones with white highlights. I added to the contrast by making his chair dark (Scott had described a "golden throne" in the script, but that would have merged into the background colours too much).

The final stage involves fine-tuning all the colour details. I felt the page lacked enough strength after the modelling, so I increased the colour saturation and pushed it further into the orange/red spectrum – I wanted an explosion of colour. I put cool highlights on Bill and Samuel in the foreground to stop them from competing with the procession. I nudged the sky in the first three panels into a deeper blue to add that extra bit of contrast with panel 4.

I also knocked back the solid black lines in many areas, turning them into lines of colour instead. Examples include the decorations on the elephant, the ticker tape, the outlines on the clouds and sun, the texture on the vizier's robes and the 'Z' logos. This added depth to the image and allowed the characters to 'pop' more.

The Soul Garden was a challenging story to colour, but also a very satisfying one. I enjoyed it!

Above:
The stages of colouring the **DWM** comic strip: 1) The black-and-white line art. 2) Adding flat colours. 3) Modelling shapes and light sources. 4) Finessing the work with special effects.

The Parliament of Fear

Scott Gray Writer

It isn't made clear in the story, so just for the record: Bass Reeves is a genuine historical figure. This may be the only time ever in *Doctor Who* where the Doctor has met a real person in a historical setting and not known who he/she was. That was quite deliberate.

A few years ago I came across an online article about Bass Reeves and was immediately struck by this rich, evocative figure: a black lawman in the late 19th century, feared by outlaws and respected by Native Americans and settlers alike. I was always on the hunt for interesting people that could spark historical stories for the comic strip, and Bass seemed a promising candidate.

Bass Reeves was born into slavery in July 1838 in Crawford County, Arkansas. He worked as a water boy and field hand. When he was eight, he and his family were moved to Texas. He learned how to shoot a gun and tend horses.

Right:
A statue of Bass Reeves stands at Fort Smith, Arkansas.

Below:
Deputy US Marshal Bass Reeves.

Bottom left:
Joey, Bass and the Doctor. Pencil art by Staz Johnson.

Bottom right:
Seth Shelton pleads for his life. Pencil art by Staz Johnson.

When the American Civil War began in 1861, Bass followed his owner, Colonel George Reeves, into combat as his servant. Bass got into an argument with him that year and laid him out cold in a fight. He fled into the Indian Territory (later to become the state of Oklahoma), seeking shelter with the Creek and Seminole tribes. He joined their struggle as they waged a guerilla war against the Confederate troops.

The Civil War ended in 1865. White and black settlers moved into the Indian Territory, breaking the agreement between the US government and the Native American tribes who had been forced to settle there. The government did nothing to remove the newcomers, and crime soon began to rapidly increase. Deputy marshals became the only active law enforcers in the massive wilderness.

Bass Reeves worked as a scout and a tracker for the deputy marshals, and in 1875 was sworn in as one himself. He was 6'2" and weighed 180 pounds. He was by all accounts a polite, moral man. He was ambidextrous and a crack shot. Bass often disguised himself as a tramp, a gunslinger or an outlaw in order to get close to his quarry. He would spend weeks at a time inside the Indian Territory, searching for men on the run from the law: mostly killers, bank robbers, horse thieves and bootleggers. Joey and Zeke are fictional, but they represent the type of men that Bass would employ to assist him. They would capture outlaws, chain them to their wagon, and continue their long trek.

It was an extraordinarily dangerous life. This was the most lawless region of America, and over 100 deputy marshals met with violent ends during Bass's time there. When the deputies reached the "dead line" – a point 80 miles from Fort Smith (the court where they would deliver their prisoners), they would find cards addressed to them personally from outlaws, telling them that if they crossed the line they would be killed.

There were other black deputy marshals operating in that era, but Bass was probably the first. A good argument could be made that he was the most successful lawman of the entire Wild West. Bass arrested over 3000 people over 32 years, but he killed only 14 men in his entire career, preferring to bring them in without violence if possible. They would often surrender when they realised who they were facing.

"Now that," I thought to myself, "is a *Doctor Who* guest star."

My bible was *Black Gun, Silver Star* by Art T Burton. The writer faced a 20-year-long uphill battle researching his book on Bass Reeves's life. A clerk at one of Oklahoma's historical societies answered an early query with, "I'm sorry, we didn't keep black people's history." Burton relied on newspaper reports, oral histories passed from one generation to the next, and federal criminal court cases still on file at the National Archives. They all tell the story of an exceptional man.

Recorded history hasn't reserved much of a place for Bass Reeves. In a better world he might have been the most famous name in Western folklore, eclipsing Wyatt Earp, Wild Bill Hickok and Davy Crockett. But the colour of his skin meant that his achievements, while occasionally reported by newspapers, were ignored by the popular press and historians of the period. Like countless other people of colour in that era, his story was buried in the past. That's why the Doctor hadn't

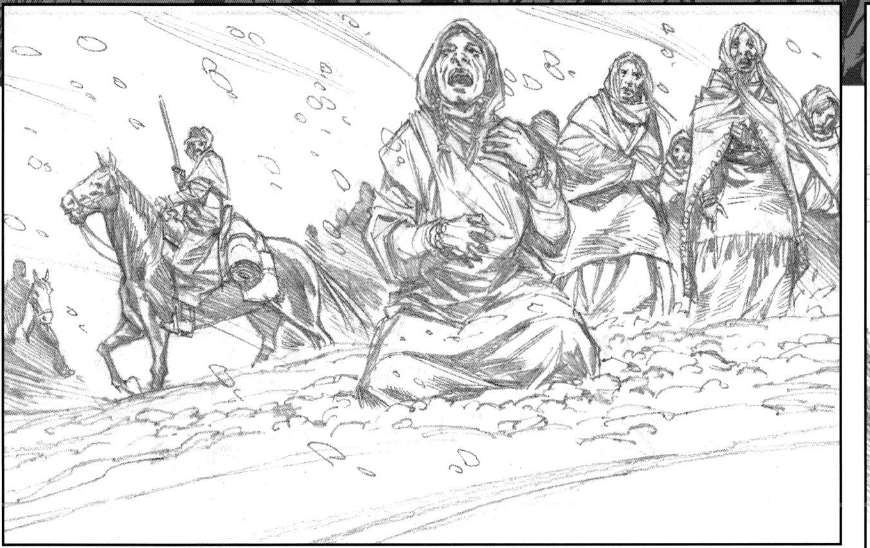

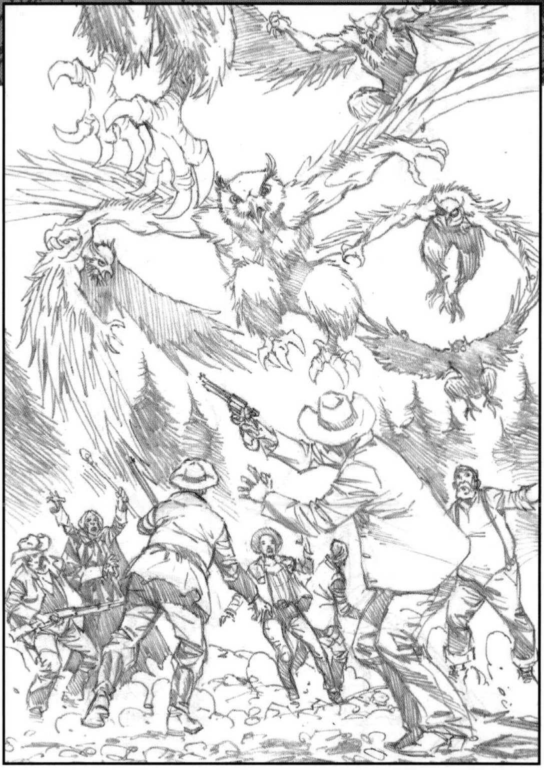

heard of Bass Reeves – it would have felt dishonest if he had.

Staz Johnson joined the posse as artist. I had been thrilled by his dynamic work with Mark Wright on two recent **DWM** stories, *Bloodsport* and *Doorway to Hell*. Staz did a superb job with this story - his textured approach was perfect for the dirty, dust-filled setting, and he absolutely nailed Bass's worldly-wise, uber-cool manner. The Stikini looked amazing too!

With photos of Bass Reeves thin on the ground, I looked around for someone that Staz could use as a model. That didn't take long – I had been looking for a comic strip role for Idris Elba for *years*, and here it was at last!

Most of our cast were based on specific actors who had been associated with Westerns. I asked Staz to make Seth Shelton look like Bruce Dern, who had played some notable baddies in several movies. Joey was Lou Diamond Phillips (from the *Young Guns* movies), and Zeke was Western great Denver Pyle (best known as Uncle Jesse in *The Dukes of Hazzard* TV show).

Sadly, Staz ran into some deadline troubles. David Roach came on board to help by inking Part Two, but other commitments meant Staz wasn't able to draw Part Three. I turned to veteran comics artist Mike Collins to rescue us. (I've long thought that the **DWM** office should have a red telephone inside a transparent case just for Mike.) He did a fantastic job picking up the reins (sorry) of the story and gave us a great conclusion. I laughed out loud when I saw Mike's "Monster Owls!!!" shot of Zeke, and the two panels that followed!

I had an ambition to write a proper horror-western; a genre mash-up I've always enjoyed. I remember several *Jonah Hex* mini-series published by DC in the 90s, written by Joe R Lansdale and illustrated by Timothy Truman and Sam Glanzman. Jonah Hex was a hard-bitten bounty hunter who had been a traditional western character for many years, but this new creative team threw him into a world of zombie gunslingers and giant flesh-eating worms. The stories were dark, exciting and very funny. I was looking forward to putting Bass, the Doctor and Bill into that kind of environment.

I started out with the intention of telling the entire story from Bass Reeves's point-of-view. He'd narrate the story and everything we would learn about the Doctor and Bill would come from his perspective. The opening scene was set in a dusty little town. A travelling salesman arrives in a colourful covered wagon. He stands up and says something like, "Good day to you, kind townsfolk! I am Doctor Caligari, and I bring you the cure for all your ills!"

He immediately starts pitching a "miracle elixir" to the townsfolk. One of the women in the crowd is dubious, but when she tries it she immediately feels fantastic! Bass is watching, instantly suspicious – he doesn't recognise the woman, and the salesman seems shifty even by shifty salesman standards.

The woman is Bill and the salesman is the Doctor, of course. (I could easily see Peter Capaldi in a top hat and fancy outfit, standing on a wagon and doing the whole snake oil routine – he'd be in his element.) Bass spots the Doctor and Bill together that night and follows them. The pair have created gallons of the elixir. They attempt to pour it into all the town wells, but Bass arrests them.

The Doctor and Bill try to explain that they have already visited another town where an alien infection has taken hold – all the people there have been transformed into monsters (I don't remember what kind). The time-travellers are secretly trying to innoculate the entire population of this town with their "elixir"; preparing them against the imminent arrival of their neighbours. After some shocking first-hand evidence, Bass realises his error and the trio battle to save the town against the monsters.

I'm sure there would have been more to it than that, but I never finished this outline. I had too many issues with it. I wanted to show Bass Reeves at his best – to demonstrate his skills, his commitment to the law and his stature among his contemporaries. Having him misunderstand the situation and

Top left:
Totika's daughter dies on The Trail of Tears. Pencil art by Staz Johnson.

Above:
The Stikini attack! Pencil art by Staz Johnson.

Below:
Bass and the Doctor. Pencils by Staz Johnson.

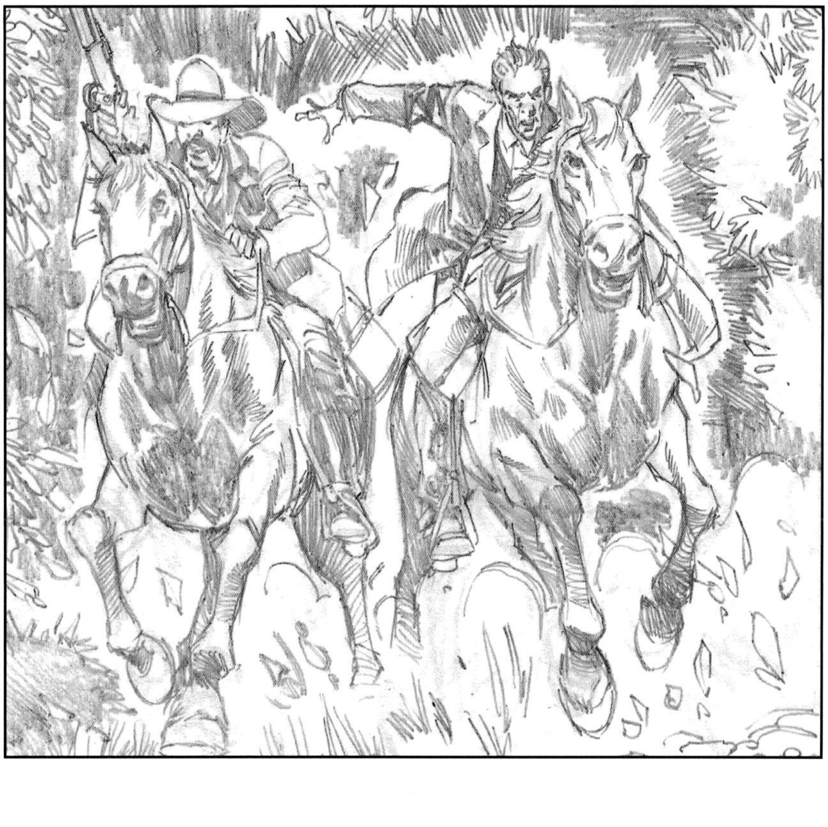

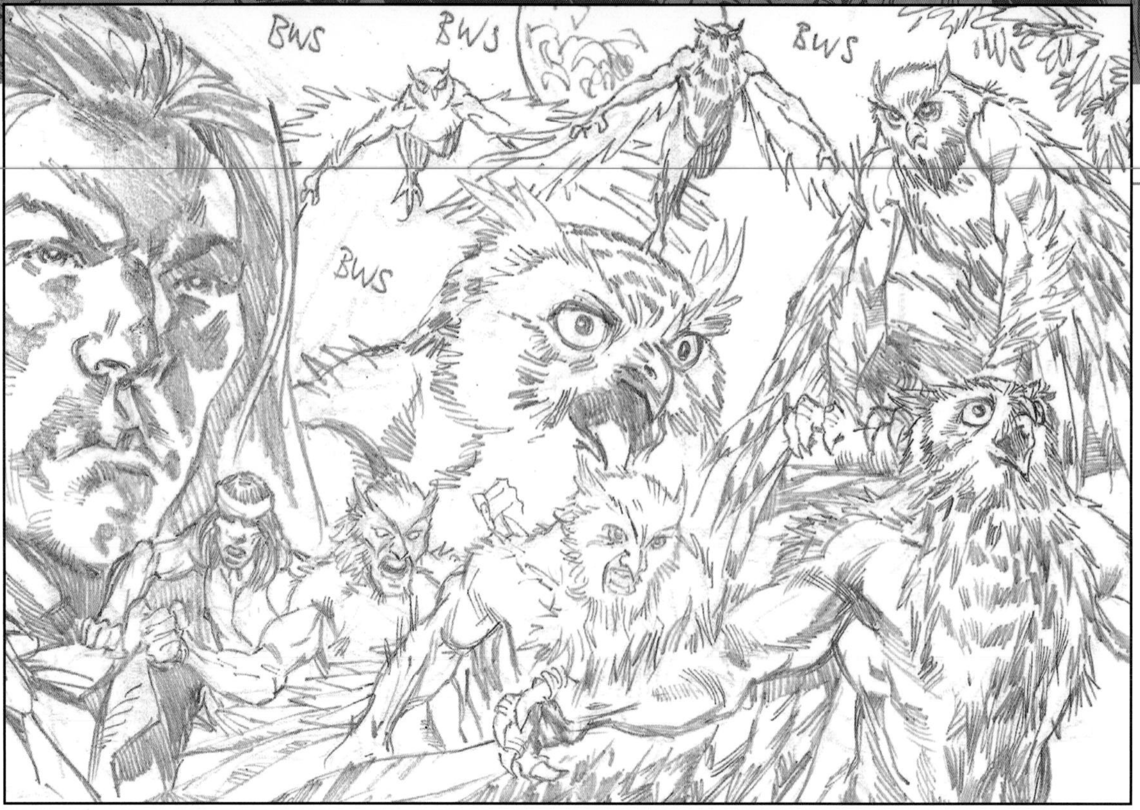
BWS
BWS
BWS
BWS

Right:
Joey tells the story of the Stikini. Pencil art by Staz Johnson.

Below:
Totika. Pencil art by Mike Collins.

Bottom:
Holata. Pencils by Mike Collins.

Bottom right:
"Monster Owls!!!" Pencils by Mike Collins.

hinder the Doctor felt like I was doing him a disservice. I had another problem with it: the more I researched the era and the region where Bass was working, the more I wanted to set the story in a concrete historical setting and have real events drive it. The generic Western town felt like a cop-out.

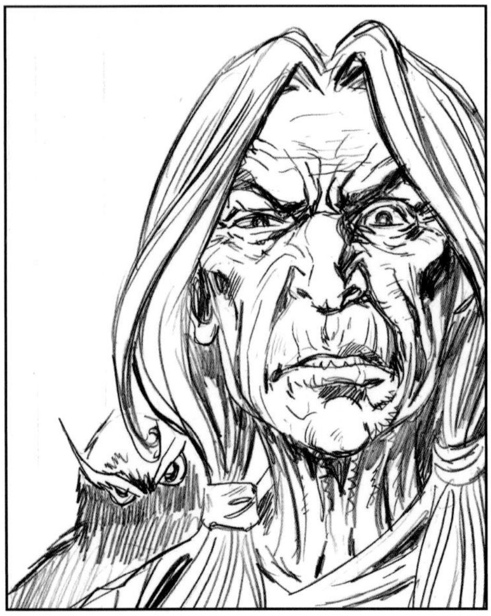

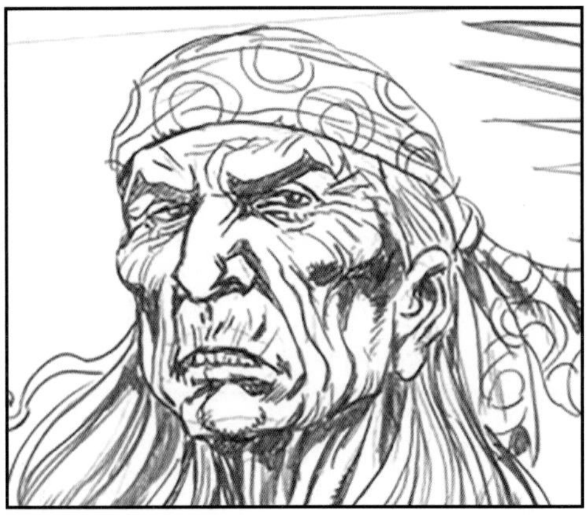

So I started over. Researching the Indian Territory led me to The Trail of Tears. I had never heard of it. (For some strange reason there don't seem to be any Western movies on the subject.) In the early 1800s the Southeastern area of the United States was becoming a more desirable place for white settlers, and also more valuable with discoveries of gold. The Native American tribes living there were seen as an obstacle to the area's exploitation. The seventh US president, Andrew Jackson, a slave-owner, pushed for their removal. Despite heavy opposition, Jackson (whose portrait is currently hanging in the Oval Office) signed the 'Indian Removal Act' in 1830. After years of bloodshed, the five tribes – the Seminole, Chickasaw, Choctaw, Creek and Cherokee – were forced out of their ancestral homelands and made to march west. Many thousands of men, women and children died of starvation, disease and exposure along the way.

Totika started out as a comedic character in the initial plot; I was going to introduce her by having Bass and the Doctor find her stuck in a large hole. They'd help her out but she'd remain cantankerous and ungrateful for the whole story. Totika was basically just there to explain the nature of the Stikini and give some advice. But with Bill Potts, Bass Reeves, Joey Two Trees and old Zeke already in the Doctor's corner, it felt like he was well-equipped for the adventure – adding Totika to his team seemed like overkill. When I made her an adversary instead, the story started to fall into place. The Trail of Tears gave her the perfect motivation for her actions – she became a tragic figure, trapped by her own pain and need for revenge.

As I was working on *The Soul Garden*, I decided that the Dreamspace would be the linking element between this group of stories. I had started playing with the concept as far back as 1996's *Ground Zero*, a Seventh Doctor story illustrated by Martin Geraghty and Bambos Georgiou (published in **DWM #238-242**). That story had been partially inspired by Swiss psychiatrist Carl Jung's theory of the 'Collective Unconscious'; an idea I've always found fascinating. Jung hypothesised that humanity's unconscious minds share common ground – this is why cultures scattered all around the world seem to have the same archetypes in their stories, myths and religions: 'The Great Mother', 'The Wise Old Man', 'The Hero' and 'The Jester' are some examples. Turning the Collective Unconscious into an independent dimension seemed like an obvious move.

I had also shown the Eighth Doctor entering the Dreamspace in another Western story, *Bad Blood* (reprinted in *The Flood* graphic novel). He and Sitting Bull left their physical bodies and

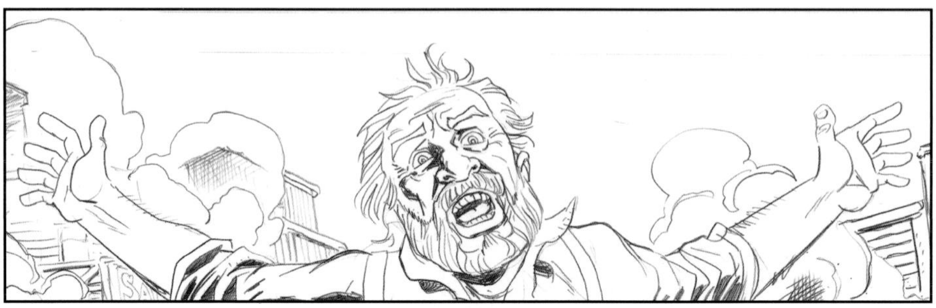

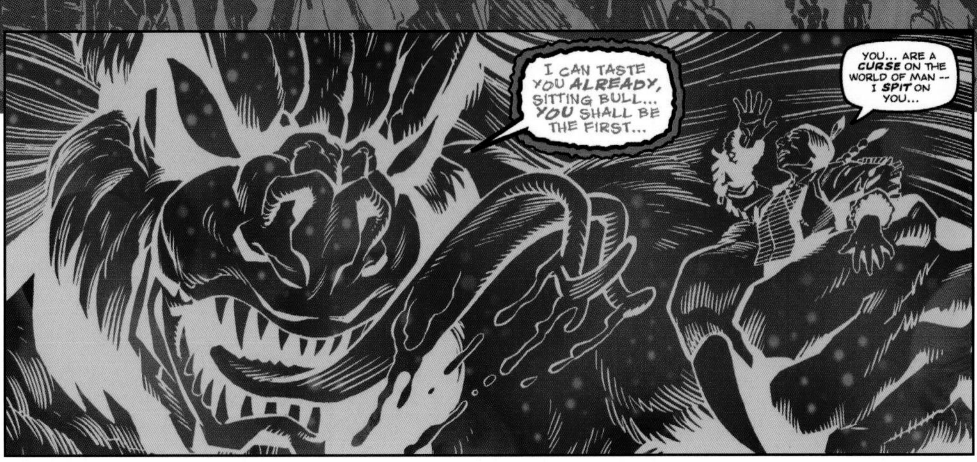
I CAN TASTE YOU ALREADY, SITTING BULL... YOU SHALL BE THE FIRST...
YOU... ARE A CURSE ON THE WORLD OF MAN -- I SPIT ON YOU...

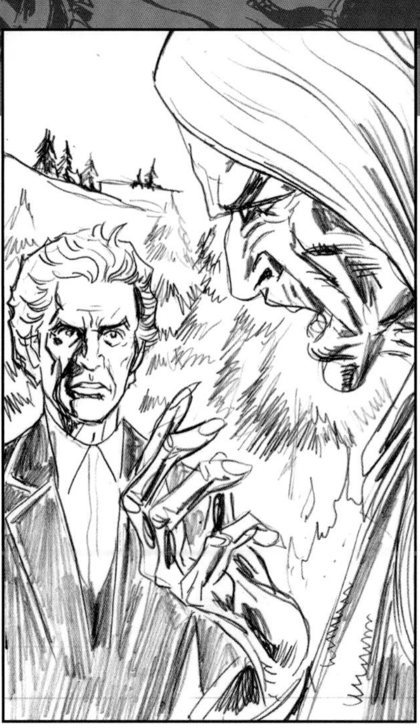

travelled as transparent astral beings into a blood-red, cosmic environment populated by spirit animals. They were attacked by the story's villain, the monstrous Windigo. As we were returning to a similar situation, I asked Mike Collins and James Offredi to stick with the visual approach established in *Bad Blood*. I reasoned that the Dreamspace was at least as big as our universe and would have countless regions with wildly different appearances. The happy, colourful world that Samuel Taylor Coleridge had travelled through was only one aspect of this realm – the Red Skies were another, far more dangerous area.

I'd liked the way the Windigo had worked out in *Bad Blood*, so I went looking for another genuine Native American legend. The Seminoles had a *fantastic* one: the Stikini. They felt like a gift from the gods. I mean, c'mon; giant Were-owls that eat human hearts?! *Wow!* There had been reports of Stikini sightings near Sasakwa, which was (and still is) a small town in Seminole County, Oklahoma, so that's where I sent Zeke.

I was really pleased with the way this story turned out – everyone involved did an excellent job. I hope it will help a little to raise awareness of a forgotten American hero.

And then maybe someone will start making a Bass Reeves TV series starring Idris Elba soon. 'Cause I want to watch the heck out of *that*.

I got lured to IDW briefly to draw *Doctor Who* for them simply because they offered me a western strip.

Unfortunately, apart from the Franco-Belgian market there's apparently little demand for Westerns these days so that itch rarely gets scratched.

You can imagine my utter jealousy at my old mate Staz Johnson getting to draw this story, eased somewhat by seeing his fantastic, dynamic art on the material. Still, a liiiiittle green... Scott, as ever, had weaved a fabulous tale involving the Doctor in a scenario that blended an authentic Western setting and aliens. When Staz fell behind and I was called in, I embraced the fantastic designs Staz had created for the owl people and had a ball getting into the cosmic alien dimension stuff. It made for a dramatic contrast with the gritty Western environment and created a powerful, emotional and exciting finale to the story.

But... you know what? I'd have been just as happy drawing the Twelfth Doctor moseying into a dusty Arizona town and taking on gunfighters (but thinking about it, that might be the domain of a much earlier incarnation), or just riding through Death Valley on a steed.

I love Westerns, and I loved drawing this story.

Top left:
The Windigo in *Bad Blood*. Art by Martin Geraghty, David Roach and Adrian Salmon.

Above:
The Doctor and Totika. Pencils by Mike Collins.

Below:
Bill meets the spirits of the Red Skies. Pencils by Mike Collins.

Mike Collins Artist

I love Westerns. Growing up, 70s TV was a mass of 'em; my favourites were *The Virginian* and *Alias Smith and Jones*. There were always cowboy movies on Saturday afternoons. I absorbed the bodies of work of John Ford, John Wayne and Audie Murphy. As I grew up, more sophisticated (see: violent) fare stirred my interest from Sam Peckinpah and Clint Eastwood.

DC and Marvel had some western strips but they had an edge of being superheroes in denim. I was more thrilled by the UK newspaper strips of the time: *Matt Marriott* by Tony Weare and *Gun Law* by Harry Bishop, both fabulous strips I'd urge you to hunt out if you can (as far as I know there's no *Gun Law* collection, but *Matt Marriott* is available in Spanish).

When I began to discover European comics in the 80s, the finest was and still is Jean Giraud's *Blueberry*. The peak of this series – *Angel Face*, *Broken Nose*, *The Long March*, *End of the Trail* and *Ghost Tribe* – are simply some of the best comics ever drawn.

I have several shelves just full of western strips (mostly in French).

I love 'em.

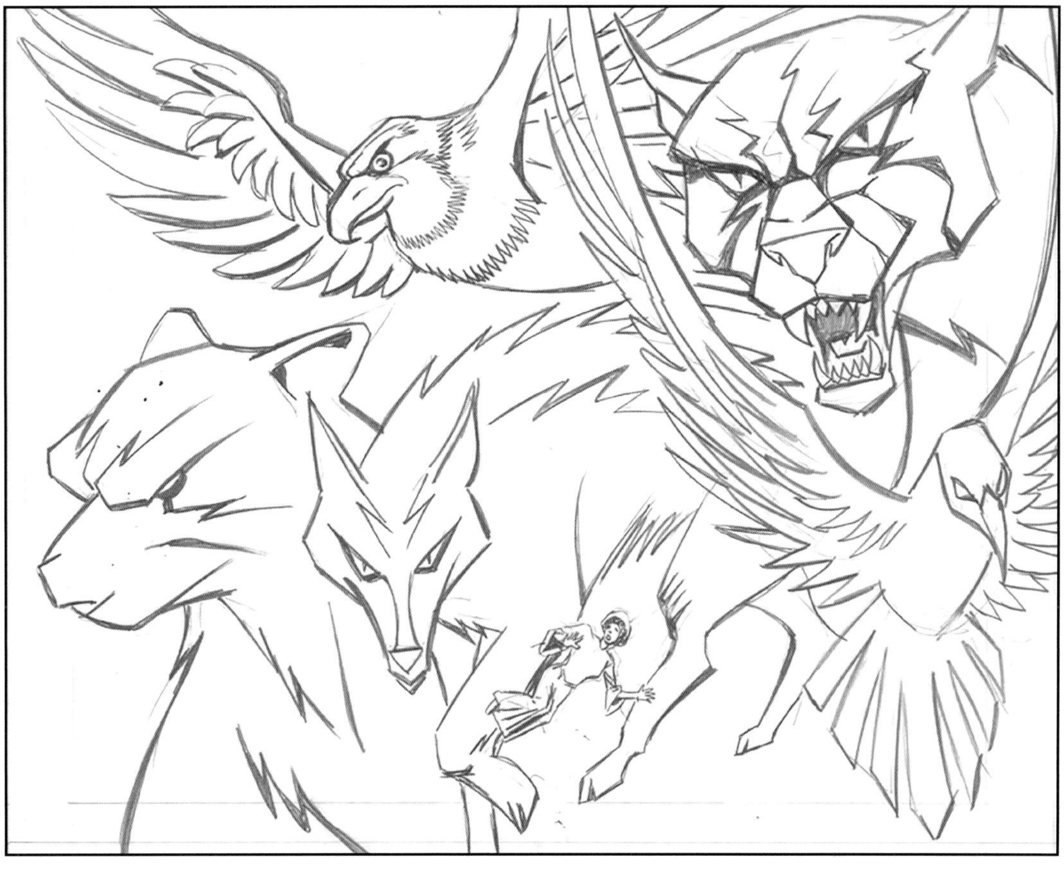

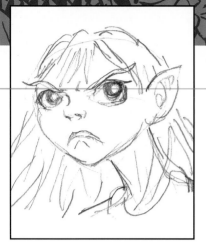

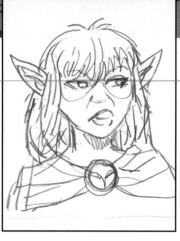

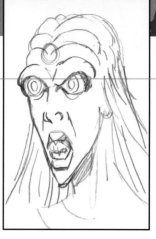

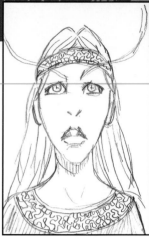

Matildus

Scott Gray Writer/Artist

After several multi-part stories in a row, I thought it'd be nice to do a one-parter as a change of pace; something relatively simple and perhaps a bit more comedic. I had wanted at some stage to have the Doctor jump back to Cornucopia, the cosmopolitan spaceport we had established in *The Cornucopia Caper*, *Hunters of the Burning Stone* and *The Blood of Azrael*. Back to outer space, then...

This story came together *very* quickly – once I had the setting and the characters figured out, it was pretty much finished. I've just gone back to my notebook and checked how many pages I took to work out the previous two stories: *The Soul Garden* was 22 pages, and *The Parliament of Fear* was 33. *Matildus* was... two. Sure, I know it's a much smaller story, but even so, that's a record for me. (But I spent far longer than usual on the character designs, so it probably balances out.)

I had designed the circular symbol that had been carved into the TARDIS and added it to the final page of *The Parliament of Fear*, using Photoshop to alter its perspective (I wasn't about to ask any artist to re-draw something that complicated on a panel-by-panel basis.) The Doctor would naturally try to identify it. Why not have him use the Renath Archive, the library he had briefly visited in *The Blood of Azrael*? I had really liked Matildus Galathea, the stern librarian who had appeared in that story – sometimes you see a walk-on character and want to learn more about them. Mike Collins had done a great job designing her. I figured Matildus could have developed a fractious relationship with the Doctor between adventures; the Doctor would borrow her books, lose them, then replace them with even more valuable ones. (I suspect that the story's opening scene isn't the first time they've gone through that routine.)

I had another reason for planning a one-parter: I wanted to draw a story. I had contributed a fair amount of visuals to the comic strip over the years; designing characters, making art corrections and sometimes even laying out pages when the artists ran out of time. But it was an unfulfilled ambition to draw a story from start to finish, and I knew I would only have time for a short one. Editor Peter Ware was thankfully enthusiastic, so I took a deep breath and jumped in...

The Kaballus Kids were my new additions to Cornucopia's growing supporting cast. I wanted the **DWM** comic strip to have a 'kid gang' like *The Little Rascals* in the 1930s movies or Joe Simon and Jack Kirby's 1940s comic characters *The Newsboy Legion*. They would be fast, street-smart and tough as nails. And they'd have a loyal dog too, of course. I took a design cue from Kirby, who always made sure that his team characters looked very different in silhouette. I asked James Offredi to give them all distinctive colour schemes too – they were deliberately very primary. I'd love to see a Kaballus Kids animated series someday!

I modified Matildus's look from Mike's original, making her look slightly more human to help with the emoting. (I think I may have unconsciously made her resemble Steve Ditko's Aunt May from the original *Amazing Spider-Man*.) She had really just been there to provide some information in *The Blood of Azrael*, but putting her in the spotlight was very satisfying. Nobody in the real world is a background character – we're all the stars of our own stories.

As I had expected, the Doctor and Bill were an absolute pleasure to draw – Peter Capaldi and Pearl Mackie look great from any angle. Lozz was based in part on TV presenter Zoe Ball, while I had Canadian comedian Katherine Ryan in mind when I was drawing Sashana.

I was overjoyed by James's colouring work, expecially the warm tones he created for the interior of the library. I also loved what he did with Bill's phone gallery images.

So the Doctor had worked out that the TARDIS symbol was really a coded message, which meant he had another old friend to visit...

Above:
Design sketches of Lozz and Sashana by Scott Gray.

Bottom:
A page layout by Scott Gray.

Bottom right:
Early design sketches of Zeddy and Sparks by Scott Gray.

Bottom far right:
The TARDIS symbol.

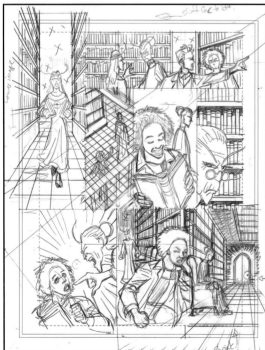

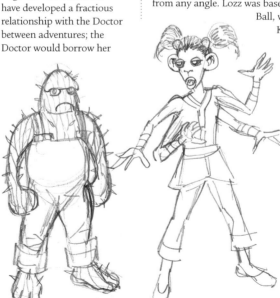

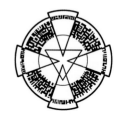

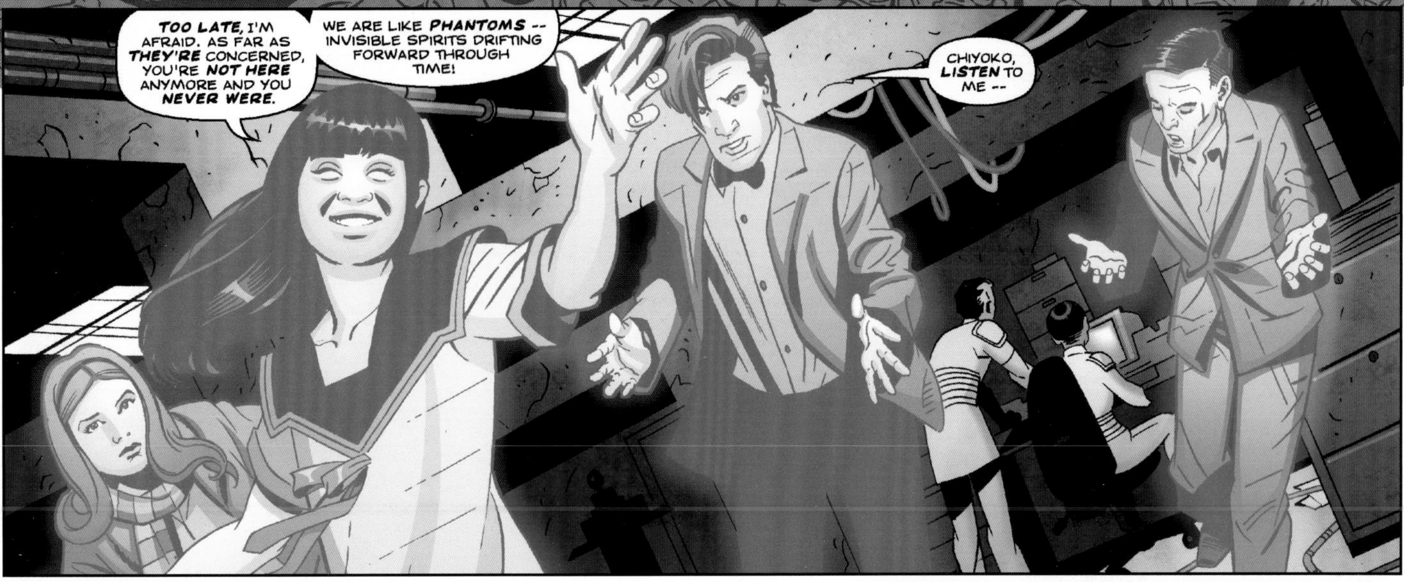
TOO LATE, I'M AFRAID. AS FAR AS THEY'RE CONCERNED, YOU'RE NOT HERE ANYMORE AND YOU NEVER WERE.
WE ARE LIKE PHANTOMS -- INVISIBLE SPIRITS DRIFTING FORWARD THROUGH TIME!
CHIYOKO, LISTEN TO ME --

The Phantom Piper

Scott Gray Writer

I had gone ankle-deep into the continuity of the **DWM** comic strip for *The Soul Garden* and *Matildus*, but I knew I'd be at least waist-high for this one. *The Phantom Piper* has its roots in *The Child of Time*, an Eleventh Doctor adventure by Jonathan Morris and Martin Geraghty. That story (and the ones leading up to it) had been a wonderfully sprawling epic for the Doctor and Amy Pond, involving a creature born out of the TARDIS (Chiyoko), history getting warped, interstellar warfare, history getting warped some more, the birth of the Galateans, history getting warped a little bit more, and a very cute dodo. It had guest-starred Alan Turing, the Bronte Sisters, Buddy Holly, Jayne Mansfield and John Keats. If you haven't read *The Child of Time*, do yourself a big favour and order a copy of the graphic novel. You won't be sorry.

I had loved the concept of the Galateans from the start, and I remember pushing Jonny (nobody calls him Jonathan) to put them at the forefront of his story. Deadly robot races are ten a penny in science fiction, but the Galateans were something genuinely fresh: the android counterparts of the human race, with their memories and personalities. They were mirror images of their creators, with all their strengths and flaws. Robots are often presented as the children of their human designers, but the Galateans were more like their brothers and sisters. It was a brilliant, juicy concept ripe for additional exploration.

I had also really enjoyed the roles Alan Turing and Chiyoko had played in *The Child of Time.* Jonny and Martin had left everyone in a very hopeful state, looking forward to a brighter future where humans and Galateans could live together in peace. The more I thought about Turing, Chiyoko and their new world, the more I wanted to revisit them and see how they were doing. Had things gone well for them...?

I started by doing my best to put myself in the position of one Galatean, waking up to find himself brand new, without any defined purpose; a copy of an original being. If he was religious, what would he think of himself? Would he believe he had a soul?

It seemed clear to me that if the first words a newly-born Galatean heard were an inspiring speech from Alan Turing, the father of artificial intelligence, then that would have quite an impact. The thought of the devoutly atheistic Alan Turing becoming a religious figure was too beautifully ironic to pass up. Turing was a man who never dealt with people all that well, and large groups of them were anathema to him. If he was put into a position where he became a global hero/messiah, his first instinct would be (I guessed) to tell the world to get lost and go hide himself away.

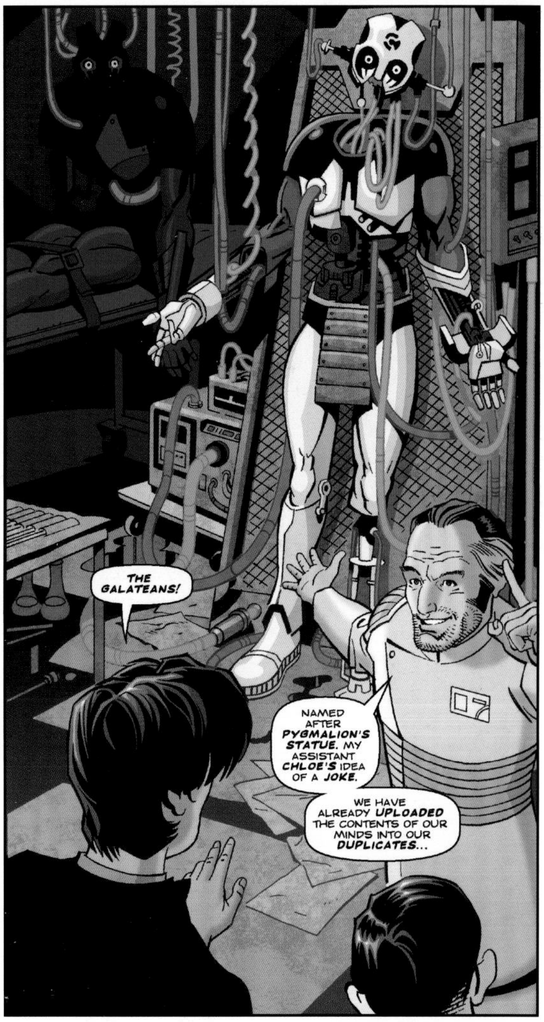
THE GALATEANS!
NAMED AFTER PYGMALION'S STATUE. MY ASSISTANT CHLOE'S IDEA OF A JOKE.
WE HAVE ALREADY UPLOADED THE CONTENTS OF OUR MINDS INTO OUR DUPLICATES...

Turing's relationship with Chiyoko was another intriguing element. In 1950 he published a paper titled *Computing Machinery and Intelligence* which speculated on the possibilities of machines generating genuine independent thought. Turing suggested that "Instead of trying to produce a programme to simulate the adult mind, why not rather try to produce one which simulates the child's?" It seemed logical that Turing would take an interest in Chiyoko's development, and the pair would stay connected.

Maggie and Delphi originated from the premise that the Galateans wouldn't age like humans, which would obviously lead to all sorts of conflicts further down the road. How would humans feel as they grew older, watching their android twins staying young and pretty? There would inevitably be resentment from many. Maggie and Delphi's relationship would have evolved over time. I imagined that they were like sisters at first, very close and mutually supportive. But as time went on, Maggie grew more mature and settled while Delphi became more frustrated and angry. They're akin to a mother and daughter right now – but Maggie might one day be more of a grandmother to Delphi.

TV *Doctor Who* hardly ever does sequels. There's *The Curse of Peladon* and *The Monster of Peladon*, and I guess *The Long Game* and *Bad Wolf*, but they're pretty thin on the ground, and it's obvious why: *Doctor Who* has intensely detailed plots, and it's hard work to recap them quickly and cleanly. I soon realised that a sequel to *The Child of Time* would mean a *lot* of recapping: I had to find ways for Bill (and the readers) to have three major things explained to them: 1) The future world shared by the Galateans and humans; 2) The unique nature of Chiyoko's

Top:
The Doctor, Amy and Alan Turing confront Chiyoko in *The Child of Time*. Art by Martin Geraghty, David Roach and James Offredi.

Above:
The Galateans are born in the same story.

The Phantom Piper

Right:
The first sketches of the Phantom Piper by Scott Gray.

Below:
Weird War Tales #42. Art by Joe Kubert. (© 2018 DC Comics)

Centre:
Jamie McCrimmon (Frazer Hines) imagines he sees the Phantom Piper in *The Moonbase* Episode 2.

Bottom left:
Block Transfer Computation was used by the Logopolitans in the TV story *Logopolis*.

Bottom right:
Ranesh and Chiyoko. Pencil art by Martin Geraghty.

creation; and 3) The origin of the Galatean version of Alan Turing. I made sure that the info-dumping took place in three separate chapters to avoid the readers getting gorged on all the explanations. (I'm not sure that helps readers of this collection, though. Sorry!)

It took me quite a while to figure out exactly what Alan Turing had been working on in seclusion. I finally reasoned that if a genius like Turing was handed futuristic computers, he'd eventually transcend them. The concept of Block Transfer Computation is well-known to fans of 80s *Doctor Who* – it comes from two TV stories written by Christopher H Bidmead; *Logopolis* and *Castrovalva*. I've always liked the premise that formulating a hyper-detailed mathematical construct could result in the creation of a real object. There's a glimpse of the same concept in the first Sixth Doctor story, *The Twin Dilemma*. In the opening scene, mathematical prodigies the Sylvest twins tell their father, "We're going to play Equations." He reacts with fear, saying, "Your mathematical skill could change events on a massive scale." It feels to me like there's a hint of genuine possibility there – it's been established in quantum physics that phenomena can be altered by the simple *observation* of that phenomena, and that's essentially what Block Transfer Computation is doing. Who knows, maybe someday...

WEIRD WAR TALES
DC
25¢
No. 42
OCT.
THE MYSTERY AND MADNESS OF...
WEIRD
WAR
TALES

I didn't want the successful conclusion of *The Child of Time* to be subverted by having war break out again between the humans and Galateans. But there would inevitably be people who *did* want a conflict, and that's how I got my villain. The Piper arrived quickly: another creature of the Dreamspace, a being who fed off the nightmares of the battlefield, angry at having the greatest war in history snatched away from him. But I wanted a playful villain this time, a Cockney geezer who could shift his appearance from panel to panel. I did a couple of quick sketches but never sent them to Martin – they were just there to help me focus on the character. I asked James Offredi to leave him completely colourless – I wanted the Piper to feel one step removed from reality. I reasoned that, even though he was constantly swapping uniforms, he would stay instantly identifiable if he remained in black-and-white.

The Piper's skeleton warriors were inspired by a DC anthology title from the 1970-80s, *Weird War Tales*. The covers (often illustrated by comics giant Joe Kubert) usually featured soldiers from all eras – past, present and future – as figures of death; skeletal and malevolent. Martin, David and James all met the challenge, creating a magnificent army. I had given them the kind of description that makes most comic artists reach for the paracetemol: "A horde of skeleton soldiers from every imaginable war, no two alike." For some reason they're still speaking to me.

I also enjoyed seeing the art team bring King's College to the Moon – and if *that* isn't a proper *Doctor Who* visual then I'll eat my anorak. Taking the Doctor and co into Turing's HQ gave me the chance to bring Tommy Flowers into the story. Flowers was the real-life engineering genius who designed and built Colossus, the world's first programmable computer.

The plots and scripts for the **DWM** comic strip are always submitted to the BBC for approval. This time around I got some notes back requesting changes. I had wanted to call the story 'The Unknown Soldier', thinking it would be a good name for the villain (I had the Sythorr make a reference to it at the end of *The Soul Garden*). The BBC weren't happy with that: 'The Unknown Soldier' is a term used to represent all the fallen soldiers who were never identified. It's a symbol of heroism, so using it as the name for the villain was felt to be inappropriate. It was a good point.

Luckily I had a back-up name: 'The Phantom Piper' comes from the Second Doctor TV story *The Moonbase*. In one scene a fearful Jamie McCrimmon sees the ghostly figure of the Piper approaching him in a dream. Jamie is convinced the Piper has

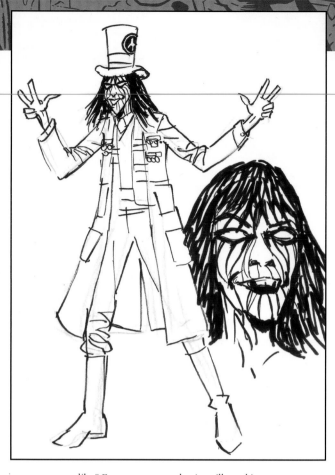

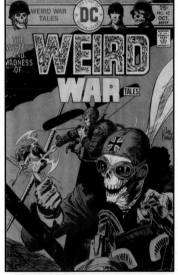

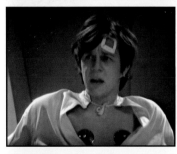

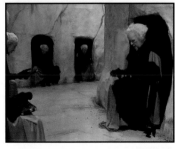

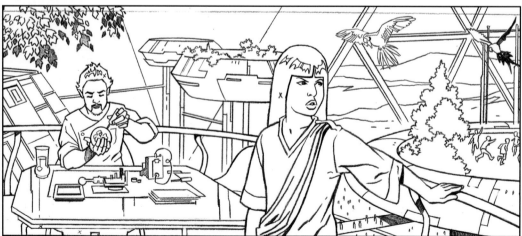

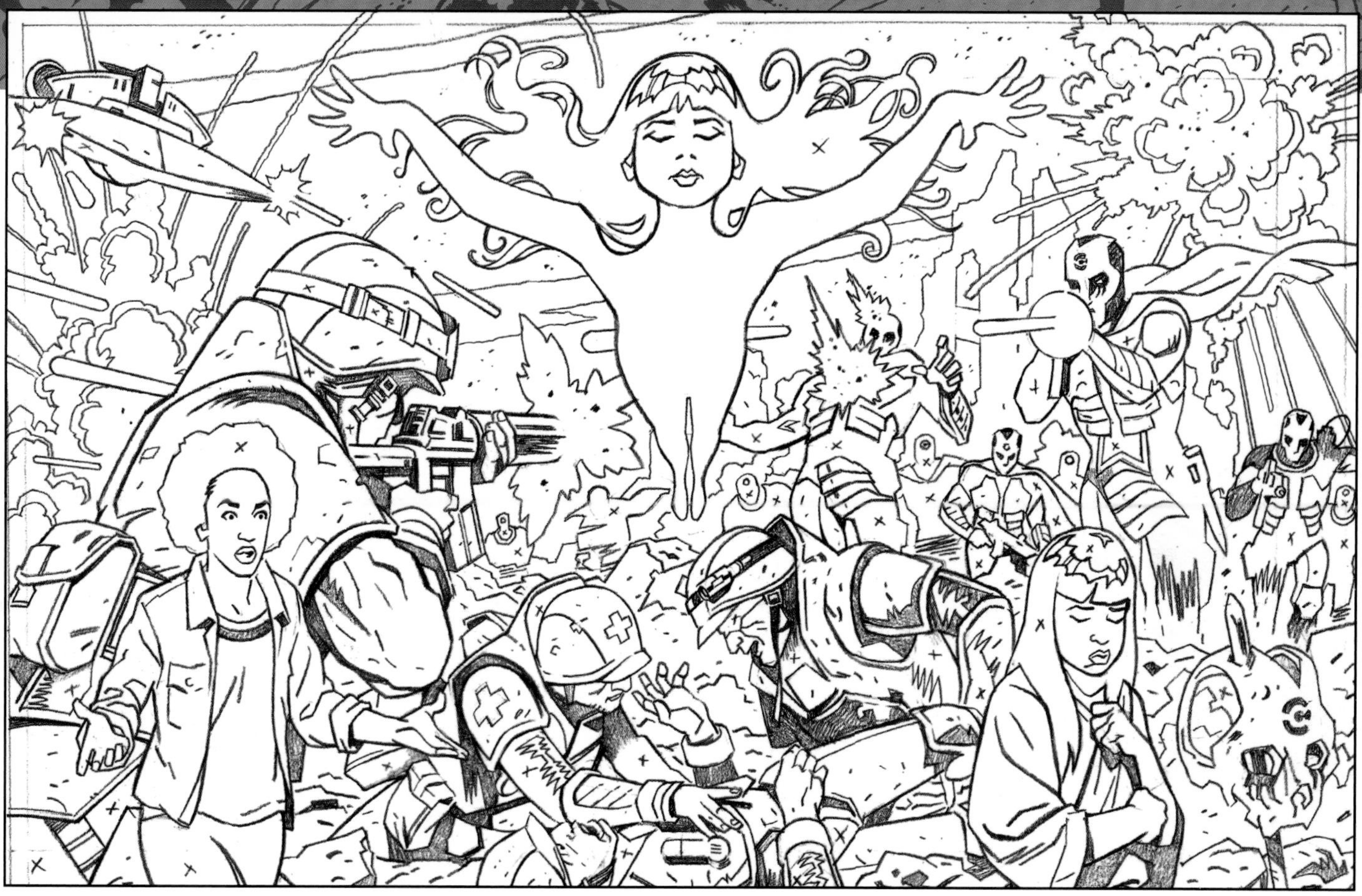

come to take him to the land of the dead. I've always liked that scene. We don't actually *see* the Piper, just Jamie's reaction to him. Was he only a dream, or something more...?

The BBC had a second, much bigger, issue with the story: Alan Turing's role in it. In the original outline, it was Alan who got grabbed by the Piper and forced to use his Block Transfer Computation abilities to create the skeleton army. The Doctor was the one who created a BTC double of himself to trick the Piper. But the BBC pointed out that Turing had been a victim of British society for most of his adult life, arrested and abused physically and emotionally. They weren't happy to see him in a similar state at the climax of the story. I admit I grumbled about this one, but I eventually realised that this was another very good story note. All along I had wanted to give Alan Turing the life that history had denied him: public recognition, a loving husband, even fatherhood. Alan really deserved to be the hero who saved the day. So Chiyoko became the Piper's captive instead, and Alan was the one who got to clobber the Piper, to the cheers of the crowd. It was a much stronger and far more satisfying ending.

But of course, it wasn't *quite* the end. While *The Phantom Piper* ties up many of the plot threads of this book, there are still more mysteries, more revelations, and more battles to come. If you've never heard of Fey Truscott-Sade before... well, be patient. *The Clockwise War* is on the way...

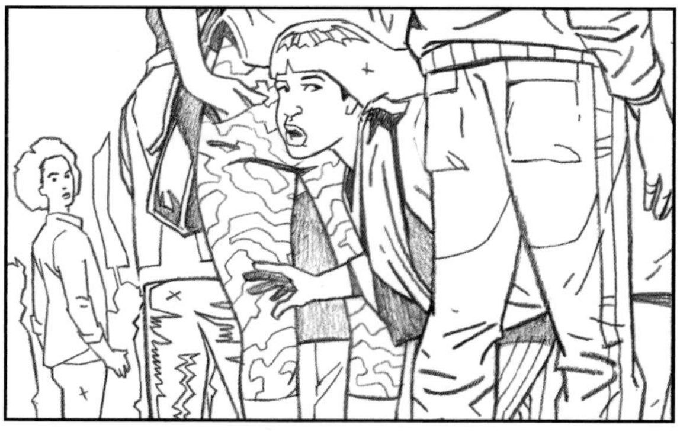

Martin Geraghty Artist

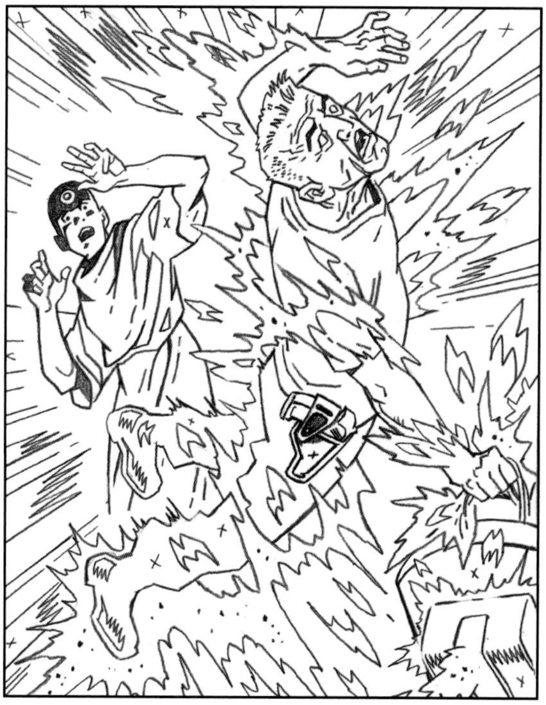

As a direct sequel to *The Child of Time* and featuring several of that story's characters, *The Phantom Piper* required me to revisit that earlier story, reacquainting myself with its visual sense in order to ensure the two stories took place in a consistent universe. I don't tend to make a habit of looking back on previous work unless specifically required to, but I thoroughly enjoyed reviewing this particular story and the themes Jonny Morris had created that Scott was now running with.

I was avidly watching *The Vietnam War*, Ken Burns's 10-part documentary that was airing on BBC4, at the time I was drawing this strip. The jaw-droppingly immediate, verite footage of close-quarter combat featured in it had a big influence on the visual feel of the war/riot panels that featured across Parts One and Two. The skeletal soldiers summoned up by the Piper evoked childhood memories of the macabre covers of the pulpy US comics that packed the wire carousels of many a UK newsagents during the 1970s.

The titular villain of the piece, rendered in David Roach's stark monochrome inks against the rich colours of the strip environment, is a spooky, costume-changing, wise-cracking ghoul who comes across as **DWM**'s very own take on the Joker. Scott specified that he be based on Noel Fielding's character the Hitcher from *The Mighty Boosh* (I was gratified to read a

Above:
Chiyoko explains her past to Bill. Pencils by Martin Geraghty.

Above:
Moxham is killed. Pencils by Martin G.

Left:
Bill spots Chiyoko. Pencils by Martin G.

Right:
Alan defeats the Piper. Pencils by Martin Geraghty,

Below:
Amie Dicke illustration.

Centre:
Alan Turing.

Bottom left:
Tommy Flowers.

Bottom right:
Design sketches of the Piper by Martin Geraghty.

correspondent to **DWM** commentating on the likeness, so job done there). I recall a degree of back-and-forth between Scott and myself before the final make-up design got the thumbs-up. Scott had sent me references of the work of Dutch artist Amie Dicke, who uses existing fashion photography which she then distorts and manipulates. The black patterning on the Piper's face was based on several striking images in her portfolio and gave him a very distinctive and malevolent appearance. A fantastic character who surely has the potential to return to the strip at some point in the future...?

It strikes me now that both the stories I contributed to for this volume feature real-life historical figures; one a poet, the other a mathematician (some may argue there is little difference between the professions). Alan Turing's return to the strip is perfectly in keeping with how the previous story left him and, like the Doctor himself, he seems equally at home looking out across the futuristic spires of a lunar city as he does throwing another log onto the fire of his quarters in King's College. I have nothing but respect for Turing the man, who has strong regional links to me, and think that the comics team treated this very real 20th-century hero with the utmost dignity and sensitivity. It's perfectly in keeping that this master cryptologist resolves the war using a fake paper plane. Almost poetically fitting, in fact.

Alan and Ranesh's kiss at the end of the tale deliberately mirrors Izzy and Fey's at the close of *Oblivion* – and who should appear over the page but Fey Truscott-Sade herself, whom I'd last drawn for the cover of a previous volume in this graphic novel series, *Oblivion*, itself well over a decade ago.

So there we have it; my final contribution to Doctor 12's wonderful comic strip run ends on a cliffhanger with the unexpected reappearance of a (friendly?) face from the Eighth Doctor's era. The **DWM** strip really is the best toy box to play in...

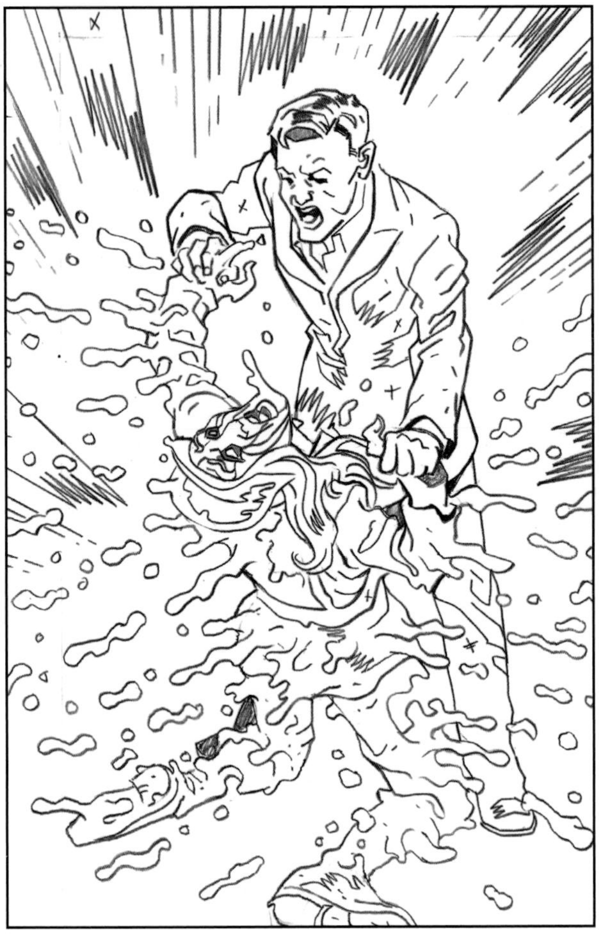

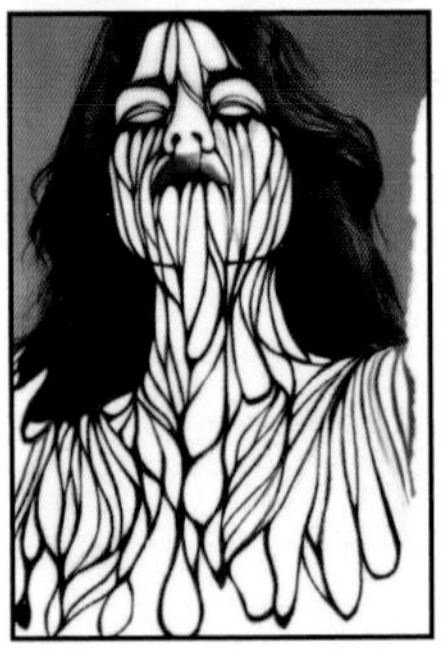

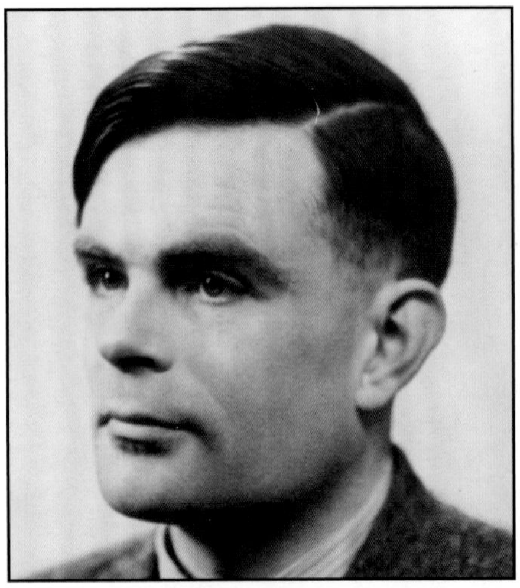

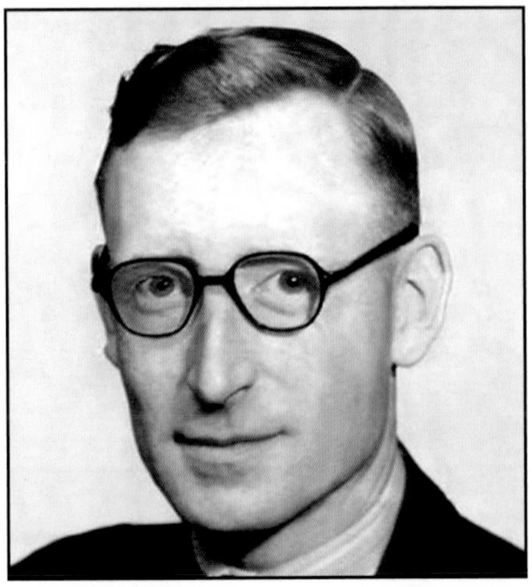

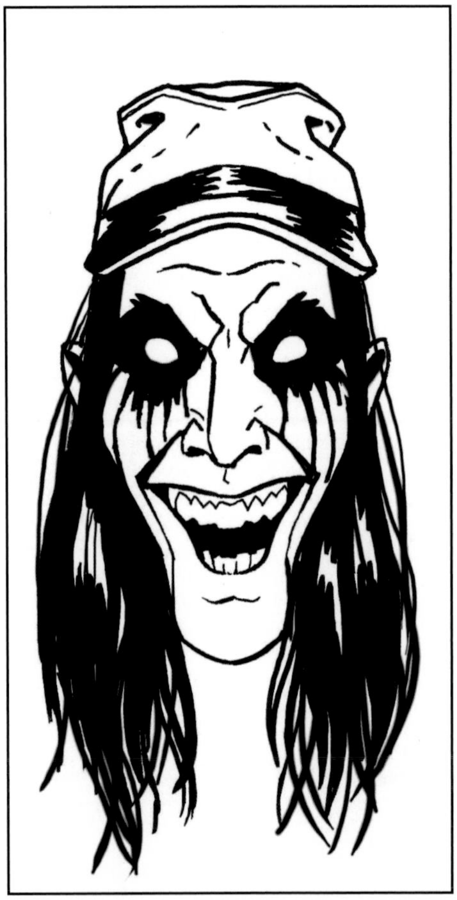

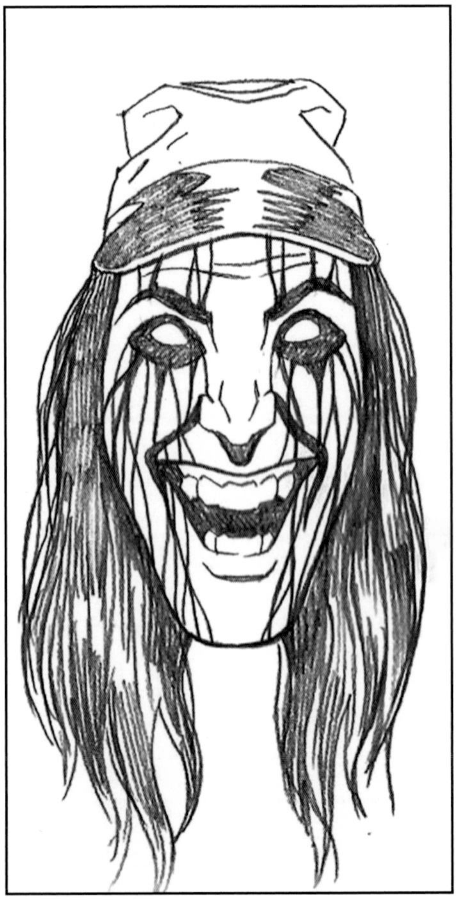

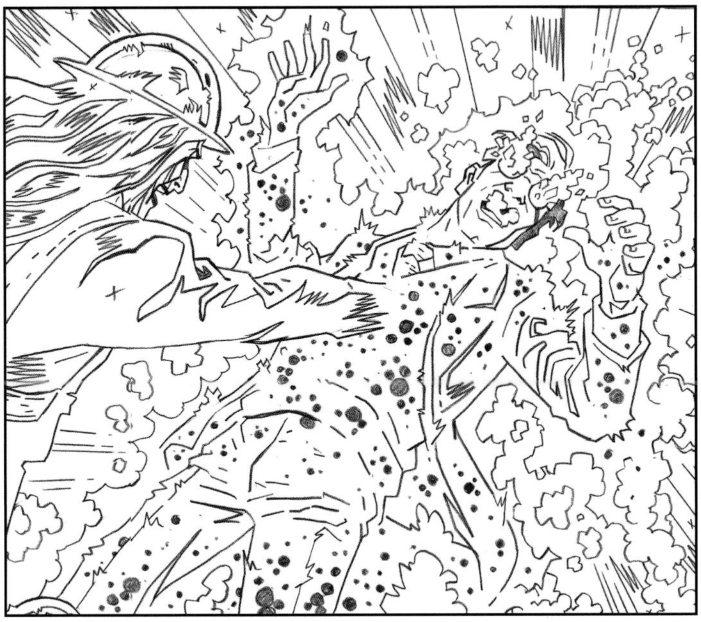

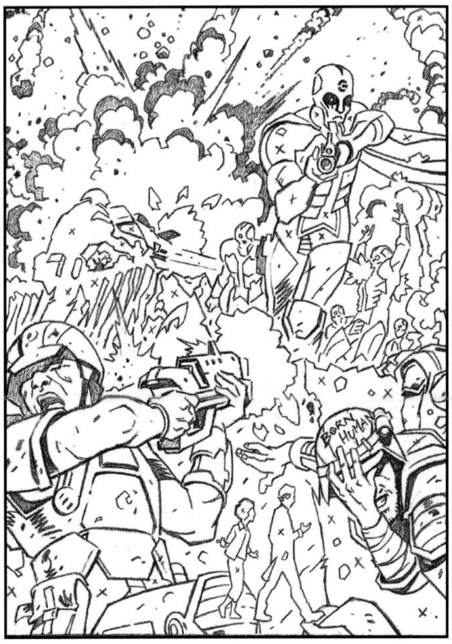

Far left:
The Piper kills Tommy. Pencil art by Martin Geraghty.

Left:
The Doctor remembers the human/Galatean war. Pencils by Martin Geraghty.

Below:
Skeletal Mongol warriors attack. Pencils by Martin Geraghty.

Bottom:
The Piper's warrior horde charges. Pencils by Martin Geraghty.

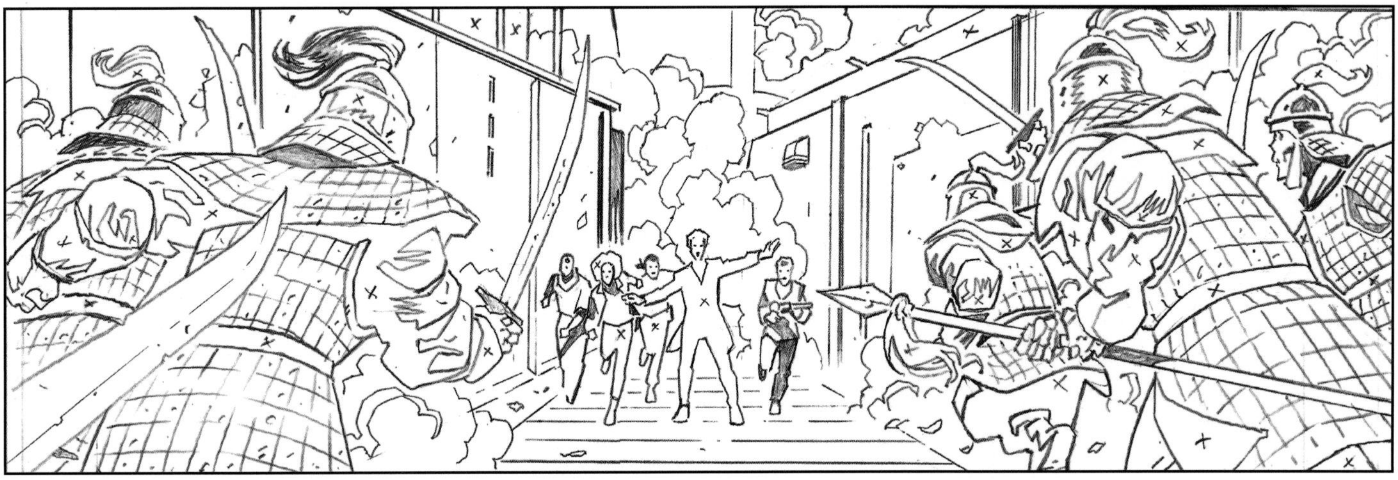

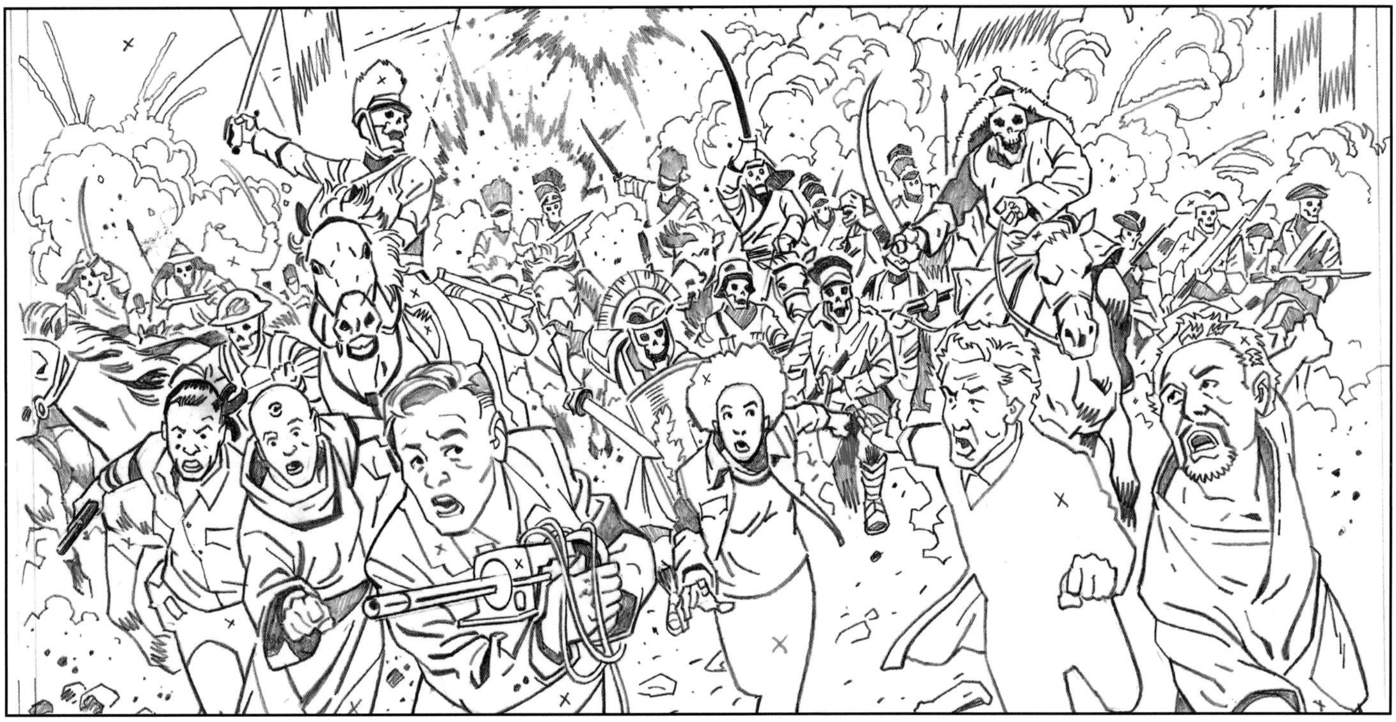

DOCTOR WHO COMIC COLLECTIONS

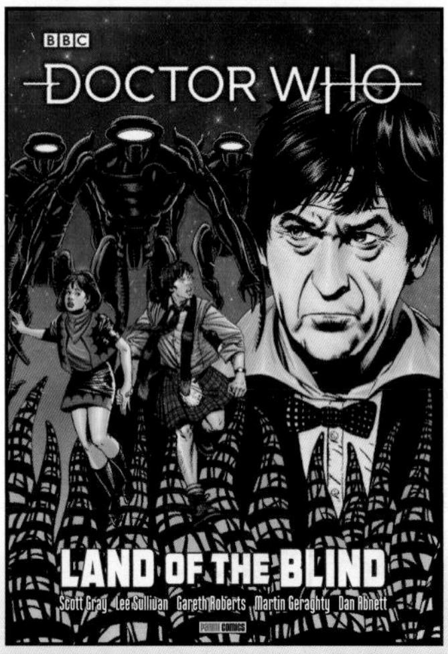
BBC
DOCTOR WHO
LAND OF THE BLIND
Scott Gray Lee Sullivan Gareth Roberts Martin Geraghty Dan Abnett

LAND OF THE BLIND (Multi Doctors: Volume 1)
Scott Gray, Lee Sullivan, Gareth Roberts, Dan Abnett
132 pages (b&w) £14.99/$19.99 ISBN 978-1-84653-886-5

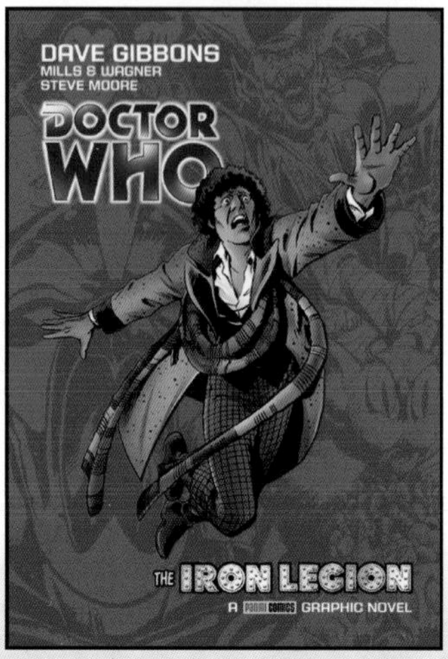
DAVE GIBBONS
MILLS & WAGNER
STEVE MOORE
DOCTOR WHO
THE IRON LEGION
A GRAPHIC NOVEL

THE IRON LEGION (The Fourth Doctor: Volume 1)
Dave Gibbons, Pat Mills, John Wagner, Steve Moore
164 pages (b&w) £14.99/$24.95 ISBN 978-1-904159-37-7

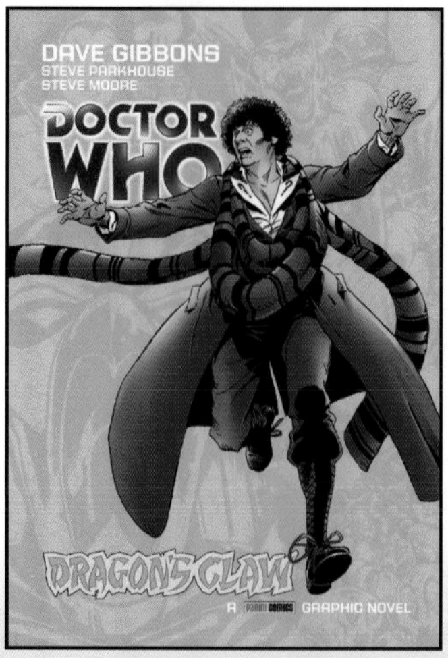
DAVE GIBBONS
STEVE PARKHOUSE
STEVE MOORE
DOCTOR WHO
DRAGON'S CLAW
A GRAPHIC NOVEL

DRAGON'S CLAW (The Fourth Doctor: Volume 2)
Dave Gibbons, Steve Parkhouse, Steve Moore
164 pages (b&w) £14.99/$24.95 ISBN 1-904159-81-8

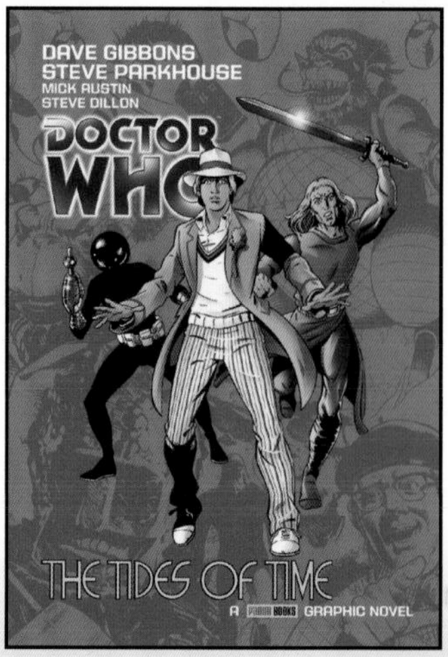
DAVE GIBBONS
STEVE PARKHOUSE
MICK AUSTIN
STEVE DILLON
DOCTOR WHO
THE TIDES OF TIME
A GRAPHIC NOVEL

THE TIDES OF TIME (The Fifth Doctor)
Dave Gibbons, Steve Parkhouse, Mick Auston, Steve Dillon
228 pages (b&w) £14.99/$24.95 ISBN 978-1-904159-92-6

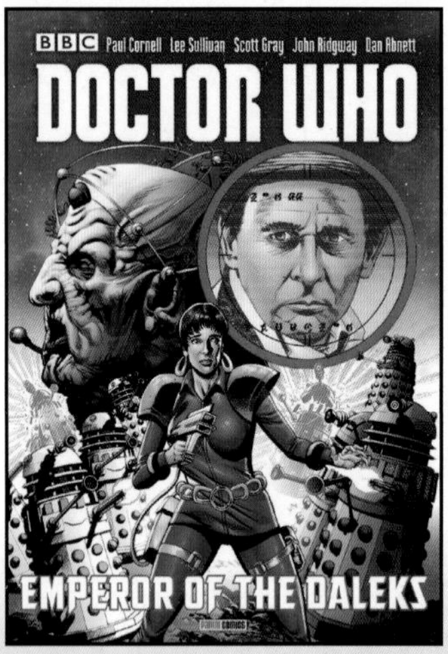
BBC Paul Cornell Lee Sullivan Scott Gray John Ridgway Dan Abnett
DOCTOR WHO
EMPEROR OF THE DALEKS

EMPEROR OF THE DALEKS (The Seventh Doctor: Volume 5)
Paul Cornell, Lee Sullivan, Scott Gray, John Ridgway
180 pages (b&w) £14.99/$19.99 ISBN 978-1-84653-807-0

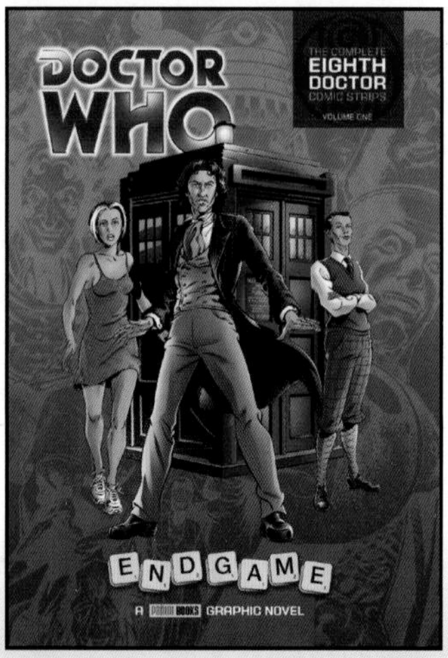
DOCTOR WHO
THE COMPLETE EIGHTH DOCTOR COMIC STRIPS VOLUME ONE
ENDGAME
A GRAPHIC NOVEL

ENDGAME (The Eighth Doctor: Volume 1)
Alan Barnes, Martin Geraghty, Scott Gray, Adrian Salmon
228 pages (b&w) £14.99/$24.95 ISBN 978-1-905239-09-2

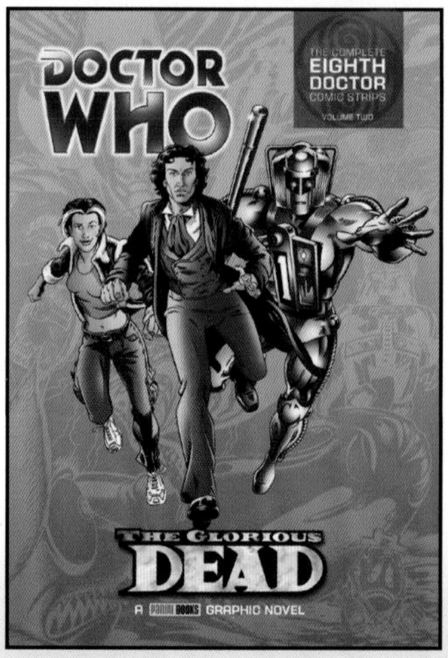
DOCTOR WHO
THE COMPLETE EIGHTH DOCTOR COMIC STRIPS VOLUME TWO
THE GLORIOUS DEAD
A GRAPHIC NOVEL

THE GLORIOUS DEAD (The Eighth Doctor: Volume 2)
Scott Gray, Martin Geraghty, Roger Langridge, Alan Barnes
244 pages (b&w) £15.99/$24.99 ISBN 978-1-905239-44-3

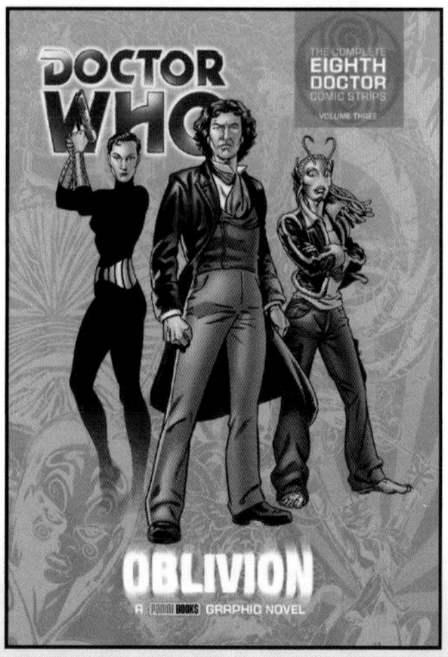
DOCTOR WHO
THE COMPLETE EIGHTH DOCTOR COMIC STRIPS VOLUME THREE
OBLIVION
A GRAPHIC NOVEL

OBLIVION (The Eighth Doctor: Volume 3)
Scott Gray, Martin Geraghty, Lee Sullivan, John Ross
228 pages (colour) £15.99/$24.99 ISBN 978-1-905239-45-0

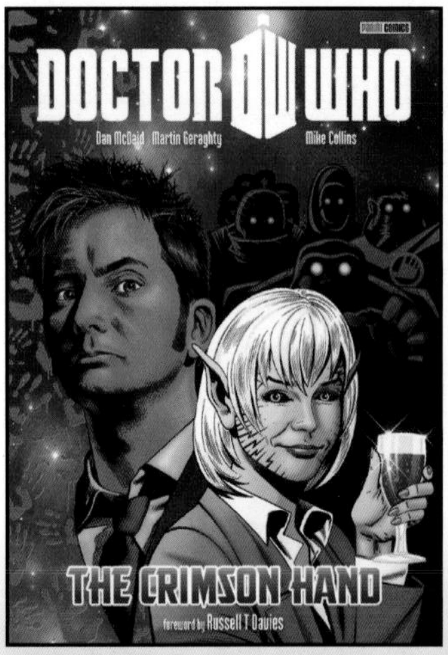
DOCTOR WHO
Dan McDaid Martin Geraghty Mike Collins
THE CRIMSON HAND
foreword by Russell T Davies

THE CRIMSON HAND (The Tenth Doctor: Volume 3)
Dan McDaid, Martin Geraghty, Mike Collins
260 pages (colour) £15.99/$31.95 ISBN 978-1-84653-451-5

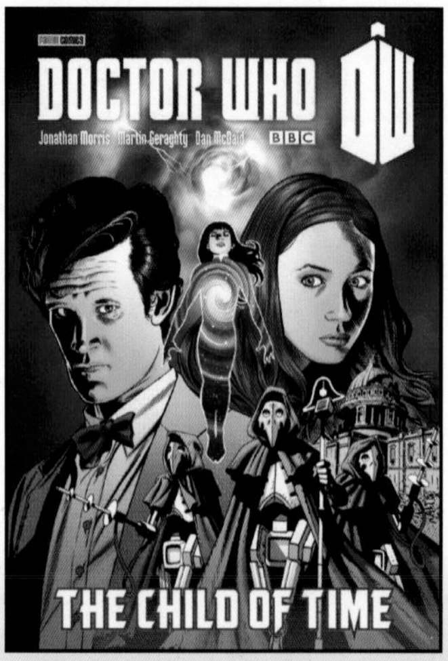
DOCTOR WHO
Jonathan Morris Martin Geraghty Dan McDaid
BBC
THE CHILD OF TIME

THE CHILD OF TIME (The Eleventh Doctor: Volume 1)
Jonathan Morris, Martin Geraghty, Dan McDaid
244 pages (colour) £16.99/$24.99 ISBN 978-1-84653-460-7

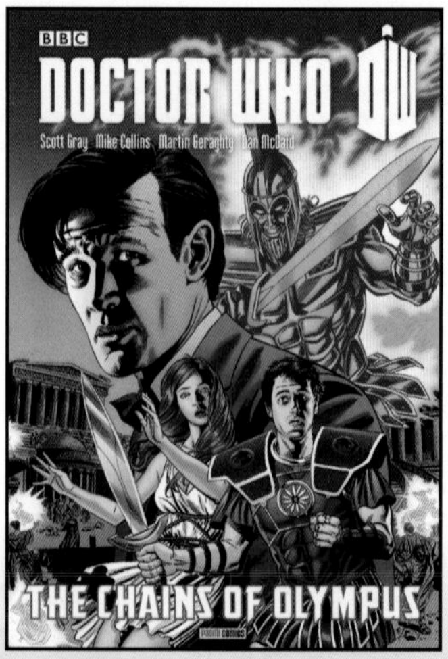
BBC
DOCTOR WHO
Scott Gray Mike Collins Martin Geraghty Dan McDaid
THE CHAINS OF OLYMPUS

THE CHAINS OF OLYMPUS (The Eleventh Doctor: Volume 2)
Scott Gray, Mike Collins, Martin Geraghty, Dan McDaid
132 pages (colour) £12.99/$18.99 ISBN 978-1-84653-558-1

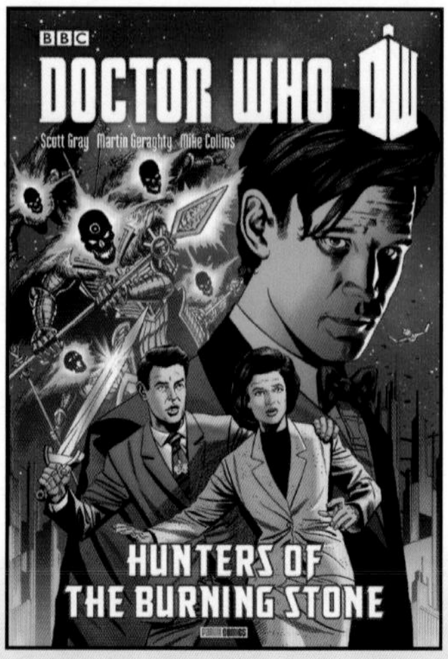
BBC
DOCTOR WHO
Scott Gray Martin Geraghty Mike Collins
HUNTERS OF THE BURNING STONE

HUNTERS OF THE BURNING STONE (Eleventh Doctor: Vol 3)
Scott Gray, Martin Geraghty, Mike Collins
164 pages (colour) £13.99/$19.99 ISBN 978-1-84653-545-1

These titles are available now from all good bookshops, specialist comic shops and online retailers! PANINI COMICS

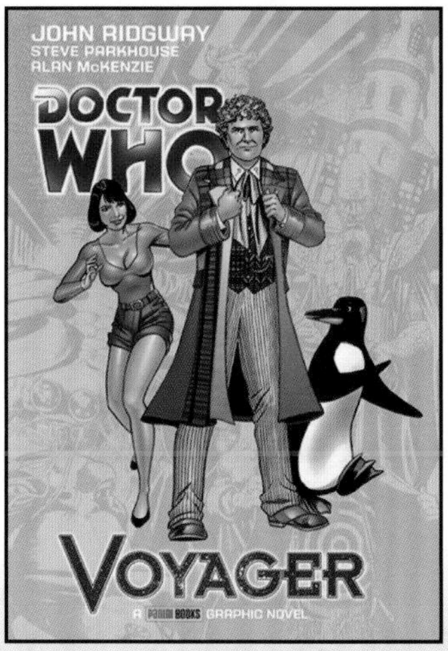
JOHN RIDGWAY
STEVE PARKHOUSE
ALAN McKENZIE
DOCTOR WHO
VOYAGER
A PANINI BOOKS GRAPHIC NOVEL

VOYAGER (The Sixth Doctor: Volume 1)
John Ridgway, Steve Parkhouse, Alan McKenzie
172 pages (b&w) £15.99/$31.95 ISBN 978-1-905239-71-9

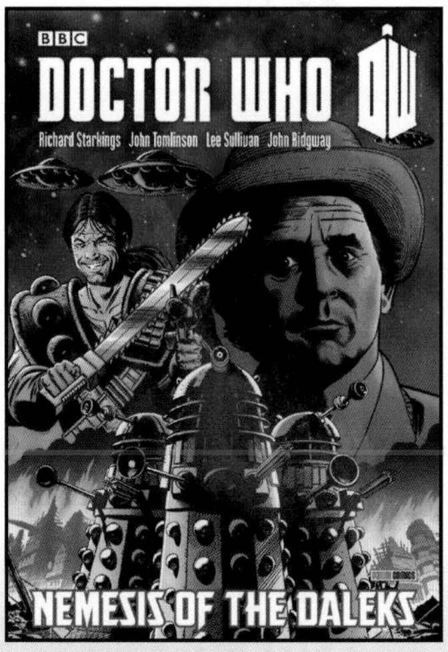
BBC
DOCTOR WHO
Richard Starkings John Tomlinson Lee Sullivan John Ridgway
NEMESIS OF THE DALEKS

NEMESIS OF THE DALEKS (The Seventh Doctor: Volume 2)
Richard Starkings, John Tomlinson, Lee Sullivan, John Ridgway
196 pages (b&w) £16.99/$24.99 ISBN 978-1-84653-531-4

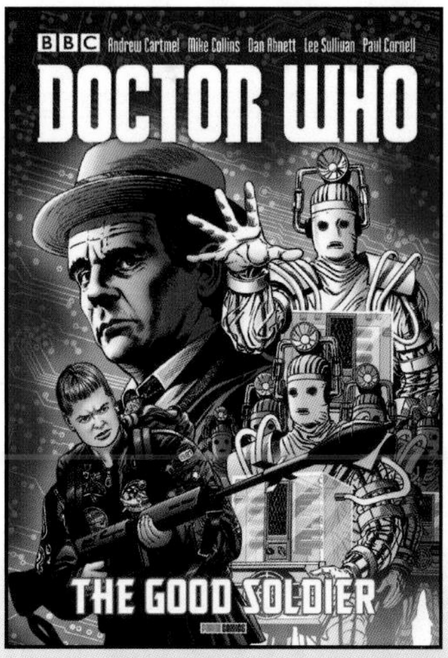
BBC Andrew Cartmel Mike Collins Dan Abnett Lee Sullivan Paul Cornell
DOCTOR WHO
THE GOOD SOLDIER

THE GOOD SOLDIER (The Seventh Doctor: Volume 3)
Andrew Cartmel, Mike Collins, Dan Abnett, Lee Sullivan
132 pages (b&w) £13.99/$19.99 ISBN 978-1-84653-659-5

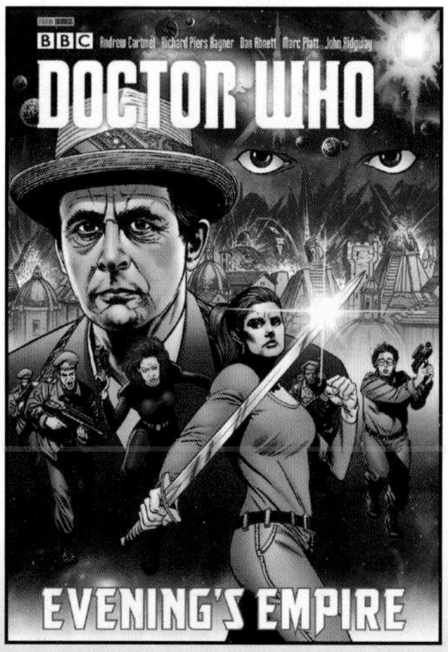
BBC
DOCTOR WHO
EVENING'S EMPIRE

EVENING'S EMPIRE (The Seventh Doctor: Volume 4)
Andrew Cartmel, Richard Piers Rayner, Dan Abnett, Marc Platt
132 pages (b&w) £13.99/$19.99 ISBN 978-1-84653-728-8

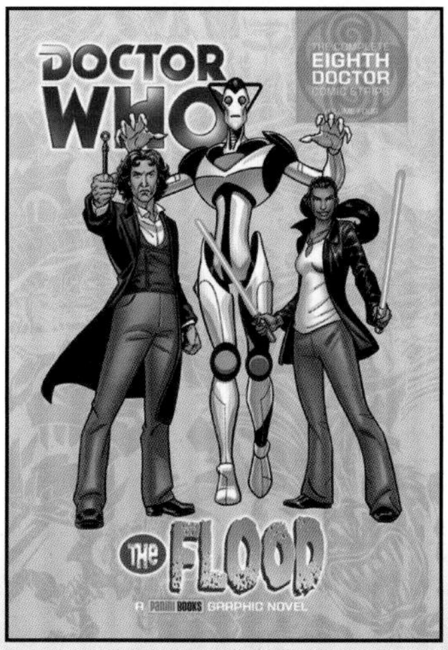
DOCTOR WHO
EIGHTH DOCTOR
THE FLOOD
A PANINI BOOKS GRAPHIC NOVEL

THE FLOOD (The Eighth Doctor: Volume 4)
Scott Gray, Martin Geraghty, Gareth Roberts, Mike Collins
228 pages (colour) £15.99/$24.99 ISBN 978-1-905239-65-8

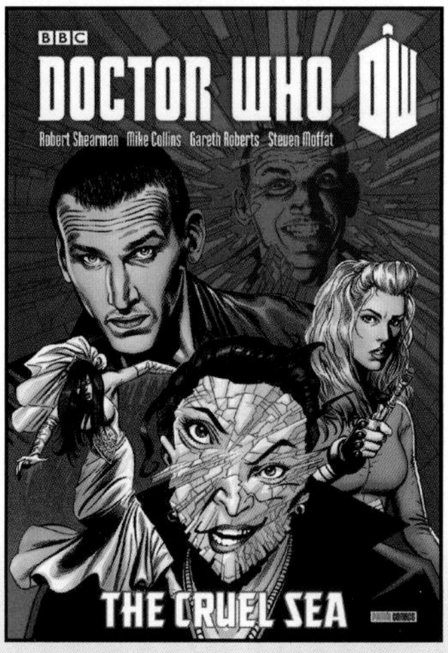
BBC
DOCTOR WHO
Robert Shearman Mike Collins Gareth Roberts Steven Moffat
THE CRUEL SEA

THE CRUEL SEA (The Ninth Doctor)
Robert Shearman, Mike Collins, Gareth Roberts, Steven Moffat
132 pages (colour) £13.99/$19.99 ISBN 978-1-84653-593-2

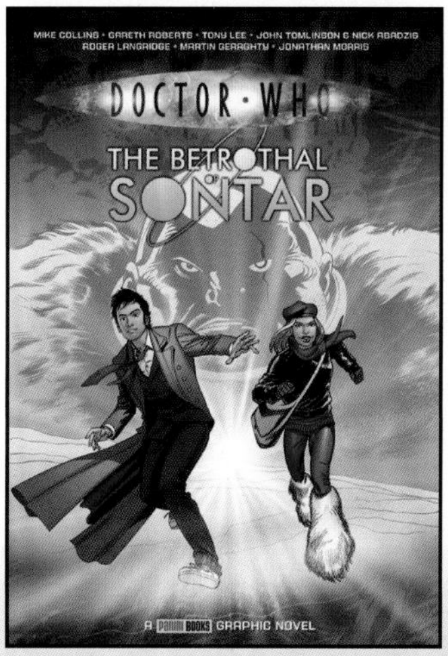
DOCTOR · WHO
THE BETROTHAL OF SONTAR
A PANINI BOOKS GRAPHIC NOVEL

THE BETROTHAL OF SONTAR (The Tenth Doctor: Volume 1)
Mike Collins, Gareth Roberts, Tony Lee, Martin Geraghty
180 pages (colour) £15.99/$24.99 ISBN 978-1-905239-90-0

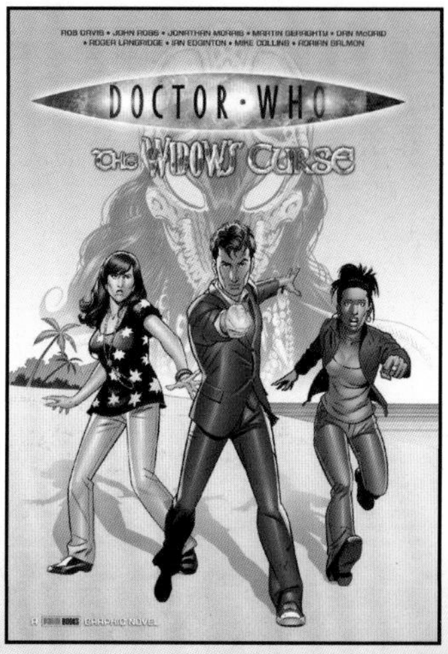
DOCTOR · WHO
THE WIDOW'S CURSE

THE WIDOW'S CURSE (The Tenth Doctor: Volume 2)
Rob Davis, John Ross, Jonathan Morris, Martin Geraghty
220 pages (colour) £15.99/$24.99 ISBN 978-1-84653-429-4

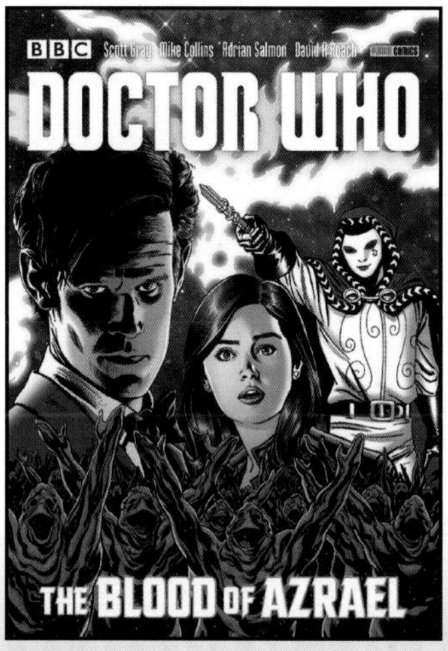
BBC
DOCTOR WHO
THE BLOOD OF AZRAEL

THE BLOOD OF AZRAEL (The Eleventh Doctor: Volume 4)
Scott Gray, Mike Collins, Adrian Salmon, David A Roach
180 pages (colour) £13.99/$19.99 ISBN 978-1-84653-625-0

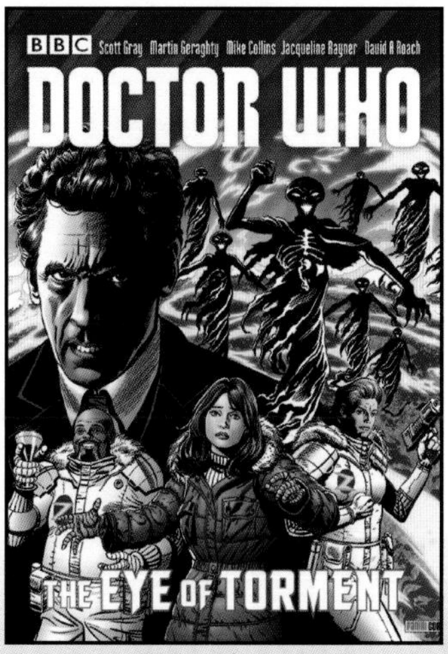
BBC Scott Gray Martin Geraghty Mike Collins Jacqueline Rayner David A Roach
DOCTOR WHO
THE EYE OF TORMENT

THE EYE OF TORMENT (The Twelfth Doctor: Volume 1)
Scott Gray, Martin Geraghty, Mike Collins, Jacqueline Rayner
180 pages (colour) £13.99/$19.99 ISBN 978-1-84653-673-1

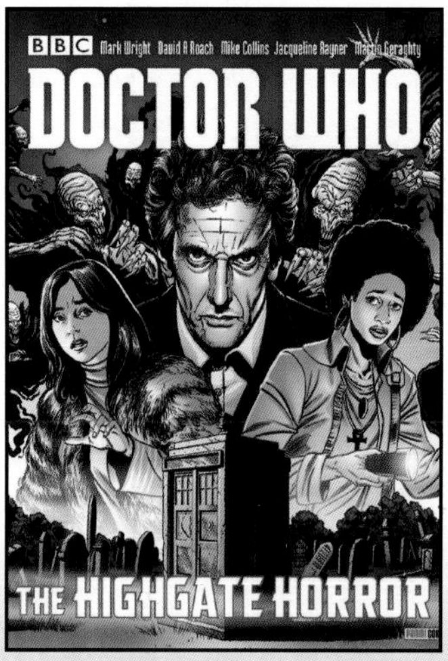
BBC Mark Wright David A Roach Mike Collins Jacqueline Rayner
DOCTOR WHO
THE HIGHGATE HORROR

THE HIGHGATE HORROR (The Twelfth Doctor: Volume 2)
Mark Wright, David A Roach, Mike Collins, Jacqueline Rayner
180 pages (colour) £14.99/$19.99 ISBN 978-1-84653-749-3

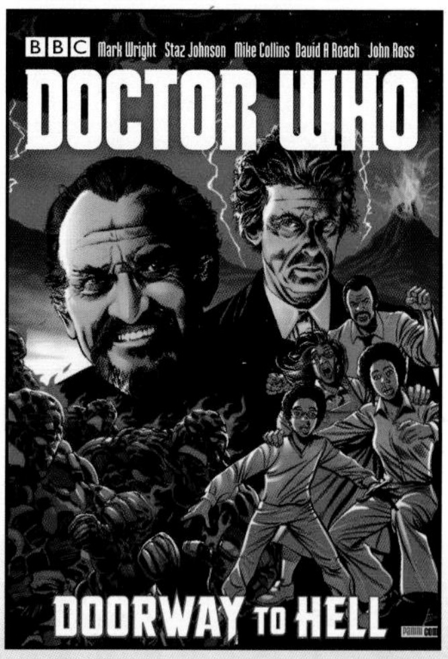
BBC Mark Wright Staz Johnson Mike Collins David A Roach John Ross
DOCTOR WHO
DOORWAY TO HELL

DOORWAY TO HELL (The Twelfth Doctor: Volume 3)
Mark Wright, Staz Johnson, David A Roach, Mike Collins
148 pages (colour) £14.99/$19.99 ISBN 978-1-84653-834-6

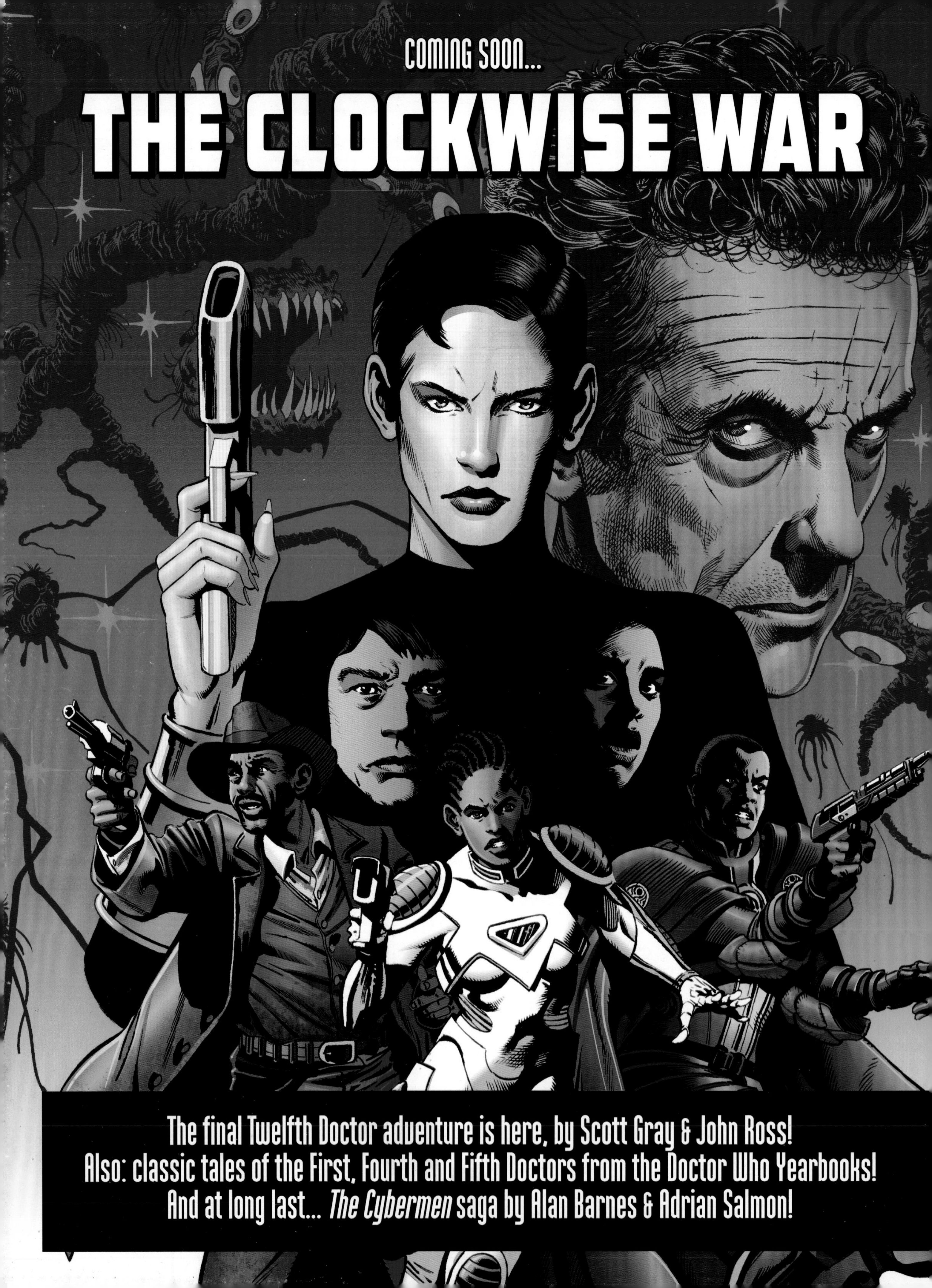
COMING SOON...
THE CLOCKWISE WAR
The final Twelfth Doctor adventure is here, by Scott Gray & John Ross!
Also: classic tales of the First, Fourth and Fifth Doctors from the Doctor Who Yearbooks!
And at long last... *The Cybermen* saga by Alan Barnes & Adrian Salmon!